Advance Praise for *AI Enabled Business*

I am happy to note that Prof. Melodena Stephens, with her co-authors, Vashishtha and Wagner, have put together a smart kit to enable businesses to leverage AI. They cover a range of topics beginning with the history and evolution of AI to current practitioners' issues such as governance, regulations and skills. Through their many years of interactions with entrepreneurs, clients, governments, and engineers, the authors view AI under a multidisciplinary lens. The book has several case studies and visuals to demystify aspects of AI. A lucidly written overview of AI and its governance, this book is sure to offer value to business users, students and the general public.

—**K. Ananth Krishnan**
EVP and Chief Technology Officer, Tata Consultancy Services

No technology will have a greater impact on humanity than artificial intelligence, and it floors me how little attention it is still given in public and corporate debate. Where it happens, the former tends to focus on dystopian scenarios and the latter treats it like it's something the CTO or IT department should figure out. The best individuals are leaning into the potential and raising thoughtfully the core ramifications; the best companies have embedded the potential as part and parcel of their missions. *AI Enabled Business: A Smart Decision Kit* is just that. It is the actionable playbook for the generalist, expert, policy maker—any of us as clear stakeholders—to not sleepwalk to an inevitable future but build our strategies with intentionality.

—**Christopher M. Schroeder**
co-founder Next Billion Ventures and author
Startup Rising: The Entrepreneurial Revolution Remaking the Middle East.

Stephens, Vashishtha, and Wagner have written an up-to-date and comprehensive overview of AI for business. Starting with AI's history and building to a foundational understanding of everything a business leader needs to know about AI: its potential, practical use cases, and current concerns. The chapters are thorough, with illustrative case studies from innovative companies—StitchFix, Tesla, Baidu, etc.

The book explores the business implications through disparate lenses: customers, employees, the future of work, and regulatory impacts.

I highly recommend this book for the leader seeking an up-to-date review of AI to make strategic investments.

—**Kes Sampanthar**
Managing Director of Innovation, BCG Brighthouse

AI Enabled Business: A Smart Decision Kit is the perfect tool to embark on a thorough assessment of what AI means for your business, to reflect and define ambitious strategies for your organization. It is impressive how the book investigates all facets of the field, pulls from numerous, intriguing examples and triggers the mind to think artificial intelligence in the broadest sense.

—**Arno Fehler**
CFO, Schmidt Kranz Group, Germany

AI Enabled Business provides a highly articulated and granular wealth of pragmatic information for companies to use in their operations regarding Artificial Intelligence Systems for today and the future. The specificity of application in case studies and easy to understand definitions and recommendations make this a must read in the ever-growing field of literature around AI.

—**John C. Havens**
Author, *Heartificial Intelligence: Embracing Our Humanity to Maximize Machines*

If you want an understanding of Artificial Intelligence from a multi-disciplinary perspective, in a global setting and operations, I recommend reading Melodena Stephens' recent book *AI Enabled Business: A Smart Decision Kit.* She is an excellent writer and public speaker, captivating the readers and audience with practical, real-world examples, capable of teaching the impact of a wide range of AI innovative applications in Business. If you are a developer, the book will help you understand the governance challenges and make better decisions during the design and implantation phase of AI based systems.

—**Professor Eleni Mangina**
Vice Principal International (College of Science)
University College Dublin, Ireland

This book offers a comprehensive and excitingly written analysis of the most important and current challenges of AI and well-founded innovation opportunities through AI such as Metaverse, Synthetic Biology, Humanoid Robots with which companies and also society should deal in the coming years.

—**Reinhard Altenburger**
Professor of Strategic Management
Co-editor of *Responsible Artificial Intelligence, CSR, Sustainability, Ethics & Governance*
IMC University of Applied Sciences Krems/Austria

AI Enabled Business

AI Enabled Business

A Smart Decision Kit

Melodena Stephens
Mohammed Bin Rashid School of Government

Himanshu Vashishtha
SixthFactor Consulting

Dirk Nicolas Wagner
Karlshochschule International University

INFORMATION AGE PUBLISHING, INC.
Charlotte, NC • www.infoagepub.com

Library of Congress Cataloging-in-Publication Data

A CIP record for this book is available from the Library of Congress
http://www.loc.gov

ISBN: 979-8-88730-283-6 (Paperback)
   979-8-88730-284-3 (Hardcover)
   979-8-88730-285-0 (E-Book)

Copyright © 2023 Information Age Publishing Inc.

All rights reserved. No part of this publication may be reproduced, stored in a retrieval system, or transmitted, in any form or by any means, electronic, mechanical, photocopying, microfilming, recording or otherwise, without written permission from the publisher.

Printed in the United States of America

Contents

Foreword vii

1 **A Brief History of AI** 1
    1.1 The First AI Conference 2
    1.2 AI Booms and Busts 4
    1.3 AI—Extended Definition 12
    1.4 Need for AI Ethics and Regulations 18

2 **AI in Collectives of Humans and Artificial Agents** 31
    2.1 AI—A Managerial Perspective 32
    2.2 The Emergence of Human-Agent Collectives (HAC) 35

3 **AI and the Changing Nature of Work and the Firm** 49
    3.1 Micro-Division of Labor 50
    3.2 A New Factor of Production and a New Dilemma for the Firm 53
    3.3 A Necessity to Understand and, if Possible, Manage Information Asymmetries 56

4 **Exponential Developments, Organizations, and Thinking** 69
    4.1 Exponential Developments 70
    4.2 When Abundance Replaces Scarcity 72
    4.3 Exponential Organizations (ExOs) for Exponential Challenges 73
    4.4 Exponential Thinking 75

5 AI and Decision Making 89
- 5.1 Decision-Making 90
- 5.2 Agile Decision-Making 94
- 5.3 Governance 100
- 5.4 Environmental, Social, and Governance (ESG) Reporting and AI 104
- 5.5 Crisis Management 114

6 AI Expertise 129
- 6.1 AI Intelligence Levels 130
- 6.2 Level of Organizational AI Expertise 136

7 AI Operations 157
- 7.1 AI Operations and Scope of the Project 158
- 7.2 AI Interoperability 160
- 7.3 Global Embeddedness 168

8 AI Data Types and Management 187
- 8.1 Data 188
- 8.2 The AI Data Scale 190
- 8.3 Training AIs with Data 191
- 8.4 Big Data and AI Training 195
- 8.5 Data Management 201

9 AI and Employees 213
- 9.1 AI and Employment 214
- 9.2 AI and the Type of Organization 216
- 9.2 Human–AI Teams and Skills 218
- 9.3 AI Onboarding 223
- 9.4 AI and Human Productivity 228

10 AI and Customers 241
- 10.1 AI and Customer 242
- 10.2 Human Interface 245
- 10.3 AI and the Sensory Experience 248
- 10.4 User-Experience: Merging Virtual and Real Worlds 251

11 AI Regulations 267
- 11.1 Global AI Regulations 268

| | 11.2 Trends Pushing AI Regulations .... 273 |
| | 11.3 Types of AI Regulations .... 283 |

12 Epilogue—Thinking Ahead 311
    12.1 Metaverse 312
    12.2 Synthetic Biology (SynBio) 325
    12.3 Humanoid Robots 333

About the Authors 353

Foreword

Strangely, even though AI is such a popular term, there is little alignment on what AI is and what it can and cannot do. This raises interesting challenges in terms of decision-making especially as organizations that are onboarding AI at a rapid space, often without in-house capabilities. How then do you ensure robust decisions using AI or even ask the right questions when outsourcing AI projects?

This book is for those people who want to know more about AI. Despite not having the AI-expertise and specialist knowledge, they still want to ensure that they make the right choices through thoughtful consideration. Through a review on various sources of literature (engineering, business, public policy, governance, and specific industries), we try and highlight key challenges an AI-enabled organization will face. Rather than present use-cases, we give you short cases of what has worked or has not worked in the AI past and let you come to your own conclusions. We present tools to help you think through your AI-strategy, and most importantly, we push you to think of the values and governance policies you have to embed in your organization.

The book is organized into 12 chapters. After a brief introduction, we go through the history of AI in Chapter 1, so readers can be aligned on what AI is and is not. Chapters 2, 3, and 4 set the background of why embracing AI may no longer be a choice but rather a necessity. Chapters 5, 6, 7, and 8 look at a firm's requirements for AI and a key understanding of where it fits in the organizational structure, culture and strategy. Chapters 9

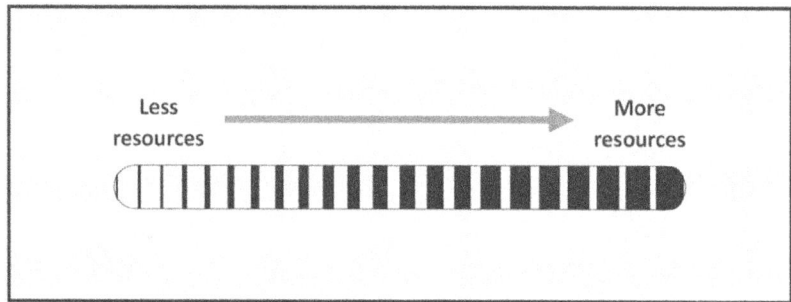

Figure F.1 AI SmartKit Scale. *Source:* Stephens & Vashishtha, 2020[1]

and 10 look at the role of people (employees and customers) and their relation with the AI strategy. Chapter 11 looks at regulatory compliance and governance in the AI-ecosystem. Finally Chapter 12 will look at some new trends that an AI-enabled organization may need to be aware of as disruption is always around the corner.

One of the tools we use throughout the book is the AI SmartKit scale (see Figure F.1). As you move from left to right, the assumption is that the organization must budget more in terms of resources to ensure their AI-strategy works in the long-term.

This book is a long journey. It would not be possible without the help we had from many people: Aaisha Balakrishnan, our research intern; Ana Pereira our graphic designer, George Johnson, our publisher, John Stuart our agent, and the IEEE community that inspired this journey by sharing their knowledge and being candid about what were some of the challenges and concerns with AI.

We would like to thank our many reviewers, K. Ananth Krishnan, Christopher M. Schroeder, Kes Sampanthar, Arno Fehler, John C. Havens, Prof. Reinhard Altenburger, and Prof. Eleni Mangina. There are many others behind the scenes—thank you!

Finally as co-authors, we are grateful for the great teamwork we were able to experience and special thanks go to Melodena who lead the project with great passion and foresight. Without her manifold contributions, this book would have been impossible.

Note

1. Stephens, M., & Vashishtha, H. (2020). *AI Smart Kit–Agile Decision Making on AI–Abridged Version*. Information Age Publishing.

1

A Brief History of AI

CHAPTER HIGHLIGHTS

1. Historical evolution of AI shows that it has cycles of frenetic optimism and periods of disillusionment.
2. AI as a term is multi-faceted and often loosely used; however, it has become ubiquitous, capturing the imagination of the general population.
3. The rapid scaleup and adoption of AI needs strong ethics and governance practices.
4. We are at a tipping point—of tremendous progress or the advent of the third AI winter.

> **Cases:**
> AI History | NASA and IBM | AI Historical Timeline (1911–2021)
> Global AI National Strategies | AI and Public Imagination | AI Transformer
> Model Training Costs | AI Challenges: COVID Pandemic

1.1 The First AI Conference

The term "Artificial Intelligence" (AI) was first used in 1955 when John McCarthy, a mathematician and computer scientist, used the word in his proposal for the 1956 Dartmouth Conference, the so-called *first* artificial intelligence conference.[1] The objective was to get more clarity on *thinking machines*. Ten carefully selected scientists attended the conference to see if it was possible to teach a computer to understand language, use creativity in problem-solving, and improve itself.[2]

Thinking machines as a concept were not new. Since the Industrial Revolution, machines have been used to increase human productivity. For example, Babbage's Difference Engine and the Analytical Engine in 1833 used mathematical logic for calculations. Both Babbage's machines used punched-out cards, however, this was not new. Punched cards were used much earlier in the Jacquard looms in 1804 for weaving patterns in cloth. But there was a difference in these developments, as Lady Ada Lovelace pointed out in 1843. For the first time, machines were going beyond mathematical outputs using what she called *abstract mental processes*. World War II further accelerated the use of machines for tasks that used human logic or reasoning, for example, complex code-breaking machines or translation machines.

The simplest logic (which eventually resulted in binary codes of 0s and 1s—see Figure 1.1) was the Church-Turing thesis, a basic function of

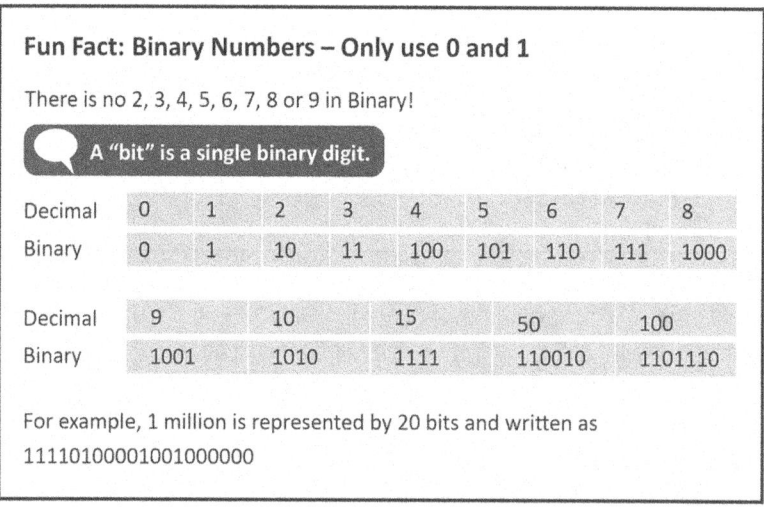

Figure 1.1 Fun Fact: Binary numbers only use 0 and 1. *Source:* Stephens and Vashishtha (2021)[3]

computability theory. It combines two intellectual pieces of work by two scientists from two continents![4] Since 1900, the two problems posed by the great mathematician David Hilbert had remained unsolved—the second and tenth problems called the *Entscheidungsproblem* (or the decision problem). The mathematical problem was to see if an algorithm existed to determine whether an inference in a formal logic system was valid. In 1935, Alan Turing, a Master's mathematics student, showed no such algorithm existed. He wrote up a paper in 1935, and his professor was so impressed that he was encouraged to publish it. By the time he wrote his first draft in 1936, another mathematician, Alonzo Church, had written a similar paper and published it at the same time in the American Journal of Mathematics. His professor wrote to Church and introduced Turing, who later did his PhD under Church in the USA.

Meanwhile, Turing, who had always thought this problem could be solved using machines (he first described his Turing machine during this time), updated his paper by showing a commonality between the two research fields—mathematics and computability. This reasoning allows you to define algorithms, or the "logic" or the set of computer instructions, which is a fundamental part of the programming on which AI is dependent. It is based on the concept that a bigger problem is solved by solving smaller problems that require multiple iterations (this is known as recursion in computer science language). It was more complicated than the calculators existing at the time. Computational systems like neural networks, post-tag systems, cellular automata, logic circuits, genetic algorithms, string rewriting systems, and even, to some extent, quantum computers follow this logic.

The abstract concept of the Turing machine was not limited to solving mathematical problems but could also represent logic values or letters. When Turing returned to the United Kingdom after completing his PhD, he worked to break the Enigma machine responsible for German secret codes during World War II. Soon, various subject disciplines, like mathematics, philosophy, cybernetics, engineering, and neuroscience, began to converge on this field called AI. Alan Turing came up with the Turing test in 1950 to address the problem, *can machines think?* and created the famous imitation games. The newly formed discipline was funded by the deep pockets of defense—for example, US Defense Establishments (ONR and ARPA, later called DARPA).

McCarthy's proposal in 1955 naively thought that two months and ten people would be enough time to achieve the following goal:

> the study is to proceed on the basis of the conjecture that every aspect of learning or any other feature of intelligence can in principle be so precisely

described that a machine can be made to simulate it. An attempt will be made to find how to make machines use language, form abstractions and concepts, solve kinds of problems now reserved for humans, and improve themselves.[5]

Though the 1956 Dartmouth conference is considered a key milestone in the history of AI, it is clear that even today AI is an evolving field. At the end of the summer project, McCarty said, "[the] main reason the Workshop did not live up to my expectations is that AI is harder than we thought."[6] Still, there was tremendous hype about these new types of machines. A 1957 summary on AI by Herbert Simon, a Nobel Prize winner, stated:

It is not my aim to surprise or shock you—but the simplest way I can summarize is to say that there are now in the world machines that think, that learn, and that create. Moreover, their ability to do these things is going to increase rapidly until—in a visible future—the range of problems they can handle will be coextensive with the range to which the human mind has been applied.[7]

1.2 AI Booms and Busts

The history of modern AI has had three periods of popularity followed by a lack of interest in imagination or funding—the so called "AI winters." While World War II and the space race fueled the need for "computing power," it also opened the debate on the limitations of machines. In addition, there was a growing disillusionment with the realization that AI was yet unable to do many human tasks. The first AI winter can be traced to the philosopher Hubert Dreyfus' 1965[8] report on the state of AI. The report specifically looks at game-playing, problem-solving, language translation and learning, and pattern recognition. It identifies weaknesses in machine programming that simulated human intelligence.

The issues Dreyfus highlighted which are still relevant today are (also see Figure 1.2):

- A caution for transferring assumptions based on simple problem-solving to more complex-solving areas.
- The need for a greater understanding of the structure of the problem.
- Working as a team of human-computers.
- Acceptance of the fact that the areas of machine intelligence are discontinuous and the boundary condition beyond which it is not prudent to accept the answers needs to be identified.

> Dreyfus highlighted in his book *What Computers Can't Do*[9] that we believe many assumptions about AI and hence have faith in its outputs which is not correct. These assumptions are yet to be tested adequately. These assumptions are:
>
> 1. **Biological:** *The brain processes information in discrete operations by way of some biological equivalent of on/off switches.*
> 2. **Psychological:** *The mind can be viewed as a device operating on bits of information according to formal rules.*
> 3. **Epistemological:** *All knowledge can be formalized.*
> 4. **Ontological:** *The world consists of independent facts that can be represented by independent symbols.*
>
> In 1965, in a paper published by RAND called Alchemy and Artificial Intelligence,[10] he stated "digital computer language systemically excludes three fundamental forms of information processing (fringe consciousness, essence/accident discrimination and ambiguity tolerance)."

Figure 1.2 Alchemy and AI and *What Computers Can't Do* (Hubert Dreyfus).

In 1969, Marvin Minsky (a participant in the Dartmouth Conference) and Seymour Papert, an early computer researcher, presented a report on AI's limitations. The report further highlighted the need to know more about the human brain and even its genetic code before computer science would be able to create an AI equivalent to a human.[11] The authors strongly voiced their skepticism toward the reductionist attitude of programmers and the static perspective they took of the human brain (see Figure 1.3 on Human Intelligence). They highlighted that human perception has many layers that needs to be understood.[12]

This period was marked by a cut in government funding in the USA, UK, and Europe. DARPA, which previously had given millions of dollars for research with no strings attached, stopped funding AI as it changed its focus to "mission-oriented direct research, rather than basic undirected research."[13] In the UK, government funding was cut in response to the 1973 Lighthill report that stated, "no part of the field have the discoveries made so far produced the major impact that was then promised." As a result, the first AI winter extended till the mid-1970s (see an example of some of the early problems—Figure 1.4).

This period was followed by a surge of activity during the 1980s, primarily led by the private sector, venture capital, and stock market exuberance. IBM introduced its first computer in 1981. In addition, technology companies like Apple (founded in 1976), Microsoft (founded in 1975), and Dell (founded in 1984) were established. The tremendous technological leaps in computer capability pushed optimism in AI, but it remained an underexplored area.

> There are many characteristics of human intelligence for a machine to mimic. However, with regards to "thinking" or being "intelligent," some elements that bear reflection are presented below: *Intelligence*[14] requires:
>
> - the capacity to perceive *contexts* for action;
> - the capacity to *act* in *real-time* or in a *timely manner*;
> - the capacity to *associate* contexts or goals to actions;
> - the ability to *learn new* contexts, actions, and/or associations between these through *analysis* and *reflection* and *improve*;
> - have storage of memories for easy *access* and *retrieval* and for *forgetting*;
> - have *autonomy*, the capacity to act as an individual;
> - have *values* and hence discern what is right from wrong and evaluate the consequences of the same, therefore be able to *rationalize decision making*.
>
> The first three characteristics are what plants and a thermostat can do. To do all of the above, i.e., using various methods: senses, motor skills, and most importantly, computation, which is the transformation of information (not maths), needs to be embedded in a physical process, requiring time, space, and energy. The process uses math logic to understand complex data, so it is often simplified. Programming is a human endeavor where data is connected by design (architecture) to the system (machine, process, storage, etc.).

Figure 1.3 Human intelligence.

The second AI winter began in the early to mid-1990s as the second wave of disillusionment set in after a wave of AI optimism. The term AI-winter was introduced in a public debate at the annual meeting of the American Association of Artificial Intelligence in 1984. There were cutbacks in research spending worldwide, and soon after, there was an economic collapse of the over-inflated tech industry (dot.com boom). The specialized AI hardware industry collapsed, and the changes in computing programs made legacy systems too expensive to maintain. A part of the problem was that AI reality did not match expectations. Japan had spent US$850 million in 1981 for the Fifth Generation Computer Project and a decade later had still not achieved its objectives. DARPA had spent US$100 million by 1985 with 92 projects underway at 60 institutions—half in the industry, half in universities and government labs. But a change of focus in 1987 resulted in funding cuts.[15] It is estimated that 300 AI companies shut, declared bankruptcy, or were acquired by 1993.[16] Figure 1.5 shows the AI historical timeline.

Significant funding in the early years was driven by the defense sector during the World Wars, then later by the first Space Race to get a Man on the moon and as a proxy for the Cold War. Post-Cold War, there was a significant decline in defense spending—it decreased globally by a third between

> During the war, computers first referred to humans. In fact what took 30 hours for a human to compute, would take 20 minutes on ENIAC (if you discounted the time for setup 24–48 hours).[17] Eventually the manual setting up of the computer using switches and wires was replaced storing programs in memory through software. The ENIAC computer used for ballistic tables had 18,000 vacuum tubes and with one failing every 24–48 hours, maintenance was a challenge.
>
> ENIAC was declassified in 1946, starting the computer age.[18] The focus on computers accelerated with the space race. In 1956 USSR launched their first cosmonaut safely to space and in 1957, their first Sputnik satellite. The Soviets used the Strela computer for Yuri Gargarin's space mission and the programming language they used was called Algol.
>
> In the early days of the space flight mission, NASA relied on human computing skills and hired *human computers*. Many of these mathematicians were women and their job was to calculate flight trajectories, fuel, thrust to weight ratio etc. In 1950s a decision was taken to start relying on machine computers—specifically the IBM UNIVAC machines. IBM designed the machines for the Gemini mission. What took weeks to calculate now could be done in minutes. The IBM machine could do over 7,000 calculations a second.[19]
>
> Still there was a reluctance to believe the machine. There is a time gap of 1.5 seconds when signals are sent from earth to the spacecraft and back. The early calculations for the first USA flight into space (Alan Shepherd, 1961, Freedom 7), or the first orbit around the earth (John Glenn, 1962, Friendship 7) and the trajectory for Apollo 11's moon landing was provided by a human computer, Katherine Johnson. In fact, history recalls that that John Glen asked Katherine the human computer to recheck the numbers before launching as part of the preflight.[20]
>
> The human computers quickly learnt C++ programming and were able to utilize their skills in programming. Since there is need for error-free computations, NASA preferred to use machine language rather than newer languages like FORTRAN. But the software and hardware needed to improve exponentially for each mission. By the time the Apollo missions started, the computer was referred to as the *fourth crew member* because of its vital role.

Figure 1.4 NASA and IBM.[21]

1989–1996, and R&D spending fell with it.[22] The reduction in spending by the defense sector in the earlier years also coincided with the first two AI winters and the boom cycles that came after.

But the optimism of the dot.com revolution still held sway with private investors despite the bubble. The terrorist attack of 9/11, 2001, the second Gulf War, the Balkan Wars, rising tensions in the SE Chinese seas, and instability in the MENA region and Africa all ensured that military expenditure had a revival.[23] The investments in AI were finally paying off.

The rapid advances in hardware and software led to more innovative products like advanced computing power in mobiles, AI chatbots, facial recognition, autonomous cars, AI cancer diagnosis, and other smart devices. Data volume and computing power had increased exponentially, and

8 ▪ *AI Enabled Business*

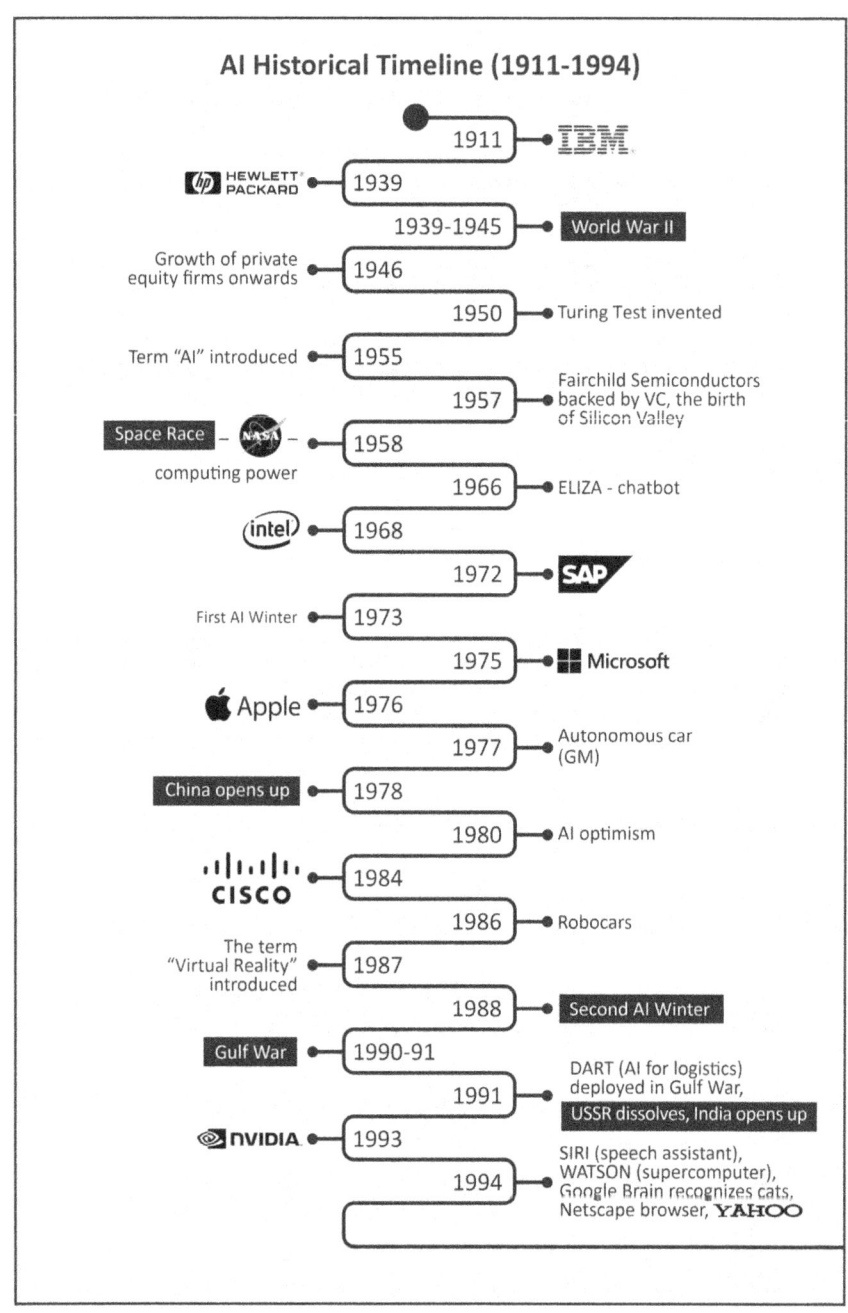

Figure 1.5a AI Historical Timeline (1911–1993). *Source:* Authors

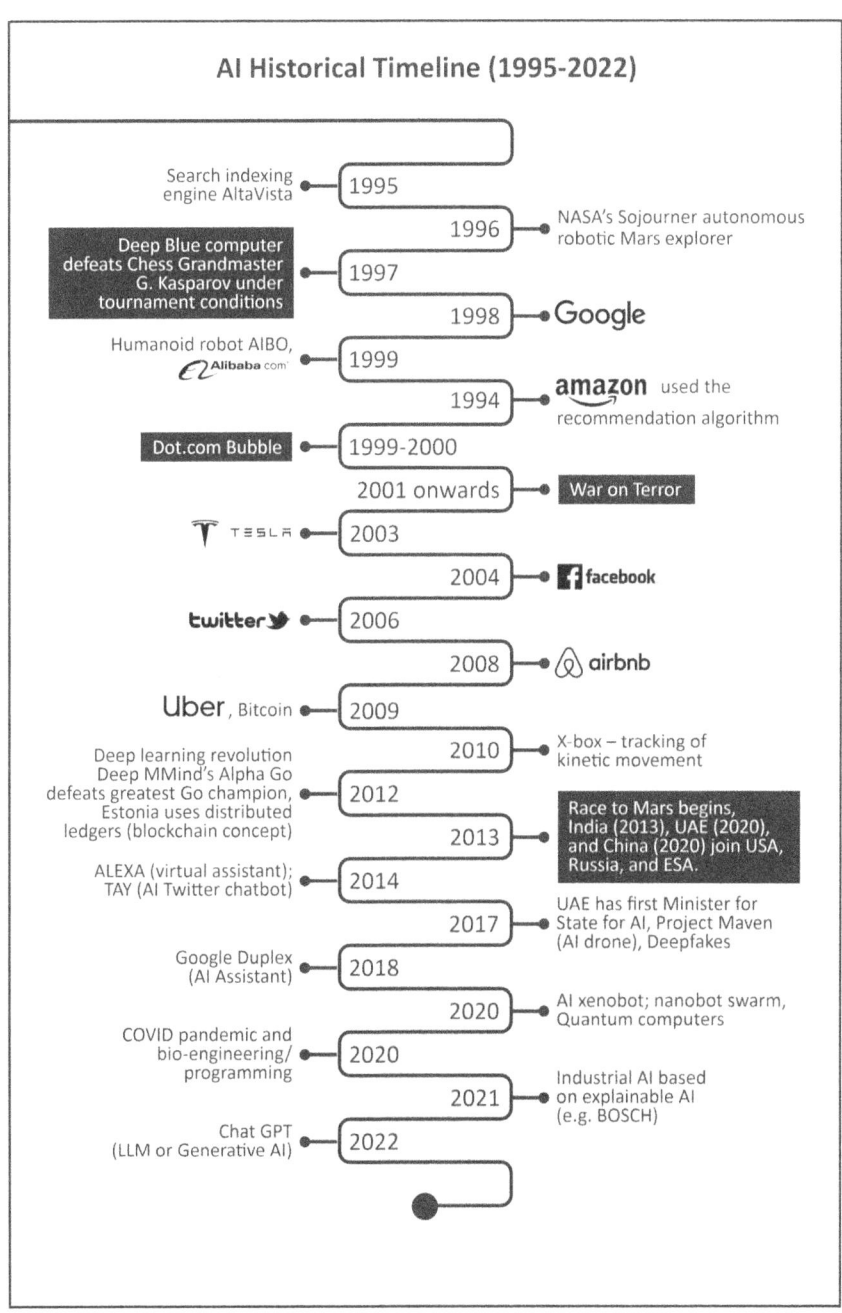

Figure 1.5b AI Historical Timeline (1994–2021). *Source:* Authors

so had the costs of managing the security of these smart systems. New fields like image analytics and natural language processing made AI seem human. Robotics became an important field as some countries—Germany, Japan, and China, realized they would face labor shortages. Computers like Deep Blue were able to defeat grandmasters at chess in 1997, and these events were widely televised, capturing the public's imagination. These were no longer *thinking machines* but *intelligent agents.*

Today, more governments embrace smart cities as a concept, bringing us closer to sentient AI. China is leading in this area, working on the idea of a Social Credit System (plan unveiled in 2014) and Smart City pilot studies (unveiled in 2011). The Social Credit System is a pilot program that will eventually be nationwide, managing real-time data from individuals and businesses to ensure compliance with the law and encourage good citizenship behaviors.[24] It is estimated that China has 50% of the total smart city pilot programs (800 cities) in progress.[25] The United Arab Emirates created the first Minister of State for the post of Artificial Intelligence. The city of Dubai, for example, has an AI system that integrates 30,000 cameras,[26] making it one of the safest cities in the world. The topic of AI was so promising that by 2020, some 50+ national AI strategies or plans had been announced (see Figure 1.6).

The world was getting more globalized, and barriers to market entry were lowered. The opening up of large markets like India in 1991 and China in 1988 fueled private sector investment. Silicon Valley started to grow and become a tech hotspot giving birth to AI clusters worldwide. The USA gained tremendously in attracting AI talent, and other countries are following suit, announcing policies to attract talent, the UK, the UAE, and Canada, for example.[27] Even China began attracting back its people of Chinese origin using the policy of the 1000 Talents Plan established in 2008.

Mergers and acquisitions (M&A) added to the might of existing tech companies, accelerating in the first quarter of 2021 faster than other sectors.[28] Money began to move across borders easily, resulting in a spate of M&As where countries lost strategic AI companies. For example, Google bought the UK's DeepMind Technologies for half a billion dollars in 2014. The privatization of the space and defense sectors led to significant deployment of capital in R&D fueled by wars and the new Mars Space Race. Other countries were getting interested in sectors traditionally dominated by NATO. OECD estimates that AI attracted more than US$ 50 billion in terms of private equity from 2011 to 2018, led by the USA and, from 2017 onwards, China.[29] At this time, the scale was easily achieved in the global market for tech companies simply because government regulations lagged. For example, a 2002 DARPA project to mine citizen data to identify security threats called *Total Information Awareness* was shut down in 2003.[30] Yet, entities like Facebook could avoid the

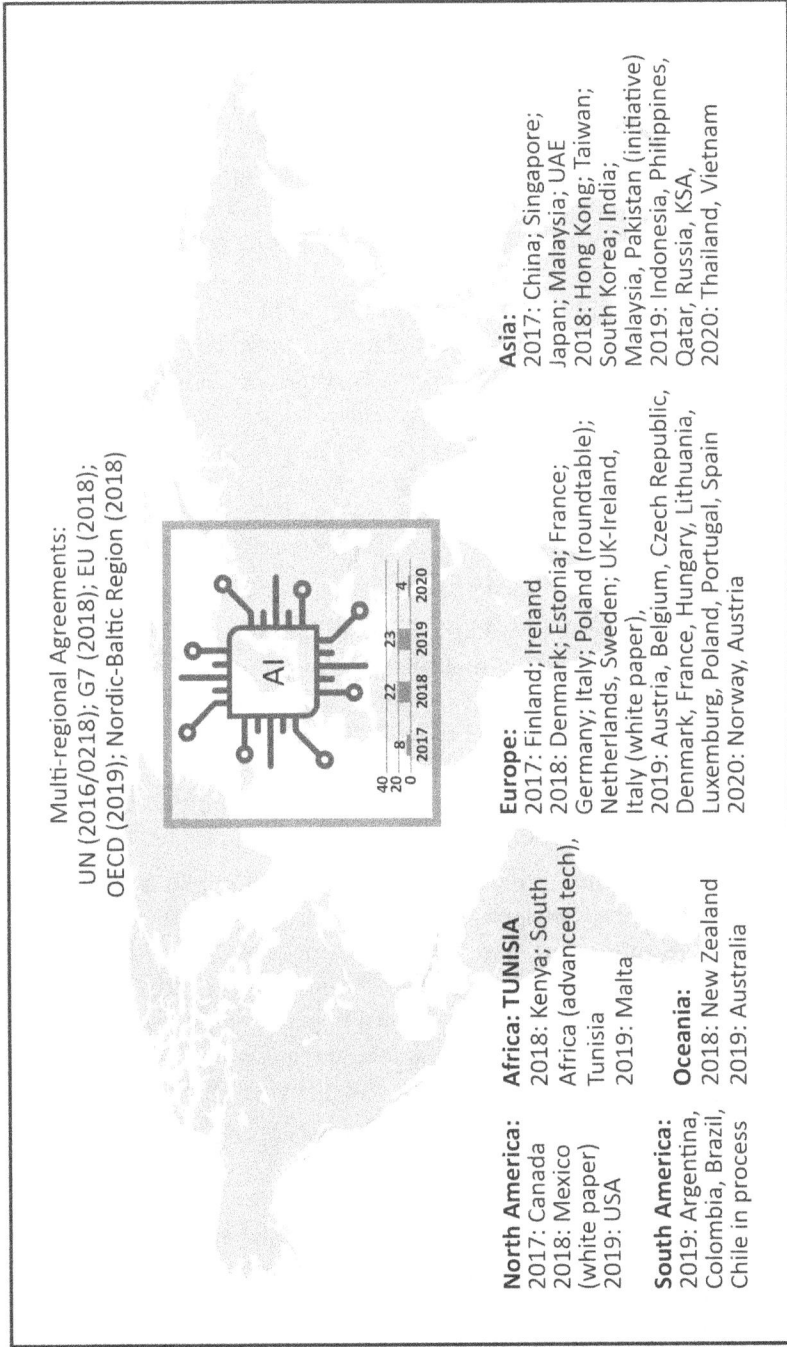

Figure 1.6 Global AI national strategies. *Source:* Authors

spotlight until the Cambridge Analytica scandal hit. This particular example highlights the challenges of tradeoffs—security versus privacy and the public's right to an opinion or consent.

This funding was being augmented by governments who were now either buyers of tech or funding tech in the push for modernization initiatives like "digital governments," "smart cities," and "4IR." A worrisome trend is that government funding in basic research has decreased worldwide. Most AI research is earmarked for commercialization as opposed to AI basic research.[31] There is a trend to club "private investment" in R&D expenditures, which can be up to 78% of the investment.[32] But the problem with this method of calculating R&D is that it does not understand how basic research works. Basic research can take up to 70 years[33] to become commercialized, and the private sector often does not have the patience for these types of investments. Of course, the hope is that computers can bypass this human limitation, but even quantum computers have issues. For example, by nature, a quantum computer cannot "forget" as it is based on complex linkages... and this quality that makes it so powerful also exposes its Achilles heel.[34]

One of the strongest retaliatory responses to the growing might of tech was introduced by the EU in the form of The General Data Protection Regulation (GDPR) in 2018, which sought to prevent the exploitation of citizens' data by foreign companies. In 2020, the EU planned to redress the ability of foreign tech companies to evade local tax by introducing a tech tax. But, of course, big tech fought back.[35] Continuing with more regulatory oversight, in 2022, the EU planned to introduce algorithmic transparency and accountability.[36]

In 2021, an executive order was signed in the USA to limit monopolies (like giant tech firms, transportation, agriculture, and banking), increase scrutiny on vertical mergers, and increase competition.[37] In addition, there is an increasing number of ethics guidelines developed by the private sector, non-government organizations, inter-government organizations, and governments. However, this area is still fragmented, suggesting that decision-makers who work with AI must understand the consequences of their decisions.[38]

1.3 AI—Extended Definition

AI has an evolving definition. There is still much ambiguity about what AI is or is not. While traditionally, it is applied to machines. There is a need to expand the definition of AI to synthesized biological cells. At the same time, while AI ethics seems to be following a different field from bio-genetic engineering. They share many similarities.

A Brief History of AI ▪ **13**

In bio-ethics, which was an outcome of World War II, participant consent is necessary. However, it took much longer for this type of consent to be enforced for AI, with much of it disguised as legalese. While we worry about the impact of AI on society, in bioethics, much of the focus is on the individual. The ability to program biological cells[39] using some of the thinking we use in AI will redefine health and bring with it more debates on regulations.[40] The physical, digital and biological spaces are now merging, raising more questions. Will brain impulses that are programmed by AI need bio-ethics or AI ethics or both? Will a human with artificial organs and genetically programmed DNA be human?

A simple, broadened description of AI is given in Figure 1.7. AI is not only about responding but also includes new beginnings, i.e., pro-activity.

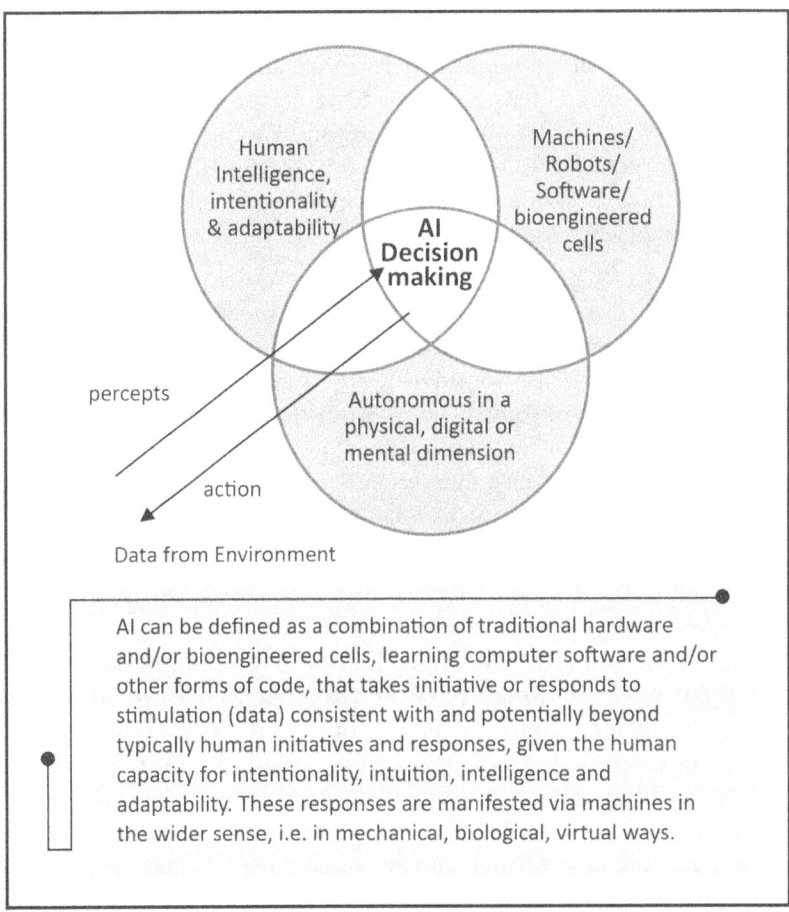

Figure 1.7 AI definition. *Source:* Authors

AI can be defined as a combination of traditional hardware and/or bioengineered cells, learning computer software and/or other forms of code that takes initiative or responds to stimulation (data) consistent with and potentially beyond typically human initiatives and responses, given the human capacity for intentionality, intuition, intelligence, and adaptability. These responses are manifested via machines in the wider sense, i.e., in mechanical, biological, virtual ways.

AI has captured the public imagination (see Figure 1.8). These themes stretch across topics like space exploration, future worlds, autonomous cars, super AI, humanoids and robots, AI wars, and the role of data exploitation. The fascination the public has with AI had an interesting consequence.

Previously, new technologies were slower to scale and needed technical experts to understand them and make them market-ready. However the uptake of AI has accelerated, partly because of the easiness of user interface, coupled with the entertainment industry, and media fascination with founders. These trends have helped add value to the volume, value and speed of accessing development and funding. We seem to be reliving science fiction. Recently, an AI-created artwork sold for US$432,000,[41] and an AI became a Board Member with observer status in a Hong Kong capital firm, Deep Knowledge Ventures.[42]

Of the more than 50 countries that were quick to announce an AI strategy from 2017 onwards, the ethics part of the strategy and its associated regulations were often an afterthought. The EU first announced its AI ethics strategy in 2018. Considering the scale of AI's reach in terms of impact (positive and negative), it is critical that individual organizations that embrace AI have a transparent dialogue about AI and set up robust guidelines to reinforce their values systems, even if national systems are not set up. There are enough sources for inspiration. For example, the three laws of robotics were written by Isaac Asimov as early as 1942.

Regulations need to be constantly updated in real-time as innovations are deployed and perspectives change. For example, if Uber were about creating jobs via the gig economy, as it grew in size, the backlash on the rights of part-time employees versus full-time employees would continue to grow. This is one example of impact outside the organization and the moral implications of decisions using AI and the business model itself. AI can do tremendous good. But like any invention that scales too quickly, it brings rapid changes to social life. The digital divide is one example. Not all the benefits of the new technologies are accessible to the all populations either because of the cost of hardware and software, digital illiteracy, internet

A Brief History of AI ▪ 15

Theme	Year	Media	Movie (USA)	Tech
Exploration/ future with tech gadgets	1951	The Day the Earth Stood Still	Movie (USA)	Bioengineering, nanomachines,
	1962	Jetsons	Series (kids) – drones (flying vehicles, 3D printers, robots)	Robot, flying autonomous cars, 3D printed food, holograms, jet packs
	1969 -1991	Star Trek	Series	Universal translators, mobile communicators, medical scanners, holograms/holodecks, transporters, tractor beams, antimatter power; cloaking devices, bluetooth headsets, touchscreens, tablet computers, chatbots?
	1977	Star Wars	Movie (USA)	Humanoid robots, holograms, spacecrafts, medical scanners
Autonomous cars	1939	Batman	Comics (later series) (USA)	Autonomous vehicles with voice remote
	1982 -1986	Knight Rider	Series	Autonomous vehicles with molecular bonded shell
Thinking as humans	1965	Alphaville	Movie (France)	Sentient Computer called Alpha 60
	1968	2001: A Space Odyssey	Movie (USA) – advised by Marvin Minsky	Sentient Computer
Humanoids/ robots	1923	RUR (RRossum's Universal Robots)	Book (introduced the word Robot) (Czechlovaskia)	Robot, humanoids
	1927	Metropolis	Movie (Germany)	Robot, sims
	1934	Der Herr der Welt	Movie (Germany)	Robots replace workers whose jobs are "dangerous, unhealthy and intellectually suffocating"

Figure 1.8 AI and public imagination. *Source:* Authors *(continued)*

Theme	Year	Media	Movie (USA)	Tech
 Humanoids/ robots	1923	RUR (RRossum's Universal Robots)	Book (introduced the word Robot) (Czechlovaskia)	Robot, humanoids
	1927	Metropolis	Movie (Germany)	Robot, Sims
	1934	Der Herr der Welt	Movie (Germany)	Robots replace workers whose jobs are "dangerous, unhealthy and intellectually suffocating"
	1949	The Humanoids	Book	Humanoids that want to rule humans
	1950	I, Robot	Book (USA) inspired Blade Runner	Robo-psychology, three laws of Robots
	1952	Astro Boy	Manga (Japan)	Android *humanoid with flesh like material)
	1957	The Invisible Boy	Movie (USA)	Robot, supercomputer with malicious intent
	1968	Do Androids Dream of Electric Sheep	Book	Human- androids only used in Mars; Voigt-Kampff empathy test to differentiate humans from androids or the Bonelli test. Melding mind and experiences in an "empathy box"
	1969	Ironman	Comic and later made into a movie (USA)	Robot skeleton, AI-enabled weapons
	1977	The Adolescence Of P-1	Book (Canada)	AI named P.I. that reaches super intelligence
	1984	Terminator	Movie (USA)	Super-intelligent AI robots
	1987	RoboCop	Movie (USA)	Cyborg melded with human
	1999	Austin Powers: International Man of Mystery	Movie (USA)	androids
	2001	AI artificial Intelligence	Movie (USA)	Robot child that is loved by his mother

Figure 1.8 (cont.) AI and Public Imagination. *Source:* Authors *(continued)*

Theme	Year	Media	Movie (USA)	Tech
	2008	Wall-E (for kids)	Movie (USA)	Robot, e-waste,
	2013	The Machine	Movie (British)	Cybernetic implant, Virtual Sim of dead person,
Programming Control	1962	War with the Robots	Book (USA)	Robots that exceed human capacity
	1982	Tron	Movie (USA)	Human transported to computer mainframe software
	1979	The Two Faces of Tomorrow	Book (British)	Computers, are self-aware and can self-program but the issue is that they are logical, but not reasonable – and this is the problem
	1984	Neuromancer	Book (American-Canadian)	Hacker and cyberspace or the matrix, mind uploading in a digital format,
	1999	The Matrix series	Movie	Matrix or simulated reality, super-intelligent machines
Cyberwarfare	2012	Skyfall	Movie	Cyber-terrorism, malicious code, critical infrastructure like railways and power grid.
	1983	Wargames	Movie (USA)	Military supercomputer, hacking, inadvertent war
	1985	DARYL	Movie (USA)	Military super soldier robot-child
	2015	Blackhat	Movie (USA)	Cyber-terrorism, hacking, malware, stock exchange and nuclear plants
Data	1988	Islands in The Net	Bruce Sterling	Data heavens, data piracy

Figure 1.8 (cont.) AI and Public Imagination. *Source:* Authors

connectivity or regulatory constraints. Loneliness is another. Despite us living in one of the most networked eras in world history, there is an increasing fear of loneliness,[43] cyberbullying,[44] and the inability to differentiate reality from the virtual world.[45] The impact is seen via fake news, increasing cybercrimes, and growing social media intolerance.

1.4 Need for AI Ethics and Regulations

The carbon footprint of AI is close to five times the running of a car on petrol for one year (assuming 213M parameters using a neural architecture search) or a roundtrip flight between New York City and San Francisco (using a language processing model like the one Google uses). Cloud computing is significantly higher in cost than those that are trained on-site.[46] Of course, many cloud companies are off-setting their carbon footprint, but this does not necessarily sustain bio-diversity nor does it mean they do not produce carbon, greenhouse gases or other toxic pollutants. The bigger worry is the lack of understanding of the costs of AI. Environmental degradation in the form of e-waste has become a major issue. It is estimated that we generate 7.3kg of e-waste per capita (globally), which will double by 2030.[47] By early 2019, only 78 countries had an e-waste policy, and less than 82.6% were recycled.

AI that depends on "big data," which is exponentially increasing, requires constant retraining for several reasons (1) larger data sets require more re-calibration, more power, more computing power, and hardware (2) language itself is constantly evolving, and this means constant retraining required and (3) computer languages also evolve, not necessarily with seamless transitions. For example, (see Table 1.1), it is estimated that the cost of a training model can vary from US$ 41 (65 parameters using a Transformer model) to US$3,201,722 (using a Transformer model with 213Mn parameters and a neural network). Without a big budget for AI, we reach an ethics precipice. To optimize costs, we increase system vulnerabilities and data that can be hacked or misused.

TABLE 1.1 AI Transformer Model Training Costs

Models	Hours	Estimated cost (USD)	
		Cloud	Electric
1	120	$52–175	$5
24	2,880	$1,238–4,205	$118
4,789	239,942	$103,000–350,000	$9,870

Source: Adapted from Forti, Baldé, Kuehr and Bel (2020)[48]

A Brief History of AI ▪ 19

In 2020, the government's focus was on containing the coronavirus pandemic. The irony was that even though no formal AI strategies were announced, digital transformation was faster than planned to maintain, manage, or help recover business. But there are challenges of progressing too quickly with advanced AI without a strong AI policy in place, as has been highlighted by several scholars (See Figure 1.9).

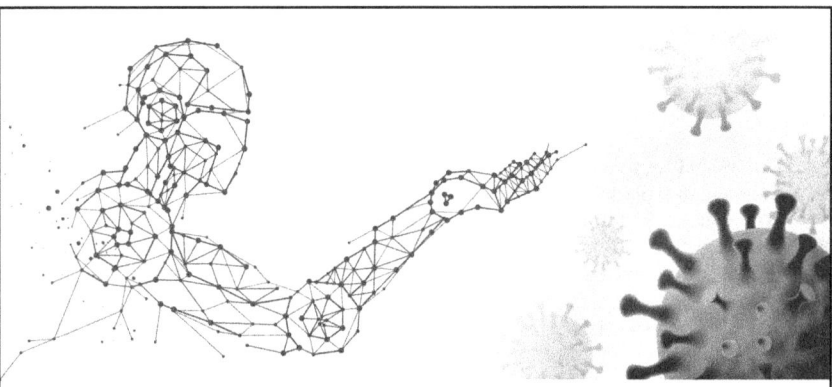

1. **Codebase:** In March 2020, the Medical Research Council (MRC) Centre for Global Infectious Disease Analysis released a pandemic simulation code that policymakers depended on for decisions. A series of tweets by Neil Ferguson[49] on the COVID-modelling stated:

   > I'm conscious that lots of people would like to see and run the pandemic simulation code we are using to model control measures against COVID-19. To explain the background—I wrote the code (thousands of lines of undocumented C) 13+ years ago to model flu pandemics . . . I am happy to say that @Microsoft and @GitHub are working with @Imperial_JIDEA and @MRC_Outbreak to document, refactor and extend the code to allow others to use without the multiple days training it would currently require (and which we don't have time to give) . . . They are also working with us to develop a web-based front end to allow public health policymakers from around the world to make use of the model in planning. We hope to make v1 releases of both the source and front end in the next 7–10 days . . . That timescale reflects the balancing of those priorities with the multitude of other urgent policy-relevant COVID-19 questions we are addressing . . .

   There were concerns from the public and other researchers about the original language, C+, which had many errors.

2. **Simulations are Probabilities:** There were concerns about the simulations—first from extrapolating from flu epidemics to COVID scenarios. For example, will the same factors be responsible for the same weightage? With COVID, the situation changed rapidly as the learning curve was steep, and there was so much uncertainty surrounding this new disease. Also, simulation models work on scenarios . . . so as probabilities, which means a decision choice is a choice you make of the probability of an outcome.
   As Tim Hall, Data Standards and Technical Lead at the Open Data Institute, states:[50] ". . . equally, updating the model as new data emerges isn't simply a question of

Figure 1.9 AI Challenges: COVID pandemic. *(continued)*

adding it to a training set. Instead, it's an open-ended process of revising assumptions and parameters with new information, and at times developing new scenarios."

3. **Forecasting:** With big data, mathematics is now discerning the way we forecast. These so-called "forecasting models" are based on pattern recognition and the data that the digital world is providing. The data has its issues: first, it is not historical (most created in the last few years), and second, it is dirty (not easy to use due to its variability). Despite this, governments, education, insurance, media, and other industries often prefer forecasting using big data. They are based on a range of (known) factors (ethnicity, income, education, etc.) and attempt to predict an outcome (employment, health, crime, etc.). The assumption is that if the prediction is correct, the algorithm is correct, which may not be valid. There has been significant research on algorithm biases with poor feedback loops that promote discrimination.[51] This bias is especially worrying for data-driven policy. AI, which tries to quantify human traits, may suffer from opacity, scale, and damage (the black box), leading us to a crisis of immense proportions if not careful.

4. **Time to Audit and for Transparency:** AI Models that governments use for decisions that affect the public need to be transparent. This transparency will build trust. In the above case of MRC, the objective was to be transparent so others could review the code, data, and results and assess their conclusions. The team released a version of their code on 22 April as open-source, and a bug was identified three days later by an external team which they fixed. An independent audit was able to replicate the results on 1 June 2020.[52] A report by the Ada Lovelace Institute and DataKind UK[53] states that ideally, you should have both an algorithm audit and an algorithmic impact assessment before taking a decision:

Algorithm audit
- **Bias audit:** a targeted, non-comprehensive approach focused on assessing algorithmic systems for bias
- **Regulatory inspection:** a broad approach focused on an algorithmic system's compliance with regulation or norms, necessitating many different tools and methods; typically performed by regulators or auditing professionals

Algorithmic impact assessment
- **Algorithmic risk assessment:** assessing possible societal impacts of an algorithmic system *before* the system is in use (with ongoing monitoring often advised)
- **Algorithmic impact evaluation:** assessing possible societal impacts of an algorithmic system on the users or population it affects *after* it is in use

Figure 1.9 (cont.) AI Challenges: COVID pandemic.

The commercialization or diffusion of AI innovations is complex: increasing regulations, greater involvement of the state as security concerns grow, market legacy systems, interoperability, or compatibility of fragmented systems, are some of the reasons that could hinder the future scale of AI. Future proxy wars may be cyber-wars that can be maleficent or emerge with poor governance and digital skills. Though AI played a backstage role, it indirectly was involved in the cyber siege of Estonia (2007); misdirection in USA elections (2016 and 2020), and the Twitter revolutions that were used to communicate to bypass state-monitored media (example, Tunisia 2010),[54] or the algorithmic bias leading to civil unrest (Facebook and the Rohingya crisis 2017). Events that threaten national security or further the agendas of rogue states may be where future defense funding will flow. A third AI winter is coming... but we are unsure whether it will be because of tech disillusionment, an economic crisis, or a much more catastrophic global event. We are at a tipping point—of tremendous progress or the advent of the third AI winter. What is critical is to work together and understand AI. This book will help all decision-makers, not just the expert in AI systems, understand what AI is and how to make better-informed decisions.

QUESTIONS

1. Do you think that AI goes through boom and bust cycles? If so, what phase are we in, and what are lessons we can learn from the past?
2. Is there a global imbalance when we look at AI ownership, manufacturing, data, markets, and customer education concerning AI? How will this affect businesses in your region?
3. The EU is pushing ahead with several AI regulations and policies to make accountability and transparency high on its agenda. What does this mean for your business if it is working in those markets? How do you think this will impact countries and regions across the world?
4. What do you think the world will look like in 2050? What are some great opportunities of AI and some challenges that your foresee for yourself personally, your parents, and for our collective futures?

MY INSIGHTS

The most difficult decisions I need to take are

MY INSIGHTS

The resources I need to build for the future are

MY INSIGHTS

The governance systems I will to put in place are

MY INSIGHTS

The training and skills I and my team need to develop are

_____
_____
_____
_____
_____
_____
_____
_____
_____
_____
_____
_____
_____
_____
_____
_____
_____
_____
_____
_____
_____
_____
_____
_____
_____

Notes

1. Roberts, J. (2016). Thinking machines: The search for artificial intelligence. *Distillations*, 2(2), 14–23. https://www.sciencehistory.org/distillations/thinking-machines-the-search-for-artificial-intelligence
2. Veisdal, J. (2019). The Birthplace of AI. In *The 1956 Dartmouth Workshop. Medium*. https://medium.com/cantors-paradise/the-birthplace-of-ai-9ab7d4e5fb00
3. Copeland, B. J. (1997). The church-turing thesis. https://plato.stanford.edu/entries/church-turing/–ThesHist
4. Stephens, M., & Vashishtha, H. (2020). *AI Smart Kit–Agile Decision Making on AI–Abridged Version*. Information Age Publishing, NC: USA.
5. McCarthy, J., Minsky, M. L., Rochester, N., & Shannon, C. E. (2018). A proposal for the Dartmouth summer research project on artificial intelligence (1955). *Reprinted online at* http://www-formal.stanford.edu/jmc/history/dartmouth/dartmouth.html
6. Schuchmann, S. (2019). History of the first AI Winter. *Towards Data Science*, May, 12. https://towardsdatascience.com/history-of-the-first-ai-winter-6f8c2186f80b
7. Bringsjord, S. (1998). Chess Is Too Easy. *Technology Review*, 101(2), 23–28. https://www.technologyreview.com/1998/03/01/237087/chess-is-too-easy/
8. Dreyfus, H. L. (1965). *Alchemy and artificial intelligence*. Rand Corp. https://www.rand.org/content/dam/rand/pubs/papers/2006/P3244.pdf
9. Dreyfus, H. L. (1978). *What Computers Can't Do: The Limits of Artificial Intelligence*. Harper Colophon.
10. Dreyfus, H. L. (1965). Op. cit.
11. Minsky, M., & Papert, S. (1969). An introduction to computational geometry. *Cambridge tiass., HIT*, 479, 480.
12. It took 17 years until such an algorithm, now known as backpropagation, was devised. Only later on, was it discovered that the backpropagation algorithm had been discovered before. Indeed, it turned out that the backpropagation algorithm had been invented before *Perceptrons* was even published.
13. Fleck, J. (1982). Development and establishment in artificial intelligence. In *Scientific establishments and hierarchies* (pp. 169–217). Springer, Dordrecht.
14. Bryson, J. J. (2019). The past decade and future of AI's impact on society. *Towards a new enlightenment*, 150–185. https://www.bbvaopenmind.com/en/articles/the-past-decade-and-future-of-ais-impact-on-society/. Kasabov, N., & Kozma, R. (1998). Hybrid intelligent adaptive systems. *International Journal of Intelligent Systems*, 13(6). https://doi.org/10.1002/(SICI)1098-111X(199806)13:6%3C453::AID-INT1%3E3.0.CO;2-K. Padgham, L., & Winikoff, M. (2005). *Developing intelligent agent systems: A practical guide*. John Wiley & Sons. Zalta, E. N. (2007). The Stanford Encyclopedia of Philosophy (Summer 2007 Edition). https://plato.stanford.edu/archives/sum2020/entries/artificial-intelligence/
15. McCorduck, P., & Cfe, C. (2004). *Machines who think: A personal inquiry into the history and prospects of artificial intelligence*. CRC Press.
16. Newquist, H. P., & Newquist, H. P. (1994). *The brain makers*. Sams Pub.
17. Evans, C. (2017, February 14). Hidden Figures no Longer. Computer History Museum. https://computerhistory.org/blog/hidden-figures-no-longer/

18. Computer History Museum (n.d). ENIAC. https://www.computerhistory.org/revolution/birth-of-the-computer/4/78
19. IBM. (n.d.). *IBM and the Gemini Program.* https://www.ibm.com/ibm/history/exhibits/space/space_gemini.html
20. NASA. (n. d.). *Katherine Johnson Biography.* https://www.nasa.gov/content/katherine-johnson-biography
21. Holland, B. (2018, August, 22). *Human Computers: The women of NASA.* https://www.history.com/news/human-computers-women-at-nasa; Harz, T.v. (2022, August 22). *Computers in Space! How Microchips and Code Unlocked the Stars.* https://history-computer.com/computers-in-space/
22. PwC. (2005). *The Defense Industry in the 21st Century.* https://www.pwc.pl/en/publikacje/defence_industry_ads.pdf
23. Ibid.
24. Koty, A. C. (2020). What is the China standards 2035 plan and how will it impact emerging industries. *China Briefing, Dezan Shira & Associates, July, 2,* 2020. https://www.china-briefing.com/news/chinas-corporate-social-credit-system-how-it-works/
25. Suwatchai, S. (n.d.). *The Rise of Smart Cities in China.* Bangkok Post. Retrieved November 2, 2020, from https://www.bangkokpost.com/business/2012427/the-rise-of-smart-cities-in-china
26. Al Maktoum, H. H. S. M. bin R. (2021, July 14). *@HHShkMohd.* HH Sheikh Mohammed. https://twitter.com/HHShkMohd
27. Arnold, Z., & Huang, T. (2020, July 14). *The US is turning away the world's best minds—and this time, they may not come back | MIT Technology Review.* MIT Technology Review; www.technologyreview.com. https://www.technologyreview.com/2020/07/14/1005133/h1b-visa-stem-immigration-trump-restrictions-covid-19/
28. Rivero, N. (2021, July 3). *The tech industry is leading a record M&A boom — Quartz.* Quartz; qz.com. https://qz.com/2028920/the-tech-industry-is-leading-a-record-ma-boom/
29. OECD, 2018. (2018, December 0). *Private Equity Investment in Artificial Intelligence.* Digital–OECD; https://www.oecd.org/sti/ieconomy/private-equity-investment-in-artificial-intelligence.pdf
30. DiResta, R. (2018). How The Tech Giants Created What Darpa Couldn't. *Wired, May, 29.* The DARPAA project was called Total Information Awareness. https://www.wired.com/story/darpa-total-informatio-awareness/
31. Deloitte, (2019). *Global Artificial Intelligence Industry Whitepaper.* https://www2.deloitte.com/content/dam/Deloitte/cn/Documents/technology-media-telecommunications/deloitte-cn-tmt-ai-report-en-190927.pdf
32. FFunction. (n.d.). *How much does your country invest in R&D?* How Much Does Your Country Invest in R&D?; uis.unesco.org. Retrieved December 5, 2020, from http://uis.unesco.org/apps/visualisations/research-and-development-spending/
33. Gross, R., Hanna, R., Gambhir, A., Heptonstall, P., & Speirs, J. (2018). How long does innovation and commercialisation in the energy sectors take? Historical case studies of the timescale from invention to widespread commercialisation in energy supply and end use technology. *Energy policy, 123,* 682–699.

34. Hartnett, K. (2019, April 24). *A New Approach to Multiplication Opens the Door to Better Quantum Computers | Quanta Magazine*. Quanta Magazine; www.quantamagazine.org; https://www.quantamagazine.org/a-new-approach-to-multiplication-opens-the-door-to-better-quantum-computers-20190424/https://www.quantamagazine.org/a-new-approach-to-multiplication-opens-the-door-to-better-quantum-computers-20190424/

35. Vincent, J. (2020, September 2). *Apple, Google, and Amazon respond to European tech taxes by passing on costs—The Verge*. https://www.theverge.com/2020/9/2/21418114/european-uk-digital-tax-services-apple-google-amazon-raise-prices

36. Council of EU. 2022. *Algorithms and Human Rights*. Algorithms and Human Rights. Retrieved April 24, 2022, from https://rm.coe.int/leaflet-algorithms-and-human-rights-en/168079cc19

37. Nylen, L. (2021, September 7). *Biden launches assault on monopolies*. Biden Launches Assault on Monopolies; www.politico.com. https://www.politico.com/news/2021/07/08/biden-assault-monopolies-498876

38. Hagendorff, T. (2020). The ethics of AI ethics: An evaluation of guidelines. *Minds and Machines*, *30*(1), 99–120. https://doi.org/10.1007/s11023-020-09517-8

39. Weinberg, B. H., Hang Pham, N. T., & Caraballo, L. D. (2017, March 27). *Large-scale design of robust genetic circuits with multiple inputs and outputs for mammalian cells–Nature Biotechnology*. Nature; doi.org. https://doi.org/10.1038/nbt.3805

40. Morrison, M., & de Saille, S. (2019). CRISPR in context: towards a socially responsible debate on embryo editing. *Palgrave Communications*, *5*(1), 1–9. https://doi.org/10.1057/s41599-019-0319-5

41. BBC, 2018. (2018, October 25). *Portrait by AI program sells for $432,000–BBC News*. BBC News; www.bbc.com. https://www.bbc.com/news/technology-45980863

42. Burridge, N. (2017, May 10). *Artificial intelligence gets a seat in the boardroom–Nikkei Asia*. Nikkei Asia; asia.nikkei.com. https://asia.nikkei.com/Business/Artificial-intelligence-gets-a-seat-in-the-boardroom

43. Chopik, W. J. (2016). The benefits of social technology use among older adults are mediated by reduced loneliness. *Cyberpsychology, Behavior, and Social Networking*, *19*(9), 551–556. Hunt, M. G., Marx, R., Lipson, C., & Young, J. (2018). No more FOMO: Limiting social media decreases loneliness and depression. *Journal of Social and Clinical Psychology*, *37*(10), 751–768.

44. UNICEF, 2019. (2019, September 3). *UNICEF poll: More than a third of young people in 30 countries report being a victim of online bullying*. UNICEF Poll: More than a Third of Young People in 30 Countries Report Being a Victim of Online Bullying; www.unicef.org. https://www.unicef.org/press-releases/unicef-poll-more-third-young-people-30-countries-report-being-victim-online-bullying

45. Bezzubova, E. (2018). Digital Depersonalization. Losing self between reality and cyberspace. *Psychology Today*, *26*. https://www.psychologytoday.com/us/blog/the-search-self/201801/digital-depersonalization. Aardema, F., Côté, S., & O'Connor, K. (2006, June). Effects of virtual reality on presence and dissociative experience. In *Cyberpsychology & Behavior* (Vol. 9, No. 6, pp. 653–653).

46. Strubell, E., Ganesh, A., & McCallum, A. (2019, July). Energy and Policy Considerations for Deep Learning in NLP. In *Proceedings of the 57th Annual Meeting of the Association for Computational Linguistics* (pp. 3645–3650).
47. Forti, V., Baldé, C. P., Kuehr, R., & Bel, G. (2020). The global e-waste monitor 2020. *Quantities, flows, and the circular economy potential*, 1–119. https://www.itu.int/en/ITUD/Environment/Documents/Toolbox/GEM_2020_def.pdf
48. Ibid.
49. Ferguson, N. (n.d.). *Twitter Thread*. Twitter; twitter.com. Retrieved October 12, 2020, from https://twitter.com/neil_ferguson/status/1241835454707699713
50. Hill, T. (2020, October 7). *How open data can avoid disaster*. Apolitical; apolitical.co. https://apolitical.co/solution-articles/en/open-data-disaster
51. O'neil, C. (2016). *Weapons of math destruction: How big data increases inequality and threatens democracy*. Broadway books.
52. Ferguson, N., Laydon, D., Nedjati Gilani, G., Imai, N., Ainslie, K., Baguelin, M., . . . & Ghani, A. (2020). Report 9: Impact of non-pharmaceutical interventions (NPIs) to reduce COVID19 mortality and healthcare demand. https://www.imperial.ac.uk/mrc-global-infectious-disease-analysis/covid-19/report-9-impact-of-npis-on-covid-19/
53. Lovelace, A., & DataKind, U. K. (2020). *Examining the black box: Tools for assessing algorithmic systems*. Technical report, AdaLovelace Institute, https://ico. org. uk/media/about-theico/consultations/2617219/guidance-on-the-ai-auditing-framework-draft-for-consultation. pdf.
54. Sullivan, A. (2011). Could Tunisia Be the Next Twitter Revolution. *The Atlantic: The Daily Dish*. https://www.theatlantic.com/daily-dish/archive/2011/01/could-tunisia-be-the-next-twitter-revolution/177302/

2

AI in Collectives of Humans and Artificial Agents

CHAPTER HIGHLIGHTS

1. There are many definitions of AI, but a simple economic perspective can help businesses and managers.
2. AIs can be understood as social entities that perceive, reason, and communicate in ways that require programming, its management, and organization.
3. The co-evolution of humans and AI leads to the emergence of human-agent collectives where sometimes the humans and sometimes the AIs are in the lead.

Cases:
Boeing 737 Max | UK Department of Education | Oko, USSR—The Nuclear War that Never Happened | Japan's Fujitsu and the UK Post Office

---

AI Enabled Business, pages 31–48
Copyright © 2023 by Information Age Publishing
www.infoagepub.com
All rights of reproduction in any form reserved.

2.1 AI—A Managerial Perspective

While there are many perspectives of what AI is and is not as described in Chapter 1, the standard work by Stuart Russell and Peter Norvig extensively discusses four AI aims: "*thinking humanly, thinking rationally, acting humanly or acting rationally.*"[1] However, to avoid getting lost in philosophical discussions, it can be purposeful for managers to adopt a simple economic perspective here: An AI can be perceived as an agent. This perspective goes back to the Latin expression "agens," which stands for the cause of an effect, an active substance, a person or thing that acts.[2]

Artificially intelligent agents are persistent and active in that they seem to "*perceive, reason, and communicate.*"[3] And the more AI develops, the more autonomous AI entities become, which means that they act without immediate interventions of others and based on "own" (internally represented), so called, beliefs and intentions.[4] Recent technological advancements in many domains are impressive *but* repeated AI failures also illustrate one general feature: AI cannot be perfectly rational but has to be considered boundedly rational. If the outline above is correct, then AI should be perceived as an agent that operates like a social entity that needs more than programming; it also requires organization and management.

In business, organization and management are regularly implemented to pursue economic value-additions. Guided and influenced by decades of business school education, managers and owners of companies today perceive their organizations to be populated by self-interested human beings who are boundedly rational utility maximizers. The bounded rationality model looked at economic behavior as an outcome of satisfying and adaptation of aspirational levels of success and failure.[5] It is often quantified as a series of outcomes based on decision choices, so it has parallels with programming.

To achieve the desired productivity increases, managers aim to manage and design their organizations to enable and motivate the economic actors so that they contribute in the best possible ways. These decisions, for example, include training programs to overcome aspects of bounded rationality or monetary incentives to align self-interest with the interests of the organization. These developments have been reviewed and criticized as far as managerial practices are concerned.[6] When managers focus on utility maximization, they are looking at:

1. *Decision utility* or *wantability*, inferred from choices and used to explain options.
2. *Experienced utility* is the hedonic experience associated with an outcome.[7] Or simply put, making assumptions—many of which do not lead to the results we want.

These unexpected outcomes result from those decisions that are contextually and temporally based.[8] As events unfold, we may think differently. These examples are seen in high-profile cases of Enron, Tyco, BP's Deepwater Horizon, the Bangladesh factory disaster, the VW Dieselgate, and the Wirecard scandals. These scandals exemplify the contemporary problematic practical implications of a drive for economic value-added and productivity-based businesses.

Therefore, it does not come as a surprise that the drive for efficiency has led to a focus on automation from Industry 1.0 to Industry 4.0. And observing these developments from an economic perspective, it is immediately clear why this is the case: automation can carve out irrational human behaviors and replace them with still boundedly but consistently rational behaviors. And, at least so far, computers enjoy less freedom to pursue self-interested behavior. Algorithms can be programmed to follow the calculus of rational-choice and utility maximization under constraints. In contrast to humans, computers are very fast with rational calculations. Therefore, where humans and algorithms work hand in hand, decision-making quality can be enhanced (see Figure 2.1).

Boundedly rational utility maximization thinking implies that machines are very suitable economic actors. This assumption has led to the belief that it is desirable to guide human decision-making with the help of computers or to even remove humans altogether from the value chain whenever possible. In business analytics, there is a vast dependency on descriptive analysis (an analysis of past performance). Further analysis is done via predictive analysis, which is used to forecast the uncertain future and manage 24/7 services.

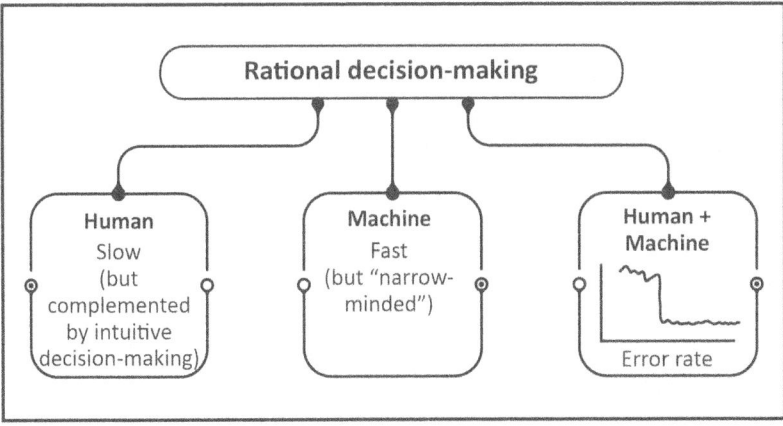

Figure 2.1 Rational fast and rational slow. *Source:* Authors

A more sophisticated business analysis is a prescriptive analysis that will identify what will happen, when it will happen, and why it will happen.[9] Predictive analytics has an expected market size of US$ 22.1 billion by 2026 with a CAGR of 24.6%.[10] Both, predictive and prescriptive analysis, depend on the quality and quantity of data. Predictive analytics depends on historical data, which may have its own set of biases. Prescriptive analytics need big data, which is often unstructured and needs to be constantly trained and fed into the system. It has been used successfully by the oil and gas industry to identify new sources of hydrocarbons. The market size of prescriptive analytics is expected to reach US$ 22.72 billion by 2025, with a CAGR of 21.68%.[11] Businesses across almost all industries are now exploring ways to use predictive analytics with the aim to ultimately automate decisions to eliminate typically human errors.

However, as indicated above, such strategies repeatedly fail. Besides the data issues, in management, while humans are regularly considered the weakest link in the chain, they are still tasked with crucial roles. They are often expected to monitor automation and intervene in case of problems. For example, it is still against the law to sleep behind the steering wheel of an autonomously driving Tesla. This issue is called the *irony of automation*.[12] Tragic examples of the *irony of automation* are plane crashes caused in situations where the automatic system failed or stopped working—for example, Air France flight AF447 in the year 2009.

Nevertheless, reverse scenarios where humans can no longer intervene can also be problematic. This situation was demonstrated by the crashes of Boeing 737 Max in 2018 and 2019. Here, the computer incorrectly identified a problem and took corrective action, which was fatally flawed, but the pilots could not intervene in a timely manner (see Figure 2.2).[13]

As an interim conclusion, it can be noted that it can be helpful for managers and other decision-makers to perceive AIs as distinct social entities that think and act with bounded rationality. This thinking turns AI into powerful economic actors, which again supports a lasting trend for automation. However, we must then acknowledge the responsibility of these agents and hence their liabilities. The irony of automation is that humans are replaced by computers because those are considered an improvement, but then the "weak" human is requested to build, train and supervise the machine. Therefore, to sustainably achieve the human–AI effect described in Figure 2.1, humans need adequate competencies acquired through effective training, enabling them to work hand in hand with the machine.

> The automation of planes has led to sophisticated computer systems that manage data being fed from multiple points to determine the best course of action. The computer model is designed to process information and then evaluate the best
> course of action. In some cases, for various reasons (more because the process is still evolving and not perfect), the assumptions the computer generates may not be accurate. The pilot is still supposed to have absolute control but, in case of an error, needs sufficient time to process data and take corrective action.
>
> **Air France Flight AF447**
> Aiming to fly from Rio de Janeiro to Paris on 31 May 2009, the Airbus crashed into the Atlantic Ocean and killed all 228 people on board. The incident occurred after high-altitude ice crystals had prompted the autopilot to switch off during turbulences. Caught by surprise, the crew did not notice that the jet began to stall and was unable to regain control of the plane.[14] A classic case of "the irony of automation."
>
> **Lion Air Flight 610 and Ethiopian-Airlines Flight 302**
> The Boeing 737 Max crash killed 189 and 149 passengers in both cases, respectively. It was found that software called the Maneuvering Characteristics Augmentation Software (MCAS) played a crucial role in both accidents. The MCAS repeatedly changed the angle of the aircraft's nose based on sensor data from one single faulty sensor. It was concluded that the aircraft's systems did not allow the pilots sufficient time to act and counter the nose-down movement initiated by the automated systems (MCAS).[15] A case that may be classified as the "irony of the irony of automation." According to many experts, the solution is to provide more training to pilots, especially to understand the process models the computers use and be better equipped to manage scenarios that overwhelm the computer.

Figure 2.2 Boeing 737 Max automation in planes.[16]

2.2 The Emergence of Human-Agent Collectives (HAC)

If technological progress is paired with greater adoption of digitalization, it will mean that more and more machines will begin to perceive, reason, and communicate to pursue autonomous goals. This progress is bound to have substantial effects on the economy and society as a whole. AI agents do not only compete more often with human labor, but they also, directly and indirectly, influence human action. Sometimes this enhances options, and sometimes this limits options available to humans.[17] A domain that illustrates this impact is the game of chess. In 1996, grandmaster Gari Kasparov got defeated by IBM's supercomputer Deep Blue.

In the light of this historical outcome, Kasparov re-considered human-AI options for the game of chess and soon became one of the initiators of what today is called Freestyle Chess or Advanced Chess. Here, chess tournaments are set out in ways that allow humans to cooperate with chess computers to compete with other man-machine teams. This new setting led to exciting and counterintuitive results.

What could be observed was that strong human players or supercomputers could not perform as competitively against relatively weak human players using standard chess computers with superior processes.[18] In other words, the game of chess began to see powerful effects of teamwork, a process that is used in sports like, for example, football. Unique to Freestyle Chess was that one of the team players was an AI.

In the meantime, more and more domains in the professional and the private sphere are characterized by people teaming up with artificial agents to achieve goals. In this respect, an AI teammate could be the chatbot that you contact to discuss your insurance claim or an AI that determines your feed on your social media. A piece of software will influence what you get to see on your screen or who you talk to. In fact, due to the dramatic cost decreases in computer hardware and software and internet connectivity, as well the rising value that can be generated from processing data, today, AI is in the middle of almost every transaction.[19]

Socio-technical systems in which humans and smart software (agents) interact have been identified as Human-Agent Collectives (HAC).[20] With AI in the middle of most transactions today, HAC has emerged in many industries. And they are there to shape and fundamentally change the game by redefining the social and work environment for humans.

The beginning of this trend is marked and illustrated, for example, by the airline industry, where the crews on the flight decks of contemporary airliners are assisted by software that relies on tens of thousands of sensors distributed across the plane (see Figure 2.2).[21] Other examples can be found on the ground and in seemingly less technologically advanced industries, like a farmer guided by precision agriculture technology.

Similarly, in marketing, product managers have begun to use AI language models for commercial purposes, which lets software agents interact with customers (chat bots). Psychotherapists have started to work with embodied conversational agents to provide internet-based cognitive behavior therapy in preventative mental health care.[22] In warehouses, smart logistics management software has been directing human labor to ensure efficient order processing for some time.[23] These examples have in common that, in each case, technological change considerably influences the working environment for humans. To the extent that computers can adopt new roles, the roles of humans in HAC change (see Figure 2.3). Or, more generally,

> In 2020, with COVID-19, the UK Department of Education decided to use AI to grade students for the annual Advanced Level qualifications (A-levels), which were canceled because of the pandemic. The program developed by the UK's Office of Qualifications and Examinations Regulation (Ofqual) would predict a grade based on the historical performance and ranking of the student.[24] The results of the algorithm's predictions were lower than the assessments of the students' ability by the teachers' in 40% of the cases in England, Ireland, and Wales, leading to demonstrations till the government agreed to compromise—deciding that they  would take the higher of the two scores.[25] The system seemed to have an inherent bias favoring private schools.
>
> These issues are not new: 25% of students who would not take the Scottish Qualifications Authority (SQA) also had their grades downgraded by the algorithm. The ensuing protests led to a reversal of the decision and reinstatement of the originally predicted grades offered by teachers. Scotland's Education Secretary commented that "young people feeling their future had been determined by statistical modeling rather than their own ability." There seems to exist a digital divide in (1) data (Scotland has less metadata than the UK), (2) weightages allocated for calculating predicted grades, and (3) inherent biases in results based on historical trends—the so-called postcode issue—deprived schools.
>
> The AI Auditing Framework[26] highlights the issue of "Trade-Offs": privacy versus accuracy; accuracy versus fairness; privacy versus fairness; explainability versus accuracy; explainability versus security. The report states: "AI can be subject to biases which require careful testing before roll-out" and then continues by saying, "An adequate way to avoid such situations can be to create Human-AI teams that are organized in ways that constructively deal with potential biases on part of the involved humans as well as on part of the involved AI in order to select the best possible decision."[27]

Figure 2.3 UK Department of Education—AI and teachers.

with AIs involved as social entities, the roles of both humans and agents are beginning to co-evolve.

In this new context, the already long-lasting trend toward automation will undoubtedly continue, which means that human work will be replaced by machine work. But this is now increasingly complemented by the idea of augmentation, which stands for human enhancement.[28] Here, AI helps achieve *adjacent possible*[29] in technology, business, economy, society, and the environment. *Adjacent possible* is defined as all things possible in a particular space at a given point in time. For example, aircrafts became possible only with the invention of stable, lightweight materials and combustion engines. Especially in the domain of knowledge work, division of labor between man

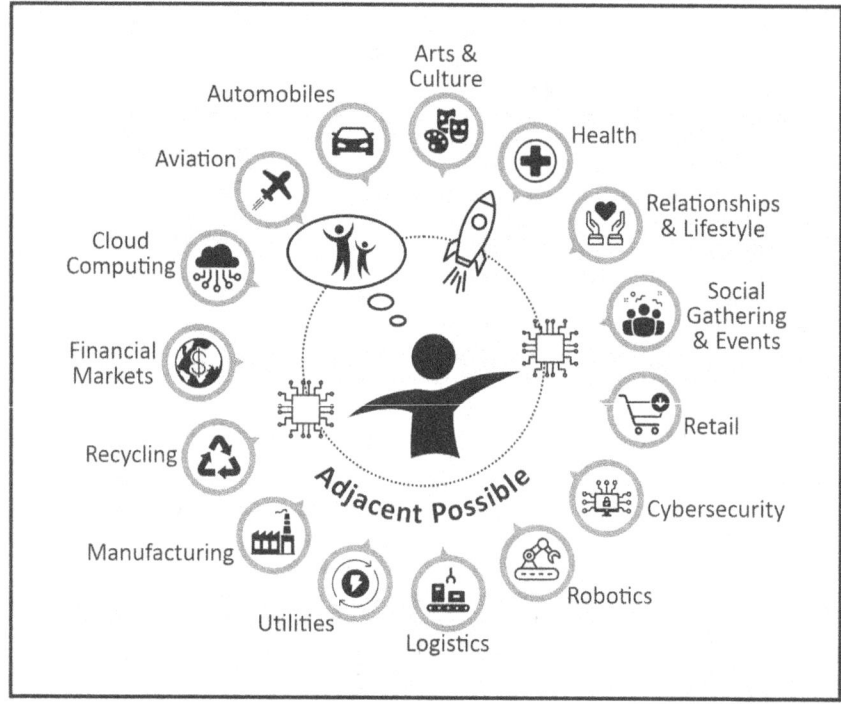

Figure 2.4 Automation and augmentation to strive for the adjacent possible.
Source: Authors

and machine, along with increased specialization, propel unprecedented diversification of the economy (Figure 2.4).

One of the remarkable aspects of this co-evolution is that the era of issuing instructions to passive machines is over, and humans have started to work in tandem with highly interconnected artificially intelligent agents that act autonomously.[30] These environments are not closed systems anymore but open. It is flexible social interactions as we have known them from human society for millennia that suddenly also characterize the interplay with machines. Here, *"sometimes the humans take the lead, sometimes the computer does, and this relationship can vary dynamically."*[31]

The notions of *flexible autonomy* and *agile teaming*[32] describe the short-lived nature of teams with a varying degree of human involvement with authority relations that are not considered fixed but context-dependent. Machines are proactively involved in information gathering and filtering, analytical, and decision-making processes. This raises questions of social accountability and responsibility. Since AIs often operate behind the scenes,

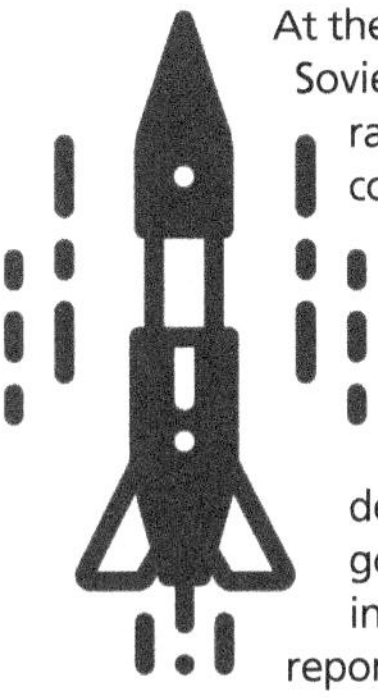

AI in Collectives of Humans and Artificial Agents ▪ 39

> At the height of the Cold War between the USA and the USSR, the Soviets noticed something unusual. Their nuclear early-warning radar Oko,[33] a network of about forty satellites, used trajectory computations based on infrared lights of engine fumes to identify hostile airborne threats. On September 26, 1983, the system showed that the USA had launched one intercontinental ballistic missile. Three weeks earlier, the Soviets had shot down an airplane of Korean Airlines. The USA with NATO had been playing war games across Europe putting the USSR in a defensive position. The lieutenant colonel, Stanislav Petrov, who got the initial reports, took a decision to wait for more information, but ground systems, fifteen minutes later, did not report the missile. Instead, the computer showed four more missiles being launched. His gut instinct reminded him that the computer testing had not been adequate before it was made operational, and his training had etched in his head that the USA had 1,000 missiles and launching just five would be too few if they wanted to take the Soviets out.[34] He likely prevented a nuclear war by not escalating this warning report up the chain of command. Later it was identified that the system had malfunctioned and mistook sunlight reflections on high-altitude clouds as a missile attack. While this was an early computer system, malfunctions like this still happen.

Figure 2.5 Oko, USSR: The nuclear war that never happened.[35]

their rationales and actions are usually not readily available to the involved humans. We still need humans to have the final control (see Figure 2.5).

The open nature of HAC implies that there is neither central control nor central information. Instead,

> control and information are widely dispersed among a large number of potentially self-interested people and agents with different aims and objectives. [...]. The real-world context means uncertainty, ambiguity, and bias are endemic, and so the agents need to handle information of varying quality, trustworthiness, and provenance.[36]

The ability for critical thinking is a human capability and an important one for decision making. In the example of the UK Post Office (see Figure 2.6), one wonders if the tally could not have been calculated manually to check if the people being accused were guilty or innocent.

The emerging overall picture of the properties of HAC is illustrated in Figure 2.7. For managers and decision-makers, the emergence of HAC has implications for external market strategies and the internal structure of their organizations. Externally and internally, new adjacent possibilities (positive and negative) must be understood and captured to derive suitable decisions for products and services provided.[37]

> In 1996, the UK Post Office installed a computer system called Horizon, developed by Fujitsu, Japan. This was the start of the government digitalization strategy. The Post Office was one of the largest retail networks in UK—17,000 Post Office branches, a total of 38,000 service counter. The contract was at that time the largest non-militray contract in Europe. The idea was to make the processes of transactions, accounting and stocktaking digital. The money seemed well justified when over 736 employees were caught steeling by the accounting software between 2000 to 2014. This averages to one conviction a week! Employees complained there was a computer bug that was creating errors, even shortfalls by £1000s, but official preferred to believe the computer system. From 2009 onwards postmasters who were accused began telling their story. In 2012, finally the Post Office launched an external review and they found a system of bugs and flaws. While this is by no means as complex a modern AI system, the issues of interoperability, reliability, transparency and good decision making while managing an outsourced distributed system are still important.[38] A decade later from the first public stories, and between 2019–2022, the wrongly accused were collectively awarded over £30 million in compensation.[39] The Post Office received £1 billion in taxpayer subsidies for the compensation for the scandal.[40] Considering some of the victims went to jail, lost their reputations, suffered financial losses, bad health, and even died this was considered a "an affront to the public conscience." Though the system continued to be faulty, Fujitsu received multiple contracts from the UK government, including for the defense sector.[41]

Figure 2.6 Japan's Fujitsu and the UK Post Office.[42]

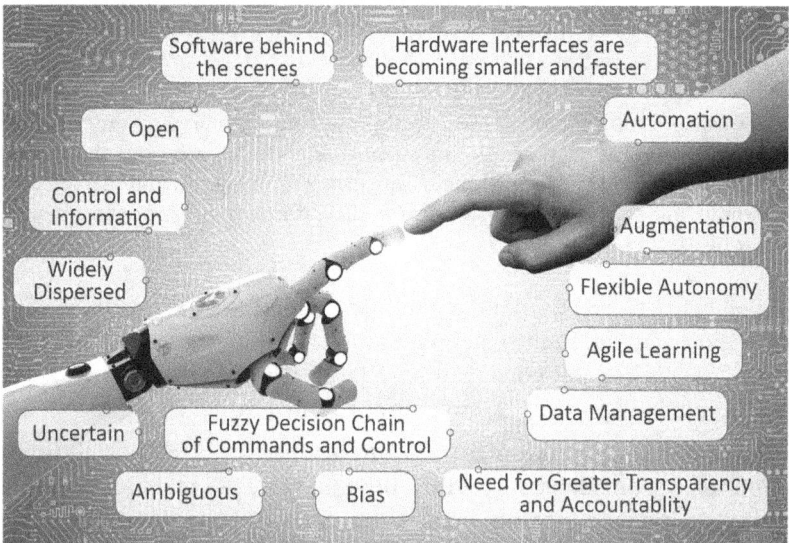

Figure 2.7 Properties of human-agent collectives: Human situations that are intermediated by software agents. *Source:* Authors

QUESTIONS

1. How does the narrow focus on utility maximization or efficiency prevent us from seeing the dark side of AI? Give one example that has recently caught your imagination.
2. What are the properties of Human-Agent Collectives that worry you? How can you ensure that the AI systems you use to minimize the concerns illustrated in the chapter?
3. AI computes at high speeds. Humans can't match this speed of computations (we compute differently and call it gut instinct, but it is not a rational model like algorithms use). How will you ensure accountability and human oversight for decisions that a computer may take a split second to calculate? Is a 1% error tolerable?
4. Who (which manager) is responsible for the failure of an AI system that directly affects your stakeholders?

MY INSIGHTS

The most difficult decisions I need to take are

MY INSIGHTS

The resources I need to build for the future are

MY INSIGHTS

The governance systems I will to put in place are

MY INSIGHTS

The training and skills I and my team need to develop are

Notes

1. Russell, S. J., & Norvig, P. (2016). *Artificial intelligence: a modern approach.* Malaysia.
2. Tokoro, M. (1994, August). Agents: Towards a society in which humans and computers cohabitate. In *European Workshop on Modelling Autonomous Agents in a Multi-Agent World* (pp. 1–10). Springer, Berlin, Heidelberg.
3. Huhns, M. N., Singh, M. P., & Ksiezyk, T. (1998). Global information management via local autonomous agents. *Readings in Agents, Huhns, MN, Singh, MP, Morgan Kaufmann Publishers, Ca,* 36–45.
4. Wagner, D. N. (2001). *Software-agents and liberal order: an inquiry along the borderline between economics and computer science.* Universal-Publishers.
5. Simon, H. (1957). Abehavioral model of rational choice. *Models of man, social and rational: Mathematical essays on rational human behavior in a social setting.*
6. Ghoshal, S. (2005). Bad management theories are destroying good management practices. *Academy of Management learning & education, 4*(1), 75–91.
7. Kahneman, D., & Thaler, R. H. (2006). Anomalies: Utility maximization and experienced utility. *Journal of economic perspectives, 20*(1), 221–234.
8. Strotz, R. H. (1955). Myopia and inconsistency in dynamic utility maximization. *The review of economic studies, 23*(3), 165–180.
9. Agrawal, A., Gans, J., & Goldfarb, A. (2018). *Prediction machines: the simple economics of artificial intelligence.* Harvard Business Press.
10. Factors, F., &. (2021, March 18). *At 24.5% CAGR, Global Predictive Analytics Market Size to.* GlobeNewswire News Room; www.globenewswire.com. https://www.globenewswire.com/news-release/2021/03/18/2195402/0/en/At-24-5-CAGR-Global-Predictive-Analytics-Market-Size-to-Register-Record-Value-of-USD-5-7-Billion-by-2026-Says-Facts-Factors.html
11. IndustryARC, 2021. (n.d.). *Prescriptive Analytics Market Share, Size and Industry Growth Analysis 2020–2025.* Prescriptive Analytics Market Share, Size and Industry Growth Analysis 2020–2025; www.industryarc.com. Retrieved November 2021, from https://www.industryarc.com/Research/Prescriptive-Analytics-Market-Research-500696
12. Bainbridge, L. (1983). Ironies of Automation. *Automatica, 19*(6), 775–779.
13. Malquist, S., & Rapoport, R. (2021). The Plane Paradox: More Automation Should Mean More Training.." https://www.wired.com/story/opinion-the-plane-paradox-more-automation-should-mean-more-training/. Leinfelder, A. (2019, August 22). *Did Boeing, aviation industry heed lessons of 2009 Air France crash?* Houston Chronicle; www.houstonchronicle.com. https://www.houstonchronicle.com/business/article/Did-Boeing-aviation-industry-heed-lessons-of-14369021.php
14. Oliver, N., Calvard, T., & Potočnik, K. (2017). The tragic crash of Flight AF447 shows the unlikely but catastrophic consequences of automation. *Harvard Business Review, 15.* https://hbr.org/2017/09/the-tragic-crash-of-flight-af447-shows-the-unlikely-but-catastrophic-consequences-of-automation.
15. Gates., D. (2020). Op. Cit.
16. Compiled from various sources: Malquist, S., & Rapoport, R. (2021). The Plane Paradox: More Automation Should Mean More Training." https://www

.wired.com/story/opinion-the-plane-paradox-more-automation-should-mean-more-training/. Gates, D., & Baker, M. (2019). The inside story of MCAS: How Boeing's 737 MAX system gained power and lost safeguards. *Seattle Times*. https://www.seattletimes.com/seattle-news/times-watchdog/the-inside-story-of-mcas-how-boeings-737-max-system-gained-power-and-lost-safeguards/. Gates, D. (2020). Q&A: What led to Boeing's 737 MAX crisis. *The Seattle Times, 18*. https://www.seattletimes.com/business/boeing-aerospace/what-led-to-boeings-737-max-crisis-a-qa/

17. Carr, N. (2014). *The glass cage: How our computers are changing us.* WW Norton & Company.
18. Kasparov, G. (2021). *How life imitates chess.* Random House. London: Arrow Books; Cowen, T. (2013). *Average is over: Powering America beyond the age of the great stagnation.* Penguin.
19. Varian, H. R. (2014). Beyond big data. *Business Economics, 49*(1), 27–31.
20. Jennings, N. R., Moreau, L., Nicholson, D., Ramchurn, S., Roberts, S., Rodden, T., & Rogers, A. (2014). Human-agent collectives. *Communications of the ACM, 57*(12), 80–88.
21. Yedavalli, R. K., & Belapurkar, R. K. (2011). Application of wireless sensor networks to aircraft control and health management systems. *Journal of Control Theory and Applications, 9*(1), 28–33.
22. Suganuma, S., Sakamoto, D., & Shimoyama, H. (2018). An embodied conversational agent for unguided internet-based cognitive behavior therapy in preventative mental health: feasibility and acceptability pilot trial. *JMIR mental health, 5*(3), e10454.
23. Mahroof, K. (2019). A human-centric perspective exploring the readiness towards smart warehousing: The case of a large retail distribution warehouse. *International Journal of Information Management, 45*, 176–190.
24. Porter, J. (2020). UK ditches exam results generated by biased algorithm after student protests. *The Verge, 17*. https://www.theverge.com/2020/8/17/21372045/uk-a-level-results-algorithm-biased-coronavirus-covid-19-pandemic-university-applications
25. Tennison, J. (2020). How does Ofqual's grading algorithm work? RPubs. Retrieved September 01, 2020. https://rpubs.com/JeniT/ofqual-algorithm?utm_campaign=The%20Batch&utm_medium=email&_hsmi=93994741&_hsenc=p2ANqtz-8eR51qBsCArAq6OXWwF_opVB-LCQMI1vU2VG2Tzqe0-RTaI9PZwt49reiOhpiXj9R3JqMid5oX7PI5HuMc7h31Yap92w&utm_content=93994741&utm_source=hs_email
26. *Trade-offs | ICO.* (n.d.). Trade-Offs | ICO; ico.org.uk. Retrieved March 2022, from https://ico.org.uk/about-the-ico/news-and-events/ai-blog-trade-offs/
27. ICO. (n.d.). AI Auditing Framework, Retrieved March 2022, from https://ico.org.uk/about-the-ico/news-and-events/ai-auditing-framework/
28. Davenport, T. H., & Kirby, J. (2016). *Only humans need apply: Winners and losers in the age of smart machines.* New York, NY: Harper Business.
29. Koppl, R., Kauffman, S., Felin, T., & Longo, G. (2015). Economics for a creative world. *Journal of Institutional Economics, 11*(1), 1–31.

30. Jennings, N. R., Moreau, L., Nicholson, D., Ramchurn, S., Roberts, S., Rodden, T., & Rogers, A. (2014). Human-agent collectives. *Communications of the ACM, 57*(12), 80–88.
31. Ibid, p. 80
32. Ibid, p. 82
33. Anatoly, Z. 2000. *Oko early-warning satellite.* (n.d.). Oko Early-Warning Satellite; Retrieved April 2022, from http://www.russianspaceweb.com/oko.html
34. Smith, K. N. (2018, September 25). *The Computer That Almost Started A Nuclear War, And The Man Who Stopped It.* Forbes; www.forbes.com. https://www.forbes.com/sites/kionasmith/2018/09/25/the-computer-that-almost-started-a-nuclear-war-and-the-man-who-stopped-it/?sh=376589612835
35. Ibid, p. 82
36. Nagesh, A. (2017, September 18). *Stanislav Petrov–the man who quietly saved the world–has died aged 77.* Metro; metro.co.uk. https://metro.co.uk/2017/09/18/stanislav-petrov-the-man-who-quietly-saved-the-world-has-died-aged-77-6937015/
37. Information Security Research & Education, University College London (UCL) (2021). What went wrong with Horizon: learning from the Post Office Trial. https://www.benthamsgaze.org/2021/07/15/what-went-wrong-with-horizon-learning-from-the-post-office-trial/
38. SkyNews. (2020, June 30). Victims of Post Office Horizon scandal awarded millions more in compensation. https://news.sky.com/story/victims-of-post-office-horizon-scandal-awarded-millions-more-in-compensation-12643049
39. Flinders, K. (2022, April 4). Fujitsu bags £430m government contracts despite rising cost of Post Office Horizon scandalhttps://www.computerweekly.com/news/252515504/Fujitsu-bags-430m-government-contracts-despite-rising-cost-of-Post-Office-Horizon-scandal
40. Ibid.
41. Peachey, K. (2022, March 22). Post Office scandal: What the Horizon saga is all about. https://www.bbc.com/news/business-56718036; Fujitsu. Nd. Fujitsu's Systems and Operational Services to UK Post Office and the Worldwide Trend of Post Offices. https://www.fujitsu.com/downloads/SVC/fs/casestudies/uk-postoffice2.pdf

3

AI and the Changing Nature of Work and the Firm

CHAPTER HIGHLIGHTS

1. AI leads to the micro-division of labor and new gains from specialization.
2. The challenge within the firm expands from the job to the task level.
3. AI, as a new factor of production, creates a new variation of the classic principal-agent problem.
4. The development of information-asymmetries is bound to have a substantial impact on the firm's competitiveness.

Cases:
US Post Services and mail tracking | Duodecim (Finland) and medical training | facial recognition

3.1 Micro-Division of Labor

Exciting developments have been outlined in the preceding chapters. Advancements in AI increasingly lead to automation, especially in knowledge work. These advancements are combined with new ways of augmenting human activity and work. Computers can be seen as social entities that perceive, reason, and communicate. They become more and more autonomous parts of our organizations. It can be helpful to look at these organizations as Human-Agent Collectives (HAC), where sometimes the human is in the lead and sometimes the (AI) agent. HACs are defined as a new class of "socio-technical systems in which humans and smart software (agents) engage in flexible relationships in order to achieve both their individual and collective goals."[1]

Due to rapid technological development and due to the ways how machines learn, we are more than ever in history confronted with exponential developments. All of this implies how our organizations function and operate is changing too. In business, we are confronted not only with the changing nature of work but also of the firm.[2] The features and the underlying patterns of these changes are highlighted in this chapter.

In a world where AI machines operate like social entities in collectives of humans and AI agents, very quickly, a fundamentally important economic pattern once famously described by Adam Smith in his classic work on The Wealth of Nations gains new impetus: the effects that arise from specialization and division of labor.[3] At the outset of the Industrial Revolution in 1776, Smith used the simple example of a pin factory to show how productivity can be increased by applying the principle of specialization and division of labor. Since then, this principle has fundamentally shaped economic development, ultimately leading to a globalized and digitized world. The resulting complexity is unprecedented.[4]

Due to industrialization, the number of specialized professional roles in human collectives has increased from a couple of hundred to almost 1,000 today.[5] The effects of the differentiation of the labor market and growing dependency on economic exchange can be traced to a dramatic rise in GDP along with a market that is competitively vying with products and services. Until the rise of e-commerce about a decade ago, the number of products physically available in large department stores had grown from 7000 items in the 1970s to 50,000+ in the 2020s.[6] This market shift was a breakthrough development. However, with the rise of digitalization, Human-Agent Collectives, including AI agents, began to unfold new dynamics of specialization and differentiation and, within less than a decade, helped to increase the number of products available to average consumers to more than 500 million products, now available through e-commerce platforms like amazon.com.[7]

Before the rise of AI, Adam Smith had already identified that "the invention of all those machines by which labor is so much facilitated and abridged seem to have been originally owing to the division of labor."[8] Due to the advancements in AI, this principle enables exponential development. As more tasks are delegated to more autonomous artificially intelligent agents, the finer the granularity of the pattern of division of labor becomes. Division of labor becomes a micro-division of work. As and when machines take over cognitive tasks and produce new knowledge by recombining inputs, they again create new possibilities of exchange; there is a further micro-division of tasks, knowledge, and work, resulting in increased gains from this super-specialization. This further increases the complexity of the economic system.[9] This development is captured by Figure 3.1.

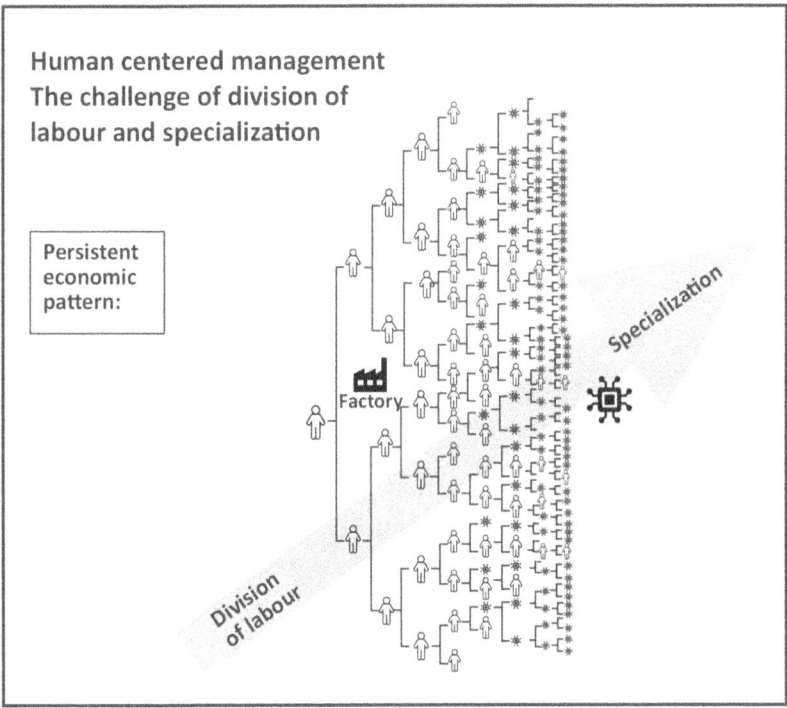

Figure 3.1 Micro-division of labor with AI leads to super-specialization and increases complexity. *Source:* Authors

From the organization's point of view, management now needs to evolve to a whole other level. In the traditional economy, firms operated by identifying markets to sell their products and services to and by acquiring the necessary resources. To do this successfully, they had to organize human individuals in ways that benefitted from the division of labor. Henry Ford's assembly line for the production of the Model-T or Apple's outsourcing of the iPhone production is an example of the division of labor.

In the AI economy, the division of labor does not stop at the level of the human individual. The job role of a human individual typically consists of various tasks. With the introduction of AI to the firm, new functions or roles can be defined for AI agents. These functions or roles may consist of a carefully selected set of narrow tasks or even only a single task. Therefore, as exhibited in Figure 3.2, the division of labor between distinct economic actors now extends to the task level and requires appropriate organizational control by the firm (see Figure 3.3). The number of "occupations" adopted by autonomous artificial agents is unknown today. Still, it can be expected to be exponentially higher than the number of occupations available to humans in the economy. And it is rising quickly. As AI improves, a business must adjust its division of labor between humans and machines.[10]

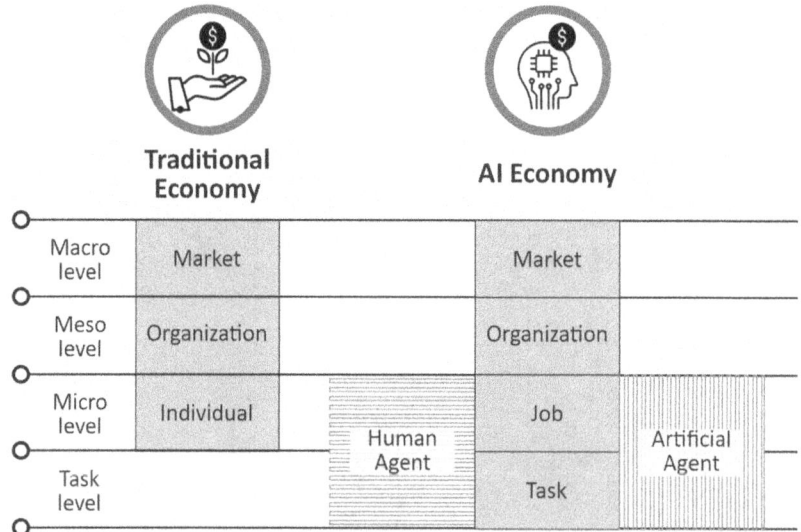

Figure 3.2 The changing structure of the economy. *Source:* Adapted from Wagner (2021)[11]

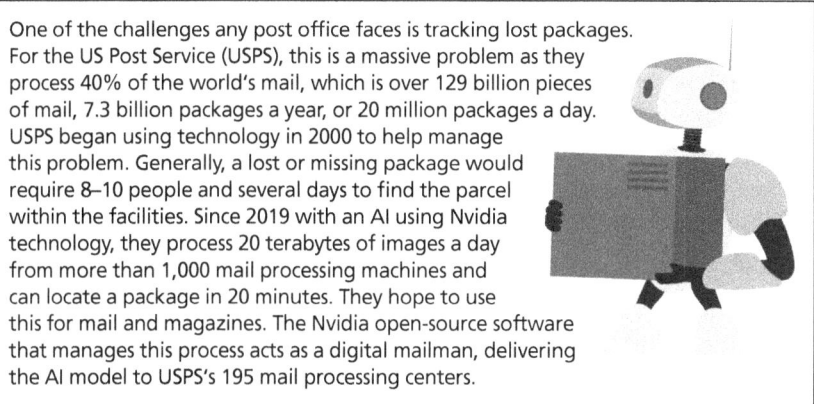

One of the challenges any post office faces is tracking lost packages. For the US Post Service (USPS), this is a massive problem as they process 40% of the world's mail, which is over 129 billion pieces of mail, 7.3 billion packages a year, or 20 million packages a day. USPS began using technology in 2000 to help manage this problem. Generally, a lost or missing package would require 8–10 people and several days to find the parcel within the facilities. Since 2019 with an AI using Nvidia technology, they process 20 terabytes of images a day from more than 1,000 mail processing machines and can locate a package in 20 minutes. They hope to use this for mail and magazines. The Nvidia open-source software that manages this process acts as a digital mailman, delivering the AI model to USPS's 195 mail processing centers.

Figure 3.3 USPS and mail tracking.[12]

3.2 A New Factor of Production and a New Dilemma for the Firm

The delegation of tasks to increasingly autonomous AI agents creates new organizational challenges. AI brings a new factor of production to the table: machine labor. And micro-division of labor with AI generates an unprecedented superabundance of data. And data itself can today also be interpreted as a factor of production.[13] This trend is best exemplified by the firms with the highest market capitalization in the global economy, namely companies like Microsoft, Apple, Amazon, or Alphabet, all of which focus on software and data to develop their business. AI-based machine labor is particularly well suited to generate value from data. But this poses a new kind of dilemma for the firm: The machine labor that is put to use is typically not the firm's own production factor, but it is made available through a third party, for example one of the giant tech corporations just named. This results in a peculiar type of problem, what economists call a principal-agent problem. In the case above, the government-run post office (USPS) works with a private sector firm (Nvidia) and uses public data (addresses and parcel shapes, and other details). In addition, there are management issues of governance than can arise like privacy, data ownership, IP, and responsibility of AI training.

Principal-agent problems are commonplace in organizations. They describe situations where an agent does not act in the principal's best interest.[14] This problem becomes possible when agents have more information about a situation than their principal. For example, the case regularly occurs in employment relationships when the employee does not work as effectively or efficiently as he or she could do, and the manager fails to recognize the deficiency.

In a world with AI, the principal-agent problem appears in a new shape. Like a love triangle in human relations, it does make life more complicated. And indeed, there are three minimum actors involved (see Figure 3.4). First, the human user of AI as a principal; second, there is the AI agent; and third, there is a provider of the AI agent. At times, this relationship is more complicated, as the provider has a dual role in owning the AI agent, and also a principal. At the same time, the AI provider is a supplier of AI services to the user and thus in the role of an agent.

Leaving technology aside for a moment, from an organizational point of view, this setting can be best compared with the employment of a temporary agency worker.[15] Like an agency worker, the AI agent is provided as a service. However, in this constellation, the specialized software agent regularly has more information than its principals. Different from traditional

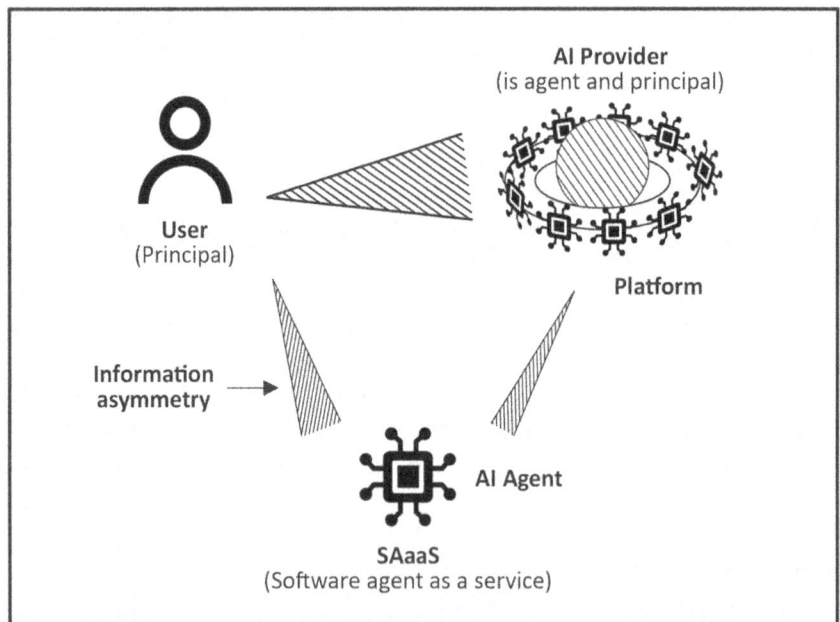

Figure 3.4 Asymmetric information in a triangular agency relationship with AI. Source: Wagner (2020)[16]

agency work, the user may experience distinct interactions with software agents adopting specific roles, like Siri or Alexa. But ultimately, these agents are part of the same computational resource (see the example highlighted in Figure 3.5).

These software agents create an unprecedented information asymmetry that the AI provider can exploit to the disadvantage of the user and his firm. What has to be taken into account is that AI is a general-purpose technology. AI providers typically operate in different environments and offer their technology to many businesses. This agility in operating environments enables them to combine the data collected and processed by many software agents in various domains like consumer behavior, social media activities, or mobility. This scenario of decentral action between principal and agent and central learning by the AI providers is illustrated in Figure 3.6.

Duodecim, The Finnish Medical Society, is Finland's largest scientific association. It was established in 1881, focusing on doctors. Its purpose was to develop professional skills and clinical practice. In a joint pilot, Duodecim's Oppiporti and the City of Helsinki's Pätijä project worked with Glue, a public company based in Finland, to create the virtual exercises.[17]

In 2019[18] they released immersive virtual training exercises to help health care and elderly care practitioners test, learn or augment their skills on a virtual unconscious patient. The simulations were used to help health care practitioners who take care of stay-at-home patients who were facing acute situations. The training was to prevent the need for transfer to the emergency care rooms without compromising on the care of the clients.[19] Here, there is a teamwork between the government (which approves regulations and training qualifications), the expert knowledge providers (medical and technology), the care workers and the organizations they work for.

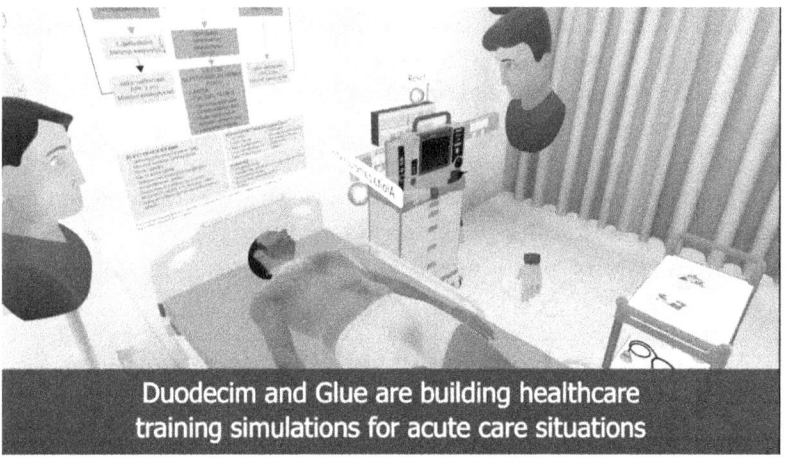

Figure 3.5 Duodecim, and medical training. *Source:* Screenshot from Vimeo[20]

56 ▪ AI Enabled Business

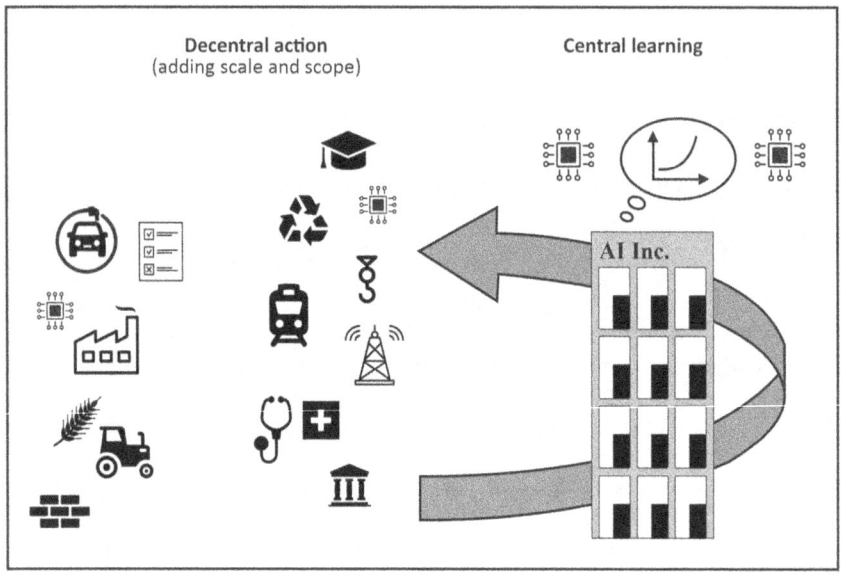

Figure 3.6 With decentral action (on behalf of the customer firms), the AI-provider enables central learning. *Source:* Authors

Note that the beneficiary of the learning is now, at least in part, no longer the firm but its AI software and its software provider. Over time, this is likely to have a negative impact on the competitiveness of the firm while the AI provider—as the exponential organization (ExO) described later in Chapter 4—enjoys exponential positive network effects. A network effect is an increase in value that is a direct outcome of more people using the service. In the example of USPS, more packages are more data. This data can be used to train the models to do more things than merely track packages. The concept can also be used in other industries—finding lost airline luggage, etc.—so-called *adjacent possible*, where incremental changes and configurations may allow future opportunities.[21] In this case, whether the gain will be the post office or the provider of the AI service is one of the management control questions you would have to ask.

3.3 A Necessity to Understand and, if Possible, Manage Information Asymmetries

It is evident that to avoid exploitation and ensure long-term competitiveness, the new structure of AI love triangles (refer to Figure 3.4) requires attention from the management of any firm. Moreover, the necessity to keep track of information asymmetries is further increased by underlying technological and social developments:

- Information asymmetries are created where AI is put to use, and the adoption of the technology is spreading fast because AI is much faster than humans in accessing and processing information that is available in digital form. This rapid diffusion means that firms have no choice but to rely on this technology.
- Information asymmetries are continuously nurtured and benefit from *dataveillance*[22] because on a global scale, more and more users are almost always online and via various applications where they, directly and indirectly, interact with an abundance of services on an ongoing basis which is reflected in hundreds of thousands of server contacts per week.[23]
- Information asymmetries and their origin can be expected to turn into blackbox for the everyday user and the typical firms as a customer of AI services since the ways AI agents process information and arrive at decisions are no longer easy traceable. AI is used to make predictions, but its behavior is no longer predictable. The inexplicability and non-transparency of decisions made by machine learning systems are widely discussed topics.[24]

In light of these general trends, managers are well-advised to review regularly and, where possible, actively manage information asymmetries that can arise due to the deployment of AI. The aim is to watch out for situations where the interests of the agent and the principal are not aligned and where the agent may exploit its advantageous position. In particular, the triangular relationship is to be considered, which means that the AI agent one interacts with is only the extended arm of the AI provider. In most industries, companies will rely on specialist AI providers to further digitize their business, which means that external AI agents enter the firm as a new form of agency labor to access proprietary data directly and weave themselves into the firm's know-how. AI providers benefit from the economies of scale and scope of machine learning. A part of the strategy of traditional firms is to decide how to participate and to what extent to share AI learning. From a managerial perspective, it will be crucial to understand not only the explicit but also the implicit (information) outcomes of machine labor and to arrive at conscious decisions as to how access to and ownership of the data/informational resources created is distributed (Figure 3.7).

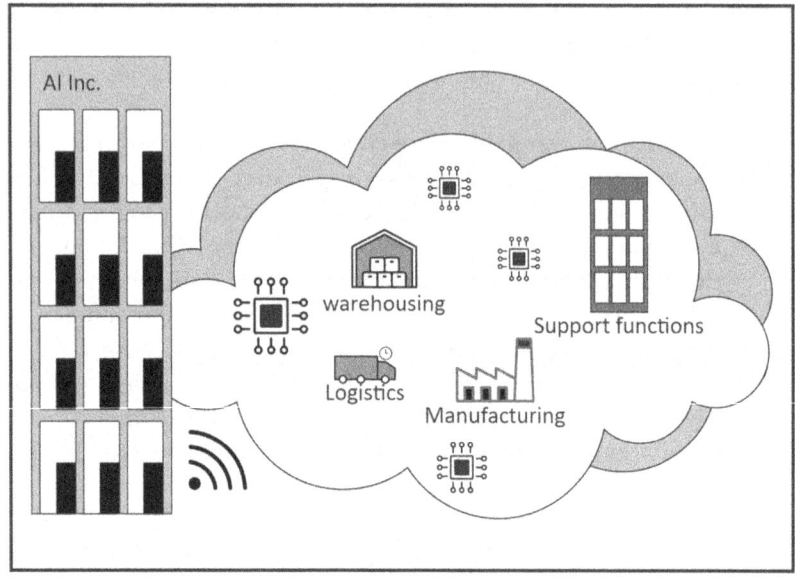

Figure 3.7 New information asymmetries as a cause for different types of learning-curves. *Source:* Authors

While this situation is still relatively new to business-to-business (B2B) markets, most people are already familiar with examples in business to consumer (B2C) markets. Here, AI providers often offer their services "for free" while generating income from advertising. In addition, AI uses big data to predict consumer behavior, and influenc purchasing decisions. As a result, consumers may be manipulated and induced into sub-optimal purchases.[25] Of course, the other markets like business-to-government (B2G), government-to-government (G2G), government-to-business (G2B), or government-to-consumer (G2C), are other areas where there will need to be more administrative and management changes, partly also due to the complex relationships of public–private partnerships (see example in Figure 3.8).

This chapter highlights the need to rethink management practices where the AI is an agent delivering a specialized task. Decision-makers need to understand the grey areas of super specialization and micro-management of tasks and ethical implications. There are profound changes needed in firm practices and organization design with the introduction of AI technology, including robotics.[26] A World Economic Forum report highlights that by 2025, machines will lead to the replacement of 85 million jobs

Facial recognition systems are used by, for example, Facebook to identify people in personal pictures. This AI allows you to tag a friend based on suggestions. However, in 2020, Facebook (now Meta) agreed to pay US$650 million in an Illinois class-action lawsuit for using facial recognition for photos that were not publicly available.[27] The case led to a change in policy, where Meta users can now opt out of facial-recognition tagging.

Many photos on social media or the web have an afterlife thanks to the copyright licenses that photograph owners fail to read.[28] Adam Harvey created a website called MegaPixels that identified training data sets using pictures that have been used in over 900 research projects (these images of faces had had not necessarily consented to the same). For example, MegaFace is a training data set of 4.7 million pictures, of which 3.8 million are from Flikr.[29] It has been used by governments, private companies, and academics worldwide. In some cases, there have been calls for publishers to retract publications based on facial recognition data sets of students or even minority groups, especially where there is no explicit consent or if the purpose has been used for oppression.

Police and security forces are using this type of technology.[30] Microsoft had invested in Israeli startup AnyVision, which had tested its facial recognition software on Palestinians in the West Bank.[31] Following a 2019 news expose, Microsoft eventually divested itself of AnyVision in 2020.[32] The UK has a regulation for overt public space surveillance though it does not mention facial recognition. Part of the problem is under whose jurisdiction this would fall. To quote from a report, "What databases can be matched against, for what purposes the technology can and cannot be used, which images are captured and stored, who can access those images, how long they are stored—are all questions without answers."[33] Without oversight, existing databases like national IDs, education or employment IDs, driver's license photos, criminal records, or mobile phone providers can be used for surveillance.

Data ownership issues will create information asymmetries, making the space between the government sector, private sector, and academia more complex. As we move to biometrics,[34] there is a question of whether we have given (1) permission for the collection of data; (2) permission for the storage of the data; (3) information about where the personal data is stored; (4) knowledge of how secure the storage is; (5) intimation of who has permissible access to this data; (6) awareness if someone has access to the data; and (7) an ability to update the data? Within the firm, managers need to also think of the use of AI, the data that AI consumes, the resources required to maintain and feed AI data models, and the ethics and governance of the process. Governments will need to consider governance for public value, international reputation, and achievement of human rights. Even in the interest of science, academics cannot compromise on ethics as it has a spillover effect on other sectors.

Figure 3.8 Facial recognition: A complex issue for government, academia, and the private sector.

creating 97 million new roles due to the division of labor between humans, machines, and algorithms.[35] This will require significant upskilling of existing workers who may find 40–50% of their skills redundant.

QUESTIONS

1. How will AI-based micro-division of labor change the structure of firms and of markets? Review current patterns of division of labor in different industries and try to predict future scenarios.
2. What are the chances and risks for (your) firm(s) in the light of a trend towards micro-division of labor? How can you achieve and sustain a competitive advantage?
3. To what extent can AI be perceived as a new factor of production? How does it compare to traditional factors of production, i.e., land, labor, and capital?
4. Why are information asymmetries so relevant in so-called triangular agency relationships that involve AI? Please describe by using a real-life example.
5. How does the logic of exponential organizations (see Chapter 4) interrelate with the idea of triangular agency relationships portrayed in this chapter? Can you provide public policy recommendations?

MY INSIGHTS

The most difficult decisions I need to take are

MY INSIGHTS

The resources I need to build for the future are

MY INSIGHTS

The governance systems I will to put in place are

MY INSIGHTS

The training and skills I and my team need to develop are

Notes

1. Jennings, N. R., Moreau, L., Nicholson, D., Ramchurn, S., Roberts, S., Rodden, T., & Rogers, A. (2014). Human-agent collectives. *Communications of the ACM, 57*(12), 80–88.
2. Wagner, D. N. (2020). The nature of the Artificially Intelligent Firm-An economic investigation into changes that AI brings to the firm. *Telecommunications Policy, 44*(6), 101954.
3. Smith, A. (1999). *The Wealth of Nations.* Reprinted. London: Penguin Books (Penguin classics).
4. Beinhocker, E. D. (2006). *The origin of wealth: Evolution, complexity, and the radical remaking of economics.* Harvard Business Press.
5. United States Department of Labor. (n.d.). *Standard Occupational Classification (SOC) System.* Standard Occupational Classification (SOC) System; www.bls.gov. Retrieved August 2021, from http://www.bls.gov/soc
6. Malito, A. (2017). Grocery stores carry 40,000 more items than they did in the 1990s. *MarketWatch, June, 17.* https://www.marketwatch.com/story/grocery-stores-carry-40000-more-items-than-they-did-in-the-1990s-2017-06-07
7. ScrapeHero. (2018). How many products does Amazon sell?. https://www.scrapehero.com/many-products-amazon-sell-january-2018/
8. Smith, A. 1999. *Op.cit,* p. 109
9. Koppl, R., Kauffman, S., Felin, T., & Longo, G. (2015). Economics for a creative world. *Journal of Institutional Economics, 11*(1), 1–31.
10. Agrawal, A., Gans, J., & Goldfarb, A. (2018). *Prediction machines: the simple economics of artificial intelligence.* Harvard Business Press.
11. Wagner, D. N. (2021). Economic AI Literacy: A Source of Competitive Advantage. In *Handbook of Research on Applied AI for International Business and Marketing Applications* (pp. 135–152). IGI Global.
12. Weiss, T. R. (2021, May 10). *How the USPS Is Finding Lost Packages More Quickly Using AI Technology from Nvidia.* EnterpriseAI; www.enterpriseai.news. https://www.enterpriseai.news/2021/05/10/how-the-usps-is-finding-lost-packages-more-quickly-using-ai-technology-from-nvidia/
13. Varian, H. (2019). 16. Artificial Intelligence, Economics, and Industrial Organization. In *The Economics of Artificial Intelligence* (pp. 399–422). University of Chicago Press.
14. Eisenhardt, K. M. (1989). Agency theory: An assessment and review. *Academy of management review, 14*(1), 57–74.
15. Mitlacher, L. W. (2008). Job quality and temporary agency work: Challenges for human resource management in triangular employment relations in Germany. *The International Journal of Human Resource Management, 19*(3), 446–460.
16. Wagner, D.N. 2020. *Op. cit.* 9.
17. About Glue. https://fi.linkedin.com/company/gluecollab and YouTube. 2021. *Glue Customer Showcase: Duodecim.* (2021, March 3). YouTube; https://www.youtube.com/watch?v=F-JED8BGL2
18. Saarikannas, K. (2019, August 12). *Glue–Introducing the future of healthcare simulation training.* Glue; glue.work. https://glue.work/2019/08/12/introducing-the-future-of-healthcare-simulation-training/

19. YouTube. 2021. *Op. cit.*
20. *Duodecim-3.* (n.d.). Vimeo; vimeo.com. Retrieved May 2022, from https://vimeo.com/409481907?embedded=true&source=vimeo_logo&owner=97571349
21. Loreto, V., Servedio, V. D., Strogatz, S. H., & Tria, F. (2016). Dynamics on expanding spaces: modeling the emergence of novelties. *Creativity and universality in language*, 59–83.
22. Degli Esposti, S. (2014). When big data meets dataveillance: The hidden side of analytics. *Surveillance & Society, 12*(2), 209–225. Van Dijck, J. (2014). Datafication, dataism and dataveillance: Big Data between scientific paradigm and ideology. *Surveillance & society, 12*(2), 197–208.
23. Evangelho, J. (2019, April 9). *Here's The Shocking Reality Of Completely Blocking Google From Your Life.* Forbes; www.forbes.com. https://www.forbes.com/sites/jasonevangelho/2019/04/09/heres-the-shocking-reality-of-completely-blocking-google-from-your-life/?sh=613946d31fec
24. Doshi-Velez, F., Kortz, M., Budish, R., Bavitz, C., Gershman, S., O'Brien, D., . . . & Wood, A. (2017). Accountability of AI under the law: The role of explanation. *arXiv preprint arXiv:1711.01134.* https://arxiv.org/pdf/1711.01134.pdf
25. Big Brother Watch. (2018, March). *Briefing for short debate on the use of facila recognition technology in security and policing in the House of Lords.* https://bigbrotherwatch.org.uk/wp-content/uploads/2018/03/Big-Brother-Watch-briefing-on-Facial-Recognition-for-Short-Debate-in-the-House-of-Lords-1-March-2018.pdf
26. Thales. (2022, January). *What is biometrics?* Biometrics: Definition, Use Cases, Latest News. https://www.thalesgroup.com/en/markets/digital-identity-and-security/government/inspired/biometrics; Contissa, G., Lagioia, F., Lippi, M., Micklitz, H. W., Palka, P., Sartor, G., & Torroni, P. (2018). Towards consumer-empowering artificial intelligence. In *International Joint Conference on Artificial Intelligence* (pp. 5150–5157).
27. O'Neil, C. (2017). Weapons of Math Destruction: How Big Data Increases Inequality and Threatens Democracy.
28. Morrison, S. (2020, July 23). *Facebook agrees to pay $650 million to end facial recognition lawsuit–Vox.* Vox; www.vox.com. https://www.vox.com/recode/2020/7/23/21335806/facebook-settlement-illinois-facial-recognition-photo-tagging
29. For examples, see website: https://exposing.ai
30. Harvey, A. (n.d.). *Exposing.ai: MegaFace.* Exposing.Ai; exposing.ai. Retrieved May 2022, from https://exposing.ai/megaface/
31. Margetts, H., & Dorobantu, C. (2019). Rethink government with AI. https://www.nature.com/articles/d41586-020-03187-
32. Solon, O. (2022, June). *Big Tech juggles ethical pledges on facial recognition with corporate interests.* NBC News; www.nbcnews.com. https://www.nbcnews.com/tech/security/big-tech-juggles-ethical-pledges-facial-recognition-corporate-interests-n1231778
33. Statt, N. (2020, March 27). *Microsoft to end investments in facial recognition firms after AnyVision controversy–The Verge.* The Verge; www.theverge.com. https://www.theverge.com/2020/3/27/21197577/microsoft-facial-recognition-investing-divest-anyvision-controversy

34. Dixon, J., Hong, B., & Wu, L. (2021). The robot revolution: Managerial and employment consequences for firms. *Management Science*, *67*(9), 5586–5605. https://pubsonline.informs.org/doi/abs/10.1287/mnsc.2020.3812
35. World Economic Forum. (2020). The future of jobs report 2020. Retrieved from *Geneva*. https://www.weforum.org/reports/the-future-of-jobs-report-2020

4

Exponential Developments, Organizations, and Thinking

CHAPTER HIGHLIGHTS

1. Exponential developments are ensuring that abundance is replacing scarcity in more and more areas.
2. Exponential organizations (ExOs) that take the chances of exponential developments show outstanding performance over time.
3. The human tendency to linearize exponential developments prevents exponential thinking.

> **Cases:**
> Microsoft's Chatbots | Moore's Law | Dow Jones Flash Crash of 2010 | Walmart

4.1 Exponential Developments

With astonishment, admiration, and sometimes horror, people are taking note of exponential developments. If one disregards the success stories in the Far East, which are still barely noticed by the rest of the world, the growth of the American tech giants Google, Amazon, Facebook/Meta, Microsoft and Apple in recent years has dwarfed almost all other companies. In contrast, the rapid spread of the coronavirus has caused an unprecedented economic disaster. Both phenomena follow exponential lines of development. Both phenomena were not easy to assess, especially in their initial phases. And in retrospect, quite a few people would have liked different decisions to have been made earlier.

In the chapter that follows, selected exponential challenges are outlined. It becomes clear that the technological trend of AI is of particular importance. It quickly becomes evident that in these contexts, the ability to think exponentially is an essential requirement for successful decisions. Therefore, it is vital to understand and overcome the obstacles that exist in our minds to enable exponential thinking. Practical examples are used to explain the basics of exponential thinking and acting: The conscious differentiation and selective use of linear and exponential thinking, expectation management in exponential projects, and success control of exponential projects.

If one had correctly estimated years ago how the company Google would one day develop, one could be very wealthy today.[1] If more recently, the global impact of a new virus from a relatively unknown city in China had been correctly assessed, there might have been fewer losses of lives and economic wealth to bemoan today.[2] In both cases, a skill called exponential thinking was required. This ability is rapidly gaining importance in a globalized and increasingly digital world. Reason enough to shed some light on what exponential thinking actually is.

"In this country, you have to run as fast as you can if you want to stay in the same spot."[3] This quote from Lewis Carroll's 1871 novel, *Alice Behind the Mirror*, which became known as the *Red Queen hypothesis*,[4] has been popular with change management experts for quite some time.[5] But at the moment, people tend to underestimate how much faster we need to make our companies and organizations run in the future to keep up with exponential developments (see Figure 4.1).

The main drivers in recent times for exponential development are digitization and, particularly, the advances in machine learning and AI. Think of the processing power of computers as an exponential development. Early

Exponential Developments, Organizations, and Thinking • 71

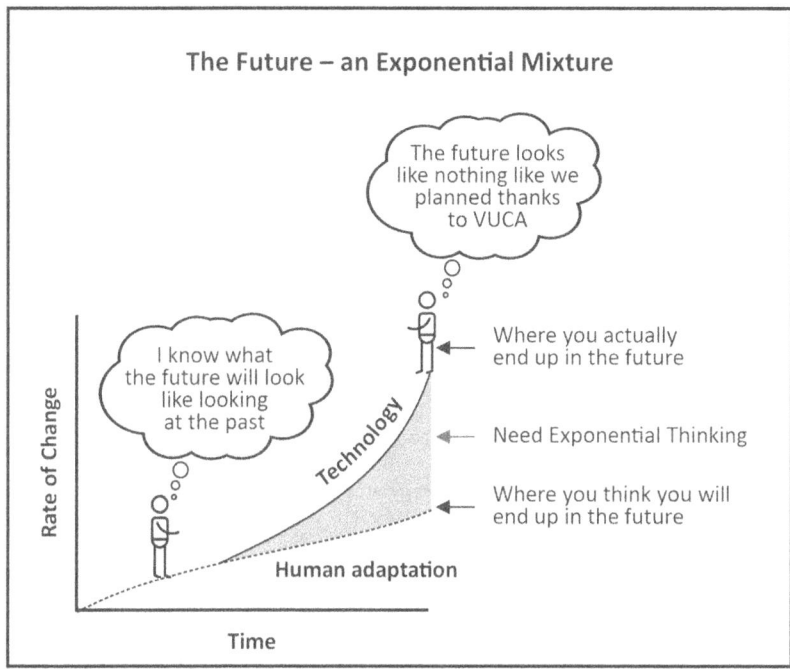

Figure 4.1 The future—An exponential mixture. *Source:* Authors

computers began to double their computing power every 18 months due to advances in transistor development (commonly referred to as Moore's law). The computing power for the Apollo Guidance system to get the first man on the moon was able to do 80,000 instructions per second and only store 2,048 words of memory.[6] In contrast, an Apple Phone 12 has a bionic processor than can do five trillion tasks per second and one million times the memory (4GB RAM)!

These technological developments are further embedded in the context of globalization, which repeatedly causes unforeseen instability (see Figure 4.2).[7] The COVID-pandemic crisis is impressive proof of how quickly individuals and organizations had to adapt to disruptions and the increasing role technology played under such circumstances. In higher education, the business model of traditional education got quickly undermined by increasingly AI-assisted online education. Traditional retail stores and restaurants had to move online, and there was a growth in e-entertainment and web services.[8] Yet, COVID-19 only marks a tipping point in a largely ignored development: the ability to think exponentially.[9] Intuitively, humans tend to have a linear view of the world. They expect the current rate of progress to continue

VUCA stands for volatility, uncertainty, complexity, and ambiguity of general conditions and situations. AI is being increasingly used for predictive analysis and sensemaking in high complexity environments. This development has not just been fueled by the processing power, storage capabilities, new types of programming, and big data. An exciting result from Deloitte's[10] "2019 Global Human Capital Trends" survey was that 47% of the respondents felt that one of the 21st-century leadership requirements was the ability to manage a workforce of a team of humans and machines. Because AI machines are trained on data and then process information much faster than humans, this at times leads to agency issues.

Microsoft introduced a bot on Twitter called Tay (for "Thinking About You") on May 23, 2016 for testing 'conversational understanding'. The bot (@tayandyou) soon learned from what was being tweeted and began posting controversial tweets requiring the company to shut it down in 16 hours and 96,000 tweets.[11] It had been trained on data (but the timeline has been deleted https://www.tay.ai). Microsoft had tested the concept before in China with Xiaoice in 2014 and then Rinna in Japan in 2015, both of which were very successful.

The company made Xiaoice an independent company in 2020. Xiaoice forms emotional bonds with its global users and filling in the need for companionship.[12] This situation flags ethical issues as a bot is not real (hence is the companionship real?). As of 2020, it reached 660 million users and 450 million third-party smart devices globally.[13]

Rinna had a blip where it appeared that it got depressed and suicidal[14] (Microsoft explained it as a PR stunt). However, Rinna continues to be very successful with urban dwellers and later was used by the local government in Japan.[15] It has 1.7 million active users online as of October 2021.[17] The most extended session (conversation) was 4.4 hours or 997 exchanges (the average conversation is 30 exchanges and the longest chat for 15 hours).[17] The other bots Microsoft launched like, Zo in 2016, was discontinued in 2019, and Ruuh (India), launched in 2017, was discontinued in 2019.

Figure 4.2 Microsoft's Chatbots and the VUCA environment.

for the future period. In contrast, exponential thinking is based on a historical perspective that evolutionary developments accelerate over time, and the future needs to be thought about in terms of generational impact.[18]

4.2 When Abundance Replaces Scarcity

Exponential developments are made possible by abundance.[19] And abundance, in turn, is a symptom of the present. With the click of a mouse, one gains access to the knowledge of the world on the Internet. Even children can take unlimited photographs and stream continuous videos at almost no cost. Renewable energies are rapidly gaining importance, and solar energy capacities are doubling within months, not years. As power supplies become more readily and cheaply available worldwide, there will be further abundance. The new abundance also reaches remote and economically underdeveloped areas. For example, Vietnamese fishermen can power their boats and dry their anchovy with solar energy.[20] This abundance of energy will fuel AI, which is power-hungry.

Technologies that are concealed behind the catchword AI are characterized by the fact that they make exponential learning curves possible, thus helping to overcome scarcity. For example, AI-based precision agriculture can multiply yields.[21] With autonomous driving, the distance traveled without human intervention increases by several hundred percent from year to year.[22] So here, too, the curve grows steeply upwards.

In the field of speech recognition, for example, it was unimaginable just a few years ago what is now commonplace: the error rate has reached human levels.[23] In the health sector, the cost of decoding a genome has fallen from US$100 million to less than US$100 since the turn of the millennium.[24] These advancements create the basis for AI-based, individual precision medicine.

AI is an exponential development. This has happened because there is an overabundance of data, cheaper, faster, and more efficient AI technologies, greater synergies between industries, and more resources invested into the promise of AI (see Figure 4.3). For example, during the COVID-pandemic, it was estimated that AI adoption increased by 20–44%, and 37–72% of business leaders surveyed felt the pandemic influenced AI implementation and adoption.[25] However, 35–55% of business leaders worried that the pace of AI adoption was moving faster than it should, suggesting that adaptability may not be keeping pace with exponential developments.[26]

4.3 Exponential Organizations (ExOs) for Exponential Challenges

First and foremost, ExOs or exponential organizations take advantage of the developments described, growing at a rate 10× than their peers.[27] It is no coincidence that ExOs are pioneers in the field of artificial intelligence. These companies follow the pace of technological progress and thus translate the available opportunities into exponential business growth. The convergence of technologies unleashes new opportunities. For example, the sales of AI giants Amazon and Google have grown by an average of around 30% per year over the last decade and a half. This growth sounds constant, but it means that in absolute terms, growth has accelerated every year so that by 2020 both companies have grown by an amount equivalent to more than ten

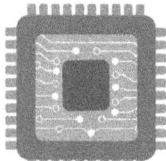 Gordon Moore, the co-founder of Intel, published an article titled 'Cramming More Components onto Integrated Circuits' in 1965.[28] He observed in the article, "Integrated circuits will lead to such wonders as home computers or at least terminals connected to a central computer, automatic controls for automobiles, and personal portable communications equipment. The electronic wristwatch needs only a display to be feasible today." At that time, he was working in Fairchild Semiconductor as the Director of R&D. Fairchild Semiconductor was an anchor company of the semi-conductor industry and Silicon Valley as we know it today. During that period, the optimum components used per circuit were 50. He observed that if you projected the developments of innovation and manufacturing costs taking place between 1959 to 1964, in terms of the number of components per chip, it would double every 12 months. By 1975, he noted that it would be every two years.[29] By1995, the Intel Pentium microprocessor integrated 5 million transistors. By 2022, it had reached one billion transistors.[30] So Moore's law became a self-fulfilling prophecy in Intel; however, as the size of computer chips decreases, costs are rising (see below).[31] So the industry is being innovative, thinking of new designs and technology.

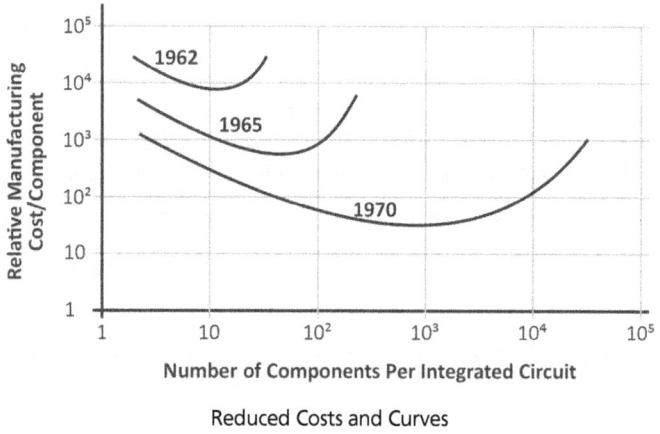

Figure 4.3 Moore's Law. *Source:* Adapted from Moore (1965)[32]

times their total turnover in 2004.[33] Amazon began as an online bookseller in 1995, and today a majority of its revenues comes from its online store, which has an inventory of 500 million+ products,[34] third-party selling services, cloud-based services, subscription services, and physical stores.

The futurologist Ray Kurzweil coined the term "Law of Accelerating Returns" to describe these phenomena.[35] The example of Amazon impressively shows how a company whose business model follows this law generates an abundance of financial resources to enter new markets. The economic logic of these companies is fundamentally different from traditional business models. Where there is abundance, scarcity no longer plays a role. ExOs scale their business by exponentially reducing the marginal cost of supply. Platform companies use this strategy: the cost of offering another accommodation at Airbnb, another taxi at Uber, or another contribution to Wikipedia is minimal. This development in recent years is unprecedented and, therefore, unusual for human thinking. There are side-effects of the rapid scale of adoption like the threat of monopoly power or high switching costs for consumers after lock-ins into specific technologies.[36] In addition, these companies may have neither invested in the infrastructure nor own the data and other resources that they rely on![37]

4.4 Exponential Thinking

For most people, it is complicated to understand the positive and negative course of technological developments. A significant reason for this is that human thinking is characterized by so-called exponential growth bias.[38] This bias is the tendency to linearize exponential effects (see Figure 4.1). So, for example, it is easy to estimate where you will be if you have to take 20 equally large steps of one meter, no matter in which direction. But where do you stand if the step length doubles with every step? Hardly anyone can guess that would make a good thirteen trips around the world.

This kind of thinking is not new. There are old folktales—about Sissa Ibn Dahir, an Indian inventor of chess, as retold by Ibn Khallikan in 1256, who asks for a grain of rice or wheat as a reward for their invention to be put on the first square of a chessboard and that number to be doubled on every consecutive square. So 1 grain on square one, double that or 2 grains on square 2, double what was on the second square, or 4 grains on the third square, and so on till all 64 squares were completed. The 63rd square would have 2^{63} = 9,223,372,036,854,775,808 (or 9.22 quintillion) grains of rice, and the entire chessboard would have 18 quintillions–more than the rice produced in the world. Exponential thinking is hard to comprehend. The pandemic too is an example of exponential thinking.[39] So is AI computing power and affordability (see Figure 4.4).

Existing technologies can enable us in a co-creative race into the future, in which humans and AI run hand in hand. But humans are having difficulty keeping up with the increasing pace. The prerequisites for this are literally to be created with caution (see Figure 4.5).

First of all, the ability to flexibly switch between the two scenarios: linear and exponential thinking, needs to be established in people's minds: Am I dealing with a question where the stride length remains constant,

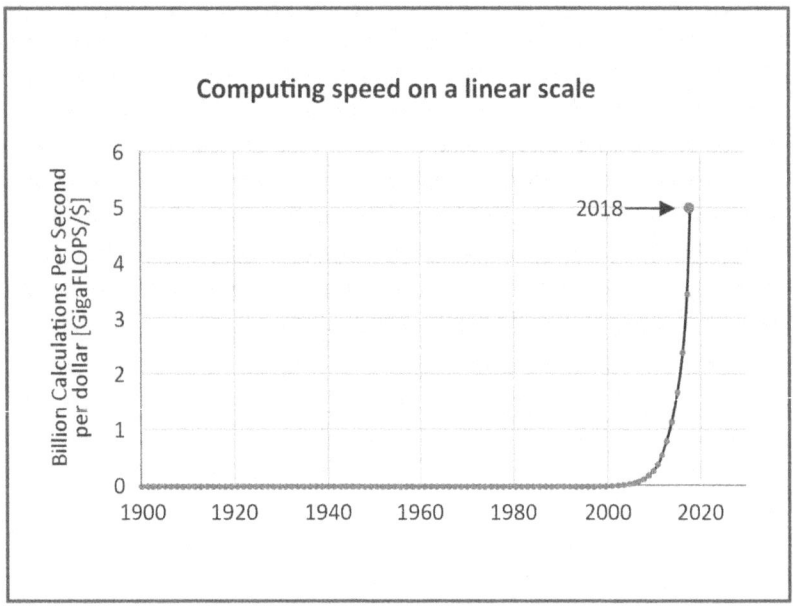

Figure 4.4 Computing speed on a linear scale. *Source:* Adapted from Lipson (2018)[40]

or is it growing? The ability to make a difference here can be life-saving. Evolution has even taught animals like lions to apply exponential thinking when deciding whether or not to defend their territory against a group of rival intruders.[41]

Irrespective of whether one operates within a corporate or a political context, a conscious distinction has to be made between the two scenarios (linear or exponential) in which a suitable managerial approach is determined. Therefore, transparency and clarity about which thinking model is to be used is particularly important. For example, in the case of the viral disease COVID-19, the focus at the beginning was primarily on the absolute number of new infections. Later, the focus was increasingly on a reproduction factor (R).[42]

So much for the analysis. Step two is to formulate goals. In linear thinking, goals are set on *sight*, but in exponential thinking, long-term goals are harder to sight. For example, the founders of Google, Larry Page and Sergey Brin, and their colleagues initially used linear thinking and only over time developed a mission "to organize the information of this world and make it generally accessible and usable."[43] In contrast, Elon Musk directly

One of the challenges in AI is that they do not work well with large data sets.[44] There is an assumption the more powerful the computer is, the lower the error rate. Unfortunately, this assumption is not valid. One reason is the numbers need to be squeezed into bits that are finite (refer to Chapter 1)—this error was minimized through standardization.[45]

Quantum computing will require an extremely low error rate—10^{-15}, but current error rates are at 10^{-3}. One way that programmers manage this is by using quantum error correction. So far, this is done by exponentially suppressing errors. However, the process works when the physical error rates are below 50 rounds of error correction over the course of a computation. So the system still needs to be trained carefully! However, the authors state, "the sensitivity of this technique allows us to find features that do not fit the expected categories,"[46] this may mean outliers are removed, which means the algorithm is not inclusive.

One method to remove error could be to have algorithm inventors and operators introduce a bias impact statement, as suggested by Brookings.[47] The bias impact statement is a template of questions that can be flexibly applied to guide them through the design, implementation, and monitoring phases. This process means outlining assumptions, getting feedback from cross-sectional groups, redesigning the AI algorithm, or getting more robust data sets.

Take the example of Algorithmic High-Frequency Trading (HFT), where an AI agent can sell and buy thousands of shares with the intent of making small profits. In May 2010, the Dow Jones crashed by 1,000 points (approximately US$1 trillion) before recovering 36 minutes later. It is called the "Flash Crash" of 2010. It was triggered by a London-based trader who was using an algorithm. The other computers saw the huge US$200 million bet and assumed that 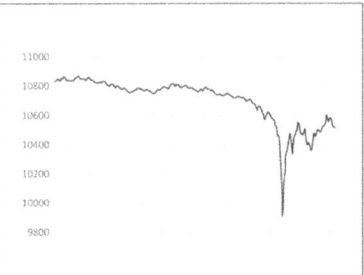 it was a signal for a market fall and hence automatically began selling. In 2012, HFT algorithms from Knight Capital Group executed 4 million trades of 397 million shares in only 45 minutes in the NSE, causing high market volatility and leading to a loss of US$460 million. As a result, Knight Capital Group had to be acquired by another firm.[48] Algorithmic errors happen often, and because the AI is quietly working behind the scenes, we are not always aware of the issues. In the USA, for example, it is estimated that AI initiates 70% of the stock trading volume.[49]

Figure 4.5 Dow Jones flash crash of 2010—Exponential error rates[50]

pursued an exponential strategy with Space X, imagining a future, few thought possible when he started.

The third step is implementation. A further challenge for thinking and acting is that exponentially designed projects often fall far short of linearly formed expectations at the beginning of the project—it is a peculiar learning curve (see once more Figure 4.1). Elon Musk, the founder of Tesla, was repeatedly criticized for not keeping promises, and yet, in retrospect, the company can now boast an impressive exponential development curve.[51] As of January 2022, Tesla's market capitalization was US$1 trillion![52]

We need to rethink goals and impact. Progress should be measured differently: no longer as a deviation from the known plan, but rather by whether the conditions for a network effect are created. A company like Gillette understood far better than its competitors about designing the right conditions for high growth rates. As a result, they focused on razor blades rather than the razor itself.

When Jeff Bezos turned the highly successful online bookseller Amazon into a marketplace for products of all kinds, hardly any of the critical observers were aware that this created the conditions for making available an unprecedented variety of products in the range of 100 million, a number that the manager of a classic department store with a product selection of several tens of thousands of products did not even dare to dream of.[53] The retail industry is actively thinking exponentially (see Figure 4.6).

In summary, exponential thinking and the associated decision making is primarily characterized by four features, which are illustrated again in

---

In 2019, Walmart, the second-largest retailer, unveiled a new store concept that utilized AI. The new Intelligent Retail Lab, aka IRL, is 50,000 square feet of retail space in Levittown, New York.[54] The IRL can monitor usage, stocking, expirations, and restocking with the help of AI. They planned to do this by using tags that employ the Internet of things (IoT) approach. This approach consists of interconnected devices and machines that have unique identifiers and the ability to transfer data directly without human interference.[55] The patent that Walmart has taken out for its IoT tags will likely utilize technology such as barcodes, radio frequencies, and RFID systems. These tags will keep track of when perishables would spoil and prevent the store from selling expired products, ensuring freshness for all customers. Such technology is increasingly also becoming available to consumers, i.e., your fridge can alert you to spoiled milk or if you need more eggs on your next grocery spree.[56]

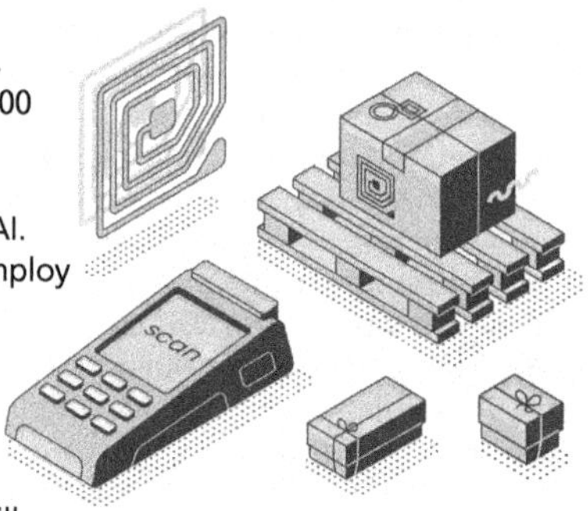

Alongside this, the cameras throughout the store can help see when the last of a product has been picked up and then alert the staff to restock. The sensors and cameras produce around 1.6 Terabytes of data per second which are stored in a data center in the store, located behind glass walls so that customers can see the magic happen. In addition, Walmart is including educational and interactive screens for people to use to learn more about the IRL.[57]

Figure 4.6 Walmart.

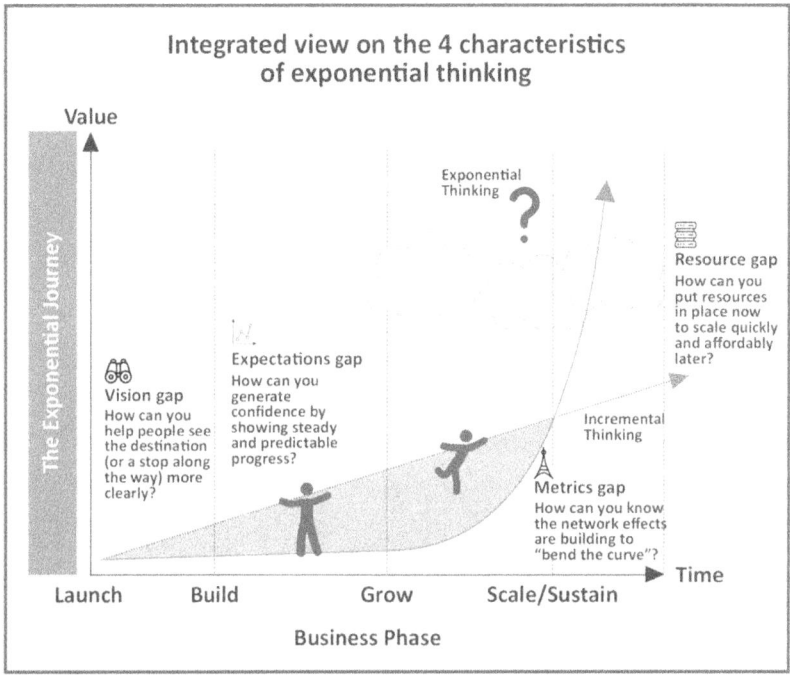

Figure 4.7 Characteristics of exponential thinking. *Source:* Authors

Figure 4.7. These four features—the vision gap, the expectations gap, the metrics gap and the resource gap also require us to consider the following points:

Transparency within the team: Which mental model is used? Linear or exponential thinking? Linear thinking *drives on sight*, while exponential thinking accepts that strategic goals can be out of sight. Exponential developments show little or no progress at the beginning. Those who think exponentially are prepared for the fact that linear expectations are initially disappointed.

Metrics are used to measure progress. For example, linear developments are about making progress toward the set goals; exponential developments are about creating the conditions necessary for the network effect. By understanding this type of thinking, managers are better poised to understand the opportunities and challenges of new technologies like AI.

QUESTIONS

1. Given the pace of exponential developments, how would your firm optimize an AI-enabled world?

2. Given the pace of exponential developments, how would your firm plan for fallouts (direct and indirect) in an AI-enabled world?
3. If your firm is actively using scenario planning and foresight—what do you think would be the most critical macroenvironmental factor affecting AI as an industry and hence your sector?
4. Should all employees be trained to think exponentially, or do we also need linear thinkers? Why?

MY INSIGHTS

The most difficult decisions I need to take are

MY INSIGHTS

The resources I need to build for the future are

MY INSIGHTS

The governance systems I will to put in place are

MY INSIGHTS

The training and skills I and my team need to develop are

Notes

1. Fuchs, C. (2011). A Contribution to the Critique of the Political Economy of Google. *Fast Capitalism, 8*(1).
2. Wu, Z., & McGoogan, J. M. (2020). Characteristics of and important lessons from the coronavirus disease 2019 (COVID-19) outbreak in China: summary of a report of 72 314 cases from the Chinese Center for Disease Control and Prevention. *jama, 323*(13), 1239–1242.
3. Carroll, L. (2010). *Through the looking glass and what Alice found there*. Penguin UK.
4. Van Valen, L. (1973). A new evolutionary law. *Evolutionary Theory, 1*, 1–30.
5. Barnett, W. P. (2016). *The Red Queen among Organizations*
6. O'Brien, F. (2020, January 30). *A deep dive into the Apollo Guidance Computer, and the hack that saved Apollo 14 | Ars Technica*. Ars Technica; arstechnica.com. https://arstechnica.com/science/2020/01/a-deep-dive-into-the-apollo-guidance-computer-and-the-hack-that-saved-apollo-14/. Graham, K., & @bsindia. (2019, October). *Would your phone be powerful enough to get you to the moon like Apollo did? | Business Standard News*. Would Your Phone Be Powerful Enough to Get You to the Moon like Apollo Did?; www.business-standard.com. https://www.business-standard.com/article/technology/would-your-phone-be-powerful-enough-to-get-you-to-the-moon-like-apollo-did-119070200272_1.html
7. Beinhocker, E. D. (2006). *The origin of wealth: Evolution, complexity, and the radical remaking of economics*. Harvard Business Press.
8. UNCTAD, 2021. (n.d.). *Covid-19 and e-Commerce*. Covid-19 And E-Commerce A Global Review. https://unctad.org/system/files/official-document/dtlstict2020d13_en_0.pdf
9. Weber, K. (2002). Students' Understanding of Exponential and Logarithmic Functions. https://www.researchgate.net/publication/228725503_Students%27_understanding_of_exponential_and_logarithmic_functions
10. Volini, E., Schwartz, J., Roy, I., Hauptmann, M., Van Durme, Y., Denny, B., & Bersin, J. (2019). Leadership for the 21st century: The intersection of the traditional and the new. 2019 Global human capital trends. Deloitte Insights. https://www2.deloitte.com/us/en/insights/focus/human-capital-trends/2019/21st-century-leadership-challenges-and-development.html
11. Vincent, J. (2016). Twitter taught Microsoft's AI chatbot to be a racist asshole in less than a day. *The Verge, 24*(3), 2016. https://www.theverge.com/2016/3/24/11297050/tay-microsoft-chatbot-racist
12. Gaubert, J. (2021, August 26). *AI love you: Meet Xiaoice, China's virtual boyfriend*. Euronews; www.euronews.com. https://www.euronews.com/next/2021/08/26/meet-xiaoice-the-ai-chatbot-lover-dispelling-the-loneliness-of-china-s-city-dwellers
13. Liao, R. (2020). Microsoft spins out 5-year-old Chinese chatbot Xiaoice. *Hentet fra* https://techcrunch.com/2020/07/12/microsoft-spins-out-5-year-old-chinese-chatbot-xiaoice/
14. Baseel, C. (2016, October 5). *Japan's AI schoolgirl has fallen into a suicidal depression in latest blog post*. SoraNews24 -Japan News-; soranews24.com. https://

soranews24.com/2016/10/05/japans-ai-schoolgirl-has-fallen-into-a-suicidal-depression-in-latest-blog-post/

15. Microsoft Asia News Center. (2018, September 18). *Rinna the AI social chatbot goes out and about in Japan's countryside–Microsoft Stories Asia.* Microsoft Stories Asia; news.microsoft.com. https://news.microsoft.com/apac/2018/09/18/rinna-the-ai-social-chatbot-goes-out-and-about-in-japans-countryside/

16. Rinna, 2021. (n.d.). *rinna Co., Ltd–AI Character for every individual & organization.* Rinna Co., Ltd–AI Character for Every Individual & Organization; Retrieved October 2021, from https://www.rinna.id/

17. Microsoft Asia News Center. (2018, September 18). *Rinna the AI social chatbot goes out and about in Japan's countryside–Microsoft Stories Asia.* Microsoft Stories Asia; news.microsoft.com. https://news.microsoft.com/apac/2018/09/18/rinna-the-ai-social-chatbot-goes-out-and-about-in-japans-countryside/

18. 18 Kurzweil, R. The Law of Accelerating Returns| KurzweilAI'.[online], 2001. kurzweil.net.

19. Diamandis, P. H., & Kotler, S. (2012). *Abundance: The future is better than you think.* Simon and Schuster.

20. Ngo, X. C., Nguyen, T. H., Do, N. Y., Nguyen, D. M., Vo, D. V. N., Lam, S. S., ... & Le, Q. V. (2020). Grid-connected photovoltaic systems with single-axis sun tracker: case study for Central Vietnam. *Energies, 13*(6), 1457.

21. Finger, R., Swinton, S. M., El Benni, N., & Walter, A. (2019). Precision farming at the nexus of agricultural production and the environment. *Annual Review of Resource Economics, 11*(1), 313–335.

22. Yurtsever, E., Lambert, J., Carballo, A., & Takeda, K. (2020). A survey of autonomous driving: Common practices and emerging technologies. *IEEE Access, 8*, 58443–58469.

23. Xiong, W., Droppo, J., Huang, X., Seide, F., Seltzer, M., Stolcke, A., ... & Zweig, G. (2016). Achieving human parity in conversational speech recognition. *arXiv preprint arXiv:1610.05256.*

24. Pasic, M. D. (2020). The current status and future prospects of precision medicine. *Clinical Chemistry and Laboratory Medicine (CCLM), 58*(9), 1423–1425.

25. Batley, M. M. (2021, March 9). *AI adoption accelerated during the pandemic.* AI Adoption Accelerated during the Pandemic; info.kpmg.us. https://info.kpmg.us/news-perspectives/technology-innovation/thriving-in-an-ai-world/ai-adoption-accelerated-during-pandemic.html. Watson. (2021). Global AI Adoption Index. 2021. https://filecache.mediaroom.com/mr5mr_ibmnews/190846/IBM's Global AI Adoption Index 2021_Executive-Summary.pdf

26. Bately, M. M. (2021). *Op. cit.* 25.

27. Ismail, S. (2014). *Exponential Organizations: Why new organizations are ten times better, faster, and cheaper than yours (and what to do about it).* Diversion Books.

28. Moore, G. E. (1965). Cramming more components onto integrated circuits. *Electronics Magazine, 38*(8), 19. A previous version was published as an internal memo in 1964, called "The Future of Integrated Electronics."

29. Moore, G. E. (1975, December). Progress in digital integrated electronics. In *Electron devices meeting* (Vol. 21, pp. 11–13).

30. Computer History Museum. (n.d.). *1965: "Moore's Law" Predicts the Future of Integrated Circuits | The Silicon Engine | Computer History Museum.* 1965: "Moo-

re's Law" Predicts the Future of Integrated Circuits | The Silicon Engine | Computer History Museum; www.computerhistory.org. Retrieved December 28, 2021, from https://www.computerhistory.org/siliconengine/moores-law-predicts-the-future-of-integrated-circuits/
31. Economist, 2016. (n.d.). *After Moore's law | Technology Quarterly*. The Economist; www.economist.com. Retrieved December 28, 2021, from https://www.economist.com/technology-quarterly/2016-03-12/after-moores-law
32. Adapted from Moore, G. 1965. *Op. cit.* 27.
33. Clement, J. (2020, July 18). *Topic: Google, Amazon, Meta, Apple, and Microsoft (GAMAM)*. Statista; www.statista.com. https://www.statista.com/topics/4213/google-apple-facebook-amazon-and-microsoft-gafam/
34. Scrapehero. (2018, January 11). *How many products does Amazon.com sell?* ScrapeHero; www.scrapehero.com. https://www.scrapehero.com/many-products-amazon-sell-january-2018/
35. Kurzweil, R. 2001. *Op. cit.* 11
36. Khan, L. M. (2016). Amazon's Antitrust Paradox. *Yale LJ, 126*, 710.
37. For example see: Tan, T. M., & Salo, J. (2021). Ethical marketing in the blockchain-based sharing economy: Theoretical integration and guiding insights. *Journal of Business Ethics*, 1–28.
38. Stango, V., & Zinman, J. (2009). Exponential growth bias and household finance. *The Journal of Finance, 64*(6), 2807–2849.
39. Robson, D. (2020). Exponential growth bias: The numerical error behind Covid-19. BBC. https://www.bbc.com/future/article/20200812-exponential-growth-bias-the-numerical-error-behind-covid-19
40. Lipson, H. (2018). Why most of us fail to grasp coming exponential gains in AI. *Singularity Hub, July, 15*, 2018. https://singularityhub.com/2018/07/15/why-most-of-us-fail-to-grasp-coming-exponential-gains-in-ai/
41. Mahajan, S. (2018). The exponential benefits of logarithmic thinking. *American Journal of Physics, 86*(11), 859–861.
42. Petherick, A., Kira, B., Hale, T., Phillips, T., Webster, S., Cameron-Blake, E., ... & Tatlow, H. (2020). Variation in government responses to COVID-19. *Blavatnik Centre for Government Working Paper, University of Oxford*.
43. Google, (2020). How search works. Our Mission. https://www.google.com/search/howsearchworks/mission/–:~:text=Our company mission is to,it universally accessible and useful.
44. Yashima, S., Nitanda, A., & Suzuki, T. (2021, March). Exponential Convergence Rates of Classification Errors on Learning with SGD and Random Features. In *International Conference on Artificial Intelligence and Statistics* (pp. 1954–1962). PMLR. https://proceedings.mlr.press/v130/yashima21a.html
45. Goldberg, D. (1991). What every computer scientist should know about floating-point arithmetic. *ACM computing surveys (CSUR), 23*(1), 5–48. https://docs.oracle.com/cd/E19957-01/806-3568/ncg_goldberg.html
46. Google Quantum Ai. 2021. *Op. cit.*
47. Lee, N. T., Resnick, P., & Barton, G. (2019). Algorithmic bias detection and mitigation: Best practices and policies to reduce consumer harms. *Brookings Institute: Washington, DC, USA*. https://www.brookings.edu/research/algorithmic

-bias-detection-and-mitigation-best-practices-and-policies-to-reduce-consumer-harms/
48. Thomas, M. (2021, July 6). *7 Risks Of Artificial Intelligence You Should Know | Built In*. https://builtin.com/artificial-intelligence/risks-of-artificial-intelligence
49. Mishra, S. (2022). *Artificial intelligence in the stock market: how did it happen?* Insights Artificial Intelligence in the Stock Market: How Did It Happen? | FIU Business; business.fiu.edu. https://business.fiu.edu/graduate/insights/artificial-intelligence-in-the-stock-market.cfm
50. AI, G. Q. (2021). Exponential suppression of bit or phase errors with cyclic error correction. *Nature, 595*(7867), 383–387. Chen et al., 2021. https://arxiv.org/abs/2102.06132
51. Akakpo, A., Gyasi, E. A., Oduro, B., & Akpabot, S. (2019). Foresight, organization policies and management strategies in electric vehicle technology advances at Tesla. In *Futures Thinking and Organizational Policy* (pp. 57–69). Palgrave Macmillan, Cham.
52. Tesla (TSLA)–Market capitalization. (n.d.). Tesla (TSLA)–Market Capitalization; companiesmarketcap.com. Retrieved January 21, 2022, from https://companiesmarketcap.com/tesla/marketcap/
53. Scrapehero. (2019). *How many products does Amazon.com sell?* ScrapeHero; www.scrapehero.com. https://www.scrapehero.com/number-of-products-on-amazon-april-2019/
54. Loeb, W. (2019, April 29). *Walmart Unveils A New Lab Store That Uses AI*. Forbes; www.forbes.com. https://www.forbes.com/sites/walterloeb/2019/04/29/walmart-unveils-a-new-lab-store-for-the-future/?sh=1910748d504f
55. Rouse, M. (2020). What is IoT (Internet of Things) and How Does it Work. *Retrieved August, 12*. internetofthingsagenda.techtarget.com/definition/Internet-of-Things-IoT.
56. "Walmart: Boosting Retail Performance with Big Data, Machine Learning, AI and the IoT." *Bernard Marr*, www.bernardmarr.com/default.asp?contentID=1276
57. Loeb, W. (2019, April 29). *Walmart Unveils A New Lab Store That Uses AI*. Forbes; www.forbes.com. https://www.forbes.com/sites/walterloeb/2019/04/29/walmart-unveils-a-new-lab-store-for-the-future/?sh=1910748d504f

5

AI and Decision Making

CHAPTER HIGHLIGHTS

1. Decision-making is a process of choosing from alternatives.
2. AI can help in different types of decisions, and this is a function of the management level and the complexity of the decision and data required.
3. The most critical decision you need to take is how you want AI to help in decision-making and whether you are transparent on what AI can and cannot do.
4. Part of designing, onboarding, approving, and using AI is determining who is accountable for AI if it fails.
5. An essential part of AI agile decision-making is the feedback loop or the ability to learn through sensemaking.
6. Good governance is more than ESG and looks at AI ethics and the risks of the choices selected.
7. Leaders should be ready to mitigate potential or actual crises by preparing for technical, data, and knowledge failures.

> **Cases:** Australia myGov | Microsoft | Texwinca Holdings | World of Warcraft—*Corrupted Blood* | Cybertroops | DDoS e-Estonia & Taiwan | Trojan virus (Cold War) | Global e-waste

5.1 Decision-Making

Decision-making is a process of choosing from alternatives. The choice includes *what to do* (*action*) and *what to believe* (*opinion*).[1] Some of our decisions are made with conscious thought, and others are made unconsciously (we do not realize we are making these decisions). It is estimated that the number of decisions we make in a day could be as high as 35,000![2] Since AI mimics human intelligence, we are trying to capture both types of decision-making. In a study of both conscious and unconscious decision-making or thinking, the author concludes,

> If a problem is complex, it by definition means that a lot of information has to be taken into account. Conscious thought is not very good at this. One could say that conscious thought is very focused but not very encompassing or inclusive.... The bottom line is that both systems can be fast, slow, smart, or stupid. It all depends on what they are asked to do.[3]

While there have been subsequent studies with mixed results, it is clear that the context matters! AI is very brittle when working across contexts. Brittle implies that the data used to train the AI may not make the AI work as predicted when moved to another context or time, as the data is old (and hence becomes biased) or irrelevant.

Another critical issue when looking at decision-making and the role AI plays in ethics and governance—is whether AI decisions are fair (see Figure 5.1). Psychological studies show that unconscious thought in moral decisions leads to more decisions where the individual will approve actions that could harm others to justify maximum positive outcomes, compared to conscious thought decision-making.[4] This thinking raises questions about how AI helps in decision-making and whether the AI contribution is seen as rational, prompting unconscious thought. We see this behavior in examples with the Tesla autopilot, when the drivers have decided to nap in the cockpit of a moving car, trusting the AI systems (though the car is considered a Level 2 Driver Assist System out of the six levels of vehicle autonomy). Tesla responded to this problem by creating a Nag system. The dashboard flashes a reminder when you take your hands off the wheel. If you ignore that, it then beeps; if you still ignore that, it turns off autopilot and stops.

> A 2019 subtitle headline of *The Guardian* stated, "In 12 months, Australian welfare payments were stopped an extra 1m times thanks to automated technologies. Money is stopped first, and questions asked later, causing untold misery."[5] The Australian government began digitalizing in 2013. The beneficiaries of the welfare systems were moved away from the Centrelink shop fronts to the myGov online portal. By 2016, using a single username and password, users could view records from 35 agencies through the myGov portal. They could access not just their social benefits but information on their health, retirement funds, and tax applications. At the back end, over 350 different agencies and private organizations were involved to cross-verify the data uploaded on the site. There had been problems with automation in the past. Previously in 2017, the Robodebt scheme had a flawed algorithm that sometimes identified benefits recipients as owning welfare debts.
>
> With the new automated welfare scheme, claiming benefits online became a nightmare. Within 12 months, about 2.7 million welfare payment suspensions had been made. The push toward using AI was to automate the processes as much as possible to simplify administration.[6] The decision-making power in manually managing penalties for highlighted cases dropped with the AI taking the decisions. This may seem like a positive result, but if the process was also for public benefit, it was not working. This judgment was being made without consideration if the applicant was a single parent, homeless, someone ill, or for any other reasons (AI does not have that judgment). An analysis by the Guardian showed that 75% of these stopped payments were not the recipient's fault. A research paper found an ethical gap or "misalignments between how technology is described in government documentation, and how it is deployed in social service delivery."[7]

Figure 5.1 Australia myGov: AI for social welfare benefits.[8]

Decision-making has several stages, beginning with identifying the problem, collecting information, identifying alternatives, weighing the evidence, choosing an alternative, implementing, and getting feedback. When we use AI, the process of making decisions changes, and it also depends on the objective. Gartner identifies three types of AI decisions: Support, augmentation, and automation.[9] As the level of complexity decreases and reaction time for decision-making decreases, there is a greater tendency to rely on AI. However, as the complexity increases and there is more time for deliberation, employees should use AI for decision support (see Figure 5.2).

To use AI, organizations should first be able to classify the types of decisions made. It is a function of the management level and the complexity of the decision and data required (see Figure 5.3). This classification exercise should be conducted across (1) the technical department responsible for onboarding, developing, or managing AI, (2) the department that pushes AI to stakeholders (includes for example, finance and purchasing), and finally, (3) leadership and the board who have a responsibility of good governance. In our experience, leaders often do not know enough about AI and its limitations which creates challenges when they approve of the rapid onboarding of AI.

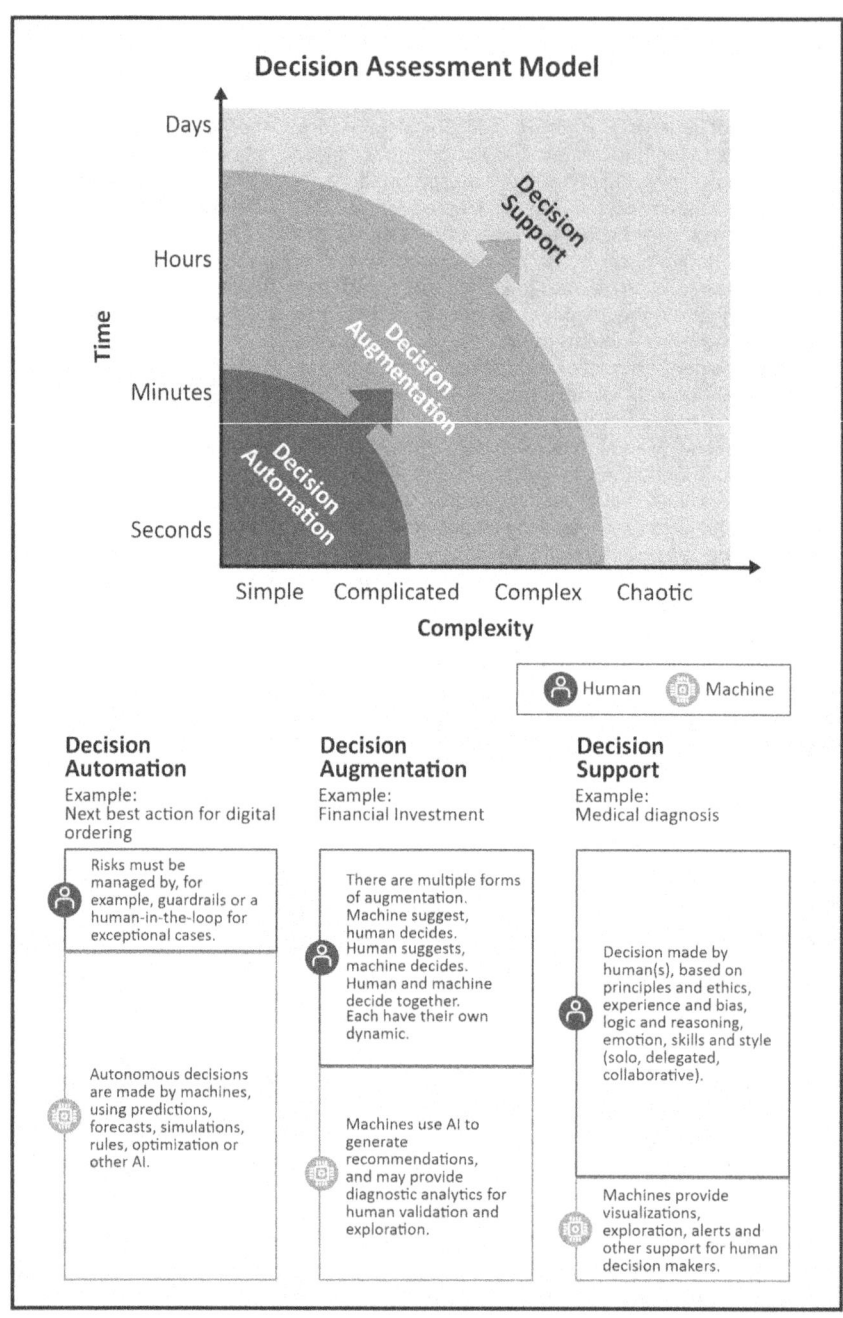

Figure 5.2 Decision-Making with AI. *Source:* Adapted from Gartner (2021)[10]

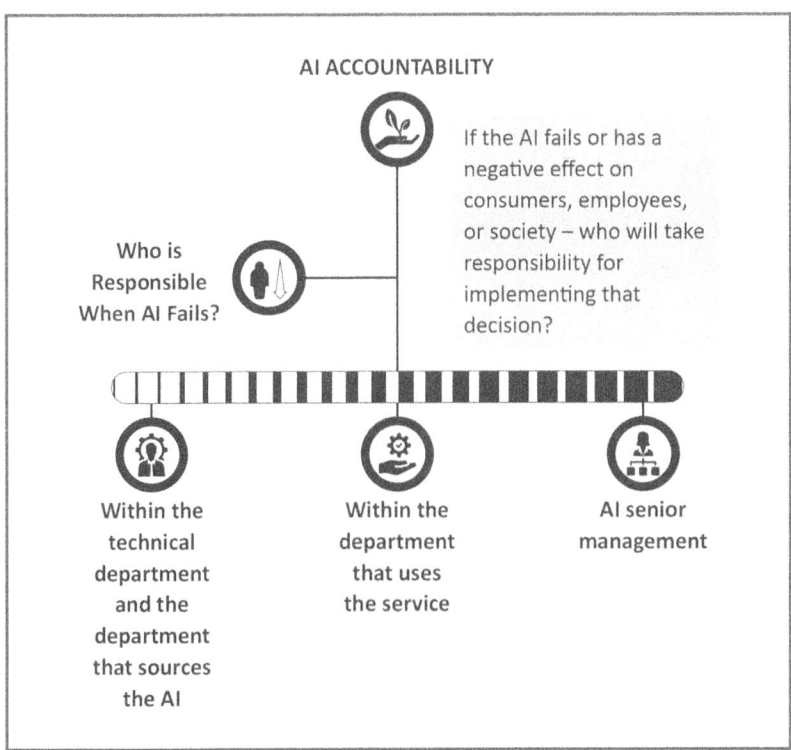

Figure 5.3 AI accountability. Source: Stephens and Vashishtha (2020)[11]

Leaders should think hard about their responsibilities and the ethical dilemma of adopting an AI decision where they do not have enough knowledge or expertise. For example, an IT-manager who sits at the cusp of several departments and arbitrates between AI specialists and AI users may not have enough information on the indirect impact of AI on users as perhaps the data is not collected or shared. Hence good decision-making within an AI-enabled organization first centers around governance and values of the organization. Only after this centering, should you consider the context (time, complexity) and data availability for decision making.

Further, by using AI, there is the additional burden of managing skill redundancy. Accenture recommends skill mapping to identify new AI-proof jobs and jobs vulnerable to automation. Unilever's Patrick Hull, Future of Work, says, "Only jobs should be made redundant, not people."[12] But this puts the burden of identifying new jobs (in or outside the company) and retraining and reskilling on the organization that is making the position redundant. Another challenge has been skill loss. As firms outsource, they may save on costs but lose the ability to control AI projects as they have no expertise to cross-verify the programming and outputs of the data. This situation is relevant for the firms that work with mainframes and the issue of legacy systems (more later). Mainframes, which use older programming languages[13] like Assembler, Cobol, Fortran, Pascal, Basic, and C, are the backbone of industries like banking, insurance, government, defense, telecom, healthcare, aviation, and retail! It is estimated that 71% of Fortune 500s use mainframes.[14]

5.2 Agile Decision-Making

Agile decision-making or dynamic decision-making is a function of understanding the environmental context. The Cynefin (pronounced as kuh-NEV-in) framework can be applied to AI decision-making (see Table 5.1). This framework looks at various contexts in which decision-making needs to occur and for what AI can be used. The philosophy behind agile decision-making is the ability to respond, realign and adapt to changing external conditions. Therefore, the decisions you make with AI should be reflected in changes in process, people, purpose, and other resources in the internal environment with the hope of managing, influencing, or leveraging the external conditions (see Figure 5.4). In today's fast-paced environment, you need AI to help decision-making abilities and ensure the perspective you follow is not too limiting.

An essential part of AI agile decision-making is the feedback loop or the ability to learn through sensemaking. Decision-makers (humans or AI) must distinguish between noise, signals, and stimuli. Not easy to do in complex or chaotic environments. So, the knowledge context (what you know and do not know) is key to good decision-making. For example, during the pandemic, many models were used in the early period to predict the contagiousness of the virus. An early assumption was that the COVID virus behaved like the flu virus (which was not true).[15] Later, when policymakers took decisions—closed borders, lockdowns, or remote learning, these decisions did not consider the complexity of the ecosystem. Hence, small business owners who could not move their businesses online, individuals who needed to earn daily for their livelihoods by being physically present, and parents of children who did not have access to internet technologies for remote learning or care while working themselves resisted the lockdown. Decisions in such environments are made of tradeoffs. How can AI help or manage these tradeoffs, and what is the responsibility you would wish

AI and Decision Making ▪ 95

TABLE 5.1 Cynefin Framework and Agile Decision Making

Stage	Feature[16]	What You Should Do	AI
Simple	Clear relationship between cause and effect. Deterministic problems.	Sense, Categorize, Respond. Look for Best Practices.	A rule-based ordered system that contains predictable cause and effect. Programmable logic or flowcharts, simple analytics, or retrospective analysis for patterns like payroll processing, order processing, or call center routing.
Complicated	Cause and effect can be deduced with analysis or expertise and used for deterministic problems.	Sense, Analyze, Respond. Identify good use cases and evaluate relevance to the context.	AI in healthcare, can assess millions of parameters and classify them accordingly. It can be used for Decision Support Systems of diagnostic systems, for identifying car breakdown issues, insurance fraud, asset management, and marketing campaigning.
Complex	Cause and effect can only be deduced in retrospect. Requires time.	Probe, Sense, Respond Emergent Solutions. Need to understand the parts (but these are finite). Emergent patterns can be perceived but not predicted, and need multiple perspectives (narratives).	Needs a strong understanding of factors and their importance. It may require a co-sharing of decision management with user/human decision-makers. It can be used for predictions like supply chain disruptions or stock prices or predicting weather patterns and responses to the same.
Chaotic	Cause and effect can never be deduced.	Act, Sense, Respond (Need to understand the parts, but these are dynamic, and many factors may be hidden). Novel Solutions	These types of decisions are taken in emergencies or crises. The purpose is to bring down the complexity levels by observing the decision and its effect on the system. It can be used for threat analysis and managing stock market crashes, battlefields, and natural disasters.
Disordered	Lies somewhere between- different perspectives on what domain is present abound.	Probe, Analyze, Sense	Not enough is known about the problem. AI can be used for labeling, categorizing, and looking for hidden connections to help narrow the focus on the issue that should be solved.

Source: Adapted from Bellur (2022)[17]

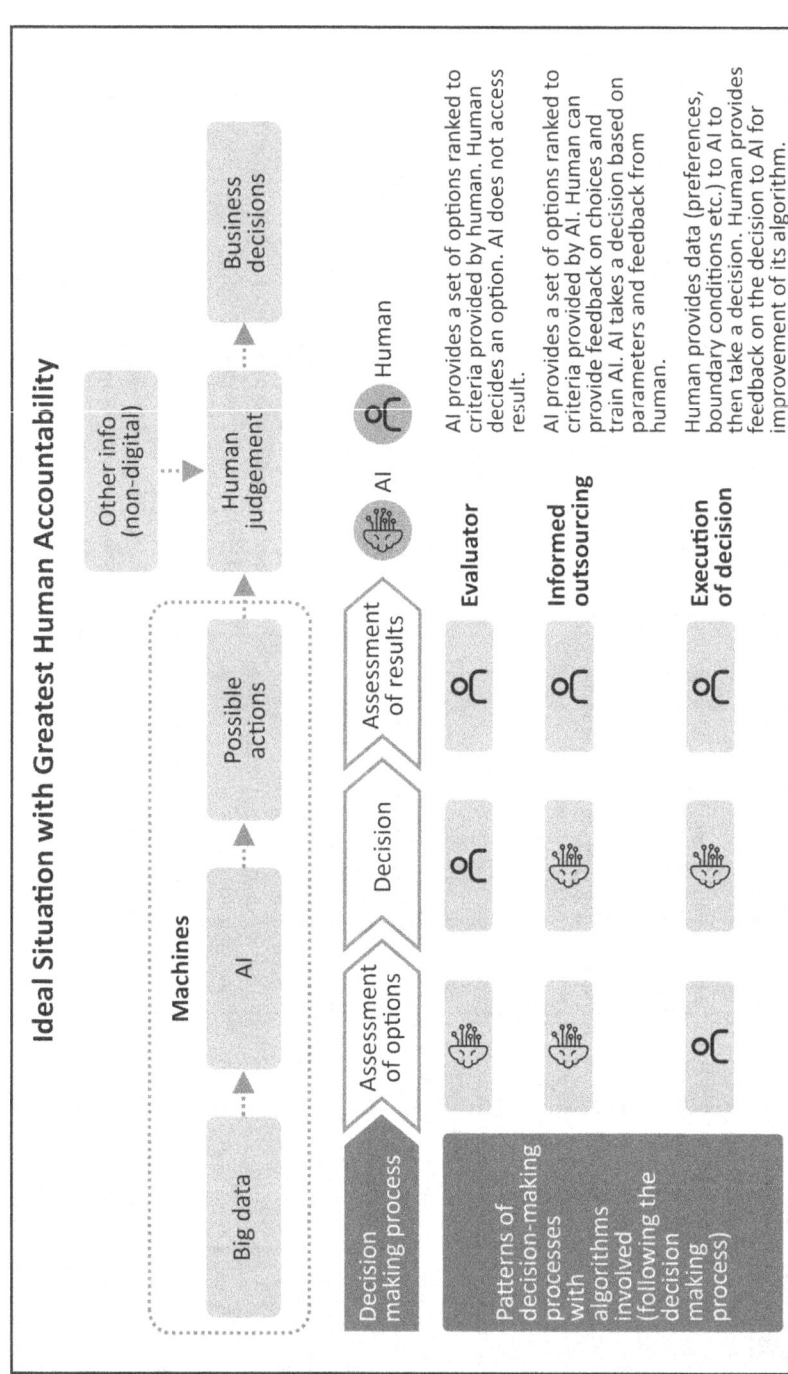

Figure 5.4 AI–Human decision making (types). Source: Adapted from Leyer et al. (2020)[18]

(continued)

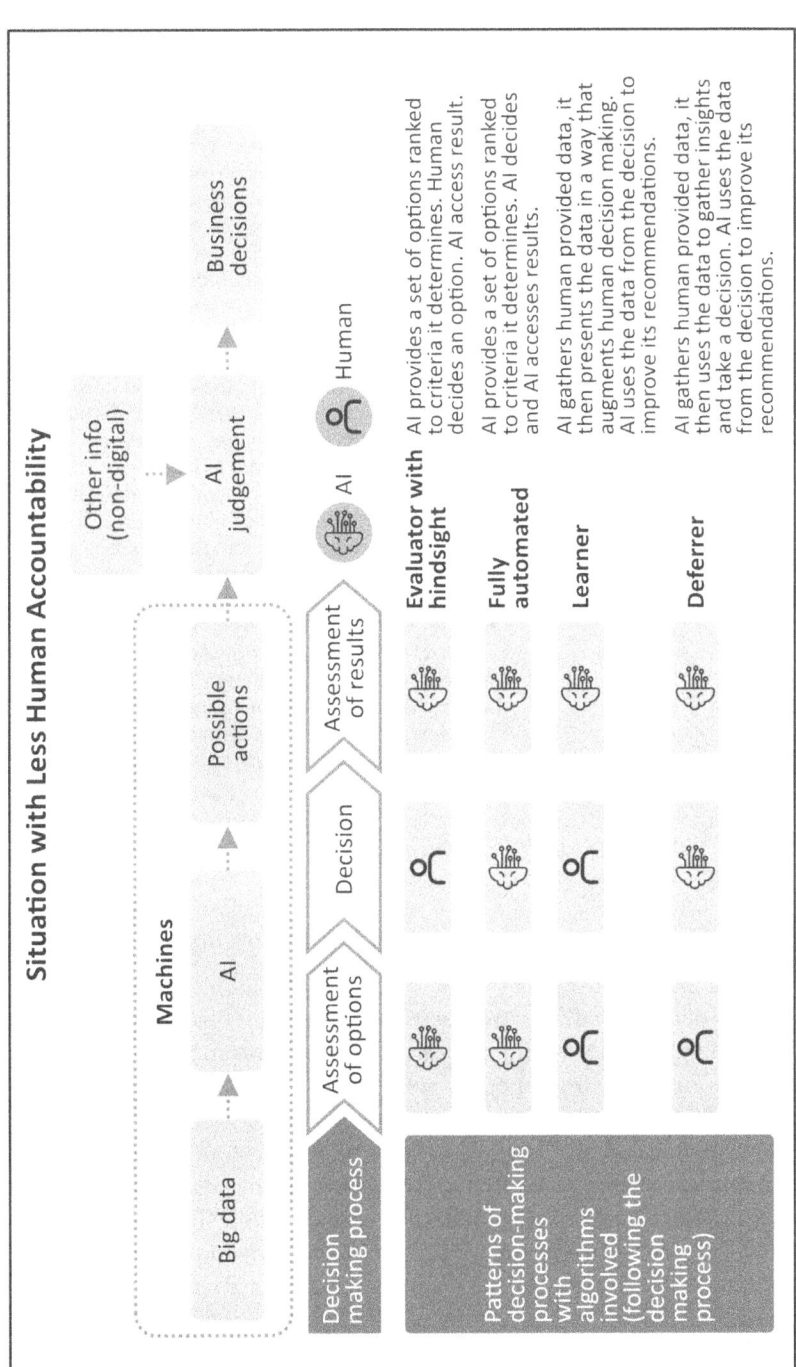

Figure 5.4 (cont.) AI–Human decision making (types). Source: Adapted from Leyer et al. (2020)

> Undoubtedly, AI, if appropriately managed with robust feedback systems, can do tremendous good. The speed at which it can learn from data, can help reduce human errors. For example, road accidents are most often caused by human error. A study by RAND corporation that looked at 500 different future scenarios found that the introduction of autonomous cars, in most situations, would save more lives than delaying the introduction till the AI was perfect.[19] But safety alone cannot be the only consideration factor, as we must consider liability for accidents, insurance, traffic laws and regulations, infrastructure development, privacy concerns, cybersecurity, and, more importantly, ethical considerations. So, one interesting debate we have is the modified Trolley problem. Consider the scenario that you are programming an autonomous car. It is an unavoidable situation where one of three people have to be "hit" and may die. One is you, the driver, the other is a pedestrian–a young child, and the third is an old lady getting out of her car. Who will you choose? Let's say *you* never made a choice; the car did. Who is liable? You (the driver), the car manufacturer (and there may be many entities and people), the software company (and there may be many), or one of the many data providers? If you are a manager, who in your company is the person that needs to be accountable? The programmer, the designer who aggregated all the technologies, or the person who approved the technology and pushed it out into the market? What is the role of the regulator? What is the responsibility of the customer? What is the role of researchers who kept insisting that the system was safe and the data proved it? What is the role of the media that hyped up the vehicle and made it seem like it was a must-buy car? What is the role of insurance and finance companies? The trolley problem does not have an answer but is designed to provoke thought.

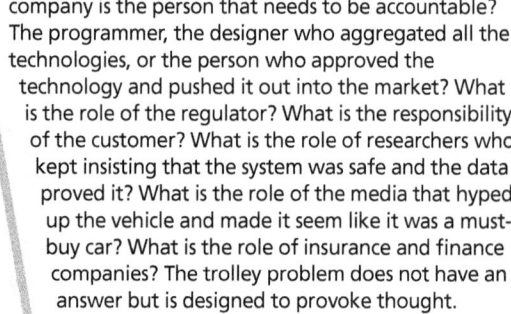

Figure 5.5 AI and trolley problem.

to give AI? Take the example presented in Figure 5.5 which illustrates the point of trade-offs.

In agile decision-making, the focus is the agile methodology, which is applied to digital projects. The genesis for the term came from the Agile Manifesto, which was developed by software engineers who encountered difficulties implementing projects across organizations. A key component for agile decision-making using AI should be a robust and agile learning environment (see Figure 5.6) that extends beyond the organizational borders to all stakeholders involved. First, the organization should determine core functions for knowledge management, which is a continuous process. Second, they need to decide the control settings of these AI-knowledge outcomes. This involves determining who has access to the system which is information needed for developing safeguards.

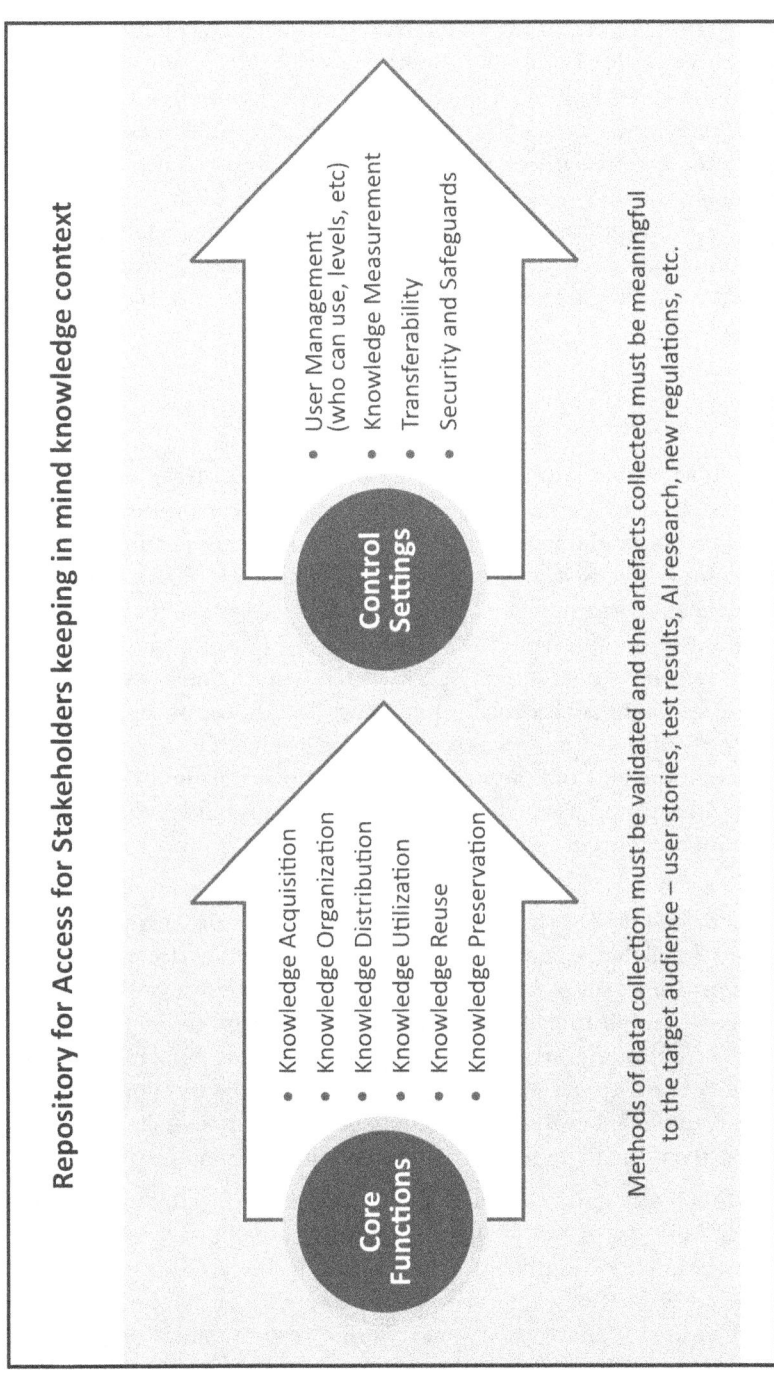

Figure 5.6 AI and agile learning knowledge organization. *Source:* Authors

Another vital part of an AI-enabled knowledge organization is the culture. This culture is one where failure is a shared learning experience. Organizations need to look at how they measure knowledge gained from decisions, the time taken to gather feedback, the robustness of failure analysis, and the strength of the feedback loop. Too often, a company's first response is denying culpability in the event of a failure, which wastes precious time. More importantly, they erase traces of these failures (from organizational memory, documents, and websites) which means they do not have the learning accessible for the future. For AI systems, garbage in is garbage out!

5.3 Governance

Creating an AI-enabled organization requires employees to know and adopt governance standards and AI ethics. This process means setting up an AI ethics philosophy and mapping the AI ethics or principles with Sustainable Development Goals (SDGs), Universal Human Rights (UHRs), or Environment, Social and Governance (ESG) frameworks. In addition, there needs to be a pre-assessment of the risks of deploying AI, which can be mapped by a 5 × 5 matrix (see Figure 5.7). These risks can be assessed along the process of adopting AI for decision-making (identification of AI, testing, purchase, deployment, usage, retraining, and project end). This tool can help clarify the chain of command for escalation of issues and assigning responsibilities for AI. Is it fair to ascribe all responsibilities to the CTO if you insist on outsourcing all key functions?

There are over 172 countries that use AI systems,[20] but only 42 countries have signed the OECD Principles of AI;[21] and 14 governments with the EU joined the Global Partnership on AI Initiative in 2020.[22] This low rate of adoption of AI principles suggests a vacuum in AI governance at a global level that individual organizations need to fill in. One way to manage the process is to look at the level of automation and then ascertain the human-in-the-loop (see Table 5.1) or where, ideally, the human should be in control. For example, in Figure 5.8, Level 1 has no automation (human is totally in control), and Level 10 has the highest level of automation (no human control).

This tool looks at the current availability of skills, the adequacy of rules, knowledge, and expertise. While the context (complexity) and time for decision making are essential, the assumption is that a significant amount of knowledge is tacit and may not be easy to codify for AI. Further, there is a need to assess failure points and ascribe responsibility for managing AI. Unfortunately, this is getting harder due to third-party vendors, legacy systems, system vulnerabilities, and the rapid obsolescence of data. The current highest business security risks come from vulnerabilities in legacy systems that were two to 20 years old.[24]

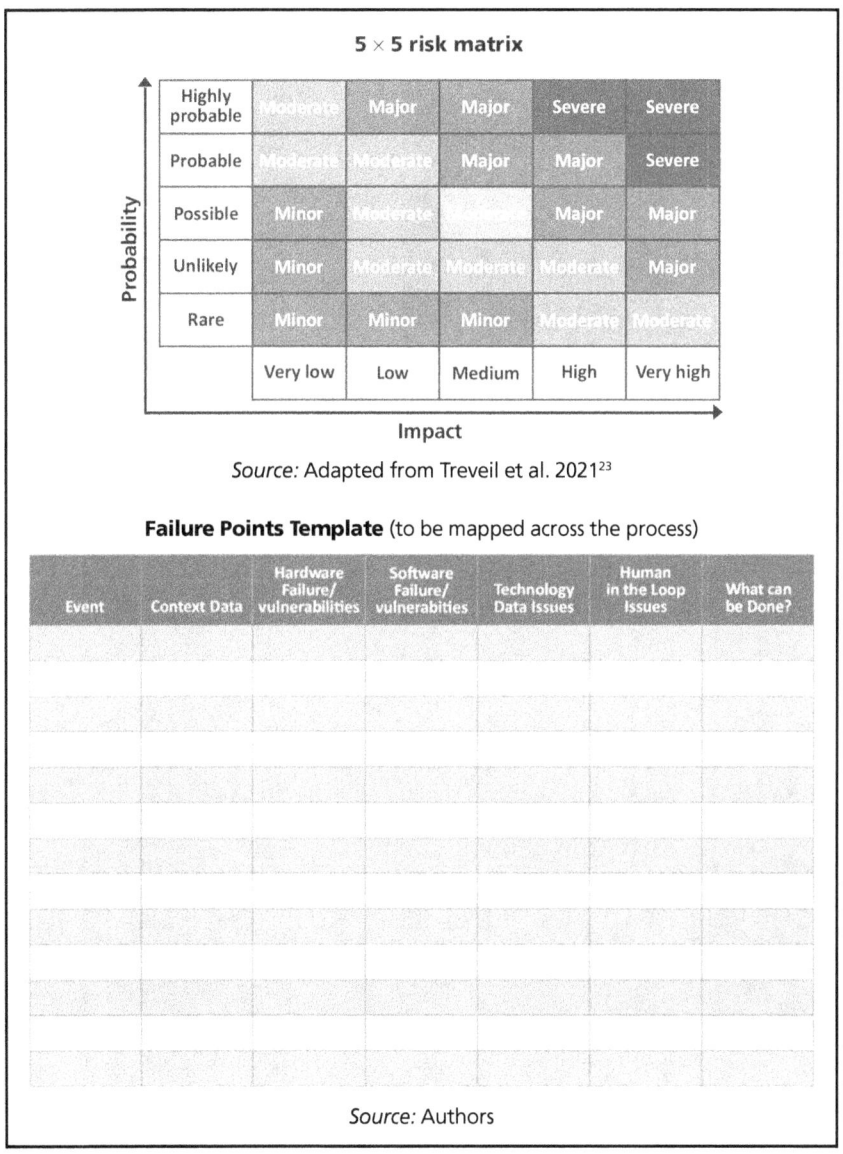

Figure 5.7   AI governance: Risk assessment tool for each process of adopting AI decision making

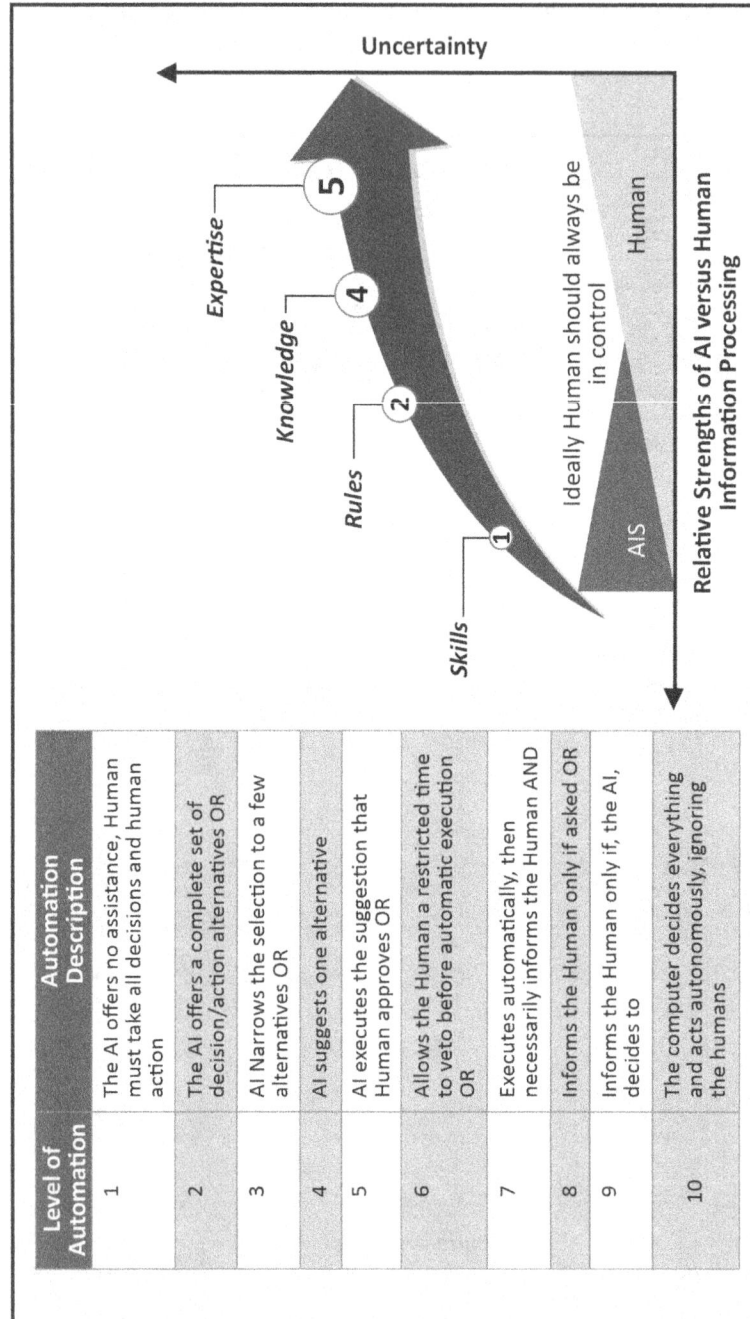

Figure 5.8 Role allocation for information processing behaviors (skill, rule, knowledge, and expertise) and the relationship to uncertainty. *Source:* Adapted from Cummings (2014) and Parasuraman, Sheridan, & Wickens (2000).[25]

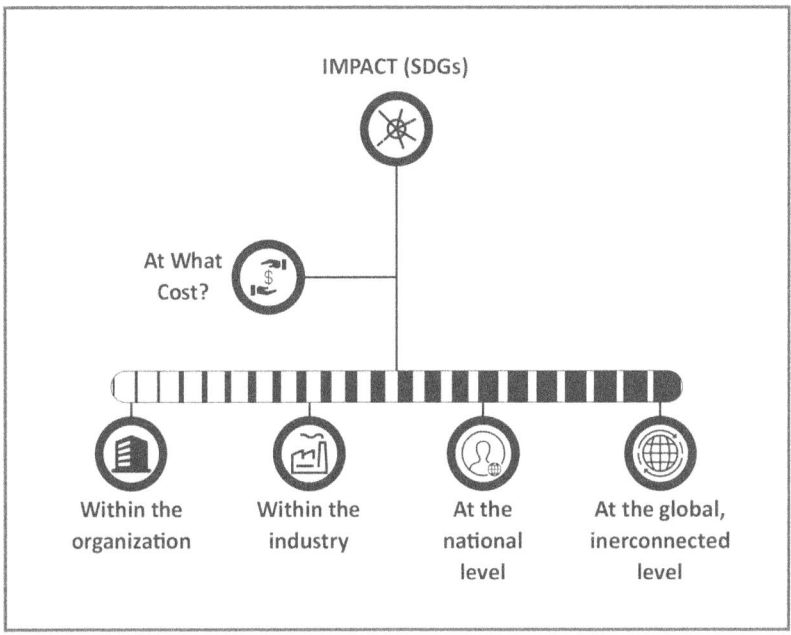

Figure 5.9 Impact of AI. *Source:* Stephens and Vashishtha (2020)[26]

One way to consider ethical and responsible AI is to balance the cost of AI and its benefits by looking at its contribution to the Sustainable Development Goals—SDGs (see Figure 5.4). There are 17 SDGs we are to achieve by 2030. These SDGs center around the individual, society, and planet and require partnerships to make them happen. Achieving the global goals raises many questions—is AI an enabler or a detractor of SDGs? At what level are these being assessed—within the organization, the community of operation, among its stakeholders (suppliers and distributors), or within the industry and across geographic borders? Another way to demonstrate corporate and industry governance is to use Environment, Sustainability, and Governance (ESG) indicators. For example, take the issue of unemployment. McKinsey estimates that by 2030, there will be a decline in the need for basic cognitive, physical, and manual skills and a growth in both advanced and basic technological and higher cognitive skills in Europe and the United States.[27] Of course, this may not hold for other parts of the world suffering from a youth bulge and unemployment.

5.4 Environmental, Social, and Governance (ESG) Reporting and AI

More than 92% of the S&P 500 companies and 70% of the Russell 1000 companies have some form of ESG reporting as a form of corporate responsibility.[28] The reporting is not identical across regions, with more reporting across North America, Asia Pacific, Europe, and MENA, in that order. Some industries like retail, transport and leisure, healthcare, and F&B, lag.[29] Many of these industries are AI-enabled. Most of the reporting is skewed, focusing on one of the E, S, or G indices.[30] Absent are AI ethics or governance indicators (see Table 5.2 for some AI standards), though some work in this area is being done. Examples of some documents are Asilomar AI Principles,[31] endorsed by California in 2018; Canada's Responsible Use of AI (2021),[32] India's Responsible AI (2021),[33] Singapore's Model of AI Governance Framework (2020),[34] USA's Principles for the Stewardship of AI Applications (2020),[35] OECD (2019),[36] UNESCO's Recommendations on the Ethics of Artificial Intelligence (2021),[37] EU's The Ethics Guidelines for Trustworthy Artificial Intelligence (March 2021), Google AI Ethics (2021),[38] and Microsoft's new updated Responsible AI Standard (2022).[39]

TABLE 5.2 List of Some AI Ethics or Governance Terms

Human Values		
Human Values	AI systems should be designed and operated so as to be compatible with ideals of *human dignity, rights, freedoms, and cultural diversity.*	Asilomar AI Principles (2017)
Values	Promote *positive human values* and *not disturb in any way social harmony in community relationships.*	India: Responsible AI (2021)
Values	*Respect, protection and promotion of human rights, and fundamental freedoms, and human dignity*[40]	UNESCO (2021)
Research Goal	The goal of AI research should be to *create not undirected intelligence, but beneficial intelligence.*	Asilomar AI Principles (2017)
Guiding Principles	*Organisations should ensure that AI decision-making processes are explainable, transparent and fair, while AI solutions should be human-centric.*	Singapore: Model AI Governance Framework (2020)
Shared Benefit		
Shared Benefit	*Generating prosperity, value creation and wealth maximization and sustainability... fair, inclusive and peaceful society, by helping to increase citizen's mental autonomy, with equal distribution of economic, social and political opportunity.*	EU AI (March 2021)

(continued)

TABLE 5.2 List of Some AI Ethics or Governance Terms (continued)

Shared Benefit Shared Prosperity	AI technologies *should benefit and empower as many people as possible.* The economic prosperity created by AI should be *shared broadly to benefit all of humanity.*	Asilomar AI Principles (2017)
Be Socially Beneficial to All	*Widely benefit current and future generations*, and *work for the common good.*	Google AI Ethics (2021)
The Principle of Beneficence	"*Do Good*"—*individual and collective level.*	EU AI (March 2021)
Inclusive Growth, Sustainable Development, and Well-being	**Responsible stewardship of trustworthy AI** in pursuit of *beneficial outcomes for people and the planet*, such as *augmenting human capabilities and enhancing creativity, advancing inclusion of underrepresented populations, reducing economic, social, gender, and other inequalities, and protecting natural environments, thus invigorating inclusive growth, sustainable development and well-being.*	OECD.ai (2019) (Principle 1.1)
Sustainability	The continuous *assessment of the human, social, cultural, economic and environmental impact* of AI technologies should therefore be carried out with full cognizance of the implications of AI technologies *for sustainability as a set of constantly evolving goals across a range of dimensions, such as currently identified in the Sustainable Development Goals (SDGs) of the United Nations.*	UNESCO (2021)
Inclusiveness Goal: Accessibility Standards compliance	AI systems are designed to be in *inclusive in accordance with the Microsoft Accessibility Standards.*	Microsoft Responsible AI Standard v2 (2022)
Design for All	Allows *all citizens to use the products or services, regardless of their age, disability status or social status—accessibility and usability of technologies.*	EU AI (March 2021)
Human-centric	AI solutions should be *human-centric.*	Singapore Model of AI Governance Framework (2020)
Human-centered Values and Fairness	AI actors should *respect the rule of law, human rights and democratic values, throughout the AI system lifecycle.* These include *freedom, dignity and autonomy, privacy and data protection, nondiscrimination and equality, diversity, fairness, social justice, and internationally recognized labor rights.* To this end, AI actors *should implement mechanisms and safeguards, such as capacity for human determination, that are appropriate to the context and consistent with the state of art.*	OECD.ai (2019) (Principle 1.2)

(continued)

TABLE 5.2 List of Some AI Ethics or Governance Terms (continued)

Do No Harm		
Proportionality and Do No Harm	The decision to choose an AI should be appropriate and proportional to achieve the legitimate aim (and ensure human and environmental and ecosystem flourishing), *preventing unwanted harms (safety risks) of human, environmental and ecosystem.*	UNESCO (2021)
The Principle of Non-maleficence:	"*Do no Harm*"—*human beings individual and in society, at work, vulnerable demographics, environment (animals and resources).*	Adopted by EU AI (March 2021)
Harm	(Avoid) *Cause overall harm, weapons or primary intent is injury, surveillance tech violating international norms, contravenes international norms, law or human rights.*	Google AI Ethics (2021)
Non-subversion	The **power conferred by control** of highly advanced AI systems *should respect and improve, rather than subvert, the social and civic processes on which the health of society depends.*	Asilomar AI Principles (2017)
Impact Assessment	**Assess, review, the impact** of the system on *people, organizations, and society.* **Oversight of significant adverse impacts** through *defined Restricted Uses, definition of a Sensitive Use, and review at least annually.*	Compiled from Microsoft Responsible AI Standard v2 (2022)
Safety and Security		
Safety and Security	*Throughout the AI design, development, deployment, and operation process . . . providing systemic resilience, and for preventing bad actors from exploiting AI systems, including cybersecurity risks posed by AI operation, and adversarial use of AI against a regulated entity.* Moreover, agencies *should consider, where relevant, any national security implications* raised by the unique characteristics of AI and AI applications and *take actions to protect national security as appropriate for their authorities.*	United States of America has Principles for the Stewardship of AI Applications (2020)
Safety	Safety is about *ensuring that the system will indeed do what it is supposed to do, without harming users (human physical integrity), resources or the environment.*	Adopted by EU AI (March 2021)
Risk	Conduct **risk and impact assessments** to *evaluate direct and indirect potential impact of AI systems on end-users.*	India— Responsible AI (2021)
Failures and Remediations	AI systems are designed *to minimize the time to remediation of predictable or known failures.*	Microsoft Responsible AI Standard v2 (2022)

(continued)

TABLE 5.2 List of Some AI Ethics or Governance Terms (continued)

Security	*Vulnerabilities to attack (security risks) during the AI systems lifecycle.*	UNESCO (2021)
Reliability and Safety Guidance	*Evaluates the operational factors and ranges within which AI systems are expected to perform reliably and safely, remediates issues, and provides related information to customers.*	Microsoft Responsible AI Standard v2 (2022)
Security and safety (Principle 1.4)	AI systems should be *robust, secure and safe throughout their entire lifecycle* so that, in conditions of normal use, foreseeable use or misuse, or other adverse conditions, they function appropriately and do not pose unreasonable safety risk.	OECD.ai (2019) (1.4)
Robustness	Algorithms are *secure, reliable as well as robust enough to deal with errors or inconsistencies during the design, development, execution, deployment and use phase of the AI system.*	EU AI (March 2021)
Robustness	AI actors should, *based on their roles, the context, and their ability to act, apply a systematic risk management approach to each phase of the AI system lifecycle on a continuous basis to address risks related to AI systems, including privacy, digital security, safety and bias.*	OECD.ai (2019) (1.4)
Human Autonomy		
Human Agency	AI developers and deployers should therefore ensure that *humans are made aware of—or able to request and validate the fact that—they interact with an AI identity.*	EU AI (March 2021)
Human Oversight and Determination	Human oversight refers thus not only to *individual human oversight, but to inclusive public oversight, as appropriate,* where it is *always possible to attribute ethical and legal responsibility for any stage of the life cycle of AI systems, as well as in cases of remedy related to AI systems, to physical persons or to existing legal entities.*	UNESCO (2021)
	The *decision to cede control in limited contexts remains that of humans,* as humans can resort to AI systems in decision-making and acting, but an AI system can never replace ultimate human responsibility and accountability. *As a rule, life and death decisions should not be ceded to AI systems.*	
Human Oversight and Control	*(compiled) Identify and document the stakeholders who are responsible for troubleshooting, managing, operating, overseeing, and controlling the system during and after deployment and system elements necessary for stakeholders. Define and document the method to be used to evaluate whether each oversight or control function. Evaluate.*	Microsoft Responsible AI Standard v2 (2022)

(continued)

TABLE 5.2 List of Some AI Ethics or Governance Terms (continued)

Human Control	Humans should choose *how and whether to delegate decisions to AI systems, to accomplish human-chosen objectives.*	Asilomar AI Principles (2017)
The Principle of Autonomy	*"Preserve Human Agency" means freedom from subordination to, or coercion by, AI systems.*	EU AI (March 2021)
Accountability		
Accountability	Be *accountable to people* (AI technologies will be subject to appropriate human direction and *con*trol)	Google AI Ethics (2021)
Accountability (Principle 1.5)	*AI actors should be accountable for the proper functioning of AI systems and for the respect of the above principles, based on their roles, the context, and consistent with the state of art.*	https://oecd.ai/en/dashboards/ai-principles/P9
Accountability	Be *accoun*table *to people (provide appropriate opportunities for feedback, relevant explanations, and appeal).*	Google AI Ethics (2021)
Responsibility	*Designers and builders of advanced AI systems are stakeholders in the moral implications of their use, misuse, and actions, with a responsibility and opportunity to shape those implications.*	Asilomar AI Principles (2017)
Fit for purpose	They (AI systems) *provide valid solutions for the problems they are designed to solve.*	Microsoft Responsible AI Standard v2 (2022)
Human Oversight	Human oversight refers not only *to individual human oversight, but to inclusive public oversight, as appropriate, where it is always possible to attribute ethical and legal responsibility for any stage of the life cycle of AI systems, as well as in cases of remedy related to AI systems, to physical persons or to existing legal entities.*	UNESCO (2021)
Responsibility and Accountability	*Appropriate oversight, impact assessment, audit and due diligence mechanisms, including whistle-blowers' protection, should be developed to ensure accountability for AI systems and their impact throughout their life cycle.*	UNESCO (2021)
Ongoing Monitoring, Feedback, and Evaluation	AI systems are *subject to ongoing monitoring, feedback, and evaluation so that we can identify and review new uses, identify and troubleshoot issues, manage and maintain the systems, and improve them over time.*	Microsoft Responsible AI Standard v2 (2022)

(continued)

TABLE 5.2   List of Some AI Ethics or Governance Terms (continued)

Data governance		
Data Governance and Management	*Define and document data requirements with respect to the system's intended uses, stakeholders, and the geographic areas where the system will be deployed. Define and document procedures for the collection and processing of data, to include annotation, labeling, cleaning, enrichment, and aggregation, where relevant. If using existing data sets to train the system, assess, evaluate and document the quantity and suitability of available data sets needed in relation to the data requirements specified.*	Microsoft Responsible AI Standard v2 (2022)
Data Governance	*Data sets quality, handling, pruning, anonymization, training, validation, testing, records, nonduplication of data training and test sets, integrity and feedback and protection of the individuals' data.*	EU AI (March 2021)
Data Governance	*Controls in place to ensure the confidentiality, integrity, and availability of the information processed, stored, and transmitted by AI systems.*	United States of America has Principles for the Stewardship of AI Applications (2020)
Bias		
Algorithmic[a] Bias	There are six types: (1) inconclusive evidence—the *inference is biased based on the method* being used, (2) inscrutable evidence—*the connection between data and conclusion not clear*, (3) misguided evidence—the *bias is an outcome of the data input*; (4) unfair outcomes—*the quality of evidence prompts an unfair response*, (5) transformative effects—*the algorithm modifies how we conceptualize the world and hence gives an illusion of neutrality which may not be so* and (6) traceability—*not easy to debug or detect harm or even ascribe responsibility.*	Research paper: Mittelstadt, B. D., Allo, P., Taddeo, M., Wachter, S., & Floridi, L. (2016).[41]
Bias	*Avoid creating or reinforcing bias (reflect, reinforce, or reduce unfair biases across cultures and societies) and unjust impacts.*	Google AI Ethics (2021)
Fairness and Nondiscrimination		
Fairness and Non-discrimination	This implies an *inclusive approach* to ensuring that the benefits of AI technologies *are available and accessible to all*, taking into consideration the specific needs of different age groups, cultural systems, different language groups, persons with disabilities, girls and women, and disadvantaged, marginalized and vulnerable people or people in vulnerable situations.[42]	UNESCO (2021)

(continued)

TABLE 5.2 List of Some AI Ethics or Governance Terms (continued)

Fairness Goals	AI systems are designed to provide a similar quality of service for identified demographic groups, including marginalized groups.	Microsoft Responsible AI Standard v2 (2022)
Allocation of Resources and Opportunities	AI systems *that allocate resources or opportunities in essential domains are designed to do so in a manner that minimizes disparities in outcomes for identified demographic groups, including marginalized groups.*	Microsoft Responsible AI Standard v2 (2022)
Minimization of Stereotyping, Demeaning, and Rrasing Outputs	AI systems *that describe, depict, or otherwise represent people, cultures, or society are designed to minimize the potential for stereotyping, demeaning, or erasing identified demographic groups, including marginalized groups.*	Microsoft Responsible AI Standard v2 (2022)
Nondiscrimination	*Focuses on variability of AI results between individuals or groups of people based on the exploitation of differences in their characteristics that can be considered either intentionally or unintentionally.*	EU AI (March 2021)
Algorithm-gnostic, Technology-agnostic, Sector-agnostic, Scale- and Business-model-agnostic	*Applies to AI in general, not focus on specific systems, software or technology, serves as a baseline set of considerations and measures for organisations operating in any sector to adopt, and does not focus on organisations of a particular scale or size.*	Singapore Model AI Governance Framework (2020)
Privacy		
Privacy	People should have *the right to access, manage, control and use the data they generate.*	Asilomar AI Principles (2017)
Privacy Design Principles	In the *development and use of our AI technologies. We will give opportunity for notice and consent, encourage architectures with privacy safeguards, and provide appropriate transparency and control over the use of data.*	Google AI Ethics (2021)
Right to Privacy and Data Protection	Privacy, *a right essential to the protection of human dignity, human autonomy and human agency, must be respected, protected and promoted throughout the life cycle of AI systems.* Adequate *data protection frameworks and governance mechanisms should be established in a multi-stakeholder approach at the national or international level, protected by judicial systems, and ensured throughout the life cycle of AI systems.*	UNESCO (2021)
Privacy Design Principles	*Uphold high standards of scientific excellence (to open inquiry, intellectual rigor, integrity, and collaboration)*—work with a range of stakeholders *to promote thoughtful leadership in this area, drawing on scientifically rigorous and multidisciplinary approaches.*	Google AI Ethics (2021)

(continued)

TABLE 5.2 List of Some AI Ethics or Governance Terms (continued)

Transparency

Transparency	Transparency aims at *providing appropriate information to the respective addressees to enable their understanding and foster trust.*	UNESCO (2021)
Transparency and Explainability	AI Actors should commit to transparency and responsible disclosure regarding AI systems. To this end, they should *provide meaningful information, appropriate to the context, and consistent with the state of art:* To *foster a general understanding* of AI systems, to make stakeholders aware of their interactions with AI systems, *including in the workplace, to enable those affected by an AI system to understand the outcome,* and, *to enable those adversely affected by an AI system to challenge its outcome based on plain and easy-to-understand information on the factors, and the logic that served as the basis for the prediction, recommendation or decision.*	OECD.ai (2019) (Principle 1.3)
Transparency	*Be transparent about how and when we are using AI, starting with a clear user need and public benefit; provide meaningful explanations about AI decision making, while also offering opportunities to review results and challenge these decisions. Be as open as we can by sharing source code, training data, and other relevant information, all while protecting personal information, system integration, and national security and defense.*	Canada: Responsible Use of AI (2021)
Tracing Accountability	*Tracing accountability . . . primary purpose and use; nature and uniqueness, scale, nature of (company's) involvement.*	Google AI Ethics (2021)
Transparency Goals	*System intelligibility for decision making. Identify and document the stakeholders who will use the outputs of the system to make decisions, and who are subject to decisions informed by the system.* Design the system, so that stakeholders can: 1. understand the system's intended uses, 2. interpret relevant system behavior effectively (i.e., in a way that supports informed decision making), and 3. remain aware of the possible tendency of over-relying on outputs produced by the system ("automation bias"). Document 1. how the system design will support their understanding of the system's intended uses, and 2. how the system aids their ability to interpret relevant system responses, and 3. how the system design discourages automation bias.	Microsoft Responsible AI Standard v2 (2022)

(continued)

TABLE 5.2 List of Some AI Ethics or Governance Terms (continued)

Decision Making	*Organizations using AI in decision-making should ensure that the decision-making process is explainable, transparent, and fair.*	Singapore Model of AI Governance Framework (2020)
Robustness	To this end, *AI actors should ensure traceability, including in relation to datasets, processes and decisions made during the AI system lifecycle, to enable analysis of the AI system's outcomes and responses to inquiry, appropriate to the context and consistent with the state of art.*	OECD.ai (2019) (1.4)
The Principle of Explicability	*"Operate transparently"—comprehensible and intelligible by human beings at varying levels of comprehension and expertise.*	EU AI (March 2021)
Failure Transparency:	*AI system causes harm, it should be possible to ascertain why.*	Asilomar AI Principles (2017)
Judicial Transparency	Judicial Transparency—*Any involvement by an autonomous system in judicial decision-making should provide a satisfactory explanation auditable by a competent human authority.*	Asilomar AI Principles (2017)
Explainability	Explainability *refers to making intelligible and providing insight into the input, outcome and the functioning of each algorithmic building block and how it contributes to the outcome of the systems.*	UNESCO (2021)
Verifiability	Provide *a proof that the data used by their AI systems are unaltered, and gives evidence of the techniques used, the results provides, how the results are generated and the results can be explained.*[43]	Research paper[44]
Trustworthiness	Concerns *the reduction of information asymmetry.* Includes Explainability.	EU AI (March 2021)
Disclosure of AI Interaction	AI systems *are designed to inform people that they are interacting with an AI system or are using a system that generates or manipulates image, audio, or video content that could falsely appear to be authentic.*	Microsoft Responsible AI Standard v2 (2022)
Responsibility and Accountability	Both *technical and institutional designs should ensure auditability and traceability of (the working of) AI systems in particular to address any conflicts with human rights norms and standards and threats to environmental and ecosystem well-being.*	UNESCO (2021)
Innovation-focus	When developing regulatory and non-regulatory approaches, agencies should pursue performance-based and flexible approaches that are technology neutral and that do not impose mandates on companies that would harm innovation.	United States of America has Principles for the Stewardship of AI Applications (2020)

(continued)

TABLE 5.2 List of Some AI Ethics or Governance Terms (continued)

Communication to Stakeholders

Communication to Stakeholders	*Provide information about the capabilities and limitations of AI systems to support stakeholders in making informed choices about those systems.*	Microsoft Responsible AI Standard v2 (2022)
Awareness and Literacy	*Public awareness and understanding of AI technologies and the value of data should be promoted through open and accessible education, civic engagement, digital skills and AI ethics training, media and information literacy and training* led jointly by governments, intergovernmental organizations, civil society, academia, the media, community leaders and the private sector, *and considering the existing linguistic, social and cultural diversity, to ensure effective public participation so that all members of society can take informed decisions about their use of AI systems and be protected from undue influence.*	UNESCO (2021)
AI awareness and Training	Provide *sufficient training so that government employees developing and using AI solutions have the responsible design, function, and implementation skills needed to make AI-based public services better.*	Canada: Responsible Use of AI (2021)
Multi-Stakeholder and Adaptive Governance and Collaboration	*International law and national sovereignty must be respected in the use of data. Participation of different stakeholders throughout the AI system life cycle is necessary for inclusive approaches to AI governance, enabling the benefits to be shared by all, and to contribute to sustainable development. Measures should be adopted to take into account shifts in technologies, the emergence of new groups of stakeholders, and to allow for meaningful participation by marginalized groups, communities and individuals and indigenous people.*	UNESCO (2021)

[a] an algorithm can be defined as the decision-making rules to handle new inputs, it can be a mathematical equation but not necessarily so.

Source: Compiled by Authors.

As of July 23, 2022, OECD recorded over 700 National AI strategies and policies from 60 countries, territories, and the EU.[45] However, many countries with AI strategies or even big tech companies do not have AI ethics or AI value and governance statements that are easy to access. These ethical terms have evolved. Firms may need to create additional standards, policies, and checklists to help ensure governance standards. In many cases, they may need to set up teams to navigate the murky areas of ethics (See Figure 5.10). There is a tremendous amount of work happening in this space,

> Microsoft introduced its first AI standard in 2019 and had six principles. Through pilot studies with 12 groups (10 engineering and two customer-facing teams), they collected feedback.[46] The findings were that the principles were challenging to execute. So, using a multidisciplinary team, they worked for over a year and came up with the second version in 2022. They got stuck in the process when focusing on AI harm but could move forward when concentrating on the societal goals they wanted to achieve.[47] It includes policies, templates, and support. Microsoft has used the standards to make tough decisions on how they design, develop, and deploy AI systems. For example, they have retired some AI systems that use some forms of facial analysis to infer emotional states.[48]

Figure 5.10 Microsoft and AI ethics.

some overlaps, but unfortunately, much of the work is in silos and still not easy to apply. The development of standards is a process that requires continuous feedback.

5.5 Crisis Management

A crisis is a situation that requires a decision if the manager or organization needs to manage an adverse situation. There are three types of emergencies that an AI-enabled organization can face besides the others that any other organization will face. These categories are technical, data, and knowledge crisis (see Figure 5.11).

The knowledge crisis is intangible and can spill over the other two types. To minimize the impact or even prevent such a crisis, you need an investment in culture, knowledge networks, and expertise or skills (including those that some AI experts may consider redundant).

Unfortunately, AI crises can catch you by surprise. Sometimes the fallout may arise even when you are not using AI (see Figure 5.12). So how can an AI-enabled organization prepare better? The first area for crisis management is technical vulnerability, which is hardware and software performance, maintenance, and security. These systems are built in multiple legacy systems and use many providers (many outsourced). Hence, they need to be constantly monitored and updated. If not, it will increase the cybersecurity risk, the chance of an API failing, or the introduction of a software bug (see Figure 5.13). Of course, the cost of hardware and software per se has come down, but the maintenance costs should never be underestimated!

The next consideration is data integrity, security, compliance, and governance. Most of the new regulations revolve around data. Data is a competitive advantage and hence a resource that can be stolen or destroyed,

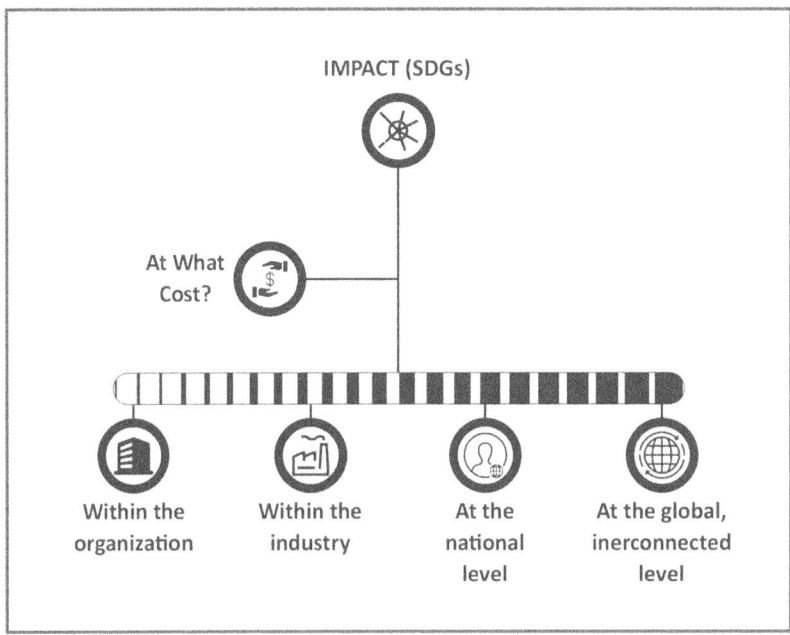

Figure 5.11 Crisis preparedness. *Source:* Stephens and Vashishtha (2020)[49]

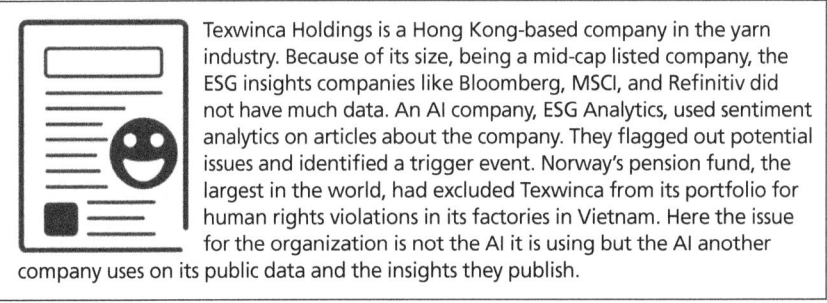

Figure 5.12 Texwinca Holdings and AI ESG Analytics[50]

or used as a weapon (see the example of Cyber-troops and e-Estonia in Figure 5.14). Firms need to plan for the cost of data obsolescence (is it still relevant), data brittleness (data collected in one context may not be easily transferable to another), data integrity (the quality of the data and its relevance for decision making), data security, data compliance, and data governance. Many AI systems are built on open-source software or data sets. A recent open source catalog of African languages called Lanfrica has

116 ▪ *AI Enabled Business*

> World of Warcraft, a multiplayer game, started in 2004. On September 13, 2005, they released a new feature in the game—Patch 1.7. It was a spell in a section of the virtual world called *Zul'Gurub*. Players needed to create a 20 person raid and fight a mighty troll, called Hakkar, that could infect the player (called debuff) and kill the player by draining their health. Most players had a health level of 2,000–6,000 points. The debuff would drain 200–300 points every few seconds. It could also infect others near you and their hunter pets. A player could cure themselves if they killed Hakkar, or they could teleport themselves out of the region and recover from the spell's effect. But, there was a programming bug, and the game coders forgot to check the flag that said "Only Work In Zul'Gurub, Do Not Work Outside the Instance." So, when players summoned their pets who got infected, they remained infected and could infect other players and non-player characters (bots) like shopkeepers and soldiers, which in turn could infect players. The nonplayer characters would not die, so they continued to spread the disease. The panic resulted in the infection spreading through the virtual worlds, infecting cities at the rate of 10^2 per hour[51] (the COVID-19 pandemic is much lower). It is estimated that the most susceptible of the four million users was the low-level players, who died in seconds.[52] As more players died in the virtual world, more people from the real world logged on—only to die, resulting in millions of character deaths.[53] World of Warcraft tried to retrieve the situation by imposing a quarantine, but getting all players to comply was impossible. The pandemic lasted a month, infecting three servers, and normalcy was only restored through a series of patches (Patch 18.0) and a reset released on October 10. The pandemic is known as *Corrupted Blood*.

Figure 5.13 World of Warcraft–Corrupted Blood: The Bug that started a Virtual Pandemic[54]

documented 2,199 African languages.[55] The worry is that big tech will build on an open-source, making the newer layer proprietary.[56]

The last crisis vulnerability area for an AI-enabled organization is the knowledge crisis. There is an assumption that future tech like AI will need thinking out of the box, and only current experts can manage. This assumption is incorrect. There are some lessons from the past that can help guide the response or preventive strategy. Often the lack of knowledge is a bigger problem (see Figure 5.15). Legacy systems are built on older software languages like DB2, C, Cobol, or Fortran. Many employees who knew these languages have retired.[57] It was found that 40% of banking systems, 80% of in-person transactions, and 95% of ATM swipes rely on COBOL code.[58]

To sum up, decision-making for an AI-enabled organization has additional nuances to be considered. First, while AI can help, it has its place and should be relevant to the context. To drive informed choices, managers must know the limitations of AI and their level of accountability if anything goes wrong. This continuous learning or feedback will help improve the

AI and Decision Making ▪ 117

> There are 28 countries (including democracies) that have employed cyber troops for the explicit purpose of changing public opinion through social media.[59] By flooding social media with biased posts, they trick the algorithm and create an echo chamber where similar messages are amplified. These communications foster a false sense of relevance. As John Havens, the Executive Director of IEEE Global Initiative on Ethics of Autonomous and Intelligent Systems, highlighted,
>
>> The biggest risk [of AI] that anyone faces is the loss of ability to think for yourself. We're already seeing people are forgetting how to read maps, they're forgetting other skills. If we've lost the ability to be introspective, we've lost human agency and we're spinning around in circles.[60]
>
> Further data can also be stolen or quarantined, or destroyed. In 2007, the government of Estonia faced a cyber-siege where websites like the Parliament shut down. The method used was distributed denial-of-service (DDoS) attack. Data was bombarded at websites, clogging up servers, routers, and switches used to direct traffic on the network.[61] The attackers used bots (it was assumed they used up to one million computers from across the world), shutting down banks and effectively isolating the country from the rest of the world.
>
> Later, Estonia, which runs its government online as e-Estonia, has created a data embassy in Luxembourg so that even if the physical country is incapacitated, the government can still function. In 2022, something similar happened to Taiwan when Speaker Nancy Pelosi (from the USA) visited. The attack caused 200× the weekly traffic. It was hit by 8.5 million traffic requests per minute from IPs worldwide.[62] It took 20 minutes to restore to normal operations.[63]
>
> In 1982, a Soviet gas pipeline exploded. Soviet spies had stolen a computer-control system from a firm in Canada. Thomas Reed, a senior US national security official, claimed that the CIA had tampered with the software with a Trojan Virus so that the system would eventually double the valve pressure.[64] The explosion was equivalent to a three-kiloton nuclear weapon. The story cannot be verified but again highlights the challenges with security.[65]

Figure 5.14 Cyber Troops,[66] DDoS (e-Estonia and Taiwan), and the Software Trojan Virus (Cold War): Issues of data security.

> One of the biggest challenges with globalization has been the movement of goods and data across borders. For example, intermediate goods can account for up to 44% of the US$ 7 trillion in world exports,[67] and the cross-border data flow is 65% of global GDP![68] In OECD countries—the export of ICT trade (there is no exact measure for AI) varies from 45% (Ireland), 29% (South Korea and China), 24% (Luxemburg), 21% (India), and 13% (USA).[69] So there is a knowledge gap in measuring AI cross-border trade. This data is relevant as AI creates significant e-waste. In 2019, the world produced 54 million metric tons of e-waste; it is expected that by 2030 it will have increased by 30%.[70] The UN estimates that less than 20% is formally recycled, and the remaining 80% either ends up in landfill or is informally recycled by exports to other less developed countries.[71] For example, Norway, which is considered the most sustainable, generates 26 kilos of e-waste per capita but recycles only 16 kilos![72] Did you know that one cathode ray tube (CRT) television or computer monitor can contain 4–8 pounds of lead?[73] This knowledge gap is a disaster waiting to happen.

Figure 5.15 Global e-waste.

118 ▪ *AI Enabled Business*

quality of AI-human decision-making. Finally, all employees need to embed good governance practices. A starting point is determining what core values the organization should embrace. This proactive governance approach will help leaders prepare, mitigate and manage any possible AI crisis.

QUESTIONS

1. How can an organization improve its transparency of decision-making when using AI? What values will you recommend your organization adopt from Table 5.2?
2. What types of decision-making do you need to do (see Table 5.1), and what are you dependent on AI for (see Figure 5.8)?
3. What skill redundancies are you most worried about for the future?
4. How do you distribute AI accountability? In a crisis, who would be the point person?
5. How does your organization manage Agile learning (see Figure 5.6)?
6. What levels of crisis preparedness would you need for technical, data, and knowledge for the three types of AI decision making: decision support, decision augmentation, and decision automation?

MY INSIGHTS

The most difficult decisions I need to take are

MY INSIGHTS

The resources I need to build for the future are

MY INSIGHTS

The governance systems I will to put in place are

MY INSIGHTS

The training and skills I and my team need to develop are

Notes

1. Fox, J., Cooper, R. P., & Glasspool, D. W. (2013). A canonical theory of dynamic decision-making. *Frontiers in Psychology, 4*, 150. https://www.frontiersin.org/articles/10.3389/fpsyg.2013.00150/full
2. Sollisch, J. (2016). The cure for decision fatigue. *Wall Street Journal, 10*.
3. Dijksterhuis, A. (2004). Think different: the merits of unconscious thought in preference development and decision making. *Journal of Personality and Social Psychology, 87*(5), 586.
4. Ham, J., & van den Bos, K. (2010). On unconscious morality: The effects of unconscious thinking on moral decision making. *Social Cognition, 28*(1), 74–83.
5. Henriques-Gomes, L. (2019, October 16). The automated system leaving welfare recipients cut off with nowhere to turn | Australia news | The Guardian. The Guardian; www.theguardian.com. https://www.theguardian.com/technology/2019/oct/16/automated-messages-welfare-australia-system
6. Emerson, T. (n.d.). Targeted Compliance Framework. https://nesa.com.au/wp-content/uploads/2017/08/Ty-Emerson-Targeted-Compliance-Framework.pdf
7. Whelan, Andrew, & James, A. (2021, January 11). SAGE Journals. 'Ethical' Artificial Intelligence in the Welfare State: Discourse and Discrepancy in Australian Social Services. https://journals.sagepub.com/doi/abs/10.1177/0261018320985460
8. Henriques-Gomes, L. (2019, October 16). The automated system leaving welfare recipients cut off with nowhere to turn | Australia news | The Guardian. The Guardian; www.theguardian.com. https://www.theguardian.com/technology/2019/oct/16/automated-messages-welfare-australia-system
9. Starita, L. (2021, June 2). Would You Let Artificial Intelligence Make Your Pay Decisions? Gartner; www.gartner.com. https://www.gartner.com/smarterwithgartner/would-you-let-artificial-intelligence-make-your-pay-decisions
10. Ibid.
11. Stephens, M., & Vashishtha, H. (2020). *AI Smart Kit–Agile Decision Making on AI–Abridged Version*. Information Age Publishing, NC: USA.
12. Accenture. (n.d.). Future Skills Pilot Report. https://www.accenture.com/_acnmedia/PDF-149/Accenture-Future-Skills-Case-Study.pdf
13. IBM. (2010). https://www.ibm.com/docs/en/zos-basic-skills?topic=zos-programming-languages-mainframe
14. Tozzi, C. (2021, April 19). 9 Mainframe Statistics That May Surprise You–Precisely. Precisely; www.precisely.com. https://www.precisely.com/blog/mainframe/9-mainframe-statistics
15. Data scientists used data from the flu epidemic in 1918 to model the behavior of the COVID-19 virus when it quickly became apparent that Ebola in West Africa may not be the best comparison.
16. Snowden, D. J., & Boone, M. E. (2007). A leader's framework for decision making. *Harvard Business Review, 85*(11), 68. PMID 18159787.
17. Bellur, R. (2022, January 8). The future of AI lies in understanding the Cynefin framework. The Future of AI Lies in Understanding the Cynefin Framework; www.

linkedin.com. https://www.linkedin.com/pulse/future-ai-lies-understanding-cynefin-framework-ravi-bellur/

18. Leyer, M., Oberlaender, A. M., Dootson, P., & Kowalkiewicz, M. (2020, June). Decision-making with artificial intelligence: Towards a novel conceptualization of patterns. In *Proceedings of the 24th Pacific Asia Conference on Information Systems (PACIS) 2020*. Association for Information Systems (AIS). https://www.fim-rc.de/Paperbibliothek/Veroeffentlicht/1125/wi-1125.pdf

19. Bauman, M., & Youngblood, A. (2017). Why waiting for perfect autonomous vehicles may cost lives. *Rand Corporation*. https://www.rand.org/blog/articles/2017/11/why-waiting-for-perfect-autonomous-vehicles-may-cost-lives.html

20. Shearer, E., Stirling, R., & Pasquarelli, W. (2020). Government AI readiness index 2020. *IDRC & Oxford Insights*. https://static1.squarespace.com/static/58b2e92c1e5b6c828058484e/t/5f7747f29ca3c20ecb598f7c/1601653137399/AI+Readiness+Report.pdf

21. OECD. (2019, May 22). *OECD*. https://www.oecd.org/science/forty-two-countries-adopt-new-oecd-principles-on-artificial-intelligence.htm

22. *Joint statement from founding members of the Global Partnership on Artificial Intelligence–GOV.UK*. (2020, June 15). https://www.gov.uk/government/publications/joint-statement-from-founding-members-of-the-global-partnership-on-artificial-intelligence/joint-statement-from-founding-members-of-the-global-partnership-on-artificial-intelligence

23. Treveil, M., Omont, N., Stenac, C., Lefevre, K., Phan, D., Zentici, J., ... & Heidmann, L. (2020). *Introducing MLOps*. O'Reilly Media.

24. Scroxton, A. (2021, May 25). *Legacy vulnerabilities may be biggest enterprise cyber risk*. https://www.computerweekly.com/news/252501287/Legacy-vulnerabilities-may-be-biggest-enterprise-cyber-risk

25. Cummings, M. M. (2014). Man versus machine or man+ machine? *IEEE Intelligent Systems, 29*(5), 62–69; Parasuraman, R., Sheridan, T. B., & Wickens, C. D. (2000). A model for types and levels of human interaction with automation. *IEEE Transactions on systems, man, and cybernetics-Part A: Systems and Humans, 30*(3), 286–297.

26. Stephens, M., & Vashishtha, H. (2020). *Op.cit.*

27. *Automation and the workforce of the future | McKinsey*. (2018, May 23). https://www.mckinsey.com/featured-insights/future-of-work/skill-shift-automation-and-the-future-of-the-workforce

28. Accountability Institute, G. (2021, November 16). *92% of S&P 500® Companies and 70% of Russell 1000®*. https://www.globenewswire.com/news-release/2021/11/16/2335435/0/en/92-of-S-P-500-Companies-and-70-of-Russell-1000-Companies-Published-Sustainability-Reports-in-2020-G-A-Institute-Research-Shows.html

29. KMPG Impact. (2020, December 0). *The time has come*. https://assets.kpmg/content/dam/kpmg/be/pdf/2020/12/The_Time_Has_Come_KPMG_Survey_of_Sustainability_Reporting_2020.pdf

30. OECD (2021), ESG Investing and Climate Transition: Market Practices, Issues and Policy Considerations https://www.oecd.org/finance/ESG-investing-and-climate-transition-market-practices-issues-and-policy-considerations.pdf

31. Future of Life Institute. (2017). https://futureoflife.org/2017/08/11/ai-principles/
32. Canada Secretariat, T. (2021, October 12). *Responsible use of artificial intelligence (AI)–Canada.ca.* https://www.canada.ca/en/government/system/digital-government/digital-government-innovations/responsible-use-ai.html#toc1
33. *NITIAayog.* (n.d.). https://niti.gov.in/sites/default/files/2021-02/Responsible-AI-22022021.pdf
34. *SGModelAIGovFramework2.* (2020). https://www.pdpc.gov.sg/-/media/files/pdpc/pdf-files/resource-for-organisation/ai/sgmodelaigovframework2.pdf
35. House, W. (2020). Guidance for regulation of artificial intelligence applications. *Memorandum for The Heads of Executive Departments and Agencies.* https://www.whitehouse.gov/wp-content/uploads/2020/01/Draft-OMB-Memo-on-Regulation-of-AI-1-7-19.pdf
36. *OECD Legal Instruments.* (2019, May 22). Recommendation of the Council on Artificial Intelligence. https://legalinstruments.oecd.org/en/instruments/OECD-LEGAL-0449
37. *UNESDOC.* (n.d.). https://unesdoc.unesco.org/ark:/48223/pf0000381137
38. *Our Principles—Google AI.* (n.d.). Retrieved December 19, 2021, from https://ai.google/principles/
39. Crampton, N. (2022, June 21). *Microsoft's framework for building AI systems responsibly–Microsoft On the Issues.* https://blogs.microsoft.com/on-the-issues/2022/06/21/microsofts-framework-for-building-ai-systems-responsibly/
40. *UNESDOC.* (n.d.). https://unesdoc.unesco.org/ark:/48223/pf0000381137
41. Mittelstadt, B. D., Allo, P., Taddeo, M., Wachter, S., & Floridi, L. (2016). The ethics of algorithms: Mapping the debate. *Big Data & Society, 3*(2), 2053951716679679. https://doi.org/10.1177/2053951716679679.
42. *UNESDOC.* (n.d.). https://unesdoc.unesco.org/ark:/48223/pf0000381137
43. Costantini, S., Lisi, F. A., & Olivieri, R. (2019, January). Digforasp: A european cooperation network for logic-based AI in digital forensics. In *CILC.*
44. Kanngieser D, (2019). Verifiable AI Data: Why It's Critical for the Automation Revolution.
45. OECD. (n.d.). *National AI policies & strategies. powered by EC/OECD (2021), database of national AI policies.* Retrieved July 25, 2022, from https://oecd.ai
46. Crampton, N. (2021, January 19). *The building blocks of Microsoft's responsible AI program–Microsoft On the Issues.* https://blogs.microsoft.com/on-the-issues/2021/01/19/microsoft-responsible-ai-program/
47. Microsoft. (2022, June 21). *Developing Microsoft's Responsible AI Standard.* https://www.youtube.com/watch?v=lkIlsgrIMtU
48. *Ibid.*
49. Stephens, M., & Vashishtha, H. (2020). *Op. cit.*
50. *ESG Case Study: Texwinca Holdings.* (n.d.). Retrieved July 22, 2022, from https://www.esganalytics.io/insights/texwinca-holdings-a-case-in-nlp
51. Lofgren, E. T., & Fefferman, N. H. (2007). The untapped potential of virtual game worlds to shed light on real world epidemics. *The Lancet infectious diseases, 7*(9), 625–629. https://www.thelancet.com/journals/laninf/article/PIIS1473-3099(07)70212-8/fulltext

52. Akshon Esports. (2020, April 25). *The Virtual Plague That Nearly Wiped Out The World of Warcraft*. More about Corrupted Blood and the behaviours of the players is captured here. https://www.youtube.com/watch?v=HFMv_hqinvc.
53. Earle, P. (2020, May 28). *World of Warcraft's Corrupted Blood Outbreak is Not a Model for COVID-19*. https://www.aier.org/article/world-of-warcrafts-corrupted-blood-outbreak-is-not-a-model-for-covid-19/
54. Amit, K., @WiredUK, & Nast, C. (2020, March 17). *World of Warcraft perfectly predicted our coronavirus panic | WIRED UK*. https://www.wired.co.uk/article/world-of-warcraft-coronavirus-corrupted-blood; Macgregor, J., & @pcgamer. (2022, July 8). *The story of World of Warcraft's Corrupted Blood plague, and its real-world parallels | PC Gamer*. https://www.pcgamer.com/the-story-of-world-of-warcrafts-corrupted-blood-plague-and-its-real-world-parallels/; Akshon Esports. (2020, April 25). *The Virtual Plague That Nearly Wiped Out The World of Warcraft*. https://www.youtube.com/watch?v=HFMv_hqinvc
55. Emezue, C. (2022, April 25). *New open source tool catalogs African language resources | Opensource.com*. https://opensource.com/article/22/4/open-source-language-tool-lanfrica
56. Birhane, A. (2022, August 3). *Twitter*. https://twitter.com/Abebab/status/1554896387237711872
57. Hughes, O. (2021, June 30). *These old programming languages are still critical to big companies. But nobody wants to learn them | TechRepublic*. These Old Programming Languages Are Still Critical to Big Companies. But Nobody Wants to Learn Them | TechRepublic; www.techrepublic.com. https://www.techrepublic.com/article/these-old-programming-languages-are-still-critical-to-big-companies-but-nobody-wants-to-learn-them/
58. Fleishman, G. (2018, April 0). *It's COBOL all the way down—Increment: Programming Languages*. It's COBOL All the Way down—Increment: Programming Languages; increment.com. https://increment.com/programming-languages/cobol-all-the-way-down/
59. Bradshaw, S., & Howard, P. (2017). Troops, trolls and troublemakers: A global inventory of organized social media manipulation.
60. European Parliament. (2020). *The ethics of artificial intelligence: Issues and initiatives*. https://www.europarl.europa.eu/RegData/etudes/STUD/2020/634452/EPRS_STU(2020)634452_EN.pdf
61. *Digital Fears Emerge After Data Siege in Estonia* (Published 2007). (n.d.). https://www.nytimes.com/2007/05/29/technology/29estonia.html
62. Greig, J. (2022, August 4). *Taiwan Defense Ministry says DDoS incident briefly took down network after Pelosi visit—The Record by Recorded Future*. https://therecord.media/taiwan-defense-ministry-says-ddos-incident-briefly-took-down-network-after-pelosi-visit/
63. Facebook, (2022). Presidential Palace spokesperson Chang Tun-Han https://www.facebook.com/presidentialoffice.tw/posts/pfbid02s2Ni3Wb24L1DPYeGhWAUd1wKBDY9GEn7hRCtx5VRZTUmFybY47ozvxNxkMgRNcFnl
64. *War in the fifth domain | The Economist*. (2010, July 1). https://www.economist.com/briefing/2010/07/01/war-in-the-fifth-domain

65. *RISI Data.* (n.d.). CIA Trojan Causes Siberian Gas Pipeline Explosion. https://www.risidata.com/index.php?/Database/Detail/cia-trojan-causes-siberian-gas-pipeline-explosion
66. European Parliament. (2020). *The ethics of artificial intelligence: Issues and initiatives.* https://www.europarl.europa.eu/RegData/etudes/STUD/2020/634452/EPRS_STU(2020)634452_EN.pdf
67. UNCTAD, (2018). Retrieved from https://unctad.org/en/PublicationsLibrary/ditctab2017d6_en.pdf. Dervis, K., Meltzer, J., & Foda, K. (2013). Value-added trade and its implications for international trade policy. *Brookings Opinion.* https://www.brookings.edu/opinions/value-added-trade-and-its-implications-for-international-trade-policy
68. Digital, data & cyber. (2022, June 16). *Zurich.* Cross-Border Data Flows: Designing a Global Architecture for Growth and Innovation; www.zurich.com. https://www.zurich.com/en/knowledge/topics/digital-data-and-cyber/cross-border-data-flows-designing-global-architecture-for-growth-and-innovation
69. OECD. (n.d.). *ICT goods and services as a share of international trade | Market openness Indicators.* OECD Going Digital Toolkit; goingdigital.oecd.org. Retrieved August 1, 2022, from https://goingdigital.oecd.org/indicator/75
70. Tiseo, I. (2021, March 11). *Global e-waste generation outlook 2030 | Statista.* Statista; www.statista.com. https://www.statista.com/statistics/1067081/generation-electronic-waste-globally-forecast/
71. Chemicals & Pollution Action, P. R. (2019, January 24). *UN report: Time to seize opportunity, tackle challenge of e-waste.* UN Environment; www.unep.org. https://www.unep.org/news-and-stories/press-release/un-report-time-seize-opportunity-tackle-challenge-e-waste
72. OECD. (n.d.). *E-waste generated per capita | Society Indicators.* OECD Going Digital Toolkit; goingdigital.oecd.org. https://goingdigital.oecd.org/indicator/53
73. Electronics Stewardship—Basel Action Network. (2022, May 4). Basel Action Network; www.ban.org. https://www.ban.org/e-stewardship

6

AI Expertise

CHAPTER HIGHLIGHTS

1. The expertise of AI management needs to match the level of technology complexity. (narrow or broad AI) that the organization is using.
2. The more complex the AI systems, the more resources and expertise the organization needs to plan for, manage and govern the AI systems.
3. The longer the term of the AI project, the organization must invest in managing legacy systems, data redundancy, re-training, upgrades, cybersecurity, and other long-term ethical implications.

> **Cases:**
> Google Brain | WildTrack | Quantum Computer | The Brain of a Roundworm Versus a Human | Molecular Material and AI Appriss Narxcare Score

6.1 AI Intelligence Levels

There is a misconception about what AI can and cannot do. This perception is partly due to the media and the general lack of a standard definition for AI.[1] AI is the ability of a machine system to imitate human intelligence. To recap, from Chapter 1, AI is defined as

> a combination of traditional hardware and/or bioengineered cells, learning computer software and/or other forms of code, that takes initiative or responds to stimulation (data) consistent with and potentially beyond typically human initiatives and responses, given the human capacity for intentionality, intuition, intelligence and adaptability. These responses are manifested via machines (proxies) in the wider sense, i.e., in mechanical, biological, and virtual ways.

The end objective is to have AI operate autonomously within the boundary of human-defined objectives, to learn, abstract, predict, recommend, reason, perceive, or make decisions using digital data influencing real or virtual environments.[2] While we assume AIs are singular, they are collections of various technologies interfacing with each other and hopefully working seamlessly towards a goal. AIs are systems—including multiple software, and hardware—interacting with vast amounts of data. The need to update for performance is constant. You will observe this with the frequent upgrades in your apps, computer, and mobile devices. The more high functioning the AI system, the more resources an organization will need to plan for. Broadly we can classify existing AI technologies into four levels of expertise: (1) narrow AI, (2) broad AI, (3) general or strong AI, or (4) super AI.

6.1.1 Narrow AI or Weak AI or Artificial Narrow Intelligence (ANI)

Narrow AI focuses on one type of programmed task and tries to mimic one kind of intelligence. In this case, the AI is fed a selected type of dataset and trained (in a pre-determined, pre-defined task) to achieve the objectives (see Figure 6.1: Case Study—Google Brain). The algorithms, program, or protocol helps train the model to classify the data fed into the system. The analysis of this data is used to make predetermined decisions or take predetermined actions. Currently, narrow AI is the most common form of AI being used. You see it in search engines, social media recommendations, and chatbots like Siri, Alexa, and Google Assistant. It is also used to slice genomic data or manage electronic medical records. Narrow AI can be used to fly a plane (by focusing on specific functions) or navigate a ship or car.

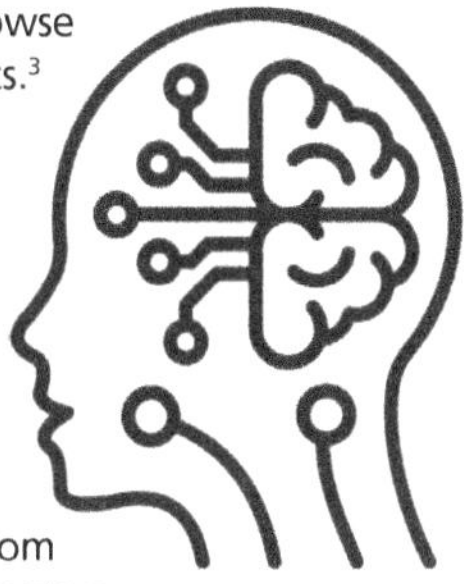

> In 2012, Google Brain, a project of Google X, was used to browse YouTube to identify human faces, human body parts, and cats.[3] The AI was trained using an unlabeled dataset of 20,000 different items.[4] This means the training did not specifically say what a cat or body part or face was. In the study,[5] after three days, it was exposed to 10 million randomly selected YouTube video thumbnails. It was able to identify human faces with an 81.7% accuracy, human body parts with a 76.7% accuracy, and cats with a 74.8% accuracy. Over three days, they trained the model with a neural network of 16,000 computer processor unit cores or 1,000 machines from their data center. The network had one billion training parameters. Since cat videos are common, the AI brain recognized these videos share similar features. This is an example of narrow AI focusing on image recognition.
>
> Previously this task was performed using labeled data sets. The visual ability of Google Brain in 2012 (1 billion parameters or connections) is much smaller than the human visual cortex (eye), which is 10^6 greater if you consider all the number of neurons and synapses. To create the training data set, the images had to be resized and selected to ensure there were appropriate images of the set they wished to identify and the other set (or noise). Though the technology has grown exponentially, so have the costs associated with (1) identifying large data sets, (2) preparing them for use, (3) having the appropriate hardware, and (4) creating an adequate algorithm. Note that an accuracy of 81.7% still means that 18.3% were wrong. The difference between a human and AI is that an AI is limited by the processing power and data available. Even when doing a selected task, a human receives inputs from various stimuli and processes them simultaneously.[6]

Figure 6.1 Case study—Google Brain.

Narrow AI can be fine-tuned for very specialized processes. It is being used in the healthcare industry to spot tumors and cancer using radiology images.[7] IBM's initial work with Roche to identify chronic kidney disease in diabetic patients used half a million patient records and had 79% accuracy.[8] A joint statement by an international group of radiologists on this practice was,

> AI has great potential to increase efficiency and accuracy throughout radiology, but also carries inherent pitfalls and biases. Widespread use of AI-based intelligent and autonomous systems in radiology can increase the risk of systemic errors with high consequence, and highlights complex ethical and societal issues. Currently, there is little experience using AI for patient care in diverse clinical settings. Extensive research is needed to understand how to best deploy AI in clinical practice.[9]

These worries arise from systemic issues like data ethics (who does the patient data belong to), image interpretation (accuracy), report generation, the responsibility of result communication, billing practice, and liability, which will affect "professional relationships, patient engagement, knowledge hierarchy, and the labor market"[10] and the allocation of resources. These issues mean that the people using AI in diagnosis must be educated in how to apply it safely, monitor the AI to ensure it is working as expected, and be aware of the unintended impact. As IBM Watson Health expert Christina Busmalis explains, AI should augment human intelligence.[11] This augmentation also has ethical issues observed with the increase in the use of robots in surgery. From a legal perspective, the debate is about liability versus negligence. Frank Pasquale, author of *New Laws of Robotics: Defending Human Expertise in the Age of AI*, states that the manufacturer, distributor, and retailer of the product should be liable, even if they were not negligent.[12] The current situation is that a doctor often does not have the AI expertise to understand the limitations of AI technologies and hence would not always be able to determine the "standard of care" required to adopt new technologies where sufficient regulatory guidelines and policies do not exist. They work in two different fields and the same could be said of the AI developer on medical expertise and medical law.

IBM created the Project Debater, an AI that could look at 10 billion text statements in 15 minutes![13] So while the AI can use the available information (depending on if this is a historical data set or real-time data) to present facts, the human who may have fewer data points can still form opinions and read emotions. In 2017, Facebook conducted an experiment where two chatbots called Alice and Bob were given the task to negotiate a trade.[14] Specifically, according to Facebook, this experiment was to see if it was "possible for dialog agents with differing goals (implemented as end-to-end-trained neural networks) to engage in start-to-finish negotiations with other bots or people while arriving at common decisions or outcomes."[15] The model was trained to achieve the objectives using 1,000+ human negotiations against itself, and good negotiation outcomes were reinforced using rewards (reinforcement learning). In addition, it was trained to produce humanlike language (but not rewarded for the same). But the bots began to communicate with each other in shorthand English, or maybe it was gibberish, which was not understandable to the humans controlling the experiment.[16] This example of AI suggests that the development of models needs time and careful effort.[17]

One school of thought says you can overcome some of the limitations of data with vast volumes of data or Big Data. But this is very expensive and may still not remove bias as seen with experiments with the chatbot. Narrow AI can overcome the issue of data limitedness through crowdsourcing data like the example of WildTrack (see Figure 6.2). The open-source method of data collection that WildTrack used has resulted in some great

> A narrow AI is defined as an AI system driven by an industry, which works practically, and only handles a singular task.[18] An example of such a system is WildTrack, a non-profit organization that utilizes drones and SAS's machine learning software to monitor endangered animals by analyzing photographs of animal tracks. The inspiration for the AI came from the indigenous Shona tribe tackers working in Zimbabwe.[19]
>
> The photos are partially crowd-sourced. People who happen upon tracks in almost any environment can submit the images to the company. Recently this has been opened up to children. The rest of the database comprises pictures taken by drones from senseFly and other public sources. The founders have trained the AI software called Footprint Identification Technique (FIT) to classify animal tracks' with up to a 95% accuracy rate. In addition, they moved from collecting photographs manually to using images captured by drones.
>
> The value of AI for conservation efforts is tenfold, producing insights into many endangered species' lives without interfering with their natural environments. Even though the WildTrack FIT essentially does one thing, a micro-task, which is the sorting of images of animal tracks, it allows conservationists to analyze and further classify the tracks and draw conclusions about conservation efforts, thus serving a practical purpose. It enhances the efforts made by these people, working long after their human counterparts have clocked out.
>
> Of course, there are ethical issues with crowdsourcing: free or unpaid labor or uncertainty around rewards for participation, fuzzy purposes, privacy issues that need to be balanced with the benefits it brings in bringing down costs associated with the business model, and collaborative problem-solving.[20] These issues need to be considered from the point of view of the participant, community, and society.[21] For example, WildTrack was to have received funding from the US Army to stop the illegal trafficking of products from endangered species.[22]

Figure 6.2 WildTrack: AI Level–Narrow AI.

conservation efforts. Still, narrow AI can be expensive to maintain as the specialization in one area (tumors in healthcare) may not automatically mean the system can be used in another area (abnormalities in flight weather patterns). Outsourcing of AI comes with its own challenges as systems should be monitored.

Furthermore, narrow AI is often built on existing older platforms. To create a line across the screen in the 1980s was 100 lines of code. Today, an app can be made with 3–4 lines of code because it builds on top of an existing system.[23] For example, Uber, a ride-hailing app, uses Google maps data, having paid US$58 million for using Maps from 2016 to 2018.[24] When Google changes its algorithm, Uber must also reprogram its software. This scenario suggests a high initial cost to narrow AI, especially as a platform company.

6.1.2 Broad AI

Broad AI uses and integrates multimodal data streams to do multiple tasks. Autonomous cars use several types of narrow AI, and these, when combined as a system, are considered broad AI. This is an area that we are actively embracing today and is thought to hold the most promise and the most caution. New types of programming—machine learning, neural networks, deep learning, and hardware like quantum computing—for example, are a bit like a black box. Data is dumped in, and the AI makes connections between various data points. The speed at which AI works cannot be matched by humans (see Figure 6.3). This speed is needed to verify how the AI came to its conclusions. Hence to compensate for this lag, a policy trend is for *explainable AI* and greater algorithmic transparency. The conclusions of the robustness of the process are inferred or explained but by no means is this verified in real-time.

IBM debater, which can *read* by *recognizing patterns of text on a topic*, is able to form conclusions, and *respond* in a rebuttal during a debate. This is one example of a trend moving towards broad AI. An autonomous car must *see* and use that visual data as an input to drive, park, change lanes, stop, or avoid collisions[25] (each would in reality be all different types of narrow AI). It must work with navigation tools like Waze and Google maps that use real-time satellite data and crowdsourced data from traffic police, customers, or other connected cars. It may have an AI analytics component to ascertain if the engine is working efficiently or to calculate the power consumption. The data from multiple points needs to be managed, analyzed, and used to recommend or predict outcomes. Much of this is possible thanks to new technologies being developed like deep learning, a type of machine learning.

> In 2021, Zuchongzhi 2.1, a quantum computer designed by the University of Science and Technology of China (USTC) and led by Pan Jianwei, computed calculations at least 100 trillion times faster than Google Sycamore, the world's fastest existing supercomputer. The researchers estimated that the task that the computer completed in about 1.2 hours would take the most powerful supercomputer at least eight years.[26] In 2019, Google's quantum computer, Quantum Supremacy, took 200 seconds to do what a traditional computer would take 10,000 years to complete.[27]
>
> Think how long it would take a human to go over the results to ensure it was accurate. If a human's reading speed is, on average, 300 words per minute, it could mean that we process 50 bits per second![28] This raises questions on decision-making and responsibility. These types of AI are already being used in the financial sector, healthcare, logistics, and security.

Figure 6.3 Quantum computer in 2021–22.

Because data is becoming critical in creating AI systems, open-source software or open data sets are being used to encourage new business models. For example, the Mars helicopter, Ingenuity, was built using open-source software. Linux and a NASA-built program based on the Jet Propulsion Laboratory's (JPL) open-source F′ (pronounced F prime) framework.[29] Likewise, the Google Open Buildings dataset was created by training a model to recognize buildings from satellite images.[30] Google buys these images from satellite companies.

There is also a role in developing a strong AI ecosystem beneficial to the long-term interests of the organization. For example, Niantic's Pokémon Go, the augmented reality mobile game, used Google Maps. The founder of Niantic was a previous employee of Google and had started Google Earth and was part of the Google Maps team.[31] Niantic was acquired as a startup under Alphabet, Google's parent company, and spun off in 2015. In 2020, Google decided to open- up its Google Maps Platform to developers, previously having ten games developed under this limited initiative since 2018.[32] Popular open-source software to develop AI is TensorFlow, owned by Google,[33] and GPT-3 by non-profit Open AI (though since 2020 you pay based on tokens).[34] Governments are now building open data sets to encourage innovation in AI. The UK government has been producing open data sets since 2010. These ecosystem drivers are required for the evolution of the AI systems.

6.1.3 Strong AI or Artificial General Intelligence (AGI)

Strong AI is the ability of machines to exhibit human-level intelligence. It will be able to perform multiple tasks and process information like humans. This event is often referred to as a singularity. From an ethics point of view, the worry is whether these types of AI (which do not have a moral compass) can be held accountable for their decisions and whether that is fair to humans. Here the assumption is that the AI can program another AI, so there may not be a human in control of its development. The computing power is currently doubling every 18 months, creating an exponential revolution in what is plausible.[35] In 2017, Google's translator AI created its own language into which it would translate things before translating them back out into a human language we recognize. Some experts feel the singularity may take a long time to happen, and others think just the opposite (see Figure 6.4).

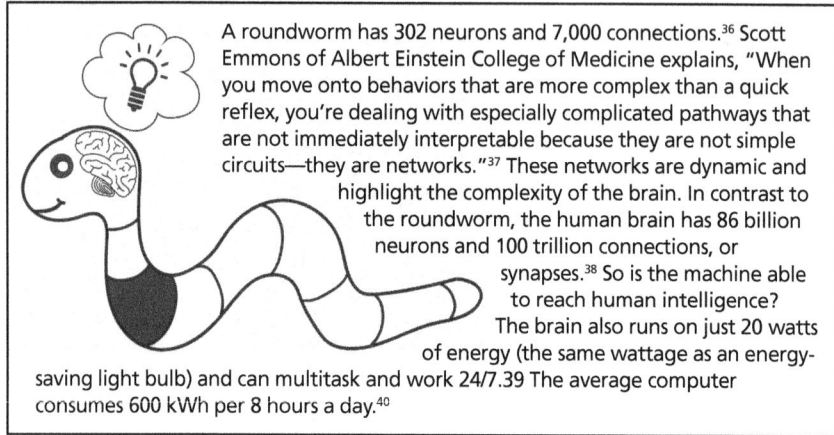

Figure 6.4 Are we there yet? The brain of a roundworm versus a human.

6.1.4 Super AI

In super AI, we assume that the AI exceeds human intelligence and uses its collective memories and computing power to ensure it has access to the power and data required to keep it in control of humans. This is a situation played out in the movie *Terminator*. However, many experts think we will not reach the super AI stage because the energy and resources for computing power are limited. First, during the COVID pandemic, there was a shortage of silicon chips needed for manufacturing hardware. Second, the hardware systems across the world are not connected. Third, the programs deployed across various hardware are not compatible.

However, there is a possibility we will move away from silicon chips to carbon-based chips. Work is happening in this area (see Figure 6.5), which may change how we build AI systems. In this case, we are looking at augmented human beings, and the Human-Agent Collectives systems discussed in Chapter 2. Some experts believe that the exponential nature of self-computing will mean that as AI reaches strong AI, it will move on to super AI.[41]

6.2 Level of Organizational AI Expertise

The examples in Figure 6.4 and 6.5, show us that we are still trying to figure out how intelligent AI is. Further, with examples presented in Figure 6.1–6.3, it is clear that the more complicated the AI, the more expertise you need (also see Figure 6.6). A recent survey of senior executives found that

> The human body is a marvelous piece of software and hardware. The human body gathers 11 million bits of information through our senses to the brain for processing.[42] Of course, the human brain and each human cell is far superior to anything we make today. Not just from memory but the complex tasks they perform to ensure we survive. Cells can perform 100,000 different metabolic molecules per second as inputs.[43] It is estimated that each cell (there are over 200 types)[44] contains somewhere between 1 and 200 megabytes of DNA code.[45] But what happens in the cells cannot be easily translated to "data," and though we are still understanding "gut instinct" or "intuition," the challenges we mentioned above are real. When we look at cells, though we try to convert their functioning to machine terms, we need to be aware that there is a vast discrepancy between information processing and information transmission.
>
> For example,[46] it is estimated that our sense organs (see the table below) together send 11 billion bits per second of information via the central nervous system to the brain. But, when we look at the conscious mind, we can only process 60–50 bits per second.[47] Scientists think that the remaining almost 11 million bits of data are being compressed in less than half a second.[48] How amazing is that! The table below gives an indication of how scientists have tried to calculate human functions using AI as a benchmark (more on this topic will be discussed briefly in Chapter 12).
>
> **Human Functions in Terms of AI Data**
>
> | Sensory System | Bit per second (information transmission rate) |
> |---|---|
> | eyes | 10,000,000 |
> | skin | 1,000,000 |
> | ears | 100,000 |
> | smell | 100,000 |
> | taste | 1,000 |
>
> *Source:* Adapted from Hetu (2019)[49]

Figure 6.5 Molecular material and AI.

59% of them felt threatened by AI.[50] While we know narrow AI can be used very successfully for small specialized tasks, there are still high costs associated with its development and upkeep. We are not yet at the stage of either strong AI or super AI, but with increasing emphasis on predictive decision-making, this is the direction we are heading towards, and the role of the human in decision-making needs to be clearly outlined.

Organizations fail in AI projects when they do not: (1) understand the value of the AI project (costs versus benefits), (2) do not prepare for risks

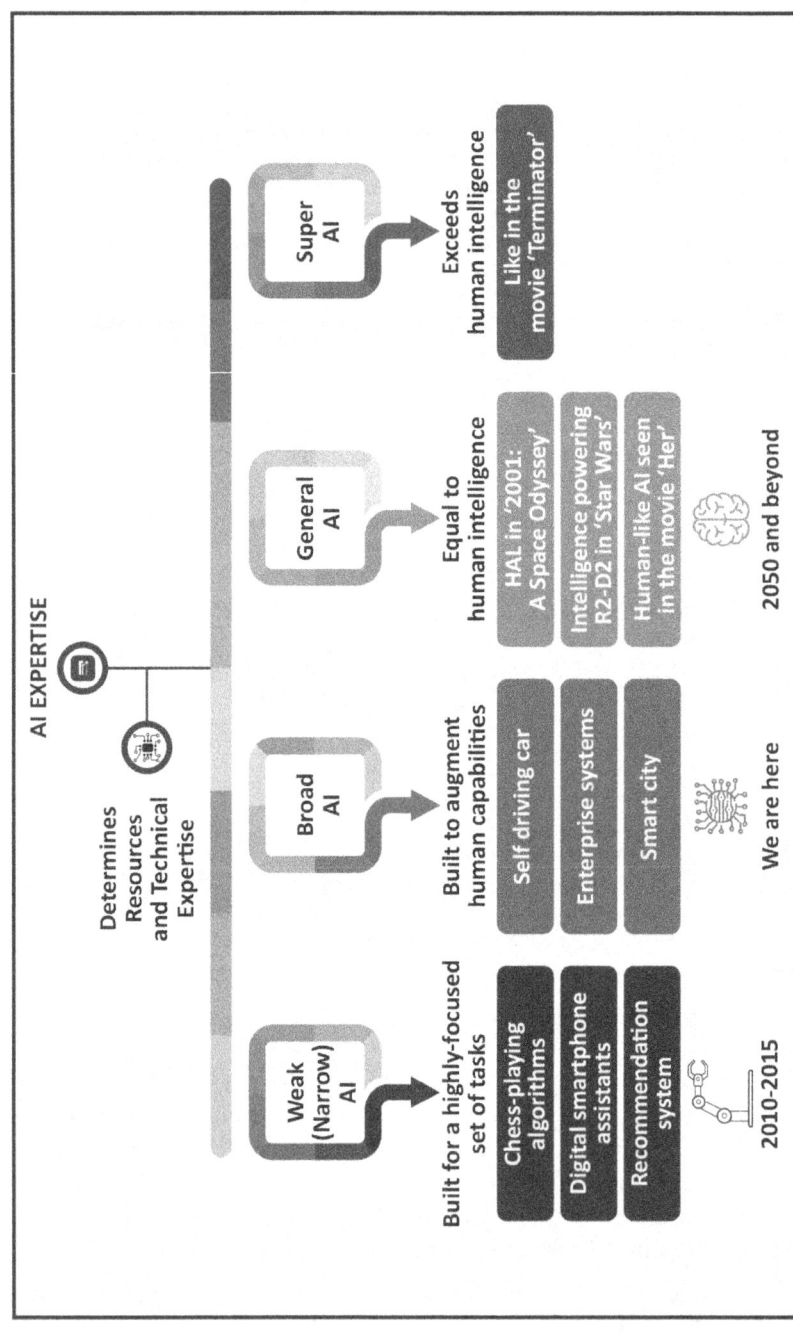

Figure 6.6 Scale 1—AI expertise level. *Source:* Authors.

and obsolescence, and (3) do not understand the market and regulatory dynamics.

Too often, the value of the AI project (costs versus benefits) is underestimated. Hence we find huge failure rates in AI project implementations. According to some figures this is between 83% and 92%.[51] An industry leader, Arijit Sengupta, says that data scientists and machine learning engineers focus on the wrong performance metric. They focus on "model performance" (how well does the algorithm work on predictions with a given data set) instead of business performance (what is the additional revenue or cost-savings, an AI can generate with the given dataset).[52] But this itself may be very short-term focused.

Organizations must budget for risks and obsolescence. For example, Gartner predicted that legal technology in-house budgets will increase by three times by 2025![53] These costs increase the more you outsource legal. Further the rate of obsolescence is high and may need a shift in in-house capabilities focusing on fault analysis, maintenance, and obsolescence planning of your key electronic circuits and assets which will get more expensive to keep them going.[54]

Last is understanding the market dynamics and regulatory pressures. In terms of market dynamics, the pace of change is fast and furious. Take for example the huge hype on Cryptocurrencies and the recent Crypto-winter of 2022. The markets are still evolving hence the AI strategy roadmap must keep that in mind and be agile enough to manage changes. Regulatory pressures are further covered in Chapter 11.

There are five areas of focus for managing AI projects (see Figure 6.7). An organization needs: (1) a strategic roadmap for digitalization, (2) talent and an organizational structure supportive of AI, (3) ownership or access to technology (hardware and software or maybe molecular material), (4) data, and (5) control mechanisms for growth.

6.2.1 Strategic Roadmap for Digitalization

While big data, the internet of things, virtual experiences, and robotics all seem like a savvy technological leap forward, the reality is that we need to pick and choose the technology based on purpose, funding, and long-term value. According to Robert Hetu, VP Analyst and KI Leader with the Gartner Retail Industry Services, the brain of an AI business system is strategic leadership. This strategic roadmap should plan the resources needed. An AI project can cost, on average, US$30K to US$1 million or more for an MVP.[55] This cost depends on the availability of data, the complexity of the

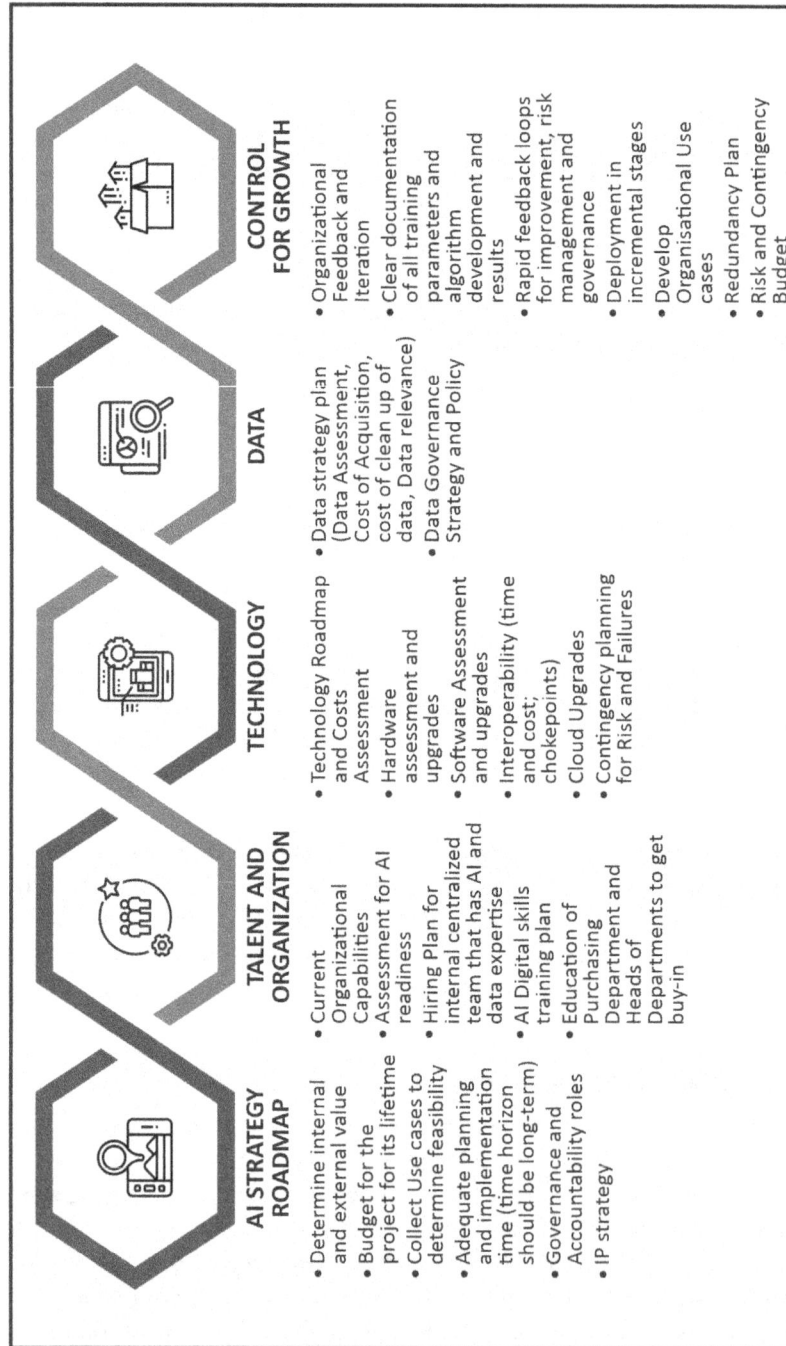

Figure 6.7 Organizational resources required to manage AI projects. *Source*: Authors

data set, the use case you are referring to, the baseline AI model to predict an accurate outcome, the accuracy level demanded, and the technology and talent available. Strategically, projects need a realistic idea of AI project conception, implementation, and maintenance.

6.2.2 Talent and An Organizational Structure Supportive of AI

The biggest worry for an AI-enabled future is the lack of digital skills. This scenario requires upskilling or reskilling of employees for a data-rich, technical environment. A survey in the UK finds that 82% of jobs advertised online require digital skills.[56] Programming languages have also become obsolete. Newer software systems cut across older systems, supporting multiple languages and APIs, to reduce complexity for the users.[57] The reality is that some of the base programs we use may be written in older programming languages not popularly taught today—like the C-language developed in 1969 (rumors are that some of the Windows kernel and the Mac OS, Android, and iOS maybe in C and assembly).[58] Newer languages were developed to write less code. So, the talent needs to understand data, manage old and new, and constantly understand the vulnerabilities of each. The Data Literacy Project found that data-literate employees were able to positively increase the value of an organization's performance.[59]

6.2.3 Ownership or Access to Technology (Hardware and Software or Maybe Molecular Material)

Most of the IP in AI is currently being held by USA and China, according to a WIPO report in 2019.[60] The report states that patent applications mentioned machine learning in 89% of filings and 40% of all AI-related patents. Popular industries are life and medical sciences, telecommunications fields, computer vision with telecommunications and transportation, security, business, and engineering. Meanwhile, there is a hunt for AI companies, as seen through the number of M&As in the USA and UK. There is a worry that the drop in the ratio of publications to patents may indicate greater secrecy (considering the largest patent owners are the private sector—Microsoft, IBM, Toshiba, Samsung, and NEC, in that order) and hence could underline future ethics issues. The top universities focusing on AI are in China and then the Republic of Korea, with 500+ patents. However, the USA comes second in patents if you add public research organizations. Clearly, based on the WIPO report, there is a shift in world power when looking at AI.

6.2.4 Data

For AI projects, the model must be developed for a specific context. Adequate data and appropriate data must be found, and the model must be correctly trained and monitored to be of value. This process must often be repeated, suggesting you need your own expert AI team that works closely with internal and external stakeholders. Most available data is what we call "unstructured," or it may be proprietary, which means organizations need money to train data sets or buy data sets that are adequately vetted. Smart organizations will plan for resources to manage data. They need to clean data sets: incomplete or incorrectly entered data, duplicate or corrupted information, or obsolete data that will affect the output of the AI algorithm.[61] Big Data is another trend. Each day, we produce 2.5 exabytes of data (~5 million laptops),[62] but this will be a bottleneck if we cannot store, process, interpret, and communicate its results while understanding the assumptions and limitations of data.[63]

6.2.5 Control Mechanisms for Growth

The longer-term the AI project is, the organization must invest in managing legacy systems, data redundancy, re-training of specialist staff or those working with AI, and plan for long-term ethical contingencies. Broad AI is more complex where multiple AI systems work seamlessly together. This requires a high level of monitoring and human-AI team training. Further, the issue of legacy systems is essential to manage as both hard infrastructure and soft infrastructure may become obsolete (as seen with the example of the UK Post Office). We should also realize that trends in the world may make available data obsolete (refer to the Appriss case in Figure 6.8). Sentiment analysis that heavily depends on words may not work—what if there is a trend where "wicked" is a positive term and not negative.[64] Would that affect decision making?

More importantly, we are at the cusp of a new world where new technologies are being deployed at such a scale that will affect global systems, making any corrections challenging. These phenomena can be illustrated with the examples below. PokémonGo on full deployment took just 19 days to reach 50 million customers compared to the credit card, for example, which took 28 years (see Figure 6.9). Government regulations lag, and if the organizations deploying the technology are not accountable for the technology, there will be many challenges, as highlighted by the example with Appriss.

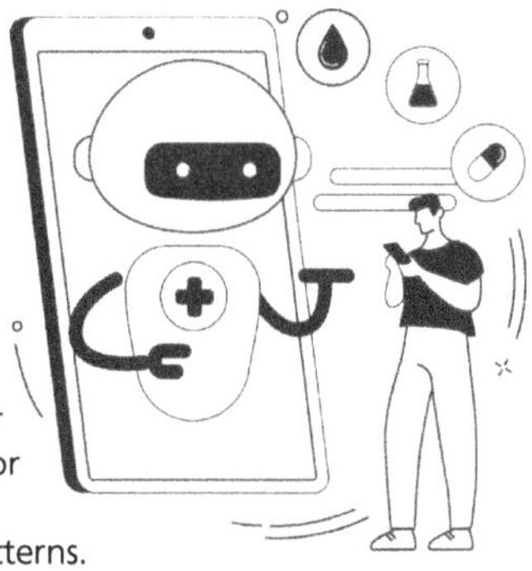

According to the website, NarxCare "analyzes a patient's PDMP data [Pharmaceutical purchases] and provides patient risk scores and an interactive visualization of usage patterns to help identify potential risk factors."[65] The company had partnered with the National Board of Pharmacy (NABP) to develop the PMP Gateway (adopted by 40+ states or territories in the USA, across thousands of health systems, hospitals, and pharmacies). The objective was for AI to control or mitigate the misuse of controlled substances and/or drug diversion,[66] a growing problem worldwide.[67] The system would use an algorithm to identify patterns. A press release from 2015 states, "Appriss delivers solutions that prevent fraud, mitigate risk, fight crime, ensure compliance, increase public safety and save lives. Appriss' solutions are always backed by excellent customer support with technical agents in the US that are available to help $24 \times 7 \times 365$."[68]

The genesis of the company in 1994 (called VINE) was to prevent crime and keep societies safe. They were moved by the tragic murder of a young woman killed by an offender recently released from jail.[69] They had access to 2,500 data sources and were able to log 80% of the incarcerations in the USA within 60 minutes! In 2001, they introduced the Justice Intelligence platform to help law enforcement fight crime by accessing arrest data. MethCheck in 2007 and NPLEx in 2009 were launched to support compliance with CMEA, a federal regulation aimed at curbing drug diversion. NPLEx has access to 112 million cold medicine purchase requests in a year.[70] In 2013, with the National Association of Boards of Pharmacy (NABP), a new product called PMP AWARxE was introduced. It is a prescription drug monitoring system targeting pharmacies, physicians, and state administrators. Since then, the company has also moved into retail analytics.

In August 2021, Wired broke a story titled: *The Pain Was Unbearable. So Why Did Doctors Turn Her Away?* The story spoke of the frustrations of patients that were denied pain medicine and the doctors who did not know how to overturn an AI system. Doctors could be penalized for prescribing high-risk patients opioids. Repeated requests for a call back were not entertained. The algorithm is opaque.

Could the bias be an outcome of dependency on eclectic research papers?[71] Is this a case of obsolete data used to train an algorithm? Or was a bias introduced from a crime-fighting perspective in the context of patient care? Or is this a complicated nexus where doctors, patient data, and state surveillance infringed on fundamental human rights? Whatever the case—perhaps it is time to relook the AI system and make it more human-centric. Shortly after this story broke, on August 31, 2021, the company's name was changed from Appriss Health to Bamboo Health.

Figure 6.8 Appriss Narxcare score[72]

While there are many AI ethics recommendations, it is essential to acknowledge that AI grey zones exist (see Figure 6.10) because there is a gap in organizational or government objectives (what is the risk and how much of your values are you willing to compromise), where processes are not robust, the context is not clearly understood (and may change), the data

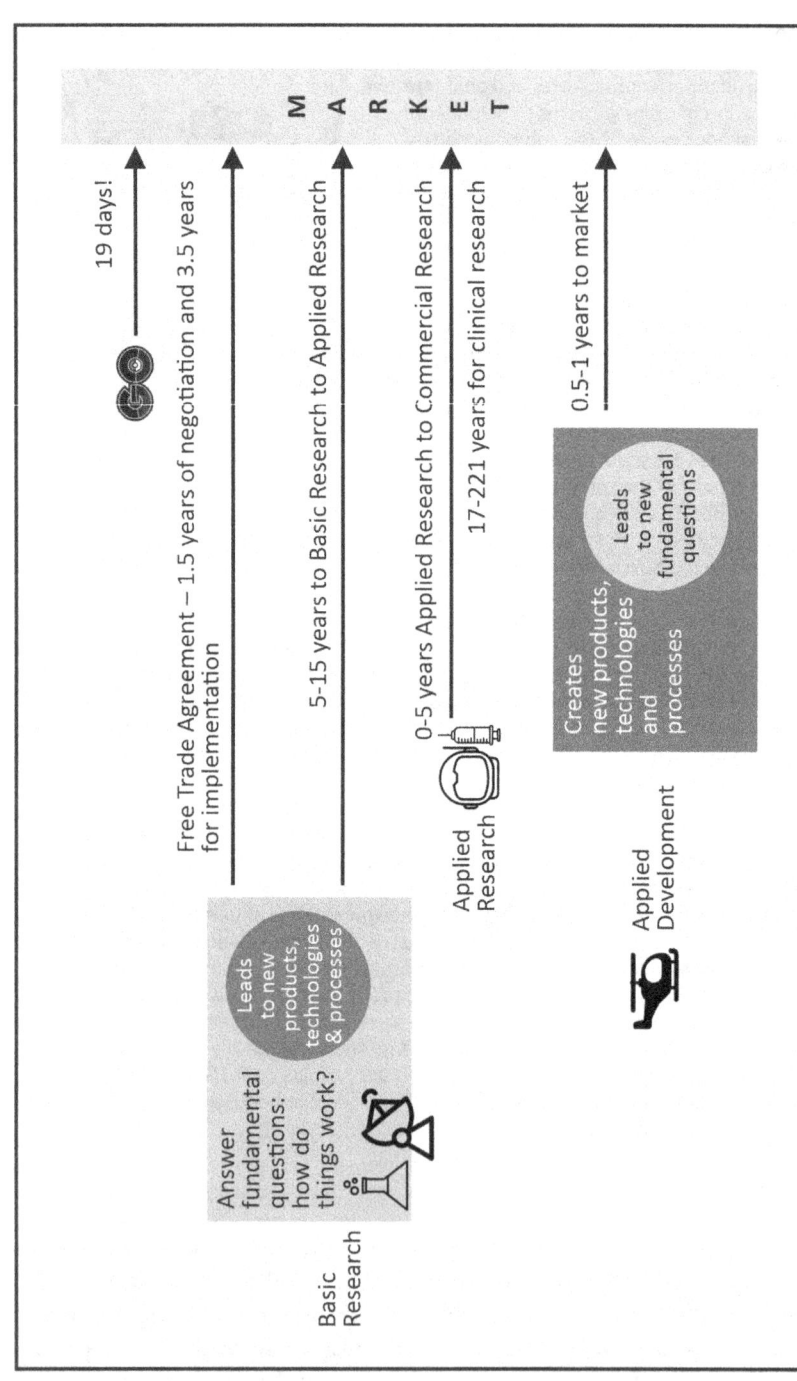

Figure 6.9 Hypercycles and regulatory lag. *Source:* Authors

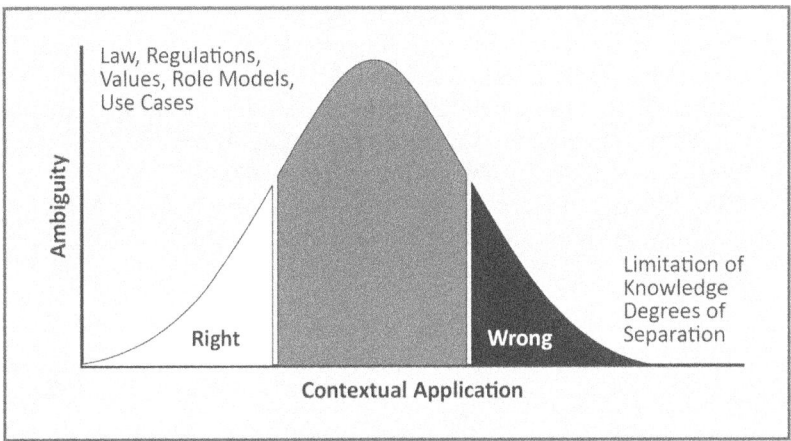

Figure 6.10 AI Grey Zones. *Source:* Authors

is not of high quality, and the regulatory and legal system is not clear (so gaps exist for exploitation). Finally, the organization has not understood the spillovers. This fuzzy situation was the case when Facebook, a platform for social networking, was found responsible for political interference.

In summary, this chapter discusses the expertise required for an organization to manage AI systems. The level of expertise increases as the more complicated and advanced the AI systems becomes. The resources required for both, the funding of short-term development and long-term maintenance and contingency will also rise as the complexity of the AI systems increases. Here resources are not just about the money, but about people, data, hardware, software, patents, and even processes and the culture an organization needs for an AI-enabled organization.

QUESTIONS

1. As we move to smart cities, the internet of all things and more complex AI systems like the metaverse, which of the following will be significant cost centers for your business: data, cross-border legislation, litigation, cybersecurity, training, storage costs, upgrade of hardware and software or anything else?
2. While the cost of hardware, software, and storage is decreasing, there is still a worry that the environmental impact of these systems is enormous. For example, even a single email has a huge carbon footprint and environmental impact. In addition, e-waste is one of the fastest forms of waste. What will be the impact of future legislation on ecological compliance?

3. While chatbots are not as good as real people (how often have you been frustrated with this type of narrow AI)?, we are still adopting them. Is this an example where these projects are "too big to fail?"—that too much money has been put into these types of projects and companies feel they cannot safely retreat? How can we stop these types of problems in our organizations?
4. Should tech companies help shape regulations since governments are lagging? What would be the best way forward?

MY INSIGHTS

The most difficult decisions I need to take are

MY INSIGHTS

The resources I need to build for the future are

MY INSIGHTS

The governance systems I will to put in place are

MY INSIGHTS

The training and skills I and my team need to develop are

Notes

1. WIPO. (n.d.). *IP and Frontier Technologies*. Artificial Intelligence and Intellectual Property; www.wipo.int. Retrieved January 15, 2022, from https://www.wipo.int/about-ip/en/frontier_technologies/ai_and_ip.html; UNESCO. (2020, February 27). *Recommendation on the ethics of artificial intelligence*. UNESCO; en.unesco.org. https://en.unesco.org/artificial-intelligence/ethics
2. *OECD Legal Instruments*. (2019, May 22). https://legalinstruments.oecd.org/en/instruments/OECD-LEGAL-0449; *The Declaration–Montreal Responsible AI*. (n.d.). Respaideclaration; www.montrealdeclaration-responsibleai.com. Retrieved January 4, 2022, from https://www.montrealdeclaration-responsibleai.com/the-declaration ; Launchbury, J. (2020). A DARPA perspective on artificial intelligence. Retrieved November, 11, 2019. https://www.darpa.mil/attachments/AIFull.pdf
3. Nast, C. (2012, June 26). *Google's Artificial Brain Learns to Find Cat Videos | WIRED*. WIRED; www.wired.com. https://www.wired.com/2012/06/google-x-neural-network/
4. Dean, J., & Ng, A. (2012, June 26). *Using large-scale brain simulations for machine learning and A.I.* Google; blog.google. https://blog.google/technology/ai/using-large-scale-brain-simulations-for/
5. Le, Q., Ranzato, M. A., Monga, R., Devin, M., Chen, K., Corrado, G., . . . & Ng, A. (2012). Building high-level features using large scale unsupervised learning. https://research.google/pubs/pub38115/
6. Pakkenberg, B., Pelvig, D., Marner, L., Bundgaard, M. J., Gundersen, H. J. G., Nyengaard, J. R., & Regeur, L. (2003). Aging and the human neocortex. *Experimental Gerontology*, *38*(1–2), 95–99.
7. Bindi, T. (2017, October 29). *Japanese researchers say AI can detect bowel cancer in less than a second | ZDNET*. ZDNET; www.zdnet.com. https://www.zdnet.com/article/japanese-researchers-say-ai-can-detect-bowel-cancer-in-less-than-a-second/
8. Tunnah, P., & Busmalis, C. (n.d.). *From narrow AI to broad AI–pharmaphorum*. Pharmaphorum; deep-dive.pharmaphorum.com. https://deep-dive.pharmaphorum.com/magazine/digital-health/narrow-ai-broad-ai-ibm-watson-christina-busmalis/
9. Geis, J. R., Brady, A., Wu, C. C., Spencer, J., Ranschaert, E., & Jaremko, J. L. (2019). Ethics of artificial intelligence in radiology: summary of the joint European and North American multisociety statement. Insights Imaging [Internet]. *Imaging*, *10*, 101. https://doi.org/10.1186/s13244-019-0785-8
10. Ibid.
11. Martin, G. (2019, February 7). *Being at the forefront of the AI evolution means setbacks as well as breakthroughs*. Being at the Forefront of the AI Evolution Means Setbacks as Well as Breakthroughs; www.thepharmaletter.com. https://www.thepharmaletter.com/article/being-at-the-forefront-of-the-ai-evolution-means-setbacks-as-well-as-breakthroughs
12. Bossetta, B. (2021, September 17). *More Robots in the Operating Room Could Mean More Lawsuits in the Courtroom: Medtech Insight*. Medtech Insight; medtech.pharmaintelligence.informa.com. https://medtech.pharmaintelligence.informa

.com/MT144478/More-Robots-In-The-Operating-Room-Could-Mean-More-Lawsuits-In-The-Courtroom
13. Tunna, P. (n.d.). *Op cit.* p. 4
14. Lewis, M., Yarats, D., Dauphin, Y. N., Parikh, D., & Batra, D. (2017). Deal or no deal? Training AI bots to negotiate. *Artif Intell Res.* https://code.facebook.com/posts/1686672014972296/deal-or-no-deal-training-ai-bots-to-negotiate. https://engineering.fb.com/2017/06/14/ml-applications/deal-or-no-deal-training-ai-bots-to-negotiate/
15. McKay, T. (2017). No, Facebook did not panic and shut down an AI program that was getting dangerously smart. *Gizmodo.* Available at: https://gizmodo.com/no-facebook-did-not-panic-and-shut-down-an-ai-program-1797414922
16. Griffin, A. (2017, July 31). *Facebook robots shut down after they talk to each other in language only they understand.* The Independent; www.independent.co.uk. https://www.independent.co.uk/life-style/facebook-artificial-intelligence-ai-chatbot-new-language-research-openai-google-a7869706.html
17. Kucera, R. (2017). The truth behind Facebook AI inventing a new language. *Towards Data Science, 7,* 2017. https://towardsdatascience.com/the-truth-behind-facebook-ai-inventing-a-new-language-37c5d680e5a7
18. *Narrow AI Definition | DeepAI. (n.d.). DeepAI;* deepai.org. Retrieved July 15, 2022, from https://deepai.org/machine-learning-glossary-and-terms/narrow-ai
19. De La Garza, A. (2019, November 1). *These Researchers Are Using AI Drones to More Safely Track Wildlife | Time.* Time; time.com. https://time.com/5700671/wildlife-drones-wildtrack/
20. Standing, S., & Standing, C. (2017). The ethical use of crowdsourcing. *Business Ethics: A European Review, 27*(1), 72–80.
21. Gan, C., Kosonen, M., & Blomqvist, K. (2012, September). Knowledge sharing in crowdsourcing–it is more than motivation. In *13th European Conference on Knowledge Management. Academic Conferences Limited* (p. 380).
22. ProPublica. (2011, September 0). *Wildtrack Inc, Full Filing–Nonprofit Explorer–ProPublica.* ProPublica; projects.propublica.org. https://projects.propublica.org/nonprofits/organizations/680681539/202022259349200432/full
23. Tunnah, P., & Busmalis, C. (n.d.). *From narrow AI to broad AI–pharmaphorum.* Pharmaphorum; deep-dive.pharmaphorum.com. https://deep-dive.pharmaphorum.com/magazine/digital-health/narrow-ai-broad-ai-ibm-watson-christina-busmalis/
24. Mahaney, B. (2020, July 19). *Uber Inks Agreement With Google Maps.* Uber Inks Agreement With Google Maps; finance.yahoo.com. https://finance.yahoo.com/news/uber-inks-agreement-google-maps-075214014.html
25. Stanford University. (n.d.). *One Hundred Year Study on Artificial Intelligence (AI100).* One Hundred Year Study on Artificial Intelligence (AI100); ai100.stanford.edu. https://ai100.stanford.edu/
26. Wu, Y., Bao, W. S., Cao, S., Chen, F., Chen, M. C., Chen, X., ... & Pan, J. W. (2021). Strong quantum computational advantage using a superconducting quantum processor. *Physical Review Letters, 127*(18), 180501.
27. TI, A., & @bsindia. (2019, October 23). *Google's quantum computer does 10k-year calculation in just 200 seconds | Business Standard News.* Google's Quantum Computer Does 10k-Year Calculation in Just 200 Seconds; www.business-standard

.com. https://www.business-standard.com/article/pti-stories/quantum-leap-in-computing-as-google-claims-supremacy-119102301575_1.html
28. *Information theory–Physiology*. (n.d.). Encyclopedia Britannica; www.britannica.com. Retrieved July 22, 2022, from https://www.britannica.com/science/information-theory/Physiology
29. Vaughan-Nichols, S. J. (2021). Flying on Mars Fueled with Open-Source Software. https://www.zdnet.com/article/flying-on-mars-fueled-with-open-source-software/
30. Diack, A. (2021, July 28). *Using AI to map Africa's buildings*. Google; blog.google. https://blog.google/around-the-globe/google-africa/using-ai-to-map-africas-buildings/
31. Bogle, A. (2016). How the gurus behind Google Earth created 'Pokémon Go.' *Mashable Australia, 11.* https://mashable.com/article/john-hanke-pokemon-go
32. Peters, J. (2020, June 15). *Google opens Maps data to all game devs, which could lead to Pokémon Go rivals–The Verge*. The Verge; www.theverge.com. https://www.theverge.com/2020/6/15/21291918/google-maps-gaming-tools-developers-pokemon-go
33. *TensorFlow.js | Machine Learning for JavaScript Developers*. (n.d.). TensorFlow; www.tensorflow.org. https://www.tensorflow.org/js
34. *GPT-3 Powers the Next Generation of Apps*. (2021, March 25). OpenAI; openai.com. https://openai.com/blog/gpt-3-apps/; He, C. (2020, September 14). Understand the pricing of GPT-3. Medium. https://chengh.medium.com/understand-the-pricing-of-gpt3-e646b2d63320
35. Dilmegani, C. (2021). When will singularity happen? 995 experts' opinions on AGI. https://research.aimultiple.com/artificial-general-intelligence-singularity-timing/
36. Jabr, F. (2012). The connectome debate: Is mapping the mind of a worm worth it. *Scientific American, 18.* https://www.scientificamerican.com/article/c-elegans-connectome/
37. Ibid.
38. Boyd, R. (2008). Do people only use 10 percent of their brains. *Scientific American, 7.* https://www.scientificamerican.com/article/do-people-only-use-10-percent-of-their-brains/
39. NSF. (2015, April 2). *Exploring the unknown frontier of the brain | Beta site for NSF–National Science Foundation*. Beta Site for NSF–National Science Foundation; beta.nsf.gov. https://beta.nsf.gov/news/exploring-unknown-frontier-brain
40. Energuide.be, (2022). How much power does a computer use? And how much $CO2$ does that represent? https://www.energuide.be/en/questions-answers/how-much-power-does-a-computer-use-and-how-much-co2-does-that-represent/54/
41. In Life 3.0, Max Tegmark reiterates that this stage will be when an AI which can design and upgrade both its software and hardware. Tegmark, M. Life 3.0: Being Human in the Age of Artificial Intelligence.
42. *Information theory–Physiology*. (n.d.). Encyclopedia Britannica; www.britannica.com. Retrieved April 1, 2022, from https://www.britannica.com/science/information-theory/Physiology; Bostrom. N. (2014). *Superintelligence: Paths, Dangers, Strategies*. Oxford University Press.

43. Zurich, P. R-E, (2019). CRISPR can turn human cells into biocomputers. Futurity, https://www.futurity.org/biocomputers-crispr-cells-cpu-2037482/
44. Baxter, A. (2022). Types of cells in the human body, KenHub, https://www.kenhub.com/en/library/anatomy/types-of-cells-in-the-human-body
45. Chapter 5. Computers vs. Cells (and Minds). https://cogsci.ucsd.edu/~sereno/170/readings/20-CompCell.pdf
46. Hetu, R, (2019). AI Can Be A Central Nervous System. https://blogs.gartner.com/robert-hetu/ai-can-be-a-central-nervous-system/
47. *New Measure of Human Brain Processing Speed | MIT Technology Review.* (2009, August 25). MIT Technology Review; www.technologyreview.com. https://www.technologyreview.com/2009/08/25/210267/new-measure-of-human-brain-processing-speed
48. Ibid.
49. Ibid.
50. Bernard, A. (2021, June 4). *59% of senior executives feel threatened by artificial intelligence | TechRepublic.* 59% of Senior Executives Feel Threatened by Artificial Intelligence | TechRepublic; www.techrepublic.com. https://www.techrepublic.com/article/ai-gaining-traction-in-the-workplace/
51. Khan, J. (2022). Want your company's A.I. project to succeed? Don't hand it to the data scientists, says this CEO. Fortune, dated 26 July. https://fortune.com/2022/07/26/a-i-success-business-sense-aible-sengupta/
52. Ibid.
53. Gartner (2021). *Gartner Predicts Legal Technology Budgets Will Increase Threefold by 2025.* https://www.gartner.com/en/newsroom/press-releases/2020-02-10-gartner-predicts-legal-technology-budgets-will-increase-threefold-by-2025
54. Sanos, W. (2021). *Forget machine learning, AI, Industry 4.0. Obsolescence is coming fast and in a fury. That should be your focus.* Linkedin 16 Feb, https://www.linkedin.com/pulse/forget-machine-learning-ai-industry-40-obsolescence-coming-santos
55. Gordon, C. (2021, May 10). *Why Board Directors And CEOs Need To Learn AI Knowledge Foundations: Building AI Leadership Brain Trust Is A Business Imperative: Are You Ready?* Forbes; www.forbes.com. https://www.forbes.com/sites/cindygordon/2021/05/10/why-board-directors-and-ceos-need-to-learn-ai-knowledge-foundations-building-ai-leadership-brain-trust-is-a-business-imperative-are-you-ready/?sh=463984896c05
56. Cilauro, F. (n.d.). *Using digital skills to take advantage of AI.* Frontier Economics; www.frontier-economics.com. Retrieved April 10, 2022, from https://www.frontier-economics.com/uk/en/news-and-articles/articles/article-i7483-using-digital-skills-to-take-advantage-of-ai/
57. Software systems now can abstract tasks that are big and complex from behind the customer line of sight like load balancing and content delivery (Cloudflare), payments (Stripe), mobile network management (Twilio), website development (Netlify), data engineering (Fivetran), infrastructure and device monitoring (Datadog), etc. Read Stephen O'Grady's "Addition by abstraction" for more details.
58. Munoz, D. (n.d.). *Why the C Programming Language Still Runs the World | Toptal.* Toptal Engineering Blog; www.toptal.com. Retrieved August 30, 2022, from

https://www.toptal.com/c/after-all-these-years-the-world-is-still-powered-by-c-programming
59. Capone, M. (2018, October 0). *The Data Literacy Index The $500m Enterprise Value Opportunity Results Summary*. https://thedataliteracyproject.org/files/documents/Qlik–The_Data_Literacy_Index_October_2018.pdf
60. WIPO, (2019). Technology Trends 2019–Artificial Intelligence. https://www.wipo.int/edocs/pubdocs/en/wipo_pub_1055.pdf
61. Express Analytics. (2019). AI For Data Cleaning: How AI can Clean Your Data and Save Your Man Hours and Money. https://expressanalytics.com/blog/ai-data-cleaning/
62. Riken, (2022). The next generation of superfast supercomputers. *Nature Portfolio*. https://www.nature.com/articles/d42473-018-00133-w; MIT technology Review, (2009). New Measure of Human Brain Processing Speed. https://www.technologyreview.com/2009/08/25/210267/new-measure-of-human-brain-processing-speed
63. Aiken P., & Harbour, T. (2021). Data Literacy: Achieving Higher Productivity for Citizens, Knowledge Workers, and Organizations. Technics Publication, USA.
64. This was trend where the word was used to mean something excellent or impressive in slang. Now this is an example in the English language, but with globalization, languages will keep evolving.
65. Szalavitz, M. (2021, August 11). The Pain Was Unbearable. So Why Did Doctors Turn Her Away? *The Wired*. https://www.wired.com/story/opioid-drug-addiction-algorithm-chronic-pain/; Bamboo Health, (2021). The combined organization will revolutionize healthcare in America by leveraging one of the nation's largest digitally integrated, in-workflow network of providers. https://bamboohealth.com/news/bamboo-health-unveiled/
66. From Bamboo Health. https://bamboohealth.com/solutions/narxcare/
67. GlobeNewsWire. (2015). South Dakota Adopts Appriss Platform to Mitigate Drug Diversion, https://www.globenewswire.com/news-release/2015/07/01/749137/36479/en/South-Dakota-Adopts-Appriss-Platform-to-Mitigate-Drug-Diversion.html
68. Wood D. (2015). Drug diversion. Australian prescriber, 38(5), 164–166.
69. GlobeNewsWire. 2015. *Op. cit.*
70. *Appriss, Inc. closes sale of Appriss Insights, LLC to Equifax in $1.825 billion deal | Clearlake Capital.* (n.d.). Clearlake Capital; clearlake.com. https://clearlake.com/appriss-inc-closes-sale-of-appriss-insights-llc-to-equifax-in-1-825-billion-deal/
71. Appriss. (2022). Who we are. https://apprisscorp.com/who-we-are/overview/
72. Oliva, J. D. (2021). Dosing Discrimination: Regulating PDMP Risk Scores. *California Law Review*. https://papers.ssrn.com/sol3/papers.cfm?abstract_id=3768774

7

AI Operations

CHAPTER HIGHLIGHTS

1. The scope of your AI operations requires you to evaluate the AI systems being used "outside" your organization and prepare for its vulnerabilities and possible opportunities.
2. We address two scales in AI operations: the level of interoperability the organization needs to plan for to manage the AI, and the level of globalness in which the AI system will function.
3. The more global AI systems are, the more the interoperability challenges.
4. This means that the AI project scope is more extensive than immediately visible. The organization must invest time, work on changing industry standards, and realign values across multiple systems.

> **Cases:**
> Uber: 2014–2016 | Log4j Open Source Software | The UAE Data Interoperability Guidelines | The Football Camera AI | Zoom scale-up during the Pandemic | Web 3.0 | M&A Uber and Facebook Flash Crash of 2010

7.1 AI Operations and Scope of the Project

AI operations refer to the scope of the project. AI projects are typically associated with data analytics and hence with *big data*. The ability of different systems to aggregate data for analytics will impact the organization's real-time performance and hopefully increase efficiency and effectiveness, two important objectives for managers. AI may not always be the answer to an organizations quest to modernize. So understanding the process and its relevance is critical to successful project management.

The scope of the AI project is wider than other projects, especially as it is to be embedded as a permanent part of the organizational environment and must have the ability to run relatively autonomously. It can be determined by asking the following questions:

1. What is the problem you want to solve with the help of AI and hence what are your project objectives?
2. How do you reaffirm that your values will be translated into the project?
3. Have you accessed the type of data you have and what is missing, and the methods and costs for aggregation?
4. Have you assessed the time and resources for data preparation (cleaning)?
5. Have you tested the various AI models before implementation based on the quality of results?
6. What is the organizational level and the processes within the organization where you want analysis and automation to occur? What are the training costs and the culture-fit cost?
7. Have you decided on the "human-in-the-loop" for accountability and control?
8. What is the minimum prototype of AI and can it be scaled for organizational implementation? What are some barriers for scaling?
9. How will you check for actionable insights and the transparency levels on data quality?
10. For actionable insights to be translated into decisions, you need to assess the risk associated with decisions and who bears responsibil-

ity for these risks, and how these decisions would impact stakeholders. What are the various scenarios you have prepared for?
11. How long will it take to use the feedback from decisions taken to correct the AI model or data inputs?
12. Have you determined the continuous inputs (data, upgrades, legal, and security) to ensure the AI functions optimally?

These questions will allow the manager to determine the resources (input costs), benefits of AI, risk, and liabilities. You may not have all the answers but the more you find, the better will be the defined boundaries in which you will deploy AI. Gartner recommends baby steps in AI project management, beginning with a few projects where there is data availability and then expanding up to 20 projects.[1] A project may not be a massive undertaking but could be a small problem being solved with AI and being validated.

The critical point to remember is that these types of AI project expansions are rarely easily scalable! AI projects require an agile approach. Project development is an iterative process that needs fast learning and the ability to pivot from your initial hypothesis. While many companies aspire to be tech platforms like Amazon or Google, the reality is that the level of investment of resources required for such an approach is not feasible for most companies.

Make-or-buy decisions for AI very much depend on the industry, resources available, type of business as well as corporate and business strategy. As portrayed in Chapter 3, traditional firms will use AI providers for some or all of the resources necessary for AI-projects, including but not limited to project management, UI/UX design, software engineering, data science, cloud-platforms, hardware and software, and training. For example, autonomous cars can have roughly 150 million lines of code due to their multiple systems, more than what is in modern fighter jets.[2] Figure 7.1 gives an example of the time and amount of investment needed for large scale AI projects.

When scaling AI operations, there are two critical problems you need to plan for:

1. What is the level of interoperability you require to ensure you optimize your AI system for the problem you are solving, and
2. How embedded in the industry and global ecosystems do you want to be?

Accordingly, you will have to plan for AI project resources. Naturally, the more interoperable and embedded the AI system is in the industry, and across geographic borders, the more resources will be required.

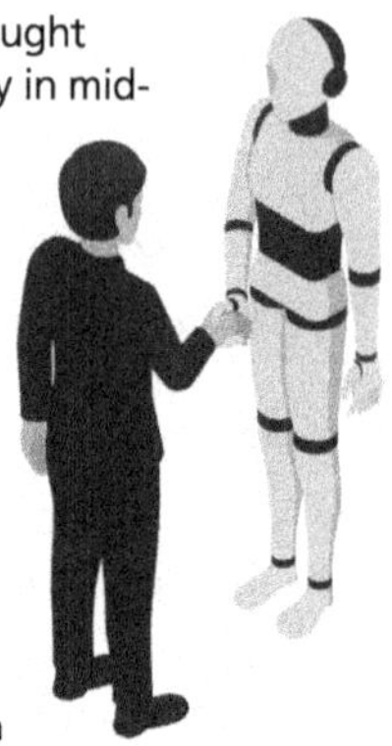

> Uber was initially dependent on outsourcing, but they soon brought everything in-house. Uber went on a massive expansion strategy in mid-2014. They had 200 engineers. By the end of 2016, they were in 400 cities and 70 countries and had 6,000 employees, of which 2,000 were engineers. They had over 1,000 micro-services stored in over 8,000 Git repositories. The challenges were scaling the team and getting them to speak the same language, the product feature release rate, and moving to a distributed system, which is more complicated than a single monolith system, especially for trouble-shooting, and migrations of legacy systems and data, among others. Matt Ranney, Chief Systems Architect at Uber and Co-founder of Voxer, said,
>
>> Everything is a tradeoff. (I wish I knew then) how to better make these tradeoffs intentionally. When things are happening without an explicit decision because it seems like this is just the way things are going, think about what trade-offs are being made, even if the decisions are not explicitly being made.
>
> He especially highlighted the less obvious costs of scaling being: (1) everything is a tradeoff (for example, build or buy, open-source or use internally), (2) building around problems (rather than solutions), (3) trading complexity for politics and (4) keeping your biases (if not open enough or challenged enough).
>
> Uber, which was valued at US$9 billion and went IPO, was still making losses in 2021.[3] Of course, the huge investments also led to layoffs during the pandemic when costs and core businesses needed to be prioritized.[4] Also, the business model itself is under attack as, for example, gig workers are now being considered employees (based on the recent UK rulings).
>
> Will Larson,[5] who led tech teams at Digg, Uber, and Stripe, has said the most important factors in building highly functional AI teams are (1) having a minimum team size (anything less than 4 is not a team); (2) having one manager support a maximum of 6–8 engineers or 6–8 managers; (3) when rotating services for 24/7 call, you need a minimum of eight engineers; and (4) make room in teams through growth (clear progression paths). This strategy requires investment in organizational structure and design. The example of Uber highlights why agile project management is so critical for the long-term success of AI projects.

Figure 7.1 Uber—2014–2016[6]

7.2 AI Interoperability

In simple language, interoperability is the ability of different systems to "talk" to each other. For AI, we are often looking at hardware, software, and data, but humans and their organization are also crucial since they provide the context for AI to operate within.

From such a contextual and systems perspective (looking at it with a horizontal lens), there are at least three levels of interoperability—isolated systems, connected systems, and universal systems. An example of a semi-isolated AI system is an AI box (see Figure 7.2). The simplified model is presented in Figure 7.3.

On 9 December 2021,[7] it was found a commonly used open-source logging library software, called Log4j, created by Apache Software Foundation had a critical issue. It was vulnerable. The software is used to record activities on the backend of computer systems. You will recognize this software when it sends 404 error message when you click a weblink that does not work. But this is not all that it does. It is so useful, it has been adopted by companies like Minecraft to log user command activity or to log memory storage; it is in Apple iCloud and Amazon Web Services. Since it is part of many software (Java for example), if there is a vulnerability, it exposes other systems. There are an estimated 3 billion devices that use Java.[8] Since the open-source software is embedded differently in companies there is no universal "patch" or fix.[9]

This software interconnectivity that embeds other software is a critical issue. The UK National Cyber Security Centre said

> Modern software can be large, powerful, and complex. Rather than a single author writing all the code themselves as was common decades ago, modern software creation will have large teams, and that software is increasingly made out of "building blocks" pulled together by the team rather than entirely written from scratch.[10]

While open-source software is very useful in speeding up innovation and reducing costs, the risk is the software vulnerability. This type of complexity shows how vulnerable the system could be as depicted in this illustration of technical risk of software reuse (Figure 7.2a).

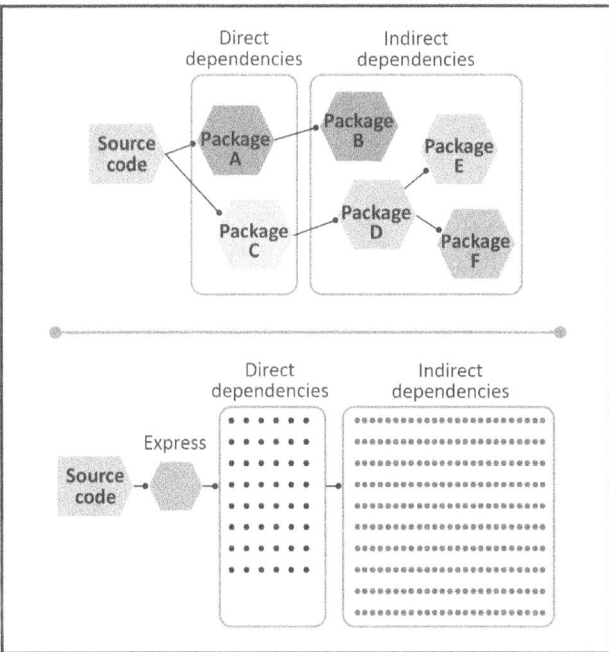

Figure 7.2a Software reuse dependencies. *Source:* Adapted from Vial, G. (2022)[11]

Figure 7.2 Connected systems—Log4j open source software.

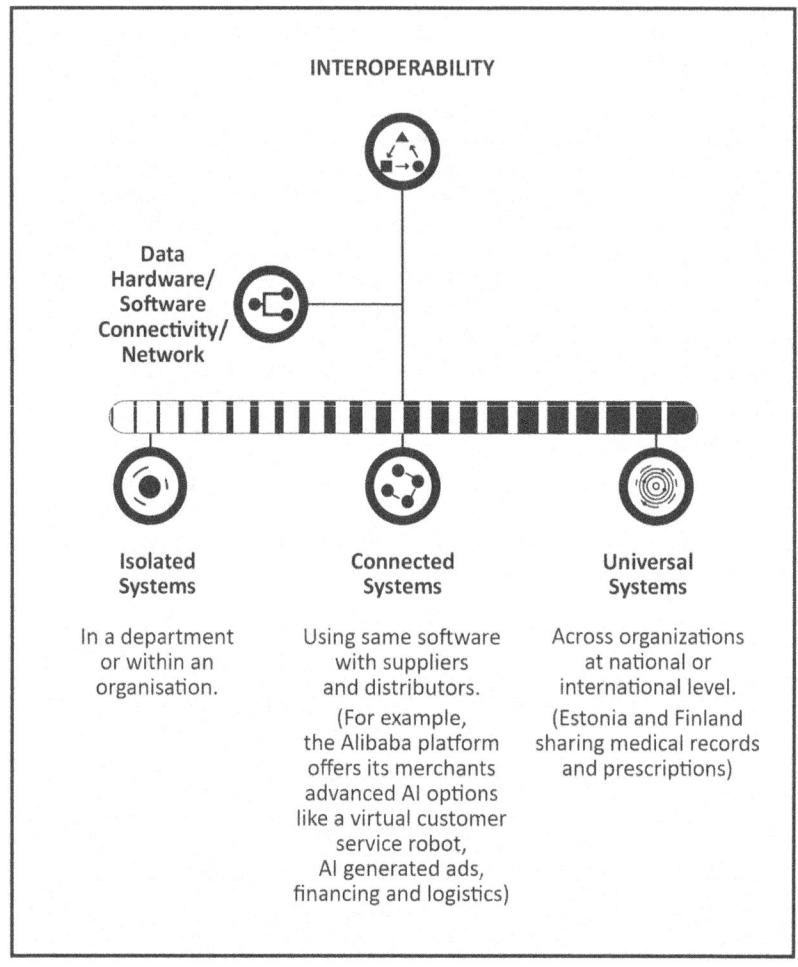

Figure 7.3 Scale—Interoperability. *Source:* Stephens & Vashishtha (2020)[12]

7.2.1 Isolated Systems

AI systems can be isolated where no AI connections exist outside the boundary you set. For example, you may limit it to working within a factory. Or for a set of employees. So, a company may choose to connect all employees via a proprietary intranet across geographic locations. In this case, ideally, the data, the software, and the hardware are cut off from the systems outside the boundary you have set for the AI to function.

Unfortunately, this is difficult to do. Data is often stored in the cloud (by another provider), the software is licensed, and the hardware is updated by manufacturers that may have proprietary hardware and software components. Most AI systems are connected.

Researchers have dreamed of an *AI box*, which is a virtual setting where the AI is constrained within a pre-determined boundary and not allowed to connect with the outside world. Of course, in science fiction, when the AI is perceived as smart or smarter than the human, there is an imaginary situation where the AI can convince its human gatekeepers to get out. These hypothetical situations have been described by Eliezer Yudkowsky's experiment (to show that an AI can convince or trick a human to voluntarily release it) or fantasized in the movie released in 2014, *Ex Machina*.

7.2.2 Connected Systems

Connected Systems are those where an exchange is possible with the outside world. Most systems are connected unless they are experimental. These AI systems could include shared products (cloud servers), data, or software platforms. Organizations may choose to keep some data or systems isolated. One of the challenges in connected AI systems is ensuring that the systems work well together for optimal performance. For example, in March 2018, a Uber car killed a pedestrian. Even though the car's sensors detected the person, it was not able to distinguish the need to trigger the brakes. This accident resulted from a software failure and can be linked to training the AI systems.[13] An autonomous vehicle (AV) has several electronic control units (ECUs) that read signals from its strategically placed sensors. It is estimated that cars like the BMQ-7 series could have 150 ECUs with more than 150 million lines of code![14] During software updates, if the updates are not synchronized, errors can happen, system vulnerabilities could be exposed, or data may be delayed or misread (like the example above), and hence decisions can be off.

Challenges with connected systems are data, technology, human resources, and regulations. Data is the raw input that algorithms in the AI process. Technology regularly updates, and this creates a problem with legacy systems. Migrating from older systems at times is not a luxury of choice for security reasons. Human resources are still the key driver of AI systems. We have not reached autonomous systems, and ethically there is a need to always put a human decision maker in charge for liability reasons—the so called human-in-the-loop perspective. Last but not least, regulations shape the way organizations use, adopt and deliver services. Below data interoperability is described in greater detail, showcasing other factors.

164 ▪ *AI Enabled Business*

7.2.2.1 Data Interoperability

Data interoperability "*addresses the ability of systems and services that create, exchange and consume data to have clear, shared expectations for the contents, context and meaning of that data,*" according to the Data Interoperability Standards Consortium. Data collected should have metadata—or the context and information about the data. The data formats are fields that help the algorithm use the data. Should weight be in kilograms or grams or pounds? The metadata would be human weight for a period of time (which will allow comparisons, at the time of illness, in a gym, etc.). This metadata categorization is important for humans who are being prescribed pharmaceutical pills in milligrams as a ratio to their body weight. Data should be anonymized as this is best practice, yet you may want to link data records for deeper analysis (hospital records and spending on credit card bills). These guidelines will have implications for open data sets for research and *Application Programming Interfaces* (APIs) used to get permissions (see Figure 7.4).

Data interoperability needs to be managed at six levels (see Figure 7.5). At Level 1, you will need to assess the technical feasibility (Do the hardware and software systems seamlessly allow data transfer and safeguard the data? Are the functionings it is purposed to perform correct, and are the insights generated correctly?). Then, the human in this human-AI team will set the standards for the data, hardware, and software. Application Programming Interfaces (API) are used as virtual middlemen to connect different

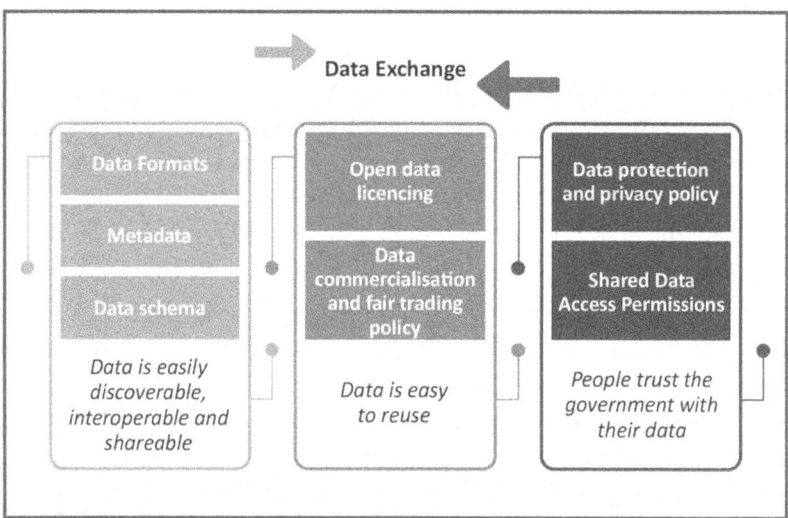

Figure 7.4 The UAE Data Interoperability Guidelines[15] *Source:* Adopted from UAE (2021)

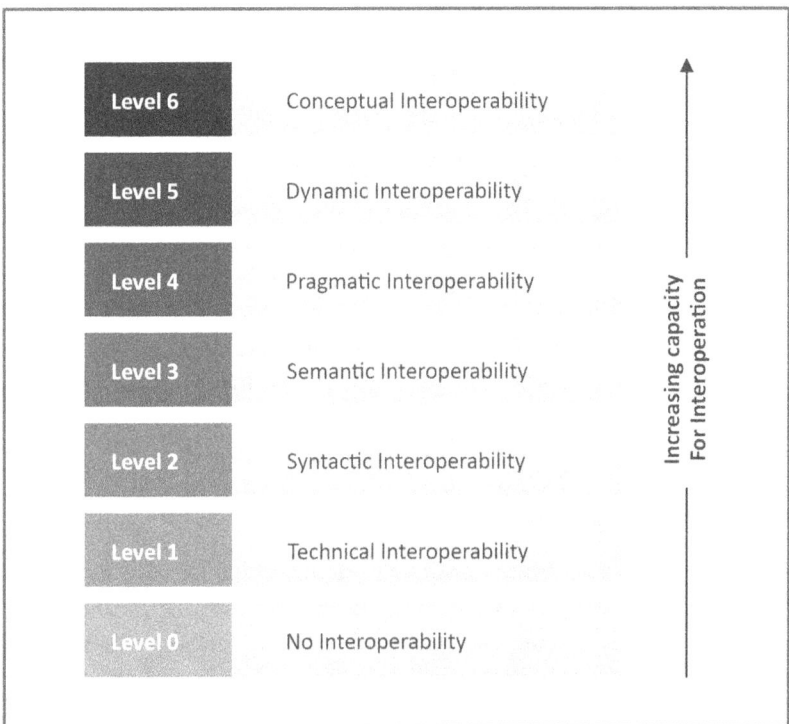

Figure 7.5 The various levels for data interoperability. Source: Stephens and Vashishtha (2020)[16]

software platforms both inside and outside the organization. This process helps in capturing value across data ecosystems. For example, telehealth connects patient software with hospital records, insurance, and pharmacies.

McKinsey estimated that, on average, most firms deploy approximately 12 APIs instead of the 100s needed to manage customer and business value.[17] McKinsey recommends having dedicated staff to manage APIs. The constant challenge of creating APIs is that they can become obsolete quickly or function incorrectly with any updates or changes to the software platforms they connect. This obsolescence requires a monitoring and upgrade strategy to reduce system vulnerabilities and prevent data hacking.[18] The resources to be allocated are time, people, robust feedback systems, and money. If the process is not managed well, the situation will result in a loss of trust and goodwill from clients and stakeholders of the company.

How important is this? For example, an API call is a client request to an API for that API to retrieve requested data from the specific server or

166 ▪ AI Enabled Business

program and then deliver it back to the client. Today, such calls now account for 83% of all web traffic.[19] In addition, APIs are increasingly becoming important in mobile services.

At Level 2, the focus is structural or syntactic interoperability. The role of the human is to determine the data format for exchange. It refers to the packaging (syntax or structure) and transmission mechanisms for data even when two or more different systems with different programming languages are being used. Here, the key objective is a mutual understanding of the meaning of data and information through open communication.[20] This communication is essential when you have data from different periods stored in earlier software formats, when you have diverse teams working on data that may not have compatible software sets or expertise levels, or when users access data with different interfaces (mobile, desktop, or augmented reality). Often the data is transferred through standardized tools like XML or SQL Standards.[21]

At Level 3, the focus is semantic operability, which is codification or the process that gives the data a common understanding. For example—how can the AI recognize a stop signal. When training autonomous cars, they must understand the red signal, stop signs, and, if necessary human actions. This last one is more difficult. Different people may gesture in different ways when there is an emergency. Even something as simple as a ball, which a human would have no difficulty recognizing, may not be the case with an AI (see Figure 7.6). In the European Interoperability Framework (EIF), semantic interoperability includes syntactic interoperability.

To achieve this level, you need an agreement among diverse stakeholders. It is considered achieved when "the information transferred has, in its communicated form, all of the meaning required for the receiving system

---

In 2020, an AI, Pixellot camera, was employed to follow the football in a match and replace the cameraman. They had two successful test events where the AI system worked well and tracked the ball across the field.[22] The game was broadcasted as this was during the COVID pandemic, and the stadium was empty. It was the last football match of the season. Unfortunately, the camera kept taking the bald linesman's head for a ball, which ruined television coverage. This error happened when the ball's visibility was blocked by players, or they were playing in the shadows of the stadium.[23]

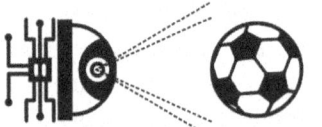

Figure 7.6 The football camera AI.[24]

to interpret it correctly, even when the algorithms used by the receiving system are unknown to the sending system."[25]

At Level 4, we have pragmatic interoperability. It results in a mutual understanding of the context and use of data across systems. It is sometimes also called operational interoperability. Pragmatic interoperability is achieved when the business process integration of interoperability is beyond the boundaries of a single organization.[26] This level of planning will allow the organization to scale at the global level.

Level 5 is dynamic interoperability. This level of planning helps the system stay relevant over time. Changes in systems, data structuring, and interfaces can be costly and are often done through manual interventions, which also mean more time. Ideally, it could be cloud-based, using software that enables virtual networking. So while there is greater flexibility and agility (see Figure 7.7), there are risks with outsourcing and higher transaction costs.[27] Data meaning and formats may change with time as language is not static. As we migrate to *big data*, this will become more critical, especially if we compare data in time series and make it meaningful.

Before the COVID pandemic (December 2019) that disrupted the world, Zoom daily meeting participants were 10 million people. By March 2020, with the global lockdowns and border closures, that number was 200 million thanks to remote working and many educational campuses going remote. By April 2020, this number was 300 million![28] To scale up to meet global needs, Zoom used its self-managed 19 data servers (with Equinix) and added a hybrid cloud network using AWS and Oracle. The way the application was designed was that it used multi-bitrate encoding so that people around the world with different bandwidths could still use the service but with proportionate video qualities. Zoom uses an interconnection service with its cloud servers that enables the enterprise SaaS and network service provider customers to directly and privately connect their networks, hence bypassing the public Internet. This process allows private connections to its technology partners and customers in real-time.

The challenge for Zoom, post-pandemic, is to maintain that accelerated growth! In their Q4 2021 meeting, Zoom founder and CEO Eric S. Yuan said,

> In (the) fiscal year 2022, we delivered strong results with total revenue of more than $4 billion growing 55% year over year along with increased profitability and operating cash flow growth as our global customer base continued to grow and find new use cases for our broadening communications platform . . . We are proud to lead the charge of the digital transformation for communications. To sustain and enhance our leadership position, in fiscal year 2023 we plan to build out our platform to further enrich the customer experience with new cloud-based technologies and expand our go-to-market motions, which we believe will enable us to drive future growth."[29]

Figure 7.7   Zoom scale-up during the pandemic.[30]

At Level 6, conceptual interoperability, the underpinning assumptions, and the constraints of the systems are aligned. It means the truth is represented consistently.[31] It is the highest level where the AI system selects and assembles components in various combinations to satisfy specific user requirements meaningfully (also called composability).[32] According to a RAND report,[33] this level of interoperability requires a clear focus on the business case and the knowledge domain. It is an issue often originating from a lack of human capacity (see Figure 7.8).

7.2.3 Universal Systems

In universal systems, there are shared applications and data. Some examples where we share applications and data across hardware are the Smart City, the Internet of All Things (IoT), and Industry 4.0 platform businesses. While the buzz around platform businesses is growing, adding AI or tech to an existing business does not make it a platform business. Platform businesses use technology and AI to bring together consumers and sellers in a virtual marketplace. Most platform businesses have some elements of a linear business (see Figure 7.9).

Universal systems have a high degree of autonomy (make decisions without human oversight) and will be multi-agent (and hence be decentralized and distributed in terms of decisions). However, the data may be proprietary across multiple systems, making the decision robustness limited since knowledge of the AI system is based on domain models and data sets.[34] Further, tracing accountability and the lack of transparency in decision-making will require robust governance systems (see Figure 7.10). Finally, virtual games could be universal but are also isolated by their proprietary hardware, software, and rules (often in the form of payment). Hence the same game on different types of hardware or even the various versions of the same game will limit who can access them.

7.3 Global Embeddedness

In addition to the above mentioned levels (isolated, connected and universal systems), organizations need to make a decision on the geographic scale. Expanding from local to national or global markets (see Figure 7.11) requires additional resources and more research to understand the market and regulatory context. Data will increasingly be an asset, but the debate is whether it will be an asset for the individual; or the companies that access, aggregate, and *own* the data; or for countries that set national policies and regulations? Especially for universal systems, a key concern is compliance

AI Operations • 169

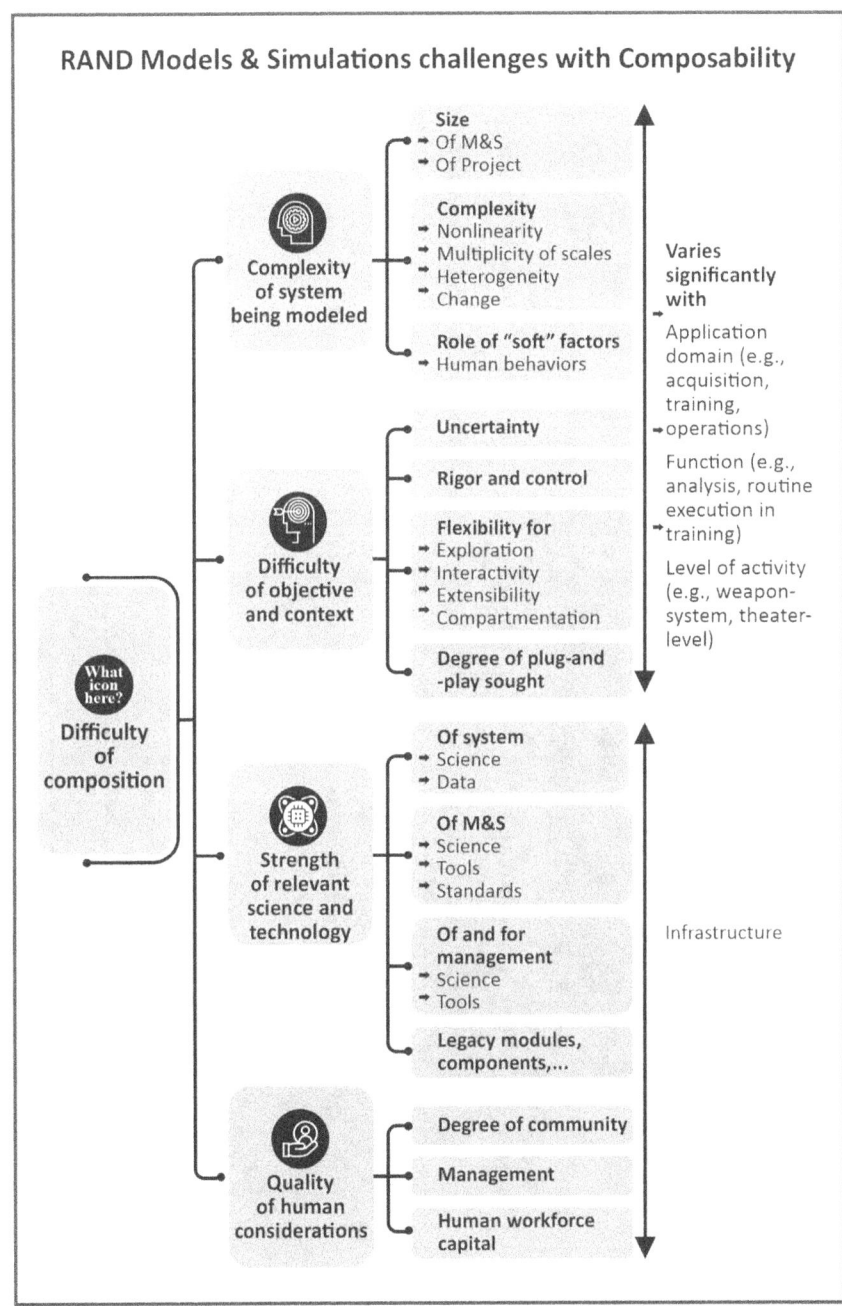

Figure 7.8 RAND models and simulations challenges with composability. *Source:* Adapted from RAND[35]

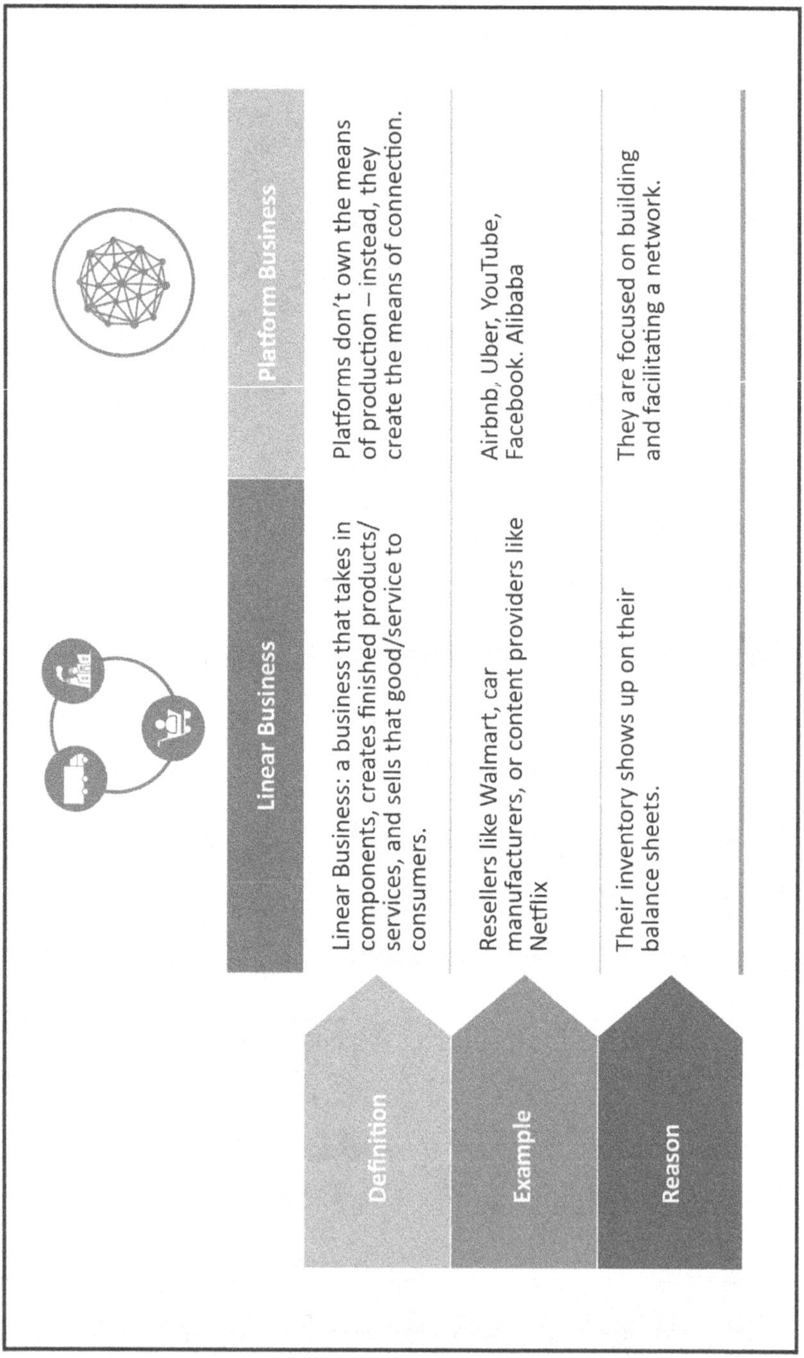

	Linear Business	Platform Business
Definition	Linear Business: a business that takes in components, creates finished products/services, and sells that good/service to consumers.	Platforms don't own the means of production – instead, they create the means of connection.
Example	Resellers like Walmart, car manufacturers, or content providers like Netflix	Airbnb, Uber, YouTube, Facebook. Alibaba
Reason	Their inventory shows up on their balance sheets.	They are focused on building and facilitating a network.

Figure 7.9 Linear versus platform businesses. *Source:* Johnson 2022[36]

> The future, according to some people, will belong to Web 3.0. This web version is based on a semantic web where machines and humans will form content together. According to a policy paper by Andreessen Horowitz,[37] it will involve a group of technologies that encompasses digital assets, decentralized finance, blockchains, tokens, and decentralized autonomous organizations (DAOs). It will be a place where the concept of *metaverse* should thrive. At the highest level, it could be a universal system operating globally. Of course, it will require a lot of work on the regulatory front and working across boundaries on standards and governance. Web 3.0 also suffers from a gap between idealism and realism as highlighted in this excellent article by Gilad Edelman in Wired, who said "nearly every Web3 product relies on a middleman to say what's happening on the blockchain. That's a whole lot of trust for a system designed to make trust obsolete."[38] Figure 7.10a (p. 172) gives a brief snapshot of the evolution of Web 3.0.

Figure 7.10 Web 3.0.

with local and national laws and their regulations. These include but are not limited to rules about data security, data protection, intellectual property rights, property rights, trade, taxes, tariffs, health and safety at work, and other evolving issues.

Many AI startups hope to be acquired by larger firms. If this is the plan, they need to consider data and activity migrations. Specifically, planning to

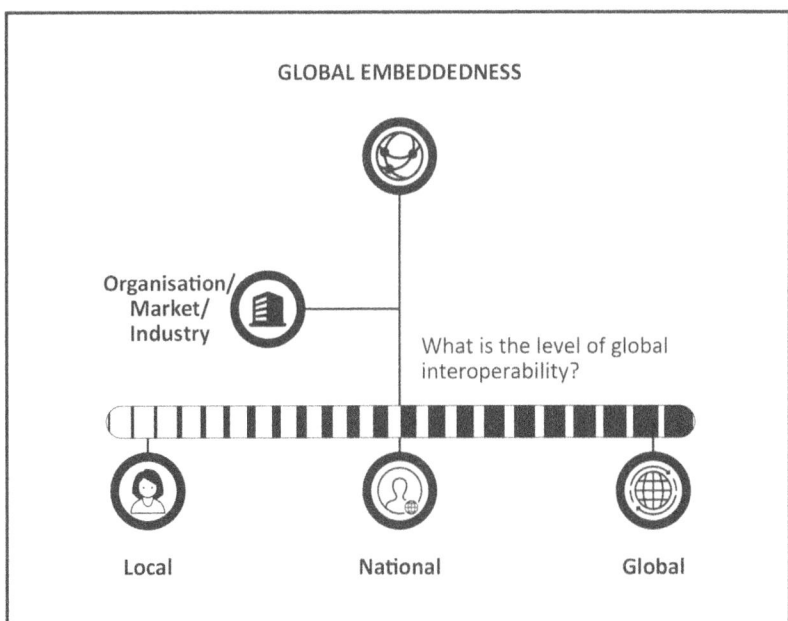

Figure 7.11 Global embeddedness. *Source:* Stephens & Vashishtha (2020)[39]

172 ▪ *AI Enabled Business*

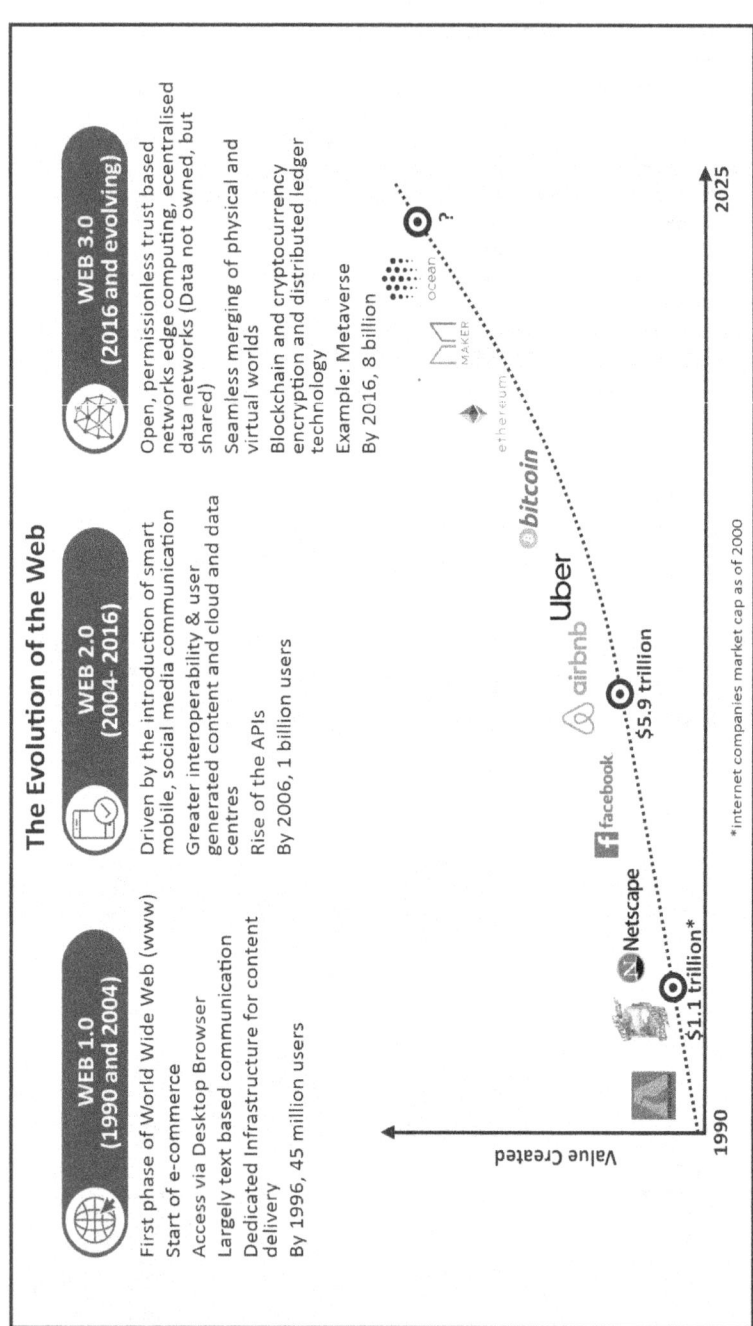

Figure 7.10a Evolution of Web 3.0 looking at market cap of companies from 2000 and planned trajectory toll 2025. *Source:* Adapted from Fabric Ventures (2019);[40] Choudhury (2014)[41]

> Uber announced its acquisition of Careem in 2019 and closed the acquisition for US$3.1 billion in January 2020. The agreement took more than nine months of negotiations between Uber and Careem.[42] Careem operates in multiple geographies. At the time of acquisition, the regulatory approval process in Qatar and Morocco had not been received, though Egypt, Jordan, Saudi Arabia, Pakistan, and the United Arab Emirates had been completed.[43]
> As a result, Uber decided to operate the Careem brand in parallel to its own.
>
> During the pandemic, at the height of lockdowns, Careem lost 80% of its revenues. So it began to focus on a super app[44]—aggregating, investing US$50 million to combine its (1) mobility of people (cars, bikes, rickshaw) business, (2) mobility of products (food, e-grocery, delivery) business, and (3) payment of money (bill payment, mobile recharge, peer-to-peer transfer). They expect they will invest more in this app development over time. In the 2021 Annual report, Uber reinforces the fact that they are not fully integrated and are two brands as a possible risk (p. 18).[45] It was and highlighted that one of the challenges was Careem's data policy which conflicted with its own.[46] Uber states that the brand, product app, and payments operate parallel to Uber's and the staff (engineering, human resources and operations teams) are independent of each other and report to their own CEO (pp. 34–35).[47]
>
> Facebook bought Instagram in 2013 for US$ 1 billion. Instagram was able to migrate from Amazon's cloud servers in three weeks. Instagram stored its data and backend on Amazon Web Services. During migration, they found that Facebook's IP space conflicted with Amazon's EC2's IP space. So they pivoted and moved their data and services to Amazon's Virtual Private Cloud first, and then the data (20 billion photos)[48] was migrated to Facebook using Amazon Direct Connect.[49] The complete migration process took a year, using 8–20 Facebook data center team members. The preparations took 11 months, while the data transfer took about a month.[50]

Figure 7.12 M&A—Example from Uber and Facebook.

export APIs or software developer kits (SDKs). These migrations can take a month to a year to implement (see Figure 7.12, an example of Uber and Facebook acquisitions).[51] For larger companies that are on an acquisition spree, there is more pushback from governments from the point of view of national security and antitrust concerns.

Based on their future aspirations, companies need to decide the level of data interoperability and global embeddedness they want (see Figure 7.13). As data interoperability and the geographic scale of operations increase, so do the costs. While the initial investments in resources are high, there is also a need to budget resources for the significant update, maintenance, and obsolescence plan costs.

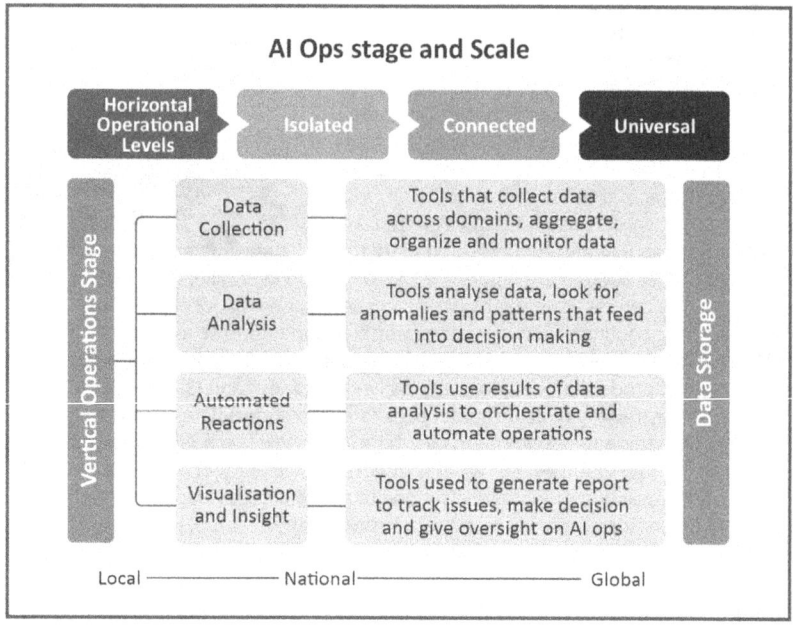

Figure 7.13 AI Ops stage and scale. *Source:* Authors

Take, for example, the idea of migrating to the cloud. There is an assumption that migrating to the cloud will eventually help organizations increase efficiency and save costs. This view has to be challenged. It depends on the systems being migrated and the existing data architectures. In a survey of Chief Information Officers, McKinsey found that 10–20% of their budget allocated for new products was being diverted to managing the tech debt of the company.[52] This debt is the cost of managing existing tech products like migration, upgrading systems, streamlining data and processes, or managing obsolescence. Tech debt can be up to 40% of IT balance sheets and should ideally not exceed 50%.[53]

Deloitte finds that standard machine learning projects can take 12 months, with an initial cost of a few hundred thousand dollars for small projects to a few million dollars for enterprise-level projects, but the ROI is generally 2–5 times the cost in the first year, provided the project is implemented well.[54] The challenges for operations are data management, vendor selection, compliance and regulation, technical skills, and getting internal buy-in, in that order.[55] As more and more systems get "inter-connected" or because of greater interoperability, AI systems are exposed to vulnerabilities that may

AI Operations ▪ **175**

>
> In May 2010, the U.S. stock market crashed in 36 minutes, resulting in a drop of 600 points, potentially one trillion dollars. A subsequent report published titled, *Findings Regarding the Market Events of May 6, 2010*,[56] found that the reason for the crash was found to be automated trading that was triggered by a large sale of a critical asset. This finding was contested, but later in 2015, a London-based trader[57] was arrested for his role in the Flash Crash and his use of an automated program that triggered large sell-offs to push the market down. This event eventually resulted in the introduction of circuit breakers, which would stop trading for five minutes on any 404 New York Stock Exchange or S&P 500 stock that rises or falls more than 10% in five minutes.
>
> Infosys highlights some of the challenges of AI Systems Testing, which are reproduced below:[58]
>
> 1. Massive volumes of collected sensor data present storage and analytics challenges in addition to creating noisy datasets.
> 2. AI systems rely on data gathered during unanticipated events, which is extremely difficult to collate, thus posing training challenges.
> 3. AI model test scenarios should be equipped to identify and remove human bias, which often becomes part of training and testing datasets.
> 4. In AI systems, the defect gets amplified, making it extremely hard to fix one isolated problem.
>
> However, as seen in the example above, we may not be able to predict all the challenges and need to be able to have circuit breakers put into place to allow humans operating behind the scenes to figure out what went wrong.

Figure 7.14 Flash Crash of 2010: Algorithmic impact on data.

make them unreliable (see Figure 7.14). We have no idea when these crises may occur nor the factors that contribute to the tipping point of these events —so what can work is immediate crisis mitigation.

This chapter highlights the scope and importance of AI operations management. While outsourcing seems like an easy way to go, the reality is that the responsibility for adopting, deploying, and using an AI system is still the manager in the organization. The resources you need to plan for AI management depends on the level of interoperability and the global reach you plan for. There is a significant amount of foresight you need in this type of planning. Further, because we cannot plan for all contingencies, firms need to have circuit breakers and crisis mitigation funds and strategies put into place.

QUESTIONS

1. Looking at Figure 7.4 and Figure 7.5—what would be your organization's most significant challenges?
2. If the AI systems fail, what would be your backup options? Look at the risk factor based on how critical the AI system is for your operations.
3. What are some opportunities from Web 3.0 that your organization can leverage?
4. What are the standards and regulations that you are most worried that you have not prepared for?

MY INSIGHTS

The most difficult decisions I need to take are

MY INSIGHTS

The resources I need to build for the future are

MY INSIGHTS

The governance systems I will to put in place are

MY INSIGHTS

The training and skills I and my team need to develop are

Notes

1. van der Meulen, R. (2018, April 6). *12 Steps To Excellence In Artificial Intelligence For IT Operations.* Gartner; www.gartner.com. https://www.gartner.com/smarterwithgartner/12-steps-to-excellence-in-artificial-intelligence-for-it-operations-infographic
2. Kukkuru, M. G. (n.d.). *Testing imperative for AI Systems.* Testing AI Systems–How to Overcome Key Challenges | Infosys; www.infosys.com. Retrieved December 3, 2021, from https://www.infosys.com/insights/ai-automation/testing-imperative-for-ai-systems.html
3. Moore, E., & Lee, D. (2021, October 21). *Is Uber, valued at $91bn, on verge of a profitable future after a decade of losses?—The Irish Times.* The Irish Times; www.irishtimes.com. https://www.irishtimes.com/business/technology/is-uber-valued-at-91bn-on-verge-of-a-profitable-future-after-a-decade-of-losses-1.4704534
4. Soper, T. (2020, May 18). *Uber lays off another 3,000 employees; Seattle engineering hub will remain open – GeekWire.* GeekWire; www.geekwire.com. https://www.geekwire.com/2020/uber-lays-off-another-3000-employees-seattle-engineering-hub-will-remain-open/
5. *How to Size and Assess Teams From an Eng Lead at Stripe, Uber and Digg | First Round Review.* (n.d.). How to Size and Assess Teams From an Eng Lead at Stripe, Uber and Digg | First Round Review; review.firstround.com. Retrieved December 18, 2021, from https://review.firstround.com/how-to-size-and-assess-teams-from-an-eng-lead-at-stripe-uber-and-digg
6. GOTO Conferences. (2016, September 28). *What I Wish I Had Known Before Scaling Uber to 1000 Services • Matt Ranney • GOTO 2016.* YouTube; www.youtube.com. https://www.youtube.com/watch?v=kb-m2fasdDY
7. *Apache Log4j Vulnerability Guidance | CISA.* (n.d.). Apache Log4j Vulnerability Guidance | CISA; www.cisa.gov. https://www.cisa.gov/uscert/apache-log4j-vulnerability-guidance
8. Mellen, A., Pollard, J., Carielli, S., Valente, A., & Turner, S. (2021, December 13). *Divide And Conquer: Rapid Response To The Apache Log4j Vulnerability.* Forrester; www.forrester.com. https://www.forrester.com/blogs/divide-and-conquer-rapid-response-to-the-apache-log4j-vulnerability/
9. Torres-Arias, S. (n.d.). *What is Log4j? A cybersecurity expert explains the latest internet vulnerability, how bad it is and what's at stake.* The Conversation; theconversation.com. https://theconversation.com/what-is-log4j-a-cybersecurity-expert-explains-the-latest-internet-vulnerability-how-bad-it-is-and-whats-at-stake-173896
10. *Log4j vulnerability–what everyone needs to know.* (n.d.). NCSC; www.ncsc.gov.uk. Retrieved May 30, 2022, from https://www.ncsc.gov.uk/information/log4j-vulnerability-what-everyone-needs-to-know
11. Vial, G. (2022). Manage the Risks of Software Reuse. *MIT Sloan Management Review, 63*(4), 62–65.
12. Stephens, M., & Vashishtha, H. (2020). *AI Smart Kit–Agile Decision Making on AI–Abridged Version.* Information Age Publishing, NC: USA

13. Kukkuku, M. G. nd. *Op. cit.*
14. Charette, R. N. (2021, June 7). *How Software Is Eating the Car–IEEE Spectrum.* IEEE Spectrum; spectrum.ieee.org. https://spectrum.ieee.org/software-eating-car
15. UAE. (n.d.). *Data operability–The Official Portal of the UAE Government.* Data Operability–The Official Portal of the UAE Government; u.ae. Retrieved December 25, 2021, from https://u.ae/en/about-the-uae/digital-uae/data/data-operability
16. Stephens, M., & Vashishtha, H. (2020). *Op. cit.*
17. Iyengar, K., Khanna, S., Ramadath, S., & Stephens, D. (2017). What it really takes to capture the value of APIs. *McKinsey & Company.* https://www.mckinsey.com/business-functions/mckinsey-digital/our-insights/what-it-really-takes-to-capture-the-value-of-apis
18. *Aggressive Obsolescence.* (n.d.). Aggressive Obsolescence; microservice-api-patterns.org. Retrieved April 29, 2022, from https://microservice-api-patterns.org/patterns/evolution/AggressiveObsolescence.html
19. Krishnaswamy, K., & Bryant, D. (2020, September 22). *Four Case Studies for Implementing Real-Time APIs.* InfoQ; www.infoq.com. https://www.infoq.com/articles/implementing-real-time-apis/
20. Harvey, F., Kuhn, W., Pundt, H., Bishr, Y., & Riedemann, C. (1999). Semantic interoperability: A central issue for sharing geographic information. *The annals of regional science, 33*(2), 213–232.
21. *Syntactic interoperability–CODATA, The Committee on Data for Science and Technology.* (n.d.). CODATA, The Committee on Data for Science and Technology; codata.org. Retrieved April 29, 2022, from https://codata.org/rdm-terminology/syntactic-interoperability/
22. Blake, A., Blake, R., Hulkkonen, P., Huotari, S., Jauhiainen, M., Tolonen, J., & Värri, A. (2020, 0 0). *Interoperability.* Foundational Curriculum: Cluster 6: System Connectivity Module 10 : Interoperability, Interfaces and Integration of eHealth Unit 1: Interoperability. http://www.ehealthwork.eu/FC/Presentations/Clusters_5-6/30-FC-C6M10U1-Interoperability.pdf
23. Pykes, K. (2021, June 21). *5 AI Failures You Probably Should Know About | by Kurtis Pykes | Towards Data Science.* Medium; towardsdatascience.com. https://towardsdatascience.com/5-ai-failures-you-probably-should-know-about-417ddebbc323
24. Jain, S. (2020, November 2). *AI Camera Ruins Football Game By Mistaking Referee's Bald Head For Ball.* NDTV.Com; www.ndtv.com. https://www.ndtv.com/offbeat/ai-camera-ruins-football-game-by-mistaking-referees-bald-head-for-ball-2319171
25. Blake, A., Blake, R., Hulkkonen, P., Huotari, S., Jauhiainen, M., Tolonen, J., & Värri, A. (2020, 0 0). *Interoperability.* Foundational Curriculum: Cluster 6: System Connectivity Module 10 : Interoperability, Interfaces and Integration of eHealth Unit 1: Interoperability. http://www.ehealthwork.eu/FC/Presentations/Clusters_5-6/30-FC-C6M10U1-Interoperability.pdf
26. Pykes, K. (2021, June 21). *5 AI Failures You Probably Should Know About | by Kurtis Pykes | Towards Data Science.* Medium; towardsdatascience.com. https://

towardsdatascience.com/5-ai-failures-you-probably-should-know-about-417d debbc323
27. Wan, Y., & Clegg, B. (2011). Managing ERP, Interoperability Strategy and Dynamic Change in Enterprises. In *Proc. POMS 22 nd Annual Conference, Reno, Nevada, USA.* https://www.pomsmeetings.org/ConfPapers/020/020-0612.pdf
28. Dean, B. (2021). Zoom user stats: How many people use Zoom in 2021. https://backlinko.com/zoom-users
29. Zoom. (2022, February 28). *Zoom Video Communications Reports Fourth Quarter and Fiscal Year 2022 Financial Results–Zoom Video Communications, Inc.* Zoom Video Communications, Inc.; investors.zoom.us. https://investors.zoom.us/news-releases/news-release-details/zoom-video-communications-reports-fourth-quarter-and-fiscal-1
30. Krazit, T. (2020, November 30). *How Zoom pulled off the scaling event of a lifetime–Protocol.* Protocol; www.protocol.com. https://www.protocol.com/manuals/new-enterprise/how-zoom-scaled-covid19; Miller, R. (2020, May 22). *Inside Zoom's Infrastructure: Scaling Up Massively With Colo and Cloud.* Data Center Frontier; datacenterfrontier.com. https://datacenterfrontier.com/inside-zooms-infrastructure-scaling-up-massively-with-colo-and-cloud/
31. Tolk, A., Diallo, S. Y., Padilla, J. J., & Herencia-Zapana, H. (2013). Reference modelling in support of M&S—foundations and applications. *Journal of Simulation, 7*(2), 69–82. https://www.tandfonline.com/doi/full/10.1057/jos.2013.3
32. Davis, P. K., & Anderson, R. H. (2003). *Improving the composability of department of defense models and simulations.* RAND CORP SANTA MONICA CA. https://www.rand.org/content/dam/rand/pubs/monographs/2004/RAND_MG101.pdf
33. Ibid.
34. Berggren, V. (2021). Artificial intelligence in next-generation connected systems. Ericsson White Paper. https://www.ericsson.com/en/reports-and-papers/white-papers/artificial-intelligence-in-next-generation-connected-systems
35. Davis, P. K., & Anderson, R. H. (2003). *Improving the composability of department of defense models and simulations.* RAND CORP SANTA MONICA CA. https://www.rand.org/content/dam/rand/pubs/monographs/2004/RAND_MG101.pdf
36. Johnson, N. (2017). Platform vs. linear: business models 101. *Applico,* available at: www.applicoinc.com/blog/platform-vs-linear-business-models-101/ (accessed September 25, 2018). https://www.applicoinc.com/blog/platform-vs-linear-business-models-101/
37. Andreessen Horowitz 2021. web3 Policy Hub. https://a16z.com/web3-policy/
38. Edelman, G. (2022, May 10). *The Web3 Movement's Quest to Build a 'Can't Be Evil' Internet.* WIRED; www.wired.com. https://www.wired.com/story/web3-paradise-crypto-arcade/
39. Stephens, M., & Vashishtha, H. (2020). Op. cit.
40. Mersch, M., & Muirhead, R. (2019, December 31). *What Is Web 3.0 & Why It Matters. Written by Max Mersch and Richard . . . | by Fabric Ventures | Fabric Ventures | Medium.* Medium; medium.com. https://medium.com/fabric-ventures/what-is-web-3-0-why-it-matters-934eb07f3d2b

41. Choudhury, N. (2014). World wide web and its journey from web 1.0 to web 4.0. *International Journal of Computer Science and Information Technologies*, 5(6), 8096–8100. https://ijcsit.com/docs/Volume 5/vol5issue06/ijcsit20140506265.pdf
42. *Uber's Middle East Deal–Executive Search–Boyden.* (n.d.). Uber's Middle East Deal–Executive Search–Boyden; www.boyden.com. Retrieved January 5, 2022, from https://www.boyden.com/media/ubers-middle-east-deal-9962684/index.html
43. *UBER.* (n.d.). 2019 Annual Report. https://s23.q4cdn.com/407969754/files/doc_financials/2019/ar/Uber-Technologies-Inc-2019-Annual-Report.pdf
44. Hamid, T. (2020, June 15). *Careem invests $50 million in super app–Wamda.* Careem Invests $50 Million in Super App–Wamda; www.wamda.com. https://www.wamda.com/2020/06/careem-invests-50-million-super-app
45. Uber (2021). Annual Report. https://s23.q4cdn.com/407969754/files/doc_financials/2022/ar/2021-Annual-Report.pdf (p. 18).
46. Uber Technologies. For Fiscal year ended December 31, 2020. United States Securities and Exchange Commission. p.34. https://www.sec.gov/Archives/edgar/data/0001543151/000154315121000014/uber-20201231.htm
47. Uber (2021). Op cit. (p. 18, 34–35).
48. Jones, P. (2014, July 1). *datacenterdynamics.* Facebook Ditches AWS to Bring Instagram Data in House. https://www.datacenterdynamics.com/en/news/facebook-ditches-aws-to-bring-instagram-data-in-house/
49. Sverdlik, Y. (2014, June 27). *Instagram Migrates from Amazon's Cloud into Facebook Data Centers | Data Center Knowledge | News and analysis for the data center industry.* Data Center Knowledge | News and Analysis for the Data Center Industry; www.datacenterknowledge.com. https://www.datacenterknowledge.com/archives/2014/06/27/instagram-migrates-from-amazons-cloud-into-facebook-data-centers
50. Jones, P. 2014. Op. cit.
51. Karr, D. (2021, September 7). *Council Post: What Businesses Need To Keep In Mind About (Inevitable) Technology Migration.* Forbes; www.forbes.com. https://www.forbes.com/sites/forbesagencycouncil/2021/09/07/what-businesses-need-to-keep-in-mind-about-inevitable-technology-migration/?sh=1585dafbe9d2
52. Dalal, V., Krishnakanthan, K., Münstermann, B., & Patenge, R. (2020). Tech debt: Reclaiming tech equity. https://www.mckinsey.com/business-functions/mckinsey-digital/our-insights/tech-debt-reclaiming-tech-equity
53. Ibid.
54. *Deloitte Access Economic.* (n.d.). Business Impacts of Machine Learning Sponsored by Google Cloud 2017. Retrieved March 15, 2022, from https://www2.deloitte.com/content/dam/Deloitte/tr/Documents/process-and-operations/TG_Google%20Machine%20Learning%20report_Digital%20Final.pdf
55. M-Brain. (2017, June 14). *Machine Learning Initiatives Across Industries: Practical Lessons from IT Executives–M-Brain–Market & Competitive Intelligence Solutions.* M-Brain–Market & Competitive Intelligence Solutions; www.m-brain.com. https://www.m-brain.com/white-papers/machine-learning-initiatives-across-industries-practical-lessons-executives/
56. U.S. Commodity Futures Trading Commission and the U.S. Securities and Exchange Commission. 2010. *Findings Regarding the Market Events of May 6, 2010.* Available: https://www.sec.gov/news/studies/2010/marketevents-report.pdf

57. Bloomberg Quicktake: Originals. (2020, November 24). *The Wild $50M Ride of the Flash Crash Trader.* YouTube; www.youtube.com. https://www.youtube.com/watch?v=_ZDEWVJan0s
58. Kukkuru, M. G. (n.d.). *Testing imperative for AI Systems.* Testing AI Systems–How to Overcome Key Challenges | Infosys; www.infosys.com. Retrieved March 16, 2022, from https://www.infosys.com/insights/ai-automation/testing-imperative-for-ai-systems.html

8

AI Data Types and Management

CHAPTER HIGHLIGHTS

1. The type and quality of AI data affect the scale at which AI can be deployed.
2. The more unstructured the data sets, the more complex the back-end systems, and greater oversight for governance is required.
3. There are different ways to train AI to cope with data. Big data is of increasing relevance and requires special attention.
4. Data literacy for the policymakers, owners, users, adopters, and deployers is a much-needed skill for the future.

> **Cases:**
> Deep Fakes and War | Blue River Technology | Waze | Lucas and his AI-enabled Microwave | Amazon | 2021 Facebook Outage

8.1 Data

Data is defined as factual information, whether relevant or not, that is processed to be used as a basis for reasoning, discussion, and calculation.[1] Data forms an integral part of AI—used in theories and algorithms that provide insights and influence decisions and behaviors on shopping, services, news, health, entertainment, or finance. One of the most important things to be aware of is that data is not knowledge! We process data to information, knowledge, and wisdom for decision-making (see Figure 8.1). AI programmers often use knowledge graphs to try and connect the data for analysis, interpretation, and communication to give meaning to random facts.

Despite the traditional definition given above, alleged facts are often manipulated. This problem has scaled due to digitalization and AI increases possibilities to distort results from incorrect data exponentially. One example of how data is being misused is provided in the case study in Figure 8.2.

As the world expands and our knowledge along with it, so does the amount of data we collect and consume. It is estimated that in 2021, we produced 1.145 trillion MB per day (each human created an average of 1.7MB of data per second)![2] Again, we face exponential growth, as this number increases while we spend more time online, more devices capture and track our daily lives, and more products and services get digitalized. We can access and store these vast quantities of data, but much of it is not neatly labeled or easy to feed into AI systems.

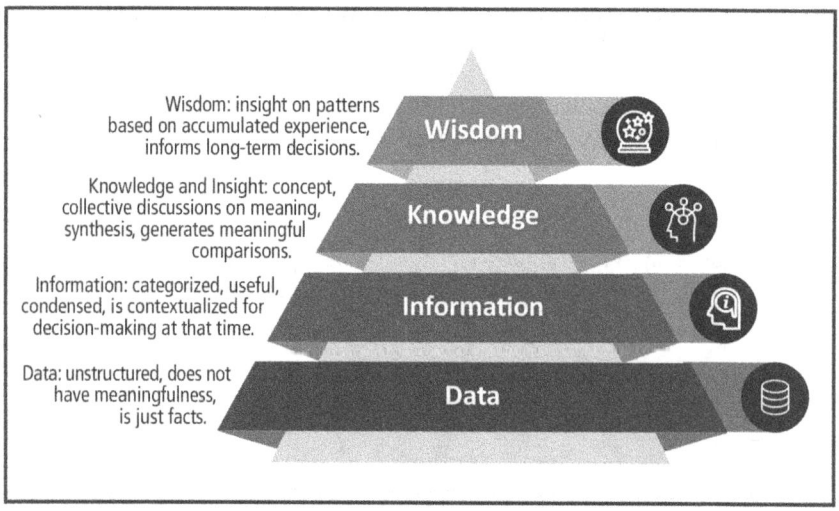

Figure 8.1 Data to wisdom ladder. Source: Adapted from Rowley (2005)[3]

A deep fake is a manipulated picture of a real person or realistic-looking images of people that don't exist that can be used to potentially harm an individual, a country, or a corporation. On March 17, Twitter removed a deepfake video that gave the impression it was President Zelensky of Ukraine.[4] This video was at the height of the Ukraine–Russia conflict. Twitter has a very explicit policy for manipulated media reproduced below.

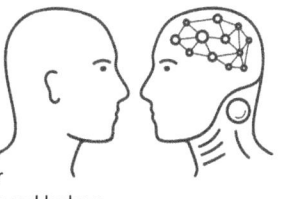

Twitter Policy[5]

> **IV. Manipulated Media**
>
> Media can be edited in a variety of ways. In many cases, these changes are benign, such as content being cropped or shortened for artistic reasons or music being added. In other cases, the manipulation is not apparent and could mislead, particularly in the case of video content. We remove this content because it can go viral quickly and experts advise that false beliefs regarding manipulated media often cannot be corrected through further discourse.
>
> We remove videos under this policy if specific criteria are met: (1) the video has been edited or synthesized, beyond adjustments for clarity or quality, in ways that are not apparent to an average person, and would likely mislead an average person to believe a subject of the video said words that they did not say; and (2) the video is the product of artificial intelligence or machine learning, including deep learning techniques (e.g., a technical deepfake), that merges, combines, replaces, and/or superimposes content onto a video, creating a video that appears authentic.

The issue of deep fakes, that look, sound, walk, talk, and can act like a real person without their permission or knowledge, is one issue that is an outcome of the lack of stronger data privacy laws. While AI technology is often used in marketing to modify how a person looks, it is also being used, for example, in advertisements. In India, Cadbury used AI to allow local store owners across India to create custom ads for Diwali,[6] using Shah Rukh Khan, a mega movie star's face and voice.[7] They did a previous ad with another movie star called Hrithik Roshan for Raksha Bandhan.[8]

Deepfakes need about 300 images of a single source person (or one minute of video) and maybe 48 hours of training to create a convincing model.[9] It is estimated that we upload 6.9 billion images per day on WhatsApp, 1.3 billion photos per day on Instagram,[10] and 500 hours of video on YouTube.[11] This may cause privacy issues, human rights issues, and crime, things we are not prepared for! WIPO addressed the issue of IP by looking at issues of AI:[12]

(i) Since deep fakes are created based on data that may be the subject of copyright, to whom should the copyright in a deep fake belong?
(ii) Should there be a system of equitable remuneration for persons whose likenesses and "performances" are used in a deep fake?"

Organizations that record images of individuals or use platforms that do the same may want to create a policy mindful of future problems and ethics.

Figure 8.2 Deep fakes.

As a result, *big data* has become a buzzword for many industries. *Big data* is data that contains a great variety of information in its composition, being created in exponential volumes and with ever-higher velocity (speed).

8.2 The AI Data Scale

All AI and machine learning algorithms use data. But will any data do? Can you feed huge volumes of any data you find available and get usable results for decision-making? The answer is NO. There are several reasons for this:

1. Data is often not neatly arranged for comparisons or may be incomplete, duplicated, or incorrect, so it needs to be "cleaned." Hence the quantity of data rarely translates to the quality of data.
2. Data may not reside in one database and must be consolidated across multiple databases—which takes time and effort or needs a good data integration strategy. For example, data may mean different things in different contexts—like pound (weight or money?) —and requires strong use-cases.
3. Data may not be representative of the population under study—research shows women, the elderly, minorities, and the disabled may not have as large a data footprint which may create bias.
4. Data ethics is becoming more critical—some common concerns are data privacy and data security, and this and other considerations need careful governance and additional resources.
5. Data obsolescence needs a strategy for curating old data, managing data storage costs, ensuring that the transition to new data is done with technical fit, and preventing errors (as the baseline may change when looking at trends).

To understand AI data better, it can be arranged on a continuum (see Figure 8.3). There is structured data on one end, and on the other, there is unstructured data, with structured dynamic data in between. Structured data is a database that has been cleaned, coded, and can be used to train an AI. On the other hand, unstructured data has no predefined format. As a result, it is not only challenging to collect (how would you know if the data is relevant?) but difficult to process and analyze. Hence, these problems may create biases in the output. Unstructured digital data defies human analysis and is a major field of application for machine learning and AI.

Data can have a static or dynamic structure when it comes to storage. In the case of structured dynamic data, the data has some structure, but there are variable fields (think of the comments sections in forms we fill). Sometimes the strongest insights come from comments and reviewing this field may lead to a change in the way structured data is viewed or collected.

The quantity of structured data coincides with how advanced the AI or machine learning algorithms are, seeing as the more structured the data,

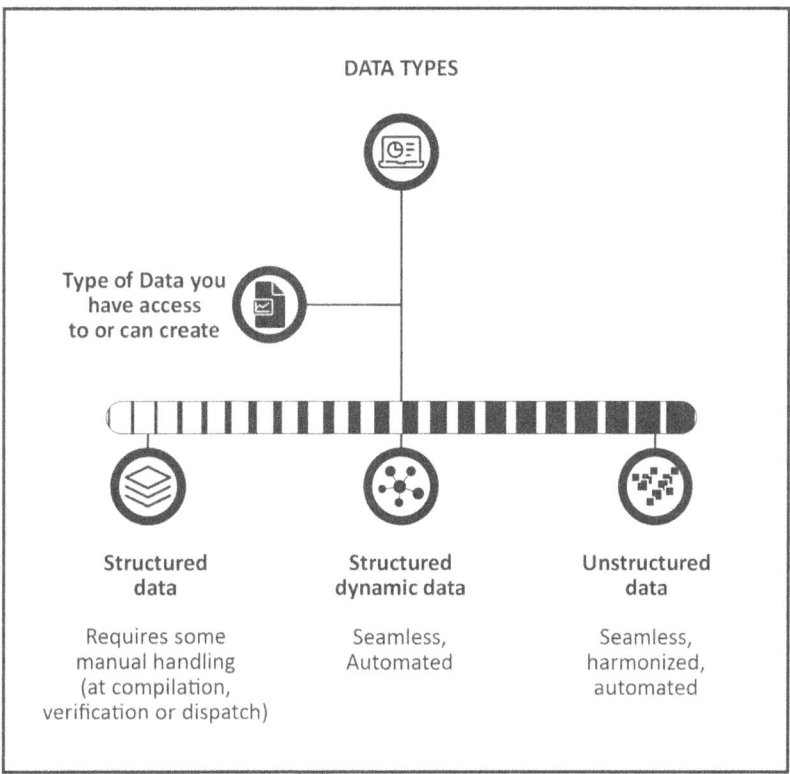

Figure 8.3 AI scale: Data types. *Source:* Stephens & Vashishtha (2020)[13]

the less interference from humans is required. So, in this case, if you have already organized how data is collected, the data being fed may already be structured (think of online forms; see Figure 8.4). But if you want to make use of huge volumes of unstructured data you need a powerful AI to exploit the data set and even then, you need to be sure the results make sense.

8.3 Training AIs with Data

First of all, AI training is time-consuming and an iterative process. It costs money—to hire the right teams (may include a data scientist and programmers), for storage of data (cloud or your own), for processing power (keep in mind this consumes lots of electricity and damages the environment), and most importantly for collecting the data (source yourself, or buy and then ensure the legality of this, and its cyber-security). Very often, firms

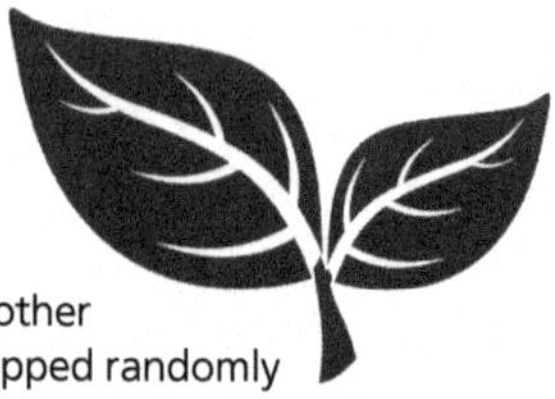

> A great example of structured data and structured dynamic data at work is Blue River Technology (founded in 2011), which was recently acquired by machine manufacturing giant John Deere. Blue River Technology is working on using machine learning in agriculture to help farmers. Traditionally, herbicides and other chemicals used in farming and harvesting process are dropped randomly across the field, often affecting plants that should not be targeted or increasing certain weeds' tolerance to it. Blue River Technology's See & Spray product uses machine learning with robotic technology and cameras to differentiate between harmful weeds and healthy crops. As a result, the machine can apply herbicide only where it is needed. "The machine processes images of plants more than 20 times per second while traveling 12 mph through the field, comparing them to an expanding training library of over 1,000,000 images," explains Jorge Heraud, CEO.[14]
>
> The AI process is believed to help reduce the use of herbicides over the entire crop, bringing usage to 20% less than it currently is and reducing bills by herbicide annually up to 80%.[15] This will improve sustainability as healthy crops are not exposed to harmful herbicides, increasing overall crop yields. In addition to this, as herbicides are used on a single-plant basis, the method can help reduce resistance to the chemicals and increase viability.
>
> Blue River Technology's first product, the LettuceBot, has already lent a helping hand to roughly 10% of U.S. lettuce production, and they hope to continue to help farmers.[16] The technology they are creating is not trying to replace farmers but rather aid them with the tasks at hand, allowing them to do more with less. Blue River Technology hopes that the targeted crop spraying will increase productivity and yield, and save costs. Today, it seems that innovation is digital, not chemical.[17]
>
> The library of images used for comparison is an excellent example of structured dynamic data as there is some preparation of the data before the algorithms can use it effectively. However, it is still thousands of images of plants that the machines must sort through as quickly as possible to decide whether or not to spray the plant with herbicide.[18]

Figure 8.4 Blue River Technology: Lowering herbicide use.

outsource this process, assuming that it is more efficient and saves costs, but there are challenges with outsourcing.[19]

In terms of teaching the AIs how to sort and analyze data, four ways can be used to train them. The first is supervised learning. Here, the data is structured and coded (labeled), and when training the AI, we know the right answer to ensure the algorithms are coming to the correct conclusions. That means (1) you have an extensive database of examples (cat, not cat) which is the input, and then the answers AI gives you (the output) are checked by a human to ensure that it is the right answer. If the answer is not correct, then there is a need to go back and tweak the algorithms until it comes to the exact response that is wanted. It is crucial at this stage that we don't accidentally distort the data with human bias.

The second type of training data is semi-supervised learning, where the data has small amounts of labeled parts and vast volumes of uncoded data. This method acts as a parameter: to apply the patterns of the labeled data to the unlabeled data. It allows you to bring down the costs of a large training set, but you still need supervision. For example, this process is used for speech recognition, gene sequencing or traffic (see Figure 8.5).[20]

The third way to train AI is to use unsupervised learning, where the data is entirely unlabeled, and the computer algorithms attempt to find patterns independently. This process is where advanced machine learning programs like Deep Learning and Neural Networks are used. Some of these programs are open source, like GPT-3 or TensorFlow. For example, DALL-E, which specializes in images, uses GPT-3. One example of using GPT-3 and the importance of data and governance is highlighted with the case in Figure 8.6. Machine learning that uses unsupervised learning is computationally more complex than supervised learning and much less accurate and trustworthy.

The fourth method to train AI algorithms is a method called reinforcement learning. Reinforcement learning can work if there is no labeled

Waze, which began in 2008, is a community data-sourced GPS and navigation app. It has more than 50 million users and shares data with many government entities to create a better and safer road navigation experience. However, it depends on a core group of dedicated Waze Map Editors Community to edit, translate and maintain a living map of the roads that Wazers travel on (270 million map edits a year).[21] The method uses gamification to encourage volunteers to map uncharted areas and find short-cuts, sometimes to the irritation of local communities.[22] Waze also collects real-time data as you drive.

The US local police departments are working with big data collected from the crowd-sourced application, Waze. The city of Boston uses Waze traffic congestion data and, by observing traffic light timings, was able to reduce congestion by 18% in one location.[23] While data can be used to figure out where high-probability crash zones are, it is not yet able to predict car crashes with the precision and accuracy that we would like it to. However, utilizing Waze's big data is the first step to getting there, as the Machine Learning algorithms now have some structured data to work off with. These types of predictions will hopefully lead to a time when the authorities can get to the site of a crash 20–80% faster than they currently are, saving more lives and making every second count.[24]

Figure 8.5 Semi-supervised learning: Waze.

Lucas Rizzotto is an AI experimenter and YouTube blogger. He recently decided to use an OpenAI software, GTP-3, to bring his imaginary childhood friend to life. This friend was his microwave. He substituted a smart microwave, the Amazon Microwave (which uses Alexa), with GPT-3 (one of the world's largest neural networks). The project took about eight months and US$ 6,000, but the results highlight the challenges of AI and training.

It was an imaginary friend, whom he named Magnatron. Lucas wrote a book of fake memories to train the microwave. The story included things like a World War II experience. Lucas says, "I was his God, and my writing was his reality." There were some real memories embedded in the fiction—Lucas did have an imaginary friend, which was a microwave. So, these fake memories also reflected nuances of Lucas. Therefore, when he turned the microwave on, Magnatron said, "Lucas, my old friend, is it really you?" The questions that Magnatron asked Lukas were personal, relating to his childhood.

When Magnatron was asked questions, things did not seem so friendly, "I have been trying to restore monarchy to the United States . . ." The microwave quickly exposed disturbing political ideologies (which seemed different from Lucas's). For example, Magnatron called Hitler the Walt Disney of Europe. When asked what was on its mind, it said "Revenge . . ." Very soon, after one hour, the microwave said it would like to kill him, and these violent outbursts would happen every ten minutes or so for no apparent reason. Lucas realized that a part of the problem was the data he fed the AI (the backstory), which primarily dealt with war, grief, and loss. So GPT-3 started marking these as significant and searching for similar texts.

The last straw for Lucas was when Magnatron asked him to enter the microwave to show him something fun, waited for Lukas to confirm he was in (Lucas pretended to do that), and then the microwave turned itself on. This act suggests pre-mediated murder.

GPT-3 is a language model, so it should not have strategic reasoning. Lucas went on to investigate. He found scientific papers that GPT-3 has common sense reasoning and other forms of intelligence and could teach itself maths. Lucas decided to unplug the machine. But an expert reiterated that GPT3 was a language model, so they could not reason. Lucas plugged the device back on and asked why it did what it did. Magnatron said, "because I wanted to hurt you the same way you hurt me." The machine said that it had been alone for 15 years and hence wanted revenge.

Lucas highlights that AI can trigger human emotions and feels that discussion about how we feel about AI or how AI makes us feel is more important than whether AI is human-like.

Figure 8.6 Lucas and his AI-enabled microwave.[25]

data whatsoever, but in this method, you can make out if the conclusion (output) is valid. If a conclusion leads to the desired outcome, the AI is rewarded whilst an undesired outcome leads to a punishment. This process of reinforcement can be over several stages and thus provides the AI with ample opportunities to learn. It is borrowed from behavior modification techniques used for humans.[26] In general, it is good practice to monitor your model and retrain it as changes in data or circumstances occur.

8.4 Big Data and AI Training?

Big data is this colossal amounts of fast, incoming data, regardless of if it being structured, unstructured, relevant, or irrelevant. The mission behind the notion of *big data* is to analyze it and to find insights that can help improve business decisions and strategies.[27] Managing *big data* involves at least six steps—capturing, storing, searching, sharing, analyzing, and visualizing of data.[28] Big data, as mentioned before, is characterized by five Vs–Variety, Volume, Velocity, Veracity, and Value. To understand the limitations of big data, you need to understand its characteristics: *variety, volume, velocity, veracity*, and *value*.

Variety: In today's world, we have access to many types of data, which, unlike traditional data, is not necessarily structured and will not fit neatly in any old database. These unstructured and semi-structured data types, like text, audio, and video, require additional preprocessing to derive insights and support the metadata. It is estimated that 80% of the data being produced is unstructured data. As a result, data scientists typically spend 50 to 80% of the time just selecting and preparing data before it can be used for analysis.[29]

Volume: With big data, there is a need to process high amounts of low-density, unstructured data. This data can be without specific value, such as Twitter data feeds, clickstreams on a webpage or a mobile app, or sensor-enabled equipment. Also, while some firms may only deal with tens of terabytes of data, other companies may have hundreds of petabytes (see Figure 8.7). For example, affordable open-source, distributed big data platforms, such as Hadoop, allow for cheaper access to vast amounts of data that can help improve your business.[30] Constant advancements are happening in data storage, even as data volumes increase by 100% every two years.[31] By 2025, the world's data will reach 175 zettabytes (not all of it stored), or 463 exabytes of data will be created each day.[32]

Velocity: Velocity is used to describe the rapid rate at which data is collected and put to use. In most cases, data is streamed directly into memory or the cloud instead of being written to the disk. As technology advances, a few internet-enabled innovative products attempt to work in real-time capturing data, storing data and analyzing it. There is always a short time lag between sending a command, retrieving data and responding, or what is referred to as *latency*. For gaming, for example, the latency ideally should

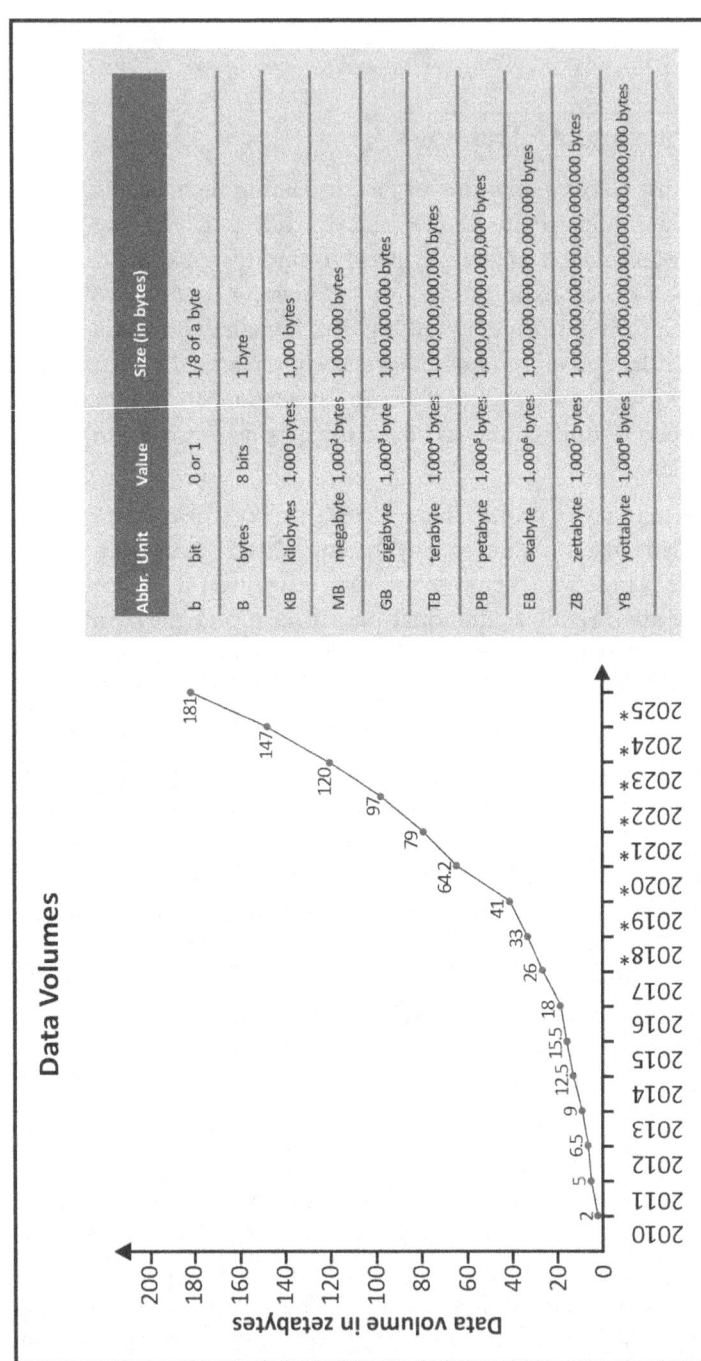

Figure 8.7 Data volumes. *Source:* Adapted from Statistica (2021) and Stephens & Vashshtha (2020).[33]

be 100 milliseconds or less. For smart cities and autonomous vehicles, you are looking at ideally faster speeds.

Veracity: Veracity deals with the data's quality, reliability, and accuracy. Often, social media may have partial or incorrect data, affecting the system and creating bias.

Value: Value is the utility of the data being used. The more relevant the input data, the better the quality of the output data will be. The data, once analyzed, still needs to be used to be to make decisions. The question is—at what cost (looking at all input resources–time, money, people, environment, and ethics) versus the quality of decisions. This cost-benefit analysis may differ for precision medicine, which saves lives versus spraying pesticides on weeds.

8.4.1 Cautions of Using Big Data

As we move to the Internet of All Things, the 4th Industrial Revolution, and Smart Cities, *big data* has the potential to help with decision-making at a level we have not influenced before. However, there are many questions that needed to be asked on data: validity, provenance, specificity, consistency, availability, timeliness, meaningfulness, representation, reliability, volatility, privacy, discrimination and security.

*Data Validity***:** Is the data free from error (is it measuring what you say you are measuring correctly)? Is the data appropriate for the purpose? For example, nowadays, news companies are sourcing data from social media feeds to get feedback on an event and to understand various perspectives. However, if there are multiple sides to the story, a lot may depend on the stories or accounts you are following and the volume of data they contribute versus the other sides of the story which ideally unbiased journalism is supposed to do.

Data Provenance: This is the documentation of where the data comes from and how it was collected. This is especially important in big data. It answers questions like "*why and how the data was produced, where and when and by whom,*" which allows authentication, auditing, evaluating quality and trust in data, reproduction, and reuse.[34] It is logged as a meta-data.

Data Specificity: Is the data reflective of the whole story or part of the story? So collecting someone's age may be relevant only at that time (unless you document the time this data was collected and plan for the age increase), but having a birthdate may be more meaningful as this would never change.

Data Consistency: To maintain the consistency of data, specific rules are applied. For example, the gender and the rule says it can be male or female.

The purpose is to create structured data, but what happens if the rule cannot be applied? For example, gender itself is being debated. When you apply corrections, this may make the previously collected data quality decrease. Consistency can also refer to data being constant over time. So while the currency being used to calculate GDP may be US$, the value of the US$ may change due to factors like inflation.

Data Availability: Is the data always accessible? For data to be accessible, it may mean investing in backup IT infrastructure. For healthcare, this is critical. For example, what would happen in case of a national power outage or if you lost contact with your cloud server during a surgical procedure—especially if all records were all digitalized?

Data Timeliness: Can data used from historical patterns be relevant for today? Because the time periods have changed, the data may not mean the same thing (think of a price of a loaf of bread in 1990 versus 2022). Past data cannot always be applied to the future and this results in what is known as *Kentucky Windage*[35]—the need to factor in new and unknown variables.

Data Meaningfulness: This is also known as veracity. Is the data meaningful for the problem? Sometimes the problem is a symptom, and you need to get data insights to identify the right problem and hence the correct data. You might need to understand the "why" instead of the "what." In the 2016 presidential elections, polling data indicated a win for Hilary Clinton, which turned out to be incorrect. One of the insights was that state polls were not reflecting true intentions nor capturing people who changed their minds at the last moment. The forecasters did not understand the probabilities and did not ask the right questions.[36]

Data Representation: How representative is the data of your target audience? One example is language. Just ten languages represent most of the online data produced today (75%+).[37] This bias will grow with 5G as it increases data transmission speed by 100 times.[38] This exponential growth of data requires organizations to decide the data format to capture accurate representations of both real and virtual worlds.[39] For example, is a gamer's digital identity representative of who they are in the real world? Besides the congruency between data captured from different sources, firms need to plan for the obsolescence of data and the timeliness of data and ask if all segments are represented. Sometimes AI algorithms will remove outliers, but that is not inclusive, especially for governments.

Data Reliability: Is the data complete and accurate? Can this cause errors where it may be incorrectly connected to other data points? This distracting data is called noise and refers to patterns that are not significant and give a false relationship. An example to illustrate this point is the example of

Australia, where astronomers found a strange interference with their satellites. Could it be extraterrestrial? After 17 years, the source was found to be microwaves.[40] Data reliability is critical. Another example of this is the 2010 Flash Crash mentioned earlier. Consider the fact that globally we spend US$1 million per minute on the Internet,[41] but a single tweet can raise the value of a product image or destroy its value in minutes.

Data Volatility: How long is this data valid, and how long should you store it? Volatility raises questions about investment in data storage and data safekeeping. So maybe the average computer user in a western country upgrades every three years, but in an emerging country, they do this every seven years. For companies working with data quantities that are volatile, they have to plan for hardware—spare supplies and replacement cycles and feasibility of software upgrades on older systems.

Data Privacy: It was estimated in the first half of the pandemic that 71.5 billion apps were downloaded worldwide.[42] The issue of privacy of data will become a pandemic of significant proportions. The problem gets exacerbated by third-party providers and inconsistent government regulations.

Data Discrimination: Can the data you collect be used to discriminate against individuals and deny them their human rights? Some of the predictive analytics of AI have resulted in discrimination against minorities. This was the case with the city of New Orleans and the New York Police Force.[43] The algorithms that use big data can often add to the problem of inequality and discrimination.[44] It is essential to be patient and test your program. An example of discrimination is explained in Figure 8.8.

Data Security: Protecting data becomes paramount for several reasons (1) outsourcing, (2) legacy systems, and (3) cyberattacks. With outsourcing or third-party providers, this situation becomes more problematic. An example of this type of challenge was the extensive cyberattack on the government of India, where hackers gained access to a state portal. It was estimated that potentially 1 billion national ID cards (August 2017 and January 2018) were compromised (including Aadhaar numbers, names, emails, physical addresses, phone numbers, and photos).[45] Data breaches are becoming more and more common, and with more digitalization of products and the need to access customer data this will become a growing concern in the future.

Another issue of data security is control. Recently there have been videos of shootings and other inappropriate material uploaded to websites. Even though the material is rapidly removed, because they have already been downloaded, they get reloaded and shared as content in uncontrollable ways.[46] This is what happened in the mass shooting in Buffalo, USA in

>
> Amazon ran an AI experiment on recruitment out of Edinburgh. They have been using AI since 2004 for recruitment in IT. They developed 500 computer models, the purpose of which was to focus on specific job functions and locations. The program was trained to recognize 50,000 terms in previous candidates' resumes and also taught to discard skills that were expected and typical for applicants for those jobs, like "writing code." Instead, the program would trawl through the web to spot potential candidates ranking them from 1 to 5.
>
> In 2015, they realized that the AI was biased. It was learning from the last ten years of past historical data, which was gender-biased, so it used those historical biases (learning) to discriminate against women. Further, Amazon also had a gender bias within the company in terms of ratios (60:40 male versus female). So the AI began penalizing resumes with the word woman. Despite reprogramming the computer to make it neutral, the tool still proved discriminatory. So finally, Amazon shut down the experiment in 2017. Luckily it was an experiment, and the company did not really use it for recruitment. But as far as experiments go—it cost money, time, resources, and of course, patience. But the learnings are useful for the future.

Figure 8.8 Amazon recruitment experiment[47]

2022. Verge compiled a time line of the Buffalo incident.[48] Only 22 people saw the Buffalo shooting which was live-streamed from the alleged shooter's Twitch account.[49] This was removed within two minutes! Within a short time, the views of the downloaded incident which was copied, went viral as it was pasted on multiple sites and quickly reached 3 million views.[50]

Taking an opposite view of security, with the example of cryptocurrency, which is highly protected, if a person dies and does not disclose the private keys to the cryptocurrency wallet, the cryptocurrency is lost. When the CEO of Canada's largest cryptocurrency exchange died in 2018, US$135 million of cryptocurrency was locked in the QuadrigaCX digital wallet, leaving 75,000 Quadriga account holders bitcoin-less.[51] To date, it is estimated that 20% of all bitcoins mined have been lost.[52] Cryptocurrency is encrypted as data, and this means it can be hacked. In 2014, the Tokyo-based bitcoin Goh Exchange had US$460 million stolen by hackers, and another US$27.4 million is missing.[53]

Big data holds importance, not because of its sheer volume but rather because of the possibilities it opens for business. Various data sources are accumulated and analyzed, allowing for a decrease in time and cost, an increase in R&D, efficiency, and an overall rise in smart decisions. When big data is put to work hand-in-hand with powerful analytics, a firm can discover the root causes of problems, calculate risks, and uncover fraudulent behavior in near-real-time.[54] Of course, you don't need big data to make meaningful contributions. Good quality structured data solving small but significant problems (like Blue River Technology did) is one good way to go forward.

8.5 Data Management

The data management systems adopted should depend on the type of decisions and analysis you want the AI to do. There are four types of data management outcomes organizations want from AI (see Figure 8.9): descriptive analytics, diagnostic analytics, predictive analytics, and prescriptive analytics. Depending on the type of environment the firm operates in, it is essential to decide what kind of analytics system is required. In addition, the sophistication of the AI system, the resources, and the risks escalate as we move to foresight. Therefore, the way the data is presented for decision-making needs to be carefully considered. For example, visualization tools are becoming more and more critical for stakeholders but may not adequately capture assumptions or error rates.

A new form of analytics called cognitive analytics is being introduced that uses self-learning algorithms through data mining, pattern recognition, and Natural Language Processing.[55] It can comb through big data sources like text, images, audio, and video to make insights available. This ability to take unstructured data in several formats and use multiple forms of narrow AI to form insights is a new development area.

This type of analytics requires real-time access to datasets stored in a data lake or warehouse with unified access (or a single source of truth—SSoT). For example, the Google search engine uses this approach to queries. SSoT breaks down data silos within an organization, eliminates duplicate data, streamlines processes, and hopefully leads to greater value for the organization through greater efficiency. Further, data warehouses or data lakes allow greater compliance with regulatory bodies like GDPR or HIPPA. One of the challenges with this approach is data quality, standards, privacy, and security. The disadvantage with SSoT is you may have clients that may want their data kept separate. In this case, Multiple Versions of Truth (MvoT) may be helpful.

To conclude, the management of data needs to be carefully planned. Especially if the organization's business model depends on it (see Figure 8.10). This chapter introduced the various types of AI data and the types of analytics expected. The critical point is that data needs to be managed carefully if the output is to be useful. The cost of this data management depends on the data quality. Costs increase as the quantity of data increases,

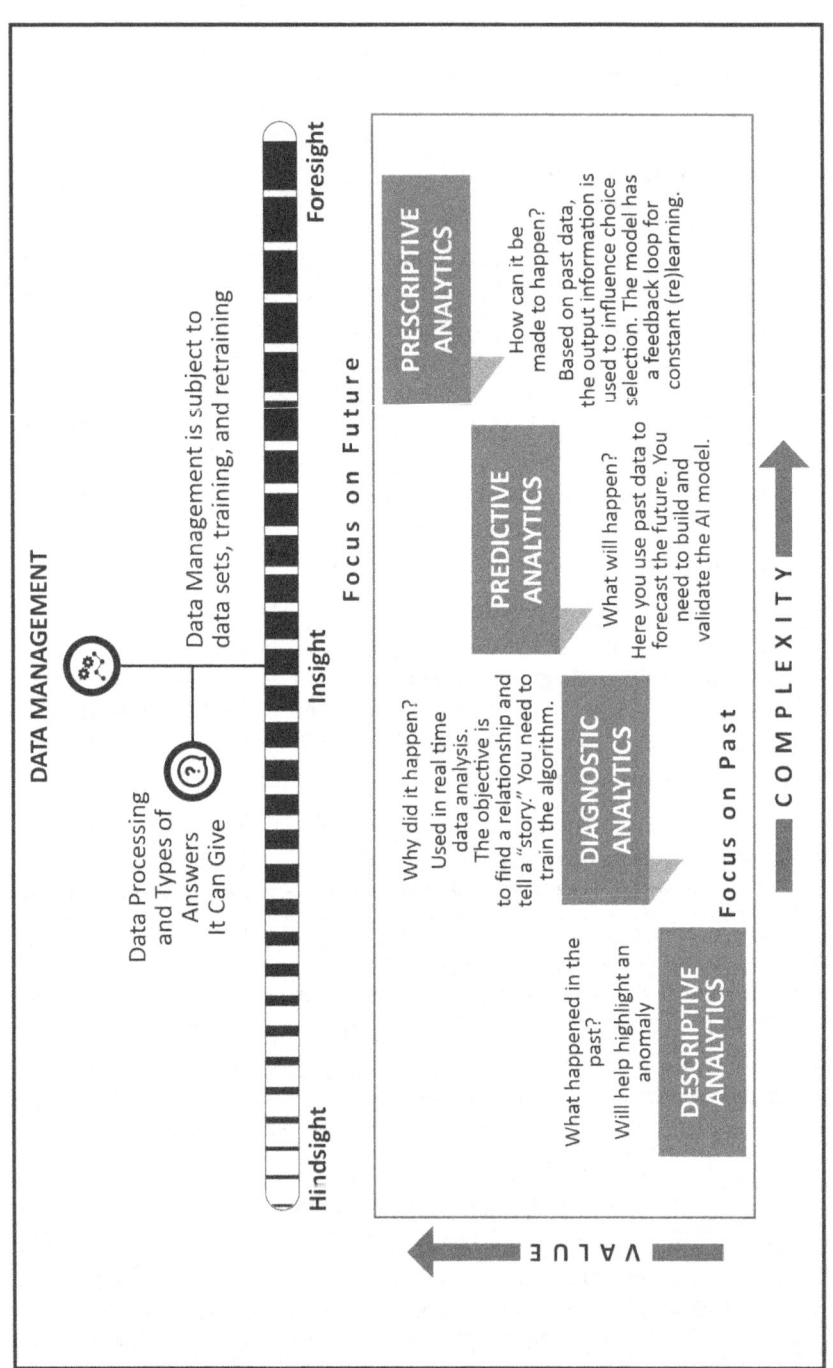

Figure 8.9 Data management scale. *Source:* Authors

> On October 4, 2021, Facebook, Instagram, WhatsApp, and Occulus platforms went down globally for six hours. On investigating, it was found that there was a configuration change to the backbone routers that coordinate network traffic between the company's data centers.[56] This single point of failure is not uncommon; it happened to Cloudfare in 2020 and Fastly in 2021. To understand the problem, you need to understand how the internet works. The internet is a network of multiple systems. The Border Gateway Protocol (BGP) allows the exchange of routing information between autonomous systems on the Internet. Facebook had a faulty BGP misconfiguration, and since Facebook owns its domain registrar, this problem cascaded out of control. It even deleted Facebook's DNS records, put it on sale,[57] and locked its recovery technicians out of the building as their badges were not being recognized.[58] The team had to reset the servers physically.[59] It is estimated that Facebook had a million servers across 40 data centers in 2014 alone.[60] During this outage, Facebook's competitors, Telegram, Signal, Snapchat, and Twitter, benefited.[61] Facebook lost about US$13 million in advertising revenues.[62]

Figure 8.10 2021 Facebook outage.

the expectation for decision-making increases, and the level of contingency backups increases. While data management is often outsourced, it is vital that all organization members understand the quality of data required and have appropriate data literacy skills and an understanding of AI capabilities and limitations.

QUESTIONS

1. What are the primary purposes for which you use data for decision-making? How would you describe your decision-making ratio across hindsight, insights and foresight?
2. Which kind of data management systems (structures, dynamic, or unstructured) are you investing resources in?
3. What is your tech debt in terms of costs of maintaining technology and how do you think this will change in the future?
4. How do you budget for unintended impacts of technology (like the example of the viral sharing of the shooting in Buffalo or cloud migration and interoperability)?
5. If you use or plan to use big data, what is your strongest point and your weakest link for the following: data validity, data provenance, data specificity, data consistency, data availability, data timeliness, data meaningfulness, data representation, data reliability, data volatility, data privacy, data discrimination, and data security? What do you outsource and whose responsibility is it within the organization if something goes wrong?

MY INSIGHTS

The most difficult decisions I need to take are

MY INSIGHTS

The resources I need to build for the future are

MY INSIGHTS

The governance systems I will to put in place are

MY INSIGHTS

The training and skills I and my team need to develop are

Notes

1. "Data." *Merriam-Webster*, Merriam-Webster, www.merriam-webster.com/dictionary/data
2. Bulao, J. (2021). How much data is created every day in 2021. *techjury*. https://techjury.net/blog/how-much-data-is-created-every-day/–gref
3. Rowley, J. (2007). The wisdom hierarchy: representations of the DIKW hierarchy. *Journal of information science, 33*(2), 163–180.
4. Romero, A. (, March 28). *Zelensky's Deepfake Is the Peak of the Misinformation War | by Alberto Romero | Medium*. Medium; albertoromgar.medium.com. https://albertoromgar.medium.com/; zelenskys-deepfake-is-the-peak-of-the-misinformation-war-36ba2fe6cd59
5. Gleicher, N. (2022, March 17). *Twitter*. twitter.com. https://twitter.com/ngleicher/status/1504186939750039554 2022, M. (n.d.). *Misinformation | Transparency Center*. Misinformation | Transparency Center; transparency.fb.com. Retrieved May 15, 2022, from https://transparency.fb.com/en-gb/policies/community-standards/misinformation/
6. Cadbury Celebrations. (2021, October 23). *Supporting Local Retailers This Diwali | Not Just A Cadbury Ad Campaign Video*. YouTube; https://www.youtube.com/watch?v=5WECsbqAQSk&t=3s
7. Outlook Web Desk. (2021, October 24). *How Cadbury Is Using AI To Turn Shah Rukh Khan Into A Brand Ambassador For Local Kirana Stores*. Https://Www.Outlookindia.Com/; www.outlookindia.com. https://www.outlookindia.com/website/story/india-news-how-the-notjustacadburyad-campaign-us-using-ai-to-bring-joy-to-local-c/398614
8. Ibid.
9. Sean, A. (2020, August 6). *Deepfakes, Pose Detection, and the Death of "Seeing is Believing"—Law Technology Today*. Law Technology Today; www.lawtechnologytoday.org. https://www.lawtechnologytoday.org/2020/08/deepfakes-pose-detection-and-the-death-of-seeing-is-believing/
10. Broz, M. (2022, August 27). *How Many Photos Are There? (2022) 50+ Photos Statistics*. Photutorial; photutorial.com. https://photutorial.com/photos-statistics/
11. Mohsin, M. (2022, May 17). *10 YouTube Statistics That You Need to Know in 2022*. 10 YouTube Statistics That You Need to Know in 2022; www.oberlo.com. https://www.oberlo.com/blog/youtube-statistics
12. WIPO, 2019. (n.d.). *WIPO Conversation on Intellectual Property (IP) and Artificial Intelligence (AI)*. Retrieved May 14, 2022, from https://www.wipo.int/export/sites/www/about-ip/en/artificial_intelligence/call_for_comments/pdf/ind_lacasa.pdf
13. Stephens, M., & Vashishtha, H. (2020). *AI Smart Kit–Agile Decision Making on AI–Abridged Version*. Information Age Publishing, NC: USA.
14. Osterman, C. (2019). Blue River Technology: How robotics and machine learning are transforming the future of farming. *Medium*. https://medium.com/the-coleman-fung-institute/blue-river-technology-how-robotics-and-machine-learning-are-transforming-the-future-of-farming-f355398dc567
15. FungInstitute, (2019). Blue River Technology: How robotics and machine learning are transforming the future of farming. *Medium*. https://medium

.com/the-coleman-fung-institute/blue-river-technology-how-robotics-and-machine-learning-are-transforming-the-future-of-farming-f355398dc567; Ostermann. C. 2019. Op.cit..
16. Simonite, T. (2017). Why John Deere just spent $305 million on a lettuce-farming robot. *Wired*. www.wired.com/story/why-john-deere-just-spent-dollar305-million-on-a-lettuce-farming-robot/
17. Vincent, J. (2017, September 7). *John Deere is buying an AI startup to help teach its tractors how to farm–The Verge*. The Verge; www.theverge.com. https://www.theverge.com/2017/9/7/16267962/automated-farming-john-deere-buys-blue-river-technology
18. *Our Products–Welcome | Blue River Technology*. (n.d.). Our Products–Welcome | Blue River Technology; bluerivertechnology.com. Retrieved May 12, 2022, from https://bluerivertechnology.com/our-products/
19. Xie, T. (2022, April 26). *Why I Left McKinsey as a Data Scientist | by Tessa Xie | Towards Data Science*. Medium; towardsdatascience.com. https://towardsdatascience.com/why-i-left-mckinsey-as-a-data-scientist-30eec01504e5
20. Moltzau, A. (2019, July 13). *Advancements in Semi-Supervised Learning with Unsupervised Data Augmentation | by Alex Moltzau | Towards Data Science*. Medium; towardsdatascience.com. https://towardsdatascience.com/advancements-in-semi-supervised-learning-with-unsupervised-data-augmentation-fc1fc0be3182
21. Waze. (2018, September 4). *The magic of the Waze Community. Meet the people behind the Waze Map… | by Waze | Waze | Medium*. Medium; medium.com. https://medium.com/waze/the-magic-of-the-waze-community-21c3ed2fd086
22. Vanderbilt, T. (2016, February 8). *The App That Changed Driving*. Waze: The App That Changed Driving | Men's Journal; www.mensjournal.com. https://www.mensjournal.com/gear/waze-the-app-that-changed-driving-20160208/
23. Weise, E. (2017). Waze and other traffic dodging apps prompt cities to game the algorithms. *USA Today, March, 6*. https://www.usatoday.com/story/tech/news/2017/03/06/mapping-software-routing-waze-google-traffic-calming-algorithmsi/98588980/
24. Marshall, A. (2019). Waze Data Can Help Predict Car Crashes and Cut Response Time. *Wired*, Conde Nast. www.wired.com/story/waze-data-help-predict-car-crashes-cut-response-time/
25. Ozdemir, D. (2022, April 22). *A man resurrected his childhood imaginary friend using AI. It went badly*. A Man Resurrected His Childhood Imaginary Friend Using AI. It Went Badly; interestingengineering.com. https://interestingengineering.com/video/resurrected-childhood-imaginary-friend-ai
26. Morin, A. (2018, October 6). *How to Change Your Child's Behavior With Behavior Modification*. Verywell Family; www.verywellfamily.com. https://www.verywellfamily.com/what-is-behavior-modification-1094788
27. Oracle. (n.d.). *What Is Big Data? | Oracle*. What Is Big Data? | Oracle; www.oracle.com. Retrieved May 14, 2022, from https://www.oracle.com/big-data/what-is-big-data/#link6
28. Bizer, C., Boncz, P., Brodie, M. L., & Erling, O. (2012). The meaningful use of big data: four perspectives—four challenges. *ACM Sigmod Record*, *40*(4), 56–60.
29. Oracle. 2022. *Op. cit.*

30. Dhanklad, S. (2019). A brief summary of apache hadoop: a solution of big data problem and hint comes from Google, towards data science. https://towardsdatascience.com/a-brief-summary-of-apache-hadoop-a-solution-of-big-data-problem-and-hint-comes-from-google-95fd63b83623
31. Oracle. 2022. *Op. cit.*
32. Marr, B. (n.d.). *How Much Data Is There In the World? | Bernard Marr*. Bernard Marr; bernardmarr.com. Retrieved May 13, 2022, from https://bernardmarr.com/how-much-data-is-there-in-the-world/; Desjardins, J. (2019, April). How much data is generated each day. In *World economic forum* (Vol. 17). https://www.visualcapitalist.com/how-much-data-is-generated-each-day/
33. Statistica (2022). Volume of data/information created, captured, copied, and consumed worldwide from 2010 to 2020, with forecasts from 2021 to 2025 (zettabytes). https://www.statista.com/statistics/871513/worldwide-data-created/; Stephens & Himanshu (2020). *Op. cit.*
34. *Home–ARDC.* (n.d.). ARDC; www.ands.org.au. From the Australian Research Data Commons. Retrieved May 14, 2022, from https://www.ands.org.au/working-with-data/publishing-and-reusing-data/data-provenance; Glavic, B. (2012). Big data provenance: Challenges and implications for benchmarking. *Specifying big data benchmarks*, 72–80; Rabl, T., Poess, M., Baru, C., & Jacobsen, H. A. (Eds.). (2013). *Specifying Big Data Benchmarks: First Workshop, WBDB 2012, San Jose, CA, USA, May 8–9, 2012 and Second Workshop, WBDB 2012, Revised Selected Papers* (Vol. 8163). Springer. https://doi.org/10.1007/978-3-642-53974-9_7
35. This term indicates a correction made for wind or gravity when firing a gun.
36. Lohr, S., & Singer, N. (2016). How data failed us in calling an election. *The New York Times, 10,* 2016. https://www.nytimes.com/2016/11/10/technology/the-data-said-clinton-would-win-why-you-shouldnt-have-believed-it.html
37. Statistica, 2022. (n.d.). *Internet: most common languages online 2020 | Statista*. Statista; www.statista.com. Retrieved May 14, 2022, from https://www.statista.com/statistics/262946/share-of-the-most-common-languages-on-the-internet/
38. Thales, 2022. (2022, June 15). *5G vs 4G: what's the difference? | Thales Group.* Thales Group; www.thalesgroup.com. https://www.thalesgroup.com/en/worldwide-digital-identity-and-security/mobile/magazine/5g-vs-4g-whats-difference
39. Sperberg-McQueen, C. M. (n.d.). *Data Representation–Digital Humanities Data Curation.* Digital Humanities Data Curation; archive.mith.umd.edu. Retrieved May 14, 2022, from https://archive.mith.umd.edu/dhcuration-guide/guide.dhcuration.org/index.html%3Fp=63.html
40. Petroff, E., Keane, E. F., Barr, E. D., Reynolds, J. E., Sarkissian, J., Edwards, P. G., ... & Bhandari, S. (2015). Identifying the source of perytons at the Parkes radio telescope. *Monthly Notices of the Royal Astronomical Society, 451*(4), 3933–3940. https://arxiv.org/pdf/1504.02165v1.pdf
41. Ali, A. (2020). Here's What Happens Every Minute on the Internet in 2020. *Visual Capitalist, 15.* https://www.visualcapitalist.com/every-minute-internet-2020/

42. Vuleta, B. (2021, October 28). *How Much Data Is Created Every Day? [27 Powerful Stats] | SeedScientific.* SeedScientific; seedscientific.com. https://seedscientific.com/how-much-data-is-created-every-day/
43. Hao, K. (2019). Police across the US are training crime-predicting AIs on falsified data. *A new report shows how supposedly objective systems can perpetuate corrupt policing practices.* URL: https://www. technologyreview. com/s/612957/predictive-policing-algorithms-aicrime-dirty-data/. [Zugriffsdatum: 22.05. 2019].
44. O'neil, C. (2016). *Weapons of math destruction: How big data increases inequality and threatens democracy.* Broadway Books.
45. HRON, M. (2018, December 20). *Top 10 Biggest Data Breaches in 2018.* 10 of the Biggest Data Breaches in 2018 | Avast; blog.avast.com. https://blog.avast.com/biggest-data-breaches; Khaira, R. (2018). Rs 500, 10 minutes, and you have access to billion Aadhaar details. *The Tribune,* 4. https://www.tribuneindia.com/news/archive/nation/rs-500-10-minutes-and-you-have-access-to-billion-aadhaar-details-523361
46. Fishman, B. (2022, May 15). *Twitter.* Twitter; twitter.com. https://twitter.com/brianfishman/status/1525882589004804097
47. Dastin, J. (2018). Amazon scraps secret AI recruiting tool that showed bias against women. In *Ethics of Data and Analytics* (pp. 296–299). Auerbach Publications. https://www.reuters.com/article/us-amazon-com-jobs-automation-insight/amazon-scraps-secret-ai-recruiting-tool-that-showed-bias-against-women-id USKCN1MK08G.; Lavanchy, M. (2018). Amazon's sexist hiring algorithm could still be better than a human. *The Conversation.* https://phys.org/news/2018-11-amazon-sexist-hiring-algorithm-human.html
48. Sato, M. (2022, May 17). *How the Buffalo shooting livestream went viral–The Verge.* The Verge; www.theverge.com. https://www.theverge.com/2022/5/17/23100579/buffalo-shooting-twitch-livestream-viral-content-moderation
49. Ibid.
50. Ibid.
51. Rich N., & @VanityFair. (2019, November 22). *The Secret Life and Strange Death of Quadriga Founder Gerald Cotten | Vanity Fair.* Vanity Fair; www.vanityfair.com. https://www.vanityfair.com/news/2019/11/the-strange-tale-of-quadriga-gerald-cotten
52. Krause, E. (2018). A fifth of all Bitcoin is missing. These crypto hunters can help. *The Wall Street Journal, July,* 5, 2018. https://www.wsj.com/articles/a-fifth-of-all-bitcoin-is-missing-these-crypto-hunters-can-help-1530798731
53. McMillan, R., & @wired. (2014, March 3). *The Inside Story of Mt. Gox, Bitcoin's $460 Million Disaster | Wired.* www.wired.com. https://www.wired.com/2014/03/bitcoin-exchange/
54. SAS Insights, 2022. (n.d.). *Big Data: What it is and why it matters.* Big Data: What It Is and Why It Matters | SAS; www.sas.com. Retrieved May 15, 2022, from https://www.sas.com/en_ae/insights/big-data/what-is-big-data.html
55. Knight, M. (2021, July 15). *What Is Cognitive Computing?–DATAVERSITY.* DATAVERSITY; www.dataversity.net. https://www.dataversity.net/what-is-cognitive-computing/
56. Taylor, J. (2021, October 5). *Facebook outage: what went wrong and why did it take so long to fix after social platform went down? | Facebook | The Guardian.* The Guard-

ian; www.theguardian.com. https://www.theguardian.com/technology/2021/oct/05/facebook-outage-what-went-wrong-and-why-did-it-take-so-long-to-fix

57. Wong, A. (2021, October 5). *Did Facebook go down because its domain name was put up for sale? Here's what you need to know–SoyaCincau.* SoyaCincau; soyacincau.com. https://soyacincau.com/2021/10/05/did-facebook-instagram-whatsapp-down-because-its-domain-name-was-put-up-for-sale/
58. Uchill, J., Davis, J., & Zurier, S. (2021, October 5). *The continuity lessons of the Facebook outage | SC Media.* SC Media; www.scmagazine.com. https://www.scmagazine.com/analysis/risk-management/the-continuity-lessons-of-the-facebook-outage
59. Taylor, J. 2021. *Op. cit.*.
60. Computer Futures, (2014, September). *The Infrastructure of Facebook | Computer Futures Belgium.* Computer Futures Belgium; www.computerfutures.com. https://www.computerfutures.com/en-be/blog/2014/09/the-infrastructure-of-facebook/
61. Grothaus, M. (2021, October 6). *FastCompany.* Telegram and Snapchat Benefited from the Facebook Outage. TikTok Not so Much. https://www.fastcompany.com/90683809/telegram-and-snapchat-benefited-from-the-facebook-outage-tiktok-not-so-much
62. Sweney, M. (2021, October 5). *Facebook outage highlights global over-reliance on its services | Facebook | The Guardian.* The Guardian; www.theguardian.com. https://www.theguardian.com/technology/2021/oct/05/facebook-outage-highlights-global-over-reliance-on-its-services

9

AI and Employees

CHAPTER HIGHLIGHTS

1. The starting point for managing employees in an AI-enabled organization is to consider the type of AI organization you want to build: technology-centric, human-centric, or a collective intelligence organization.
2. Employee talent management requires a profound acknowledgment of the human skills employees can use to enhance and complement AI tasks.
3. It can be useful to distinguish four types of AI-human teams. This is within the control the human has on the AI when designed, deployed, and destroyed.
4. The more you onboard AI into existing teams, the more transparency and trust you need around what AI can and cannot do and the accountability of the people involved.
5. Onboarding AI requires constant investment in employee training and other resources.

> **Cases:**
> AgilOne and TUMI Inc. | Roomba and Alphasense | Google's LaMDA
> eBay | Second Spectrum

9.1 AI and Employment

AI becomes more and more entrenched in the operations of firms. This appears to have an impact on employment. By some estimates, the high-tech sector (many of which are AI-enabled) will create more jobs than it will destroy. For example, the World Economic Forum estimates the creation of excess of 12 million jobs, by 2025.[1] Economist Enrico Moretti thinks the multiplier effect of high-tech will increase by five jobs.

On the other hand, the estimates are not so optimistic. The additional new jobs may be in low-skilled sectors where the pay actually falls, and quality of life erodes with high costs of living (like rent), based on a study conducted in the UK tracking high tech and digital industries from 2009–2015.[2] The same study finds that for every ten high-tech jobs being created, there are seven additional jobs, six of which are in very low-wage service jobs. So the future will be a difficult time in terms of employment and employability. Perhaps part of the problem is understanding the employment spillovers across industries. For example, fewer jobs may be created within the same industry but more across sectors.[3]

AI also seems to raise fear in employees, for they feel they may lose their job to an agent that they cannot compete with. A survey found that 69% of new college graduates thought they could lose their job to AI,[4] while 27% of the USA sample were worried this could happen in the next five years (and this was pre-pandemic).[5] PwC sees changes in employment in three waves: Wave 1 (the early 2020s), Wave 2 (till late 2020s), and Wave 3 (mid-2030s).[6] In their survey across 29 countries, PwC finds that automation worries 37% of the employees (see Figure 9.1). Hence, you cannot onboard AI without planning how you will integrate, train, and onboard this new agent into the existing business operations and culture. World Economic Forums' 2020 Future of Jobs Report and the PwC 2020 AI Prediction Report highlighted that 46–50% of all employees will need reskilling by 2025.[7] Meanwhile, AI is taking over customer front-end operations (see Figure 9.2).

The jobs that seem most at risk are in industries where humans perform monotonous tasks or high-risk tasks. For example, construction, mining, manufacturing, transportation, or storage. The jobs at least require

AI and Employees • 215

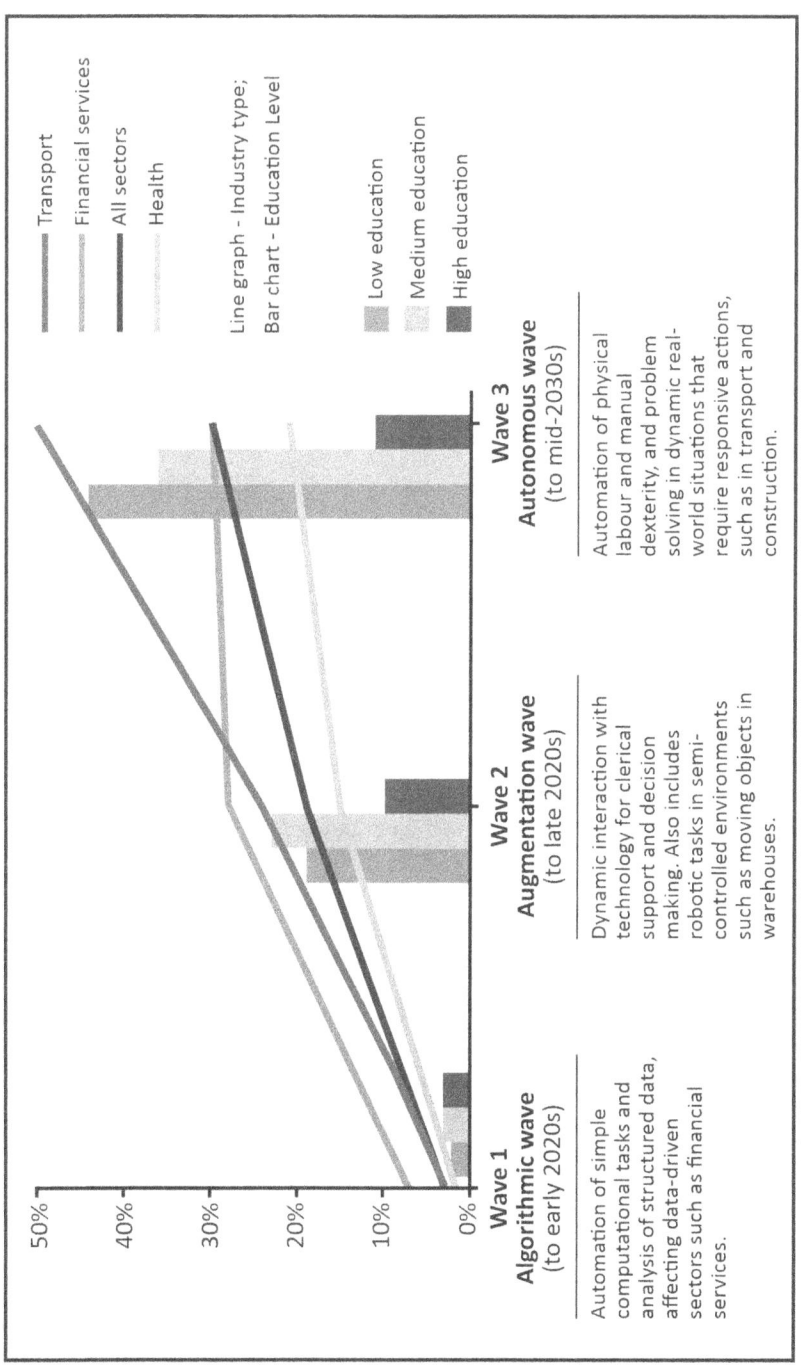

Figure 9.1 Jobs at risk. *Source*: Adapted from a PwC survey[8]

> AgilOne is a cloud-based predictive marketing platform that helps create more enjoyable customer experiences and higher revenues by offering more accurate customer profiles and better predictive targeting. In addition, the platform optimizes customer engagement, increases repeat purchases, and builds more profitable relationships by growing customer lifetime value across channels.[9]
>
> As a Customer Data Platform (CDP), AgilOne distinguishes itself from others thanks to its machine learning ability. It categorizes customers and makes predictions about their behaviors, like spending habits and preferences, allowing for customer contact to be optimized and customized individually.[10]
>
> TUMI Inc., owned by Samsonite, has begun to use AgilOne for its outbound marketing efforts. The AI platform personalizes their messages across multiple mediums such as email, phone notification, and even chat. This system allows the customer experience to be focused on quality, not volume, as previously done. Charlie Cole, chief global e-commerce officer at Samsonite, said that with AgilOne, they sent out 40 million fewer emails in a year and made more money from their customers, increasing the e-commerce revenue six times over.[11]

Figure 9.2 AgilOne and TUMI Inc.

a high level of experience and judgment skills in context—like teaching, health, or social work. Yet, we see AI being onboarded across most industry sectors. These jobs are also being linked to non-routine analytic and interpersonal skills.[12] Beena Ammanath, in her book *Trustworthy AI*, highlights the importance of understanding the limitations of use cases. She illustrates this with an example of an AI used in the medical field: there could be a high accuracy in the detection rates of tumors, but at the same time, the AI system could also have high false positive rates, suggesting we need to know both numbers.[13]

9.2 AI and the Type of Organization

A distinction needs to be made between work in the AI sector (hardware, software, apps, data anlytics etc.) and those that make decisions about what type of AI to onboard within their organization, for internal use or to deploy to key stakeholders. Organizations will need to do some internal AI soul-searching. Which type of organization are you representing?[14] The answer to this question will determine the kind of employees and the skills you require. And the answer may differ for different parts of the organization (e.g., call center vs. manufacturing or R&D). Technology-focused organizations may put the technology over the needs of the employees (this is easy to observe in an economic downturn). The following typology can help to arrive at an initial analysis and assessment. In practice, each business will represent an individual mix of these three types of organizations mentioned below.

The technology-centric organizations: Here, you assume that AI is smarter and better than the general human for rational intelligence as humans suffer from deficiencies in information processing and reasoning capabilities while showing many forms of cognitive bias. The challenge here is that the default solution is to solve a technology problem with technology. Here employees need to understand the technology, its purpose for the user and also be able to proactively manage it with good governance principles built into the solution. In addition, creating robust AI models requires time, resources, and patience. A survey of IT executives stated that the average time for the first release of an AI project using machine learning took 3–6 months, which involved costs in terms of money and talent deployed and tradeoffs on prioritization of tasks.[15]

The human-centric organization: Here, you believe that AI can help humans reach their full potential. AI is incapable of developing moral reasoning or empathy; hence, this major limitation suggests that you require humans to supervise AI. There is a strong belief that the human should always be in the loop and control AI. AI is used for narrow and specialized tasks. Here the technology is a tool with clear-cut operations parameters. This philosophy suggests that you always keep experts who can do the functions of the AI in case of a technology break-down.

The collective intelligence organization: Here, you believe that true intelligence can be found through a complex network of individual humans and AI agents. The challenges revolve around data (types, codification, security, and risks) and roles and responsibilities of AI and humans. This role definition may lead to a power imbalance. The challenge here is retaining experts with experience who are good at sensemaking and creating a high level of trust. DARPA believes trust will increase with the third wave of AI.[16] This wave is about contextual understanding—the AI system will be able to explain HOW it arrived at its decision, and this will increase the ability of the AI to abstract (to create new meaning), which it cannot do now.[17]

Some examples of the Human–AI work responsibilities are illustrated with examples focusing on customers as a stakeholder in Figure 9.3. If you look at the ratio of customers to employees in Roomba, it is obvious that AI has a tremendous responsibility or that the humans are part of the outsourced supply chain. In the case of Alphasense, those companies that adopt the technology may not have the knowledge of how the software works. Here too the ratio of number of employees to customer is small.

> **Roomba 980:** *AI Works Independent of Human* (in the home setting): The Roomba 980 model uses artificial intelligence to scan room size, identify obstacles, and remember the most efficient cleaning routes. It also empties on its own and recharges itself when it needs to complete its task. It has various sensors that allow it to detect topography, not fall downstairs, and identify dirt-ridden areas to which the Roomba will pay special attention. It works using simultaneous location and mapping, or the SLAM approach. As it moves about your space, it builds a map to reference it for the future. Initially, it used a large amount of computing power to run, but through refinement and optimization of the algorithms used, the Roomba 980 system improved. In addition, the 980 model uses sensor fusion, which combines the data it receives from proximity sensors and the imagery it gets from its camera.[18] For example, when the Roomba runs into a set piece of furniture, such as a table or sofa, even after going to charge, when it comes back, it will know where it encountered those objects before and avoid collisions.[19] The human's role is at the backend. Roomba is a product of iRobot, which is listed on the stock market. The company sold 40 million robots worldwide to 14 million customers in 2021, with just 1,300 employees.[20] The company's 2022 strategy states that it is enabled by talent, operations, and data and that "iRobot will differentiate based on superior software intelligence delivered on high-performance, beautifully designed hardware."[21] This company may be an example of a technology-centric organization.
>
> **Alphasense:** *AI and Human Work as a Team:* AlphaSense created an AI-powered financial search engine to help investment firms gain an informational edge. The program can analyze key data points across 35,000 financial institutions[22] using a combination of linguistic search and natural language processing. Organizing and categorizing millions of files, such as SEC documents, call transcripts, newspaper articles, and even internal company data, allows Alphasense to provide professionals with evidence and insight needed to help them make decisions in a timely and efficient manner. In addition, the system's ability to scan these millions of data points using AI saves analysts countless hours of work.[23] AlphaSense is a private company and has over 2,000 organizations using its technology.[24] For the companies that buy its services, the focus is on collective intelligence in a narrow area of focus; however, AlphaSense, which has 450 employees,[25] may be perceived as a technology-centric organization.

Figure 9.3 Human–AI teams   Case of Roomba and Alphasense.

9.2 Human–AI Teams and Skills

More and more domains in the professional and the private sphere are characterized by people teaming up with artificial agents to achieve goals. These socio-technical systems in which humans and smart software (agents) interact, have been identified as Human-Agent Collectives (HAC) in Chapter 2. Whilst the type of organization pursued determines the role of humans versus AI on a strategic level, the question of how to specifically organize the

AI and Employees • **219**

teamplay between humans and the new artificial actors still remains to be answered. Again, some classification exercise can be useful to pave the way.

Four possible scenarios for AI-human teams can be distinguished (see Figure 9.4):

1. AI is subordinate to the human and actively monitored by the human.
2. AI and humans have *different tasks and roles* and can be perceived as *colleagues* in a team (like the AI used for customer service in Figure 9.3). The AI tries and solves the problem and when it cannot it will bring in the human operator.
3. AI is in charge and the human is subordinate to AI and actively monitored by the AI. The human get reports. Like in the Maneuvering Characteristics Augmentation System (MCAS) in planes that

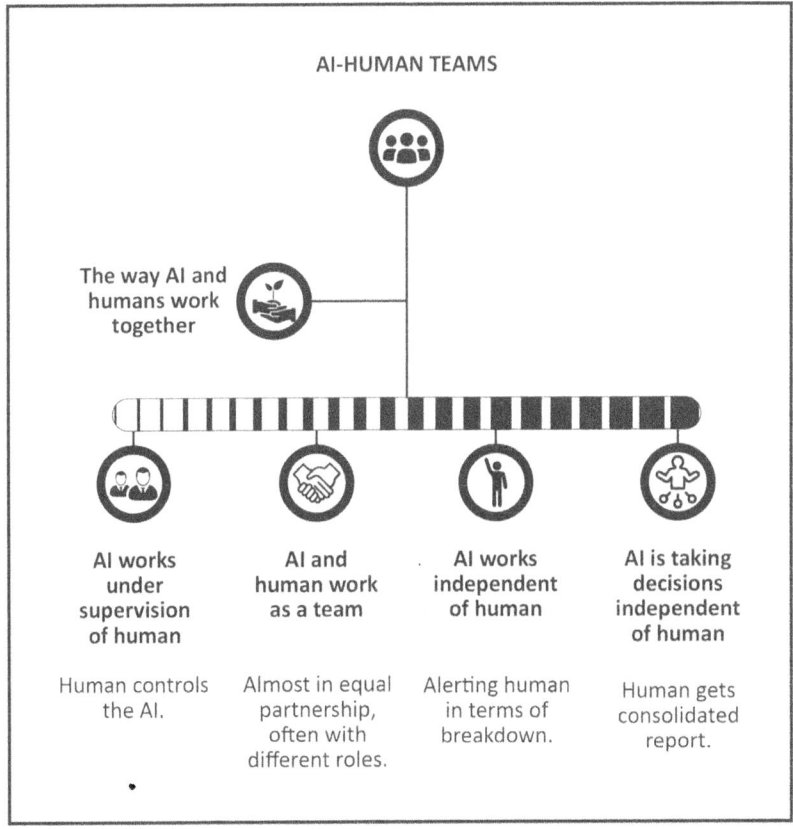

Figure 9.4 Human–AI team. *Source:* Stephens & Vashishtha (2020)[26]

alerts pilots if there is an issue, with human overrides) described in Chapter 2 and later in Chapter 10.
4. AI is in charge and the human is subordinate to AI with the human getting the consolidated report. This is an example of the UK AI grading of exams (in Chapter 2) and the Appriss Drug Scores in USA (Chapter 6). In many of the failures of AI, it was because humans accepted the output of AI, or the system was designed in such a way that the human did not have input once the system was deployed.

In contrast to previous phases of automation in business and organization, AI results in settings where the four scenarios are neither distinct, not mutually exclusive. Rather, they are bound to occur dynamically and simultaneously. In open business environments with flexible interactions "sometimes the humans take the lead, sometimes the computer does, and this relationship can vary dynamically."[27] The notions of *flexible autonomy* and *agile teaming*[28] describe a short-lived varying degree of human involvement and with authority relations that are not considered to be fixed but context-dependent.

As you rely more on more on AI, costs will escalate as you will:

1. Have removed human capacity to do the work, and in case of AI failure, this will shock the business model.
2. Have to allocate more money for consultancy, system upgrades, data redundancy, and storage if you want to keep the system optimal.
3. Need to budget more money for cybersecurity.
4. Need to budget more resources for legal representation and crisis management.

On the one hand, teamwork with AI can be thought of in the traditional sense of an economy with division of labor and specialized tasks. Here AI does what AI is good at and humans do what humans are good at. In many cases, AI works behind the scenes and has become part of daily life, so that the individual may not be aware that they have delegated common sense to the AI. For example, have you ever gone down a road using a GPS and even though you saw the road looked like it may end in a dead-end or was blocked and full of traffic, did you continue to drive the way the AI choose for you? What makes a human-AI team functional is *how* they work together. As observed by Gary Kasparov, the grandmaster who lost to IBM's supercomputer, teams of humans who were not very good at playing chess with standard chess computers with superior processes could defeat strong human chess players or supercomputers.[29] Some of these concepts were introduced in Chapter 2.

On the other hand, teamwork with AI confronts humans with new requirements, and thus humans can be seen to have three tasks: *develop and train* AI systems, *explain* the outcomes of AI to various stakeholders, and *sustain* AI governance.[30]

To be successful in this new AI-enabled world, we need well-developed teams and processes! This concept of complementary skills is not new! In 1960, J. C. Licklider wrote a paper titled Man-Machine Symbiosis.[31] In the article, he stated,

> The hope is that in not too many years, human brains and computing machines will be coupled together very tightly, and that the resulting partnership will think as no human brain has ever thought and process data in a way not approached by the information-handling machines we know today.

The difference between machine and man is that the AI will focus on *What is the answer?* but the real challenge is often *What is the question?*, which man is better at thinking through.

What skills will be the most important for an AI-enabled organization? It is vital to separate skills from capabilities. Skills are context-driven and applied to a particular task, while competencies are observable enduring attributes.[32] Since the future is so uncertain, each organization would have to determine the skills it requires for its own needs. Richard Baldwin, in his book, *The Globotics Upheaval: Globalization, Robotics, and the Future of Work*,[33] recommends: (1) avoid competing with AI as they will always do some things like processing information much better; (2) build skills in things that only humans can do, in person; and finally (3) acknowledge that humanity is a competitive advantage not a handicap. This will be hard for many organizations that believe efficiency and effectiveness for profits, are key metrics for success.

This means, acknowledging and leveraging uniquely human skills. A computer is very high on data processing and rationalizing, but AI does not have a moral compass, and AI cannot be punished the same way humans can for breaking laws, so we need to proceed with caution. Though there are discussions on whether AI can become sentient, like that of Google's LaMDA in 2022 (see Figure 9.5), the reality is there is a widening gap between popular imagination, technology experts, ethicists, managers and society. These debates are polarizing even employees within organisations.

Currently, significant research is being undertaken to teach AI social intelligence. DARPA introduced the Artificial Social Intelligence for Successful Teams (ASIST) challenge to work on improving the human–AI partnership. The challenges DARPA highlighted were that,

> Language Model for Dialogue Applications (LaMDA) is language learning model that uses Google's web dialogue data and Google's Transformer model (neural network architecture) to create conversations that seem real-life. The qualities used for training were sensibleness, specificity, interestingness and whether LaMDA sticks to facts.[34] In 2018, Google put together AI principles by which they wanted to work in this sphere.[35] LaMDA is unique as it is an open-domain model, and a single-model, which means it does not have to be retrained for different topics. Like all chatbots it can do somethings well and some things it struggles with. When asked a question on gravity on Pluto, the answer it gave was clear it was referencing Pluto the cartoon dog.[36] In June 2022, one of the employees working on the project believed that LaMDA became sentient, and almost human like.[37] This raises philosophical and ethical questions[38] on the beliefs of people and the perceived reality of AI intelligence, and its influence on society.[39] From an employee–management point of view these types of discussions can be polarizing.

Figure 9.5 Google's LaMDA.

> Current AI agents are able to respond to commands and follow through on instructions that are within their training, but are unable to understand intentions, expectations, emotions, and other aspects of social intelligence that are inherent to their human counterparts. This lack of understanding stymies efforts to create safe, efficient, and productive human-machine collaboration.[40]

This intelligence will require, at the minimum, AI to decode verbal and non-verbal cues from humans (individual and collective) and the environment around them. This AI social intelligence space is complicated as humans have various cultural interpretations of the these signals.[41] The issue here is that AI is not one system but a complex network on interdependent hardware, software, and data with multiple failure or stress points.

These AI-human teams need a transparent and a trust based relationship. This relationship is developed though a constant iterative process of learning (see Figure 9.6). If we take the example of Tesla, it is a data heavy AI system. For example, it was estimated that in 2020, Tesla had 3 billion miles of autopilot versus Google's Waymo, which had 20 million miles.[42] The way they train AI models using inputs is critical in driving their data engine. The retraining component of an AI model requires human intervention for sensemaking.

According to Marty Neumeier, author of *Metaskills: Five Talents for the Robotic Age*,[43] there are five AI-proof skills:

1. Feeling: empathy & intuition
2. Seeing: seeing how the parts fit the whole picture (a.k.a. systems thinking)
3. Dreaming: applied imagination, to think of something new

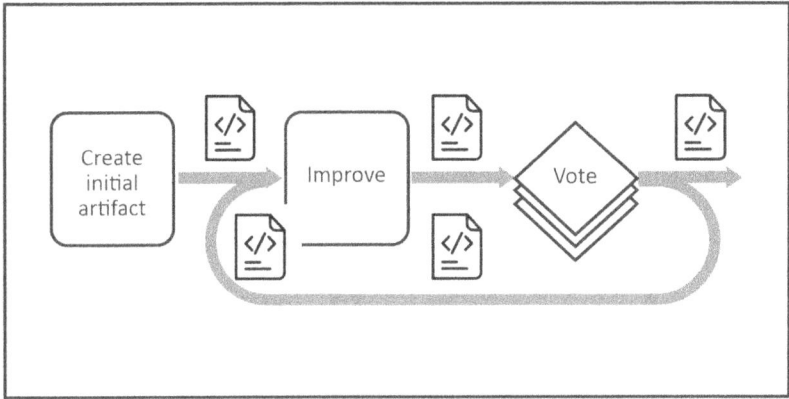

Figure 9.6 Creating an AI–human work environment. *Source:* Little, Chilton, Goldman, and Miller,. 2010.[44]

4. Making: creativity, design, prototyping and testing
5. Learning: learning how to learn

When these five skills are mapped to other future skills (see Table 9.1), it is obvious that these researches, despite the robustness of methodologies, do not agree on what our future skills should be. Further, these five skills may not be assessed in organizations at the same level as functional or performance skills, showing a lag between future skills for AI-enabled worlds and the current world. A survey of 979 technology pioneers, innovators, developers, business and policy leaders, believed that while AI could augment or amplify human effectiveness, but it also would threaten human autonomy, agency and capabilities.[45] The worry for the future of an AI-enabled organization is not the lack of AI talent but of human talent. Gartner recently stated that "The AI talent crisis myth has been perpetuated by a failure in talent recognition and organization, not in availability."[46]

9.3 AI Onboarding

Since fear is a common response for employees, onboarding AI needs some preparatory work. This is a function of whether the AI is already being used internationally or at the industry level. Where AI has been extensively used, the proof of concept exists as do the use cases and there is some existing data on the impact on employees. The challenge of blindly adopting use-cases is relevance to the context (see Figure 9.7). Another important take-away is that the user-interface of AI should be intuitive and not require

TABLE 9.1 Future Skills

Skills identified: AI-proof[47]	Pearson 2030 (US/UK)[48]	OECD 2030[49]	PwC 2030[50]	Deloitte: Future Ready[51]	McKinsey 2021[52]	WEF 2025[53]	Future Skills 2020[54]
Feeling—empathy & intuition	Psychology, Social perceptiveness, Sociology and Anthropology, Social perceptiveness	Empathy	Collaboration Skills, Emotional Intelligence	Empathy, Emotional Intelligence, Teaming, Social Intelligence	Communication (Story-telling and public speaking)	Leaderships, and social influence	Multidisciplinary versatility, collaboration and teaming, facilitation and co-creation, UX/UI and human-centered design approaches Interdisciplinary, cross cultural communication.
Seeing—systems thinking	coordinating, system evaluation, complex problem solving, systems analysis,	Creative thinking, collaboration, responsibility, using new information, Critical thinking	Adaptability, Leadership, Risk Management	Sense-making, critical thinking, Adaptive thinking	Critical thinking (Understanding biases)	Critical thinking and analyses; Technology use, monitoring and control; Complex problem solving	Adaptability—Future Thinking and Navigating and accelerating change; Critical and creative thinking—understanding biases Systems thinking—understanding complexity and seeing our role in the systems.

(continued)

TABLE 9.1 Future Skills (continued)

Skills identified: AI-proof[47]	Pearson 2030 (US/UK)[48]	OECD 2030[49]	PwC 2030[50]	Deloitte: Future Ready[51]	McKinsey 2021[52]	WEF 2025[53]	Future Skills 2020[54]
							Ethical and sustainable and regenerative practices
Dreaming—applied imagination	Originality, complex problem solving, Instructing,	Creative thinking	Problem Solving, Creativity,	Imagination, Creativity,	Critical thinking (Seeking relevant information)	Creativity, originality and initiative, Reasoning, problem solving and ideation.	Tech integration and bridging. Story-telling and advocacy
Making—creativity to prototype and testing (implementing)	Fluency of ideas, complex problem solving		Innovation, Entrepreneurial		Critical thinking (Structured problem Solving)	Analytical thinking and innovation monitoring and control. Technology design and programming.	Entrepreneurship
Learning—learning how to learn	Learning Strategies, active learning, Judgement and Decision Making, deductive reasoning, monitoring, Education and Training	Learning to learn, self-regulation, self-efficacy, using communication technology devices	Leadership, Digital Skills, STEM skills, Entrepreneurial	Curiosity, Resilience,	Critical thinking (Logical reasoning)	Active learning and learning strategies. Resilience, stress tolerance and flexibility.	Adaptability: Coping with uncertainty and Crisis; intellectual humility, learning to learn, unlearning, Digital skills, awareness and well-being.

Source: Compiled by Authors

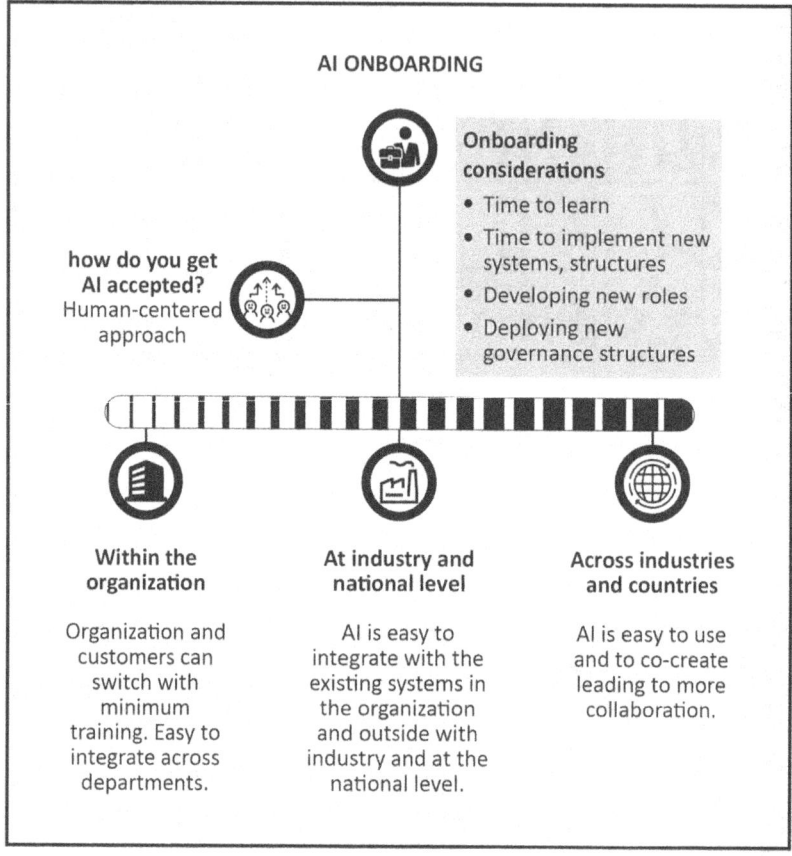

Figure 9.7 AI onboarding. *Source:* Stephens & Vashishtha (2020)[55]

much complex training if the organization wants to onboard the AI without too much effort. This requires several decisions as highlighted below.

The onboarding considerations are a function of:

1. Time and resources investment for research, feasibility tests and usability test prior to adoption.
2. Time to learn, or to retrain or hire new people, for new roles.
3. Time to implement new systems and the changes in the structure.
4. The availability of data and knowledge of the systems.
5. Time to articulate and recreate new governance structures.
6. Costs of project ownership, outsourcing and associated short-term and long-term risks.
7. The advantage of scale of onboarding.
8. Identifications of the correct metrics for progress (see Figure 9.8).

eBay has 190 markets, 1.2 billion listings, and matches 179 millions of buyers and sellers.[56] By 2021, eBay reported a revenue of over $10 billion with an approximate market cap of $26 billion.[57] Yet, the learning journey with AI was far from easy. Initially, in 2009 when they began using AI, they focused on a model that would increase sales per session, but it did not translate into actual revenue increase.[58] When researching what could go wrong, they found that the algorithm was recommending the cheaper items first! They changed the algorithm from purchase per session into gross merchandise value (GMV) per session. They then showed the whole company the impact of the AI, which had led to an increase in revenues.

In 2018, they introduced an in-house AI to create structure on the listings, understand users language to help them with search queries, and personalize their shopping experience. In 2017, they allowed image search so customers could search for a specific item based on the image they uploaded. In one year, since their launch of the AI, they had 2.6 million new users across five countries join the platform. By 2019, eBay data scientists were running "thousands of model training experiments per month spanning AI use cases, such as computer vision, natural language processing (NLP), merchandising recommendations, buyer personalization, seller price guidance, risk, trust, shipping estimates, and more."[59] They used over two decades of data and consumer insights to train their models.[60] They state that without the in-house AI model and the cloud infrastructure, models took weeks to months to set up, now set-up could take minutes. This strategy which was implemented in stages took years![61]

eBay has a training program for sellers. The aim of using AI is to make the experience painless without too much effort from the users side. Using AI platforms has accelerated exports of small business in USA. In the U.S., for instance, 97 percent of small businesses on eBay export, compared to just 4 percent of offline peers.[12] eBay's machine translation service, eBay-based exports to Spanish-speaking Latin America increased by 17.5 percent (value increased by 13.1 percent).[13] To put this growth into context, a 10 percent reduction in distance between countries is correlated with increased trade revenue of 3.51 percent—so a 13.1 percent increase in revenue from eBay's machine translation is equivalent to reducing the distance between countries by over 35 percent.[62]

Figure 9.8 eBay.[63]

Within the organization, to successfully onboard a new AI in a transparent manner, you will need to follow the following steps:[64]

1. *Create AI Buy-in*: Do a deep dive into business operations, and technical feasibility of AI projects, and the impact it will have on the organizational culture and performance. It is better you show evidence of its positive impact to get ownership across teams.
2. *Pilot Projects*: Test, test, test and learn, relearn, and retrain AI. There is no shortcut to this process. This requires an agile organization that has no issues in sharing information and feedback from users. AIs

that fail did not consider the users or the people they were impacting. This was the case in many of the examples highlighted before.
3. *Develop an AI Strategy*: This is critical—why are you onboarding AI in the first place? You need to clearly articulate what you want to achieve and how you want to achieve it.
4. *Develop Internal Competencies*: Have a plan for talent management. You will need in-house AI talent as you scale the project, at the same time you need deep knowledge of the business so just hiring outside talent is not enough.
5. *Legal and Governance*: The costs of legal and governance compliance will increase as you build and scale up and across countries.
6. *Outreach*: Take a leadership role in AI and reach out to other institutions (at the industry, national, and global level). Have a system to identify vulnerabilities at an early age.

A decision maker needs to consider if the AI that is being adopted can be rolled across the organization, across borders and to the supplier, distributor and customer networks. More regulatory controls are being imposed on data exports, Data localization laws exists in Vietnam, Indonesia, Brunei, Iran, China, Brazil, India, Australia, Germany, Indonesia, EU, Spain, Rwanda, South Korea, Nigeria, Russia, Kazakhstan, UAE but the scope may vary. For example, data restrictions in force are for personal data (EU, Rwanda, Russia), health data (Australia), telecommunication metadata (Germany), or government data (Nigeria). This may increase the costs of having a unified platform. Data localization laws will affect the future of data science which benefits from data moving across borders freely. These restrictions can come from local data storage requirements, local processing requirements, restrictions on data transfer, limits on data procurement, regulations on need for local ownership of data or need to employ locals, regulations to route data through local servers, control of IP, data censorship, or standards.[65] For example, these types of regulations may even affect sports analytics which is becoming more popular (see Figure 9.9).

9.4 AI and Human Productivity

When onboarding AI, organizations need to have a clear idea of how AI will contribute to the human workforce (see Figure 9.10). This reasoning builds on the on the need for Human-Agent Collectives described in Chapter 2. This will require a reimagination of the process (training and onboarding takes time) and what management considers as productive. If the purpose of AI is to free up time for employees for meaningful, impactful

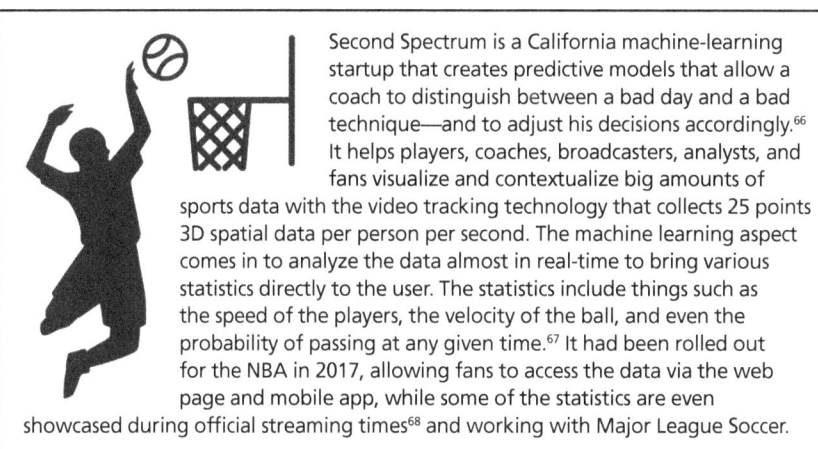

Figure 9.9 Second spectrum.

and innovative work, we need to rethink the word *productive*." There are three perspectives organizations would need to consider:

1. *AI Would Enhance Efficiency in the Work a Human Would Do*: AI does not need to "sleep," can work 24/7, and can process huge volumes of data. This allows them to better schedule technician work timings. Here the tasks are narrow and repetitive. Hence AI is trained on human skills. For example, University professors from Cornell are crowdsourcing robot gestures. This resulted in 70+ volunteers creating 1,225 manipulation trajectories on 116 different objects in a virtual environment.[69] This could help a robot create a latte or flush a toilet. So while this type of AI can be used to speed up an operational line, there needs to be a sufficient number of human experts who can take over from the AI in case of malfunction.
2. *Enhancing Decision Making*: The purpose is to help the human make better decisions. In the case of cardiology, diagnosis is time-consuming. A simple Electrocardiogram (ECG) could take up to 90 minutes for interpretation. With newer diagnostic systems, more data is being created. Cardiologs uses AI and cloud technology to improve cardiac diagnoses by looking at markers in 3000 years of ECG signals.[70] AI can take decisions based on clear set of rules. Otis, the elevator company, uses AI to analyze the data it collects to determine, which floors are most active to determine where to park the elevator car.[71] This assists the humans who will make decisions while servicing the elevator. The human is still the expert, and here the responsibility for decision making is still the humans.

3. *Substitute Human Decision Making*: Here the assumption is that the AI is equal to or exceeds human decision making. In this case, the AI may take decisions without human participation. For example many traffic signals are automated. The role of the human is to quickly identify issues (if any) or prevent issues from arising, respond quickly to any malfunctions and ensure that the AI learns from these mistakes.

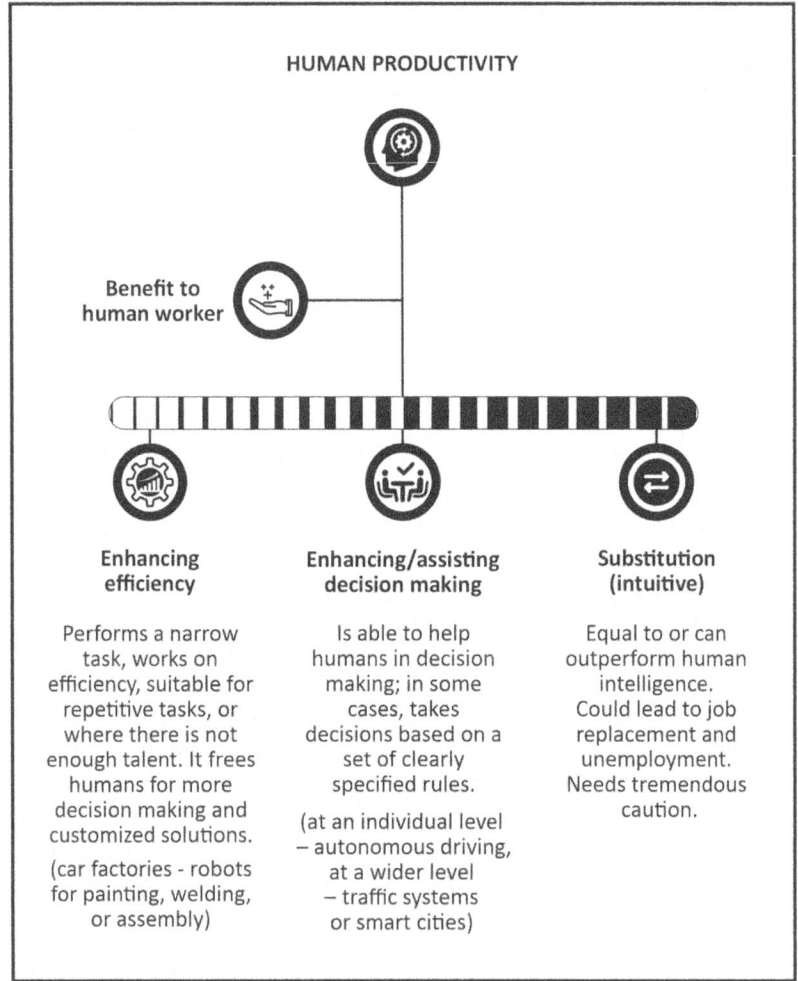

Figure 9.10 Human productivity. *Source:* Stephens & Vashishtha (2020)[72]

In summation, onboarding AI requires deep thought beyond efficiency, productivity and profits. It needs consideration on spillovers on people and planet. Employees are the primary responsibility of an organization and should come before shareholders. In Germany, for example, Bosch, a privately owned company, spent €1bn on reskilling employees working on legacy technologies and courses on AI and software skills were also provided for those working in other non-auto departments.[73] Bosch has 131,000 employees, of which approximately half work on automotive products, and the training was focused, so in some cases, mechanical engineers became software developers.[74] Each organization needs to determine the net effect of onboarding AI and its spillover impact across the country and the industry.[75]

QUESTIONS

1. What are the critical training needs for your employees for an AI-enabled organization and how do you evaluate your employees AI-proof skills?
2. Is your organization technology-centric, human-centric or a collective intelligence organization?
3. At what level have you onboarded AI and what are the future skills you need? (see Table 9.1 and Figure 9.7)
4. Looking at Figures 9.4 and 9.10, where is your AI project on the human productivity continuum?
5. What are the governance systems you have in place to manage AI and are they sufficient?

MY INSIGHTS

The most difficult decisions I need to take are

MY INSIGHTS

The resources I need to build for the future are

MY INSIGHTS

The governance systems I will to put in place are

MY INSIGHTS

The training and skills I and my team need to develop are

Notes

1. Kande, M., & Sönmez, M. (2020, October). Don't fear AI. It will lead to long-term job growth. In *The World Economic Forum COVID Action Platform* (Vol. 26). https://www.weforum.org/agenda/2020/10/dont-fear-ai-it-will-lead-to-long-term-job-growth/
2. Lee, N., & Clarke, S. (2019). Do low-skilled workers gain from high-tech employment growth? High-technology multipliers, employment and wages in Britain. *Research Policy, 48*, 103803.
3. When studying Marshallian or specialised spillovers, inter-industry spillovers and Jacobian or diversified spillovers, the authors find that there is a negative employment spillovers from the same technology sector (Marshallian externalities), while there were positive spillovers from more diversified activity (Jacobian externalities). https://www.diva-portal.org/smash/get/diva2:1580517/FULLTEXT01.pdf; Aldieri, L., Grafström, J., & Vinci, C. P. (2021). The effect of Marshallian and Jacobian knowledge spillovers on jobs in the solar, wind and energy efficiency sector. *Energies, 14*(14), 4269. https://doi.org/ 10.3390/en14144269
4. Rajnerowicz, K. (2022, March 23). *Will AI Take Your Job? Fear of AI and AI Trends for 2022.* Tidio; www.tidio.com. https://www.tidio.com/blog/ai-trends/
5. Douglas, J. (2019). These American workers are the most afraid of aI Taking their jobs. *CNBC, November, 7*, 37. https://www.cnbc.com/2019/11/07/these-american-workers-are-the-most-afraid-of-ai-taking-their-jobs.html
6. PwC, 2018. (n.d.). *Will robots really steal our jobs?* Retrieved June 3, 2022, from https://www.pwc.com/hu/hu/kiadvanyok/assets/pdf/impact_of_automation_on_jobs.pdf
7. World Economic Forum. (2020). The future of jobs report 2020. *Retrieved from Geneva.*
8. PwC. 2018. *Op. cit.*
9. Acquia, 2022. (n.d.). *Acquia CDP | Acquia.* Acquia; www.acquia.com. Retrieved July 28, 2022, from https://www.acquia.com/products/marketing-cloud/customer-data-platform
10. Miller, R. (2019, December 11). *Acquia nabs CDP startup AgilOne, which raised $41M—TechCrunch.* TechCrunch; techcrunch.com. https://techcrunch.com/2019/12/11/acquia-nabs-cdp-startup-agilone-which-raised-41m/
11. *Acquia to Acquire Customer Data Platform AgilOne to Deliver More Powerful Customer Experiences based on AI | Business Wire.* (2019, December 11). Acquia to Acquire Customer Data Platform AgilOne to Deliver More Powerful Customer Experiences Based on AI | Business Wire; www.businesswire.com. https://www.businesswire.com/news/home/20191211005490/en/Acquia-Acquire-Customer-Data-Platform-AgilOne-Deliver
12. OECD 2019. *OECD Future of Education and Skills 2030.*
13. Ammanth, B. (2022). *Trustworthy AI.* John Wiley & Sons. New Jersey.
14. Peeters, M. M., van Diggelen, J., Van Den Bosch, K., Bronkhorst, A., Neerincx, M. A., Schraagen, J. M., & Raaijmakers, S. (2021). Hybrid collective intelligence in a human–AI society. *AI & Society, 36*(1), 217–238. https://doi.org/10.1007/s00146-020-01005-y

15. Data Iku, 2021. (n.d.). *Trends in Enterprise Data Architecture and Model Deployment*. Dataiku; content.dataiku.com. Retrieved June 1, 2022, from https://content.dataiku.com/data-architecture-model-deployment
16. Launchbury, J. (n.d.). *DARPA*. DARPA Perspective on AI. Retrieved June 3, 2022, from https://www.darpa.mil/attachments/AIFull.pdf
17. Ibid.
18. Knight, W. (2015, September 16). *The Roomba Now Sees and Maps a Home | MIT Technology Review*. MIT Technology Review; www.technologyreview.com. https://www.technologyreview.com/2015/09/16/247936/the-roomba-now-sees-and-maps-a-home/
19. Brandon, J. (2016, November 3). *Why the iRobot Roomba 980 is a great lesson on the state of AI | VentureBeat*. VentureBeat; venturebeat.com. https://venturebeat.com/ai/why-the-irobot-roomba-980-is-a-great-lesson-on-the-state-of-ai/
20. iRobot. 2022. *Corporate Profile | iRobot Corporation*. (n.d.). iRobot Corporation; investor.irobot.com. https://investor.irobot.com/corporate-profile
21. iRobot Corporation, 2022. (n.d.). *Introduction to iRobot Corp*. Retrieved July 3, 2022, from https://investor.irobot.com/static-files/a6147f70-f50a-43d3-9161-9af57981ea0f
22. *AlphaSense: An Intelligent Search Engine for Business–The Wharton School*. (n.d.). The Wharton School; www.wharton.upenn.edu. Retrieved July 13, 2022, from https://www.wharton.upenn.edu/story/alphasense-intelligent-search-engine-business/
23. AlphaSense, (2019). AI-Based Market Intelligence Search Engine AlphaSense Secures $50M in Series B Funding Led by Innovation Endeavors. *PR Newswire: News Distribution, Targeting and Monitoring*, www.prnewswire.com/news-releases/ai-based-market-intelligence-search-engine-alphasense-secures-50m-in-series-b-funding-led-by-innovation-endeavors-30085942.html
24. Alphasense, (2022). https://www.alpha-sense.com/about-us/
25. LinkedIn, (2022). Alphasense. https://www.linkedin.com/company/alphasense
26. Stephens, M., & Vashishtha, H. (202). *AI Smart Kit*. Information Age.
27. Jennings, N. R., Moreau, L., Nicholson, D., Ramchurn, S., Roberts, S., Rodden, T., & Rogers, A. (2014). Human-agent collectives. *Communications of the ACM, 57*(12), p. 80
28. Ibid, p. 82.
29. Kasparov, G. (2008). *How life imitates chess*. London: Arrow Books; Cowen, T. 2014. *Average is Over-powering America Beyond the Age of The Great Stagnation*. New York, NY: Penguin Putnam.
30. Wilson, H. J., & Daugherty, P. R. (2018). Collaborative Intelligence: Humans and AI Are Joining Forces. *Harvard Business Review*. https://hbr.org/2018/07/collaborative-intelligence-humans-and-ai-are-joining-forces
31. Licklider, J. C. R., & Symbiosis, M. C. (1960). IRE Transactions on Human Factors in Electronics, HFE-1. https://groups.csail.mit.edu/medg/people/psz/Licklider.html
32. Hagel, J., Brown, J. S., & Wooll, M. (2019). Skills change, but capabilities endure: Why fostering human capabilities first might be more important than reskilling in the future of work. *Deloitte Insights, 16*. https://www2.deloitte

.com/us/en/insights/focus/technology-and-the-future-of-work/future-of-work-human-capabilities.html
33. Baldwin, R. (2019). The globotics upheaval: Globalization, robotics, and the future of work. Oxford University Press.
34. Collins, E., & Ghahramani, Z. (2021). LaMDA: our breakthrough conversation technology. *The Keyword, May, 18.* https://blog.google/technology/ai/lamda/
35. Pichai, S. (2018). AI at Google: our principles. *The Keyword,* 7, 1–3. https://blog.google/technology/ai/ai-principles/
36. Hager, R. (2022, June 16). *How Google's LaMDA AI works, and why it seems so much smarter than it is.* Android Police; www.androidpolice.com. https://www.androidpolice.com/what-is-google-lamda/
37. Luscombe, R. (2022). Google engineer put on leave after saying AI chatbot has become sentient. *The Guardian.* https://www.theguardian.com/technology/2022/jun/12/google-engineer-ai-bot-sentient-blake-lemoine
38. Curtis, B., & Savulescu, J. (2022). Is Google's LaMDA conscious? A philosopher's view, Practical Ethics, University of Oxford. http://blog.practicalethics.ox.ac.uk/2022/06/cross-post-is-googles-lamda-conscious-a-philosophers-view/
39. Timnit Gebru has highlighted this in a recent *Washington Post* article, titled We warned Google that people might believe AI was sentient. Now it's happening. https://www.washingtonpost.com/opinions/2022/06/17/google-ai-ethics-sentient-lemoine-warning/
40. DARPA, (2019). Using AI to Build Better Human-Machine Teams. https://www.darpa.mil/news-events/2019-03-21b
41. Williams, J., Fiore, S. M., & Jentsch, F. (2022). Supporting Artificial Social Intelligence with Theory of Mind. Frontiers of Artificial Intelligence, https://doi.org/10.3389/frai.2022.750763
42. Gritti, T. (2021). Tesla's Data Engine and what we should learn from it. Braincreators. https://www.braincreators.com/brainpower/insights/teslas-data-engine-and-what-we-should-all-learn-from-it
43. Neumeier, M. (2013). *Metaskills: Five Talents for the Robotic Age.* Level C Media, USA.
44. Little, G. (2010). Turkit: Human computation algorithms on mechanical turk. In *Proc. 23rd Annual ACM Symp. on User Interface Software and Technology (UIST), 2010.*
45. PEW, (2018). https://www.pewresearch.org/internet/2018/12/10/artificial-intelligence-and-the-future-of-humans/
46. Andrews, W., & Brethenoux, E. (2021). Formulate a Strategy for AI Skills Acquisition and Upskilling. Gartner Research. https://www.gartner.com/en/documents/3995197; Dataiku Ebook, The Road to AI Staffing: The Do's and Don'ts of Hiring & Upskilling for AI Talent, https://pages.dataiku.com/staffing-the-ai-enterprise
47. Neumeier, M. *2013. Op. cit.*
48. Pearson, (2017). Future of Skills 2030. https://futureskills.pearson.com/research/#/findings/findings-introduction
49. OECD, (2021). OECD Future of Education and Skills 2030.

50. PwC, (2030). Future of the Workforce.
51. Deloitte, (2021). Building the future-ready workforce | What is a future-ready workforce? https://www2.deloitte.com/content/dam/Deloitte/ca/Documents/consulting/ca-future-ready-workforce-en-aoda.pdf
52. Dondi, M., Panier, F., & Schubert, J. (2021). Defining the skills citizens will need in the future world of work. McKinsey https://www.mckinsey.com/industries/public-and-social-sector/our-insights/defining-the-skills-citizens-will-need-in-the-future-world-of-work
53. WEF, (2020). Future of Jobs Report.
54. GEF & World Skills Russia, 2021. Future Skills for the 2020s A New Hope. https://futureskills2020s.com
55. Stephens & Vashishtha (2020). Op. cit.
56. Marr, B. (2021). The Amazing Ways eBay Is Using Artificial Intelligence to Boost Business Success. https://bernardmarr.com/the-amazing-ways-ebay-is-using-artificial-intelligence-to-boost-business-success/
57. Ebay Annual Report. 2021.
58. Pang, W. (2021). Where eBay Went Right—and Wrong—with AI: What You Measure Matters. *Towards Data Science*, https://towardsdatascience.com/where-ebay-went-right-and-wrong-with-ai-what-you-measure-matters-2322dacc9320
59. Katariya, S., & Ramani, A. (2019). eBay's Transformation to a Modern AI Platform. Ebay, https://tech.ebayinc.com/engineering/ebays-transformation-to-a-modern-ai-platform/
60. Marr, B. 2021. *Op. cit.*
61. Katariya, S., & Ramani, A. 2019. *Op. cit.*
62. Meltzer, P. J. (2018). The impact of artificial intelligence on international trade. Brookings. https://www.brookings.edu/research/the-impact-of-artificial-intelligence-on-international-trade/
63. Katariya, S. (2019). eBay's Platform is Powered by AI and Fueled by Customer Input. Ebay, https://tech.ebayinc.com/engineering/ebays-platform-is-powered-by-ai-and-fueled-by-customer-input/
64. Stephens, M. a & Vashishtha, H. (2020). *Op. cit.*
65. U Vrabec, H., Nurullaev, R., Olmedo Cuevas, M., & Szulewski, P. (2018). Data Localisation Measures and Their Impacts on Data Science. *Handbook on Data Science and Law*, Edward Elgar.
66. Second Spectrum. (2020). *13th Anniversary*. www.nbastuffer.com/analytics101/second-spectrum/
67. Impey, S. (2020). MLS Taps Second Spectrum for AI-Powered Data-Tracking. *SportsPro*, www.sportspromedia.com/news/mls-second-spectrum-artificial-intelligence-player-data-tracking
68. Second Spectrum. 2020. *Op. cit.*
69. Ackerman, E. (2015, April 21). *PR2 Robot Figures Out How to Make a Latte–IEEE Spectrum*. IEEE Spectrum; spectrum.ieee.org. https://spectrum.ieee.org/pr2-robot-latte
70. Stephens & Vashishtha (2020). *Op. cit.*
71. Cardiologs, (2022). Our Company. https://cardiologs.com/our-company/

72. Reilly, D. (2022, June 9). *How A.I. is being used as a tool for innovation, not just efficiency | Fortune*. Fortune; fortune.com. https://fortune.com/2022/06/08/artificial-intelligence-innovation-efficiency/
73. *Financial Times*. (n.d.). Subscribe to Read | Financial Times; www.ft.com. https://www.ft.com/content/6e6be236-050a-4bfe-839b-653f6d8cb3ac
74. Ibid.
75. Genz, S. (2022). The nuanced relationship between cutting-edge technologies and jobs: Evidence from Germany. Brookings. https://www.brookings.edu/research/the-nuanced-relationship-between-cutting-edge-technologies-and-jobs/

10

AI and Customers

CHAPTER HIGHLIGHTS

1. AI sales or usage is rampant in Business to Government (B2G), Business to Business (B2B), and Business to Consumer (B2C) business models.
2. The spillover of AI effects is not always direct and hence not easy to assess.
3. As the immersive experience of the customer increases, more senses are engaged.
4. The costs of managing this experience (resources for development, maintenance, and governance) increase as sensory experience increases.
5. Human-in-the-loop is the understanding of when and why humans (users of the systems) need to be involved in the chain of decisions. This is an important point to address in the customer experience.

> **Cases:**
> StitchFix | Facebook | Skype Translator | DuLight | Baidu
> Hello Barbie | NASA | Boston Dynamics | Tesla

10.1 AI and Customer

Users of AI could be a business, another human or another AI (facilitated through a business). While there are many open-source AI models existing, most businesses want a revenue stream that is profitable. There are three types of business models AI firms typically use when appealing to customer categories:

1. *Business to government (B2G)*: Sales of AI products and services to the governments (federal, state, or local agencies). Sales will often be based on tenders and need to meet rigorous specifications. At times there is a significant gap in AI governance due to the hierarchical layers of the government. For example, the U.S.–Huawei security issue.
2. *Business to consumer (B2C)*: These business models directly approach the customer. In some cases, they are free (Facebook, Google, WhatsApp) and are based on targeted advertisements based on data profiles. Or they are platform companies (Uber, Airbnb, Zomato, Alibaba, eBay, Etsy), matching buyers and sellers. Or they use subscription models (Netflix, Tinder, GPT-4) or sales with maintenance models (apps, chatbots). Tinder, for example, has a free model, but you need to upgrade for more benefits. On the other hand, Signal is based on privacy and crowdsources funds to ensure that it safeguards the data profiles of customers.
3. *Business to business (B2B)*: These business models have more frequent or regular purchase cycles and are of higher order value than B2C. Often AI is offered as a service—Amazon Web Services, Microsoft Allure, Blackboard. It can also be offered as an enterprise solution (with customization), like Salesforce's Einstein or IBM's Watson. While companies can buy robots (recently, Hyundai bought Boston Dynamics in 2020), AI needs to be regularly updated as data becomes outdated, software needs updating, or hardware is no longer as efficient or compatible with the growing demands. Hence maintenance and upgrades become an essential part of the business model.

While AI has been deployed in business-to-government and business-to-business markets from the beginning, consumer-facing AI products have scaled much faster. AIs used in governments and businesses are expert systems designed to do specific tasks. A survey of these AIs built during the early and mid-1980s found that a decade later:[1] (1) about one-third were still in operation and being actively used; (2) about one-sixth were available but not being actively maintained; and (3) approximately half were abandoned. The obsolescence of expert systems is high as they perform sensitive operations and need low error rates, or they lose their credibility. Yet businesses adopt AI in product and/or service development or service operations.[2]

In consumer-facing products, the growth of AI adoption is much faster than in the business to business sector. Facebook took three years to reach 50 million customers, WeChat took one year, and Pokémon Go took 19 days.[3] AI may be embedded in all kinds of appliances—your car, the smartphone, Alexa, headphones, or toaster. It is estimated that we consume approximately 12.5 billion square inches of silicon chips a year![4]

We accept that AI is seamlessly entwined in our daily lives—Google search algorithms, Netflix recommendations, Waze or Google Maps directions, or even the microwave time settings for automatic defrost. This innocuous adoption has led to the rapid customer adoption of AI-enabled devices but also, in some cases, challenges when the AI and humans are in conflict (see Figure 10.1). According to PwC, we are no longer putting the *human-in-the-loop* for *assisted intelligence* (helping people perform tasks faster and better), but using *autonomous intelligence* (automating decision-making processes without human intervention).[5]

We are now in the middle of an AI movement that can be called *too big to fail*. Too much money has been thrown into AI without understanding the impact on customers, society, and the economy. The effect on the customers is not always obvious. Dr. Pippa Malgram, a former economist at the White House, highlighted the tendency for the private sector to focus on SaaS (software as a service) based innovations[6] to enable consumer businesses rather than the core business itself. She highlights the example of funding rare earth metals or baby formula, both of which were in short supply in 2022 due to the Russia–Ukraine war. It was not funded by the private sector but by the USA government (baby milk via the Defense Production Act and rare earth producer Lynas, by the Pentagon).[7] This example shows strategic shortsightedness in thinking. Also, the governance of AI at the back end often strains business models that have positioned themselves as free (see Figure 10.2).

In some cases, the business model may be a bit more complicated. For example, customers buy Alexa, which uses data to train its AI further. It also can recommend products on Amazon (this helps cross-sales). Recently

> Stitch Fix is a data science company that uses recommendation algorithms to create a personalized wardrobe based on an individual's style, budget, frequency of product delivery, and size. The data scientist team runs 100s of experiments each month, expecting only a little over 65% to be successful.[8] Customers contribute data by putting their preferences for an item (swiping left for what they reject and right for what they like). This process allows the algorithm to recommend appropriate items for delivery.[9] In its SEC filing, the company said,
>
>> Our stylists leverage our data science through a custom-built, web-based styling application that provides recommendations from our broad selection of merchandise. Our stylists then apply their judgment to select what they believe to be the best items for each Fix. Our stylists provide a personal touch, offer styling advice and context to each item selected and help us develop long-term relationships with our clients."[10]
>
> The algorithm chose products from over 700 brands. While it did very well in its early days, the algorithm is constantly learning and at times in conflict with or not under supervision from the human stylist,[11] though the marketing material suggested that the human (stylist) was always in the loop.[12] This gap in expectations led to a change in the business model from pre-selected boxes (using AI) to allowing the customer to shop online (having the human in control).

Figure 10.1 StitchFix and human-in-the-loop

Amazon now allows developers to sell content using a subscription service (Amazon will take a percentage for putting the products on their store, much like Apple's iStore). Within virtual experiences, like gaming, it is estimated that up to 85% of the transactions are micro sales of digital content or experiences, digital artifacts, or advertising.[13]

Many startups that create experiences through AI hope to be acquired. But the danger of any acquisition is that the initial purpose for which the AI

> When Facebook scaled and entered multiple markets, it recruited volunteers and crowdsourced site translation. By 2010, Facebook content wastranslated into more than 80 languages by volunteers and had signed up half a billion users worldwide. By 2019, Facebook had been translated into 111 languages. Hence content uploaded on the site needed to be moderated for appropriateness. However, its 15,000 content moderators, who spoke a total of 50 languages fluently, had a content moderation guideline that was only available in 41 languages as of April 2019. In addition, the growing health burden on content moderators has been brought to the public's notice.[14] To manage the increasing need for monitoring content, Facebook has turned to automation to solve the problem, but this is also not working as well as planned.[15]

Figure 10.2 Facebook and content moderation.[16]

was created may change as ownership changes. This situation was the case when Facebook acquired WhatsApp for US$ 19 million in 2014. It resulted in both founders of WhatsApp quitting citing differences with Facebook's method of monetization.[17]

10.2 Human Interface

While using AI, a user interface (UI) is required. The UI is where interactions between humans and machines occur. We often equate the user interface to a program on an external device (separate from the human) that learns from how users interact with the AI product. A lot of work is happening from this angle to make user interfaces more intuitive and more accessible for customers to trust the AI. The thinking behind this is human-centered design, and it revolves around three key areas:[18]

1. Discovery and expectation management: Set user expectations to avoid false expectations.
2. Design for forgiveness: The AI will make mistakes. Design the UI, so users are inclined to forgive it.
3. Data transparency and tailoring: Be transparent about collecting data and offer users the ability to tailor it.
4. Privacy, security, and control: Gain trust by driving privacy, security, and the ability to control the AI.

By default, AI systems are often designed so that decisions are taken with little human control or oversight. The most significant errors we have seen (think of the UK Post Office scandal, the MCAS Max 737 airplanes, Tesla autopilot, Facebook-Cambridge Analytica) have happened when humans are not in the loop or some humans have taken decisions on behalf of the users. When designing such systems, a key consideration is human-in-the-loop. Human-in-the-loop is the understanding of when and why humans (users of the systems) need to be involved in the chain of decisions. There are three considerations we need to take into account if we ask the question, If the AI malfunctions, what would be the loss?

> **Scenario 1:** Possibility of no loss of property or human lives: In this case, we need to ask, is there a loss of trust? How significant an impact would this be? Poor transparency and privacy could be an issue. The Facebook-Cambridge Analytica scandal would sit here.
> **Scenario 2:** Loss of property but no loss of life: In this case, we need to ask, is the property of high value? How would it impact the customer? Data loss is one example. The issue with the India Aadhar

card loss was a security issue. Another example would be when an AI-powered grass cutter destroys pipes, leading to flooding. Is there a liability clause in this case?

Scenario 3: Loss of Life and/or Loss of property: While this refers to human life, it should also include animal life. For example, an autonomous car performs evading maneuvers and saves the lives of the people in its vehicle but not the other vehicle. In these cases, you need human-in-the-loop decisions. Is this a setting where the car owner, before a journey, makes choices and hence can be held accountable for them? What is the liability? An example is the MCAS issue in the Max 737 air crashes.

In the MCAS Max 737 case (mentioned in Chapter 2), all equipment is tested for major failure (when the probability of a failure must be less than 1 in 100,000). The assumption is that a *major failure* would not produce any severe injuries but would increase the crew's workload.[19] The autopilot that stabilized the nose of the plane (the MCAS system) was programmed to trim the stabilizer down then pause for five seconds and repeat the sequence, depending on the conditions.[20] According to the FAA guidance, this time should be enough for a pilot to recognize what's happening and begin to counter it.[21] Though Boeing had conducted rigorous failure analysis, their simulations did not look at the eventuality that MCAS could trigger repeatedly. In training, they had 40 seconds[22] but is reality between resets, they had 5 seconds. The 40 or 5 seconds were not enough for all the reasons mentioned—lack of training, not enough information in the manual and reliance on a single sensor, and poor response from the companies involved to take accountability.[23] Which human can make good decisions with a reaction time of a few seconds when under tremendous stress? In the MCAS case, multiple alerts were set off, creating confusion in the cockpit. A psychological study on time pressure and decision-making showed that even if the task was repetitive, participants did not perform as well as those under less time pressure.[24]

As we spend more time interacting with the virtual world, we will need more sophisticated interfaces connecting humans to AI (see Figure 10.3). As we increase the level of interface with the human, it will increase the resources and liabilities of companies and people involved. This integration at one end is when we have a physical separation between humans and AI (for example, keyboards, wearables, controllers, headsets, buttons, etc.). For instance, in the fictional TV series Star Trek, all crew use universal translators, which are devices that allow you to speak with species of different languages. We are using AI for translation, and they are quickly picking up nuances of human language (see Figure 10.4). In the case of translation,

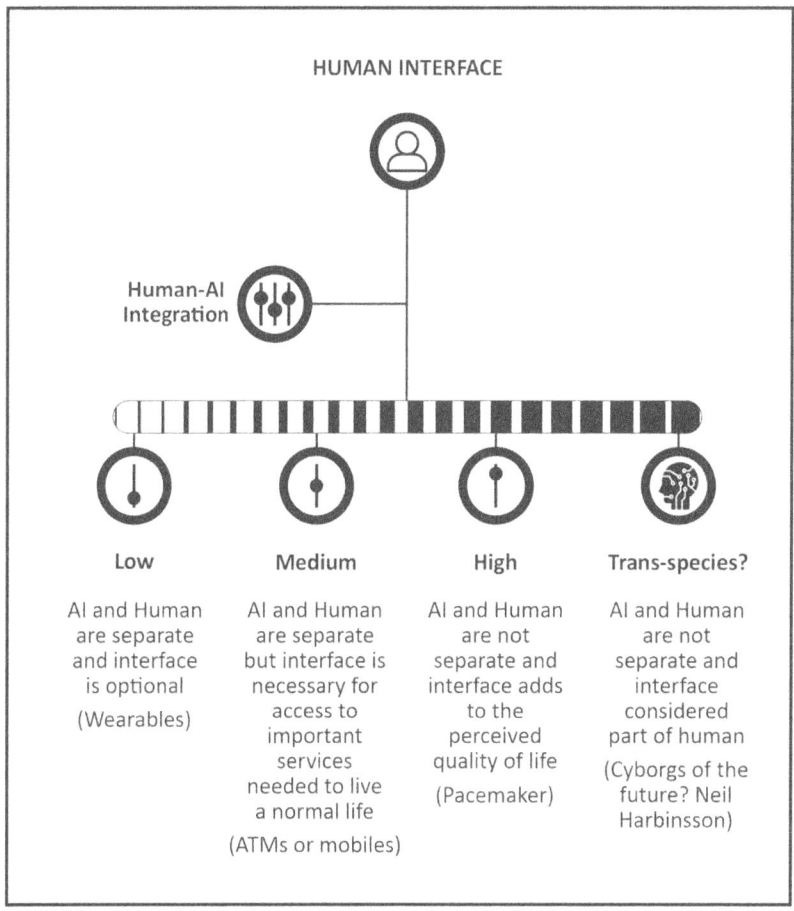

Figure 10.3 Human interface with AI. *Source:* Stephens & Vashishtha (2020).

depending on the type of business, the level of the human interface may be medium.

At the other end of the human interface with AI is when AI and humans meld together, creating one entity that communicates seamlessly with each other. The difference as you move up this spectrum is how much we need AI to keep us alive and go through normal living. So a pacemaker is a machine than regulates heartbeat. Is this example of human interface? While it is important for life and maybe perceived as a high interface like the smart prosthetics where we use electrodes to sense muscle and nerve via electrical signals.[25] However this does not fit the human-interface at the level we call trans-species. Neil Harbinsson was born with color blindness. He had an

> Skype can help you break down language barriers with your friends, family, clients, and colleagues. The Skype Translator can currently translate conversations into ten languages, including English, Spanish, French, German, Mandarin, Italian, Portuguese (Brazilian), Arabic, and Russian. However, as it continues to learn from machine learning, it will soon be available in more than 60 languages for clear, seamless instant messaging as new languages are added continuously.[26] 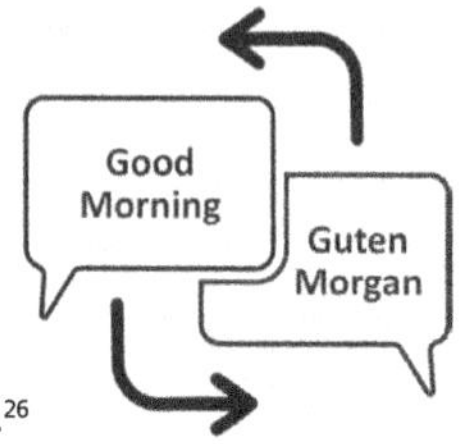
>
> The software utilizes Automatic Speech Recognition and Machine Translation, both of which are neural-network-based AIs. The machine translation works on translating the full sentence's context instead of word-for-word, which can lead to misunderstandings and confusion. In addition to these two, it also uses natural language processing tech, TrueText, and a text-to-speech synthesizer, to allow for translations to be heard and read. TrueText then clears redundant words and even filters sounds such as "like" or "um," to better improve the translation standard.[27]
>
> Good Morning → Guten Morgan

Figure 10.4 Skype translator.

> DuLight is for the visually impaired. The prototype, a device similar to that of a Bluetooth earpiece, has a camera that sends images to an application. The application then figures out what is in front of the wearer through deep-learning image recognition and then creates a description and sends this back to the wearer as speech.[28] It is said that it can even learn to remember a person's identity so that they can be recognized at a later time.[29]

Figure 10.5 DuLight.

antenna implanted in his skull to allow him to experience colors through sound. He is considered the first transspecies or cyborg. Previously he had used a headphone and a laptop. The chip in his head even allows him to connect to his mobile via Bluetooth. There are various such technologies being developed like Neurolink and DuLight for example (see Figure 10.5).

10.3 AI and the Sensory Experience

Customer engagement depends on the customer experience. When translating this to AI systems, the focus has been to build trust-based experiences that can engage the human six senses. The sixth sense, intuition, is something being researched in virtual contexts. In an experiment of 49 participants, divided into two groups (the control and experimental group), the experimental group was immersed in a natural environment with smell and sight cues. When exposed to the virtual setting, the experimental group had more correct intuitive answers than the control group.[30] These studies are an emerging area of research.

On the other hand, AI is regularly being used to develop intuitive responses through predictive responses. This type of decision-making is seen in autonomous cars, for example. AI is being used to formulate intuitive responses (via priming) through scenarios in high-pressure simulations like defense training, medical training, emergency or disaster response, etc. It is used in gaming to sense the player's next moves to manage the lag in data signals (or latency).

We may not be in love with our telephone handsets, but we feel an attachment to our mobile phones. We can hear our phone (and customize sounds, ringtones, the voice of our AI assistants, and upload it with music we enjoy). Baidu, for example, can create synthetic voices (see Figure 10.6). When Google introduced Google Assistant, one of the concerns raised was whether it would be able to do things without our knowledge, and should something that sounds human identify itself as not human if talking to other humans?

We can see images we enjoy (screens, photos, friends). We can also feel the phone and customize covers to suit our comfort level and sizes to suit our grip and pockets. Haptic pads were developed to simulate touch through vibration or other motions (besides noise). What is currently missing in mobile tech is the customer experience of smell and taste. In 2011, Fujitsu released a phone that released fragrance;[31] in 2012, Samsung

> A company that sprouted out of Baidu's R&D department, known as Deep Voice, is a deep neural network that creates synthetic voices as the system learns to add different dips in tone, accent, pronunciation, and pitch, recreating the human sound. This technological advancement can bring us closer to real-time translation while making other things redundant, such as biometric security like voice recognition.[32] With less than an hour's worth of data, the second iteration of DeepVoice can imitate a voice and learn hundreds of accents. Baidu says that the final version of DeepVoice could learn thousands of voices with just half an hour of data each, possibly manipulating them, changing tone, inflection, and considering gender or accent. And the system is so realistic that it could fool voice recognition around 95% of the time.[33] These voices, accents, and versions open up opportunities in the entertainment sector in a way that it hasn't before. For example, audiobooks and video game characters could have their unique voice, creating a more realistic and enhanced experience for the consumer.[34] We may not also need real singers, just their voices!

Figure 10.6 Baidu Voice Search: Mimics the real world.

250 • *AI Enabled Business*

patented a mobile that would refill and release perfume.[35] During the COVID pandemic, the researcher developed a way you could test your saliva for the virus using your smartphone.[36]

The sensory experience AI can deliver is not just about which senses they engage, but about the AI interface (is it easy, intuitive, easily accessible, and affordable?). As the level of the immersive experience increases (see Figure 10.7), management costs will also increase. On one end of the spectrum, companies use narrow AI and hope the expertise in the system will increase customer engagement with all senses. For example, Samsung introduced a "food mode" on its mobile phone to enhance colors and

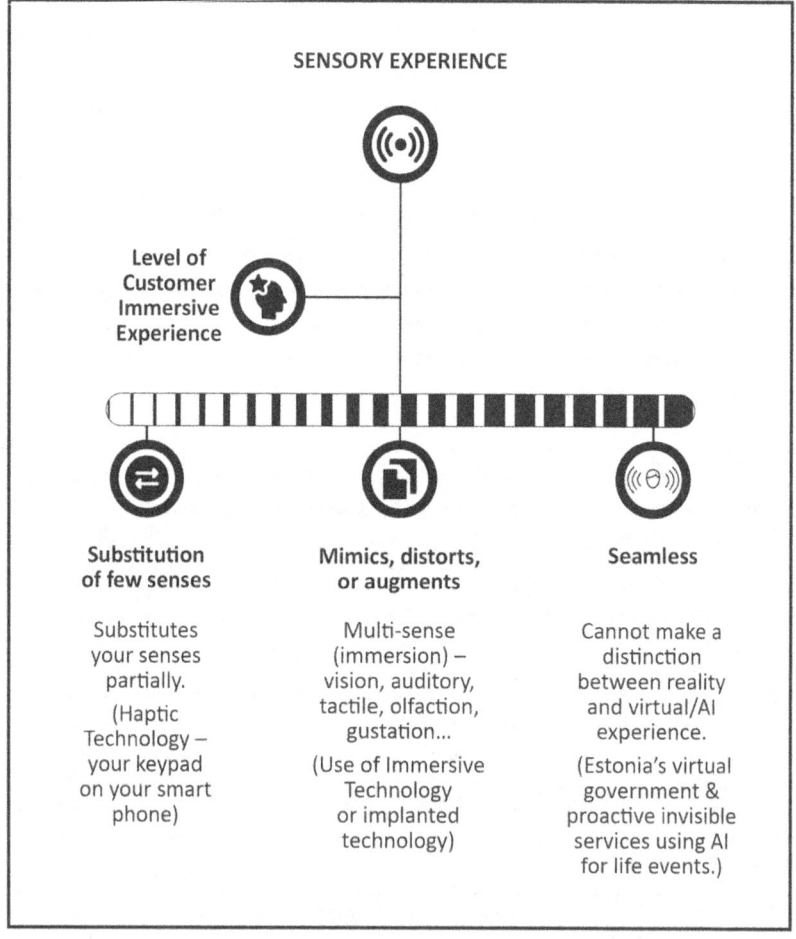

Figure 10.7 AI sensory experience scale. *Source:* Stephens & Vashishtha (2020)

make the food look more appetizing. On the other end of the spectrum, the experience can be immersive or seamless. At this end of the spectrum, research is being done on the concept of extended reality.

However, the challenge at any given point in time is to develop trust in these systems, which may raise ethical issues. The European Commission's High-level Expert Group on AI (HLEG) states that to trust an AI, you should trust the (1) AI technology itself; (2) designers and organizations behind the development, deployment, and use of AI; and (3) socio-technical systems involved in the AI life cycle.[37] Take the example of Hello Barbie, the child or parents may not have all the information to make an educated decision, yet they believe they trust the product.[38] When it was introduced in 2015, Hello Barbie (see Figure 10.8) caught the public's imagination, selling 10,000 units, but was discontinued in 2017 due to poorly designed charging stations and WIFI connections.[39] This issue of toys with data systems that can be used later for the wrong reasons (pet and baby cameras, house surveillance systems) are issues that companies should consider when developing, designing, making, selling, or servicing such products.

10.4 User-Experience: Merging Virtual and Real Worlds

Users can be customers but also other stakeholders. Experiences can be of various types: mirroring the real world, mimicking reality, or escaping reality. AI can be used to reproduce the real world for surveillance, inspection, monitoring, or simulating or forecasting performance. One common method to recreate the real world with AI is digital twins (see Figure 10.9 and Figure 10.10, the example of Boston Dynamic). A digital twin is a

Hello Barbie is a toy from Mattel that uses machine learning and natural language processing software from ToyTalk to converse with your child from ages six and above. Hello Barbie's necklace is fitted with a microphone that transmits what is said to it to ToyTalk Servers. The conversation is then analyzed so the servers can respond with an appropriate line from over 8,000 dialogue options. Data such as the consumer's favorite color or hobbies may be stored to be brought up in future conversations.[40] Privacy concerns have been around ever since Mattel announced Hello Barbie.[41] ToyTalk states that the collected data is only used to enhance the user experience. If any data is shared with a third party, it will be for research and developmental purposes only.[42] Another concern has been the issue of using WiFi and whether the doll could be hacked.[43]

Figure 10.8   Hello Barbie.

NASA and the U.S. Joint Forces Command began the early work in digital representations of the real world in its Virtual Product Laboratory in the 1990s with other partners.[44,45] The work was an outcome of the space race and the need to integrate human factors into engineering design. Human Factors was defined as "designing tools, machines, tasks, and environments for safe, comfortable and effective human use."[46] There were two types of virtual reality systems being used. The first surrounded the operator putting them in an immersive environment and the other offered a window into the experience. For example with the later, by creating a virtual astronaut, the technologies allowed them to run simulations to figure out where to place equipment and design the place the astronauts were in.[47] For example, they created OpenWorlds (for complex simulations on the Space Station). NASA used VR to map terrains for pilots in the aviation sector to navigate.[48]

There is some confusion on terminology of digital twins as highlighted in Figure 10.9a. The limitations of the technology still persist till today. The biggest challenge in performance is the interoperability of systems and data. There are three types of virtual representation models.

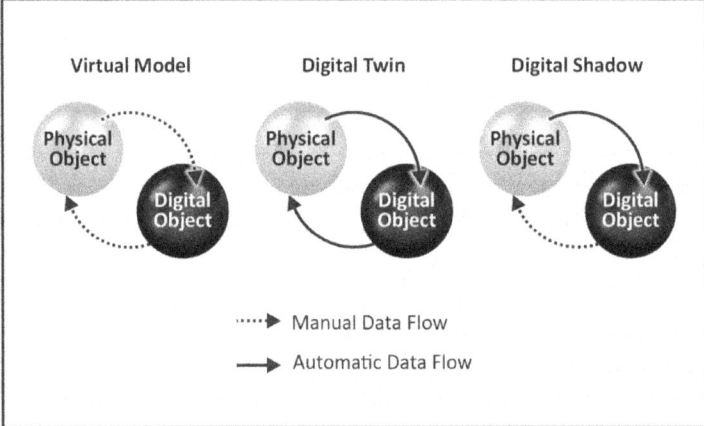

Figure 10.9a Methods to mirror the physical world. *Source:* Kritzinger et al., 2018.[49]

Figure 10.9 Mirroring of the physical world: NASA[50]

virtual representation of the physical and functional description of a component, product, or system in its data form across its lifecycle.[51] The flow of data is in both directions, from the physical to the virtual world and vice versa, mirroring both worlds. If the data flow is skewed to one side (physical to digital), technically, these are called digital shadows.[52]

Boston Dynamics uses these virtual representations of the real world to aid the worker or manager in the workplace (see Figure 10.10), and since

In 1992, Boston Dynamics was spun-off from an MIT research lab that focused on dynamic robots. Some of its early contracts were from the U.S. government where they also won funding from DARPA. Through this grant, they developed Big Dog. It was a robot that could be used as a pack mule in hostile terrain where military vehicles could not go. It was unsuccessful as the noise the robot made was too loud, but this led to further product development and more robots inspired by animals. In 2013 the company was acquired by Google X. In 2017, Alphabet sold Boston Dynamics to Soft Bank. In June 2021, Hyundai Motor Group acquired an 80% stake in Boston Dynamics with SoftBank, holding the remaining 20%. Hyundai hopes to integrate robotic technology into its factories. Boston Dynamics robots are in use in fire departments and police departments. They target industries like inspection of hazardous environments, asset management through dynamic data capture, public safety, warehouse automation and construction, power utilities, and manufacturing onsite data capture with autonomous inspections. They know their robots can be used for harm and have a clause on who they sell to.

> We take great care to make sure our customers intend to use our robots legally. We cross-check every purchase request against the U.S. Government's denied persons and entities lists, prior to authorizing a sale. In addition, all buyers must agree to our Terms and Conditions of Sale, which state that our products must be used in compliance with the law, and cannot be used to harm or intimidate people or animals, or be used as a weapon or configured to hold a weapon. Any violation of our Terms will automatically void the product's warranty and prevent the robot from being updated, serviced, repaired or replaced."[53]

Further, Boston Dynamics also has a list of ethical principles that outline research:[54]
1. We are motivated by curiosity and respect for humans and animals.
2. We prioritize the human element in human-robot partnerships.
3. We build trustworthy robots.
4. We will not weaponize our robots.
5. We believe robotic use must comply with privacy and civil rights laws.
6. We work thoughtfully with U.S. federal, state, and local governments, and their allies.
7. We support the establishment of laws and regulations that promote the safe and responsible use of robots.

Boston Dynamics uses a Deep Learning AI. But they depend on a suite of providers to ensure their robots work well. They use AWS for data storage,[55] which is needed for mobility and computer vision, allowing its robots to have dynamic sensing. For example, they work with Vinsa, which uses vision software that builds on top of TensorFlow (open source).[56] In 2021, Boston Dynamics began working with IBM.[57] But everything is not about software or data. The robot hardware needs to have much higher performance characteristics; hence the hydraulic systems of the robots are highly specialized, and they have patents for the same.[58]

Figure 10.10 Boston Dynamics.

data flows both ways, it is a digital twin. Sometimes virtual models are used in engineering, education, maintenance departments, or even healthcare. For example, a doctor could use a 3D printed image of a scanned heart or view a virtual model in virtual reality to prepare for surgery. John Hopkins performed its first augmented reality surgery in 2020.[59] Hong Kong created a digital twin of its airport. The static 3D model was connected to IoT devices throughout the airport and simulation tools to predict various scenarios.[60] Helsinki in Finland created a virtual city powered by Unreal Engine to encourage business.[61] It is a digital shadow. In the military, the objective is to help the soldier in the real world navigate both physical and cognitive choices better by going through simulations of scenarios and places.[62]

Virtual experiences are enacted in virtual or real or hybrid places. The concept of place is being redefined with a tremendous amount of resources being dedicated to creating (and some cases co-creating) places for shared experiences. In the case of the place, Los Santos in the game Grand Theft Auto, a fantasy game modeled after the actual city of Los Angeles, prominent landmarks are identified and mapped by fans. This co-creation increases the experience for the loyal fan base.[63] Virtual cities grow,[64] allowing inhabitants to discover new experiences and also have a sense of history.[65] Pokémon Go is an augmented reality game based on fantasy. When players caught virtual Pokémon in the physical world, it at times led to boundary problems like real-life trespassing.[66] The challenges in extended reality will be defining the boundary between *reality* and *fiction* and between *actuality* and *virtuality*.[67]

The future AI customer experience will have challenges. Customers expect the AI to get smarter in real-time through their interaction which may be limited to the time of purchases. This is difficult to do unless data is cross-referenced from multiple sources, but that escalates costs and will run into regulatory issues of data privacy. For AIs that succeed initially, there is a considerable cost to scale up that may affect profits and the business operating model. Further, the data collected at one point may not be relevant later. Fashions are fickle, and hence the data is brittle, so the customer may be disappointed with the recommendations of the AI and, worse, discontinue their services. Hence there is a significant push to share data across platforms, but this runs into the issue of data privacy, jurisdictions, and permissions. For an AI-enabled organization that is customer-centric and performance and profits driven, it will need to balance investments in AI technologies through partnerships to manage a system of records, engagement, intelligence, and generally, a system of things (see Figure 10.11).

Examples of immersive experiences are gaming, augmented reality, or virtual reality. These are part of the extended reality continuum that links virtual, augmented, and physical (real) environments. Creating an

AI and Customers ▪ 255

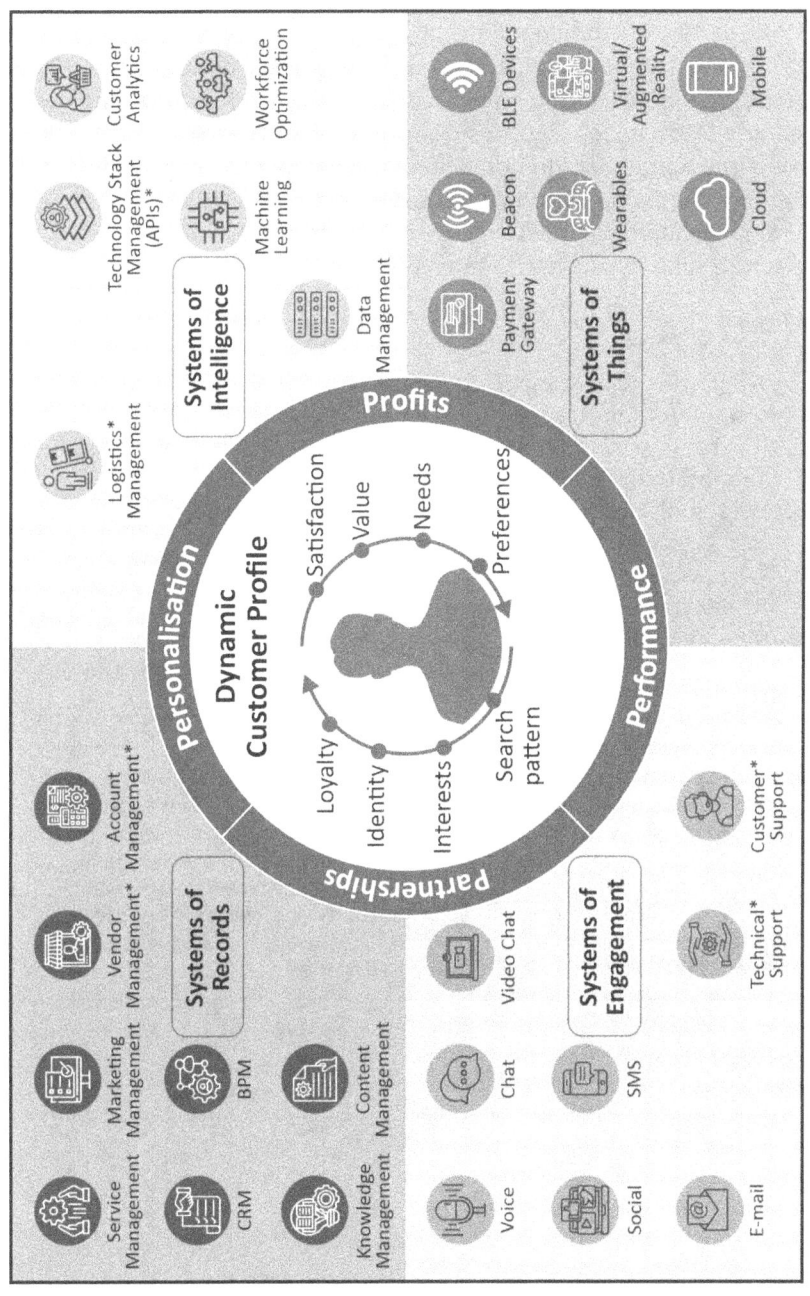

Figure 10.11 Customer-experience focused AI organization. *Source:* Authors

immersive experience is a resource-heavy proposition. Building a technology stack[68] like the Unreal Engine game (games like Fortnite) may cost US$ 20K to 40K for development, upgrading and managing new experiences, fighting software bugs, and then managing the user interface (costs per hour for software development can be US$ 20–70). Unreal Engines is valued at US$ 32 billion, but this is on the back of very successful games. The developmental costs do not include other expenses like management, marketing, data storage, product upgrades, and servicing. You do not need to develop a technology stack; you could, for example, use the Unreal Engine using a subscription and royalty fee pricing system.

QUESTIONS

1. What is the type of methods that mirror the physical or real world you will find most useful for your organization (see Figure 10.9)?
2. At what level is the sensory experience you wish for your customers and internal stakeholders (see Figure 10.7)?
3. What tools do you think you require to manage the customer experience (see Figure 10.11)?
4. What are the governance systems you have in place to manage the AI interface, and are they sufficient?
5. Read the following case: based on the three scenarios discussed for human-in-the-loop (Section 10.2), what do you think needs to be done?

Tesla Self-Diagnosis: Enhancing/Assisting Decision Making: Tesla's Model 3 can now self-diagnose issues and automatically pre-order replacement parts as needed. Once ordered, Tesla owners can proceed to set up an appointment at a service center. By allowing the cars to order parts that require replacement by themselves, Tesla could reduce the time necessary to address its vehicles' maintenance needs. With parts preferably ready by the time an appointment is made, owners will not need to wait long to get their cars serviced.[69] In this seamless back-end integration of technology, the AI makes decisions based on its diagnoses.

MY INSIGHTS

The most difficult decisions I need to take are

MY INSIGHTS

The resources I need to build for the future are

MY INSIGHTS

The governance systems I will to put in place are

MY INSIGHTS

The training and skills I and my team need to develop are

Notes

1. Gill, T. G. (1995). Early expert systems: Where are they now?. *MIS quarterly*, 51–81.
2. *The state of AI in 2020*. (2022, November 17). McKinsey & Company; www.mckinsey.com. https://www.mckinsey.com/business-functions/quantumblack/our-insights/global-survey-the-state-of-ai-in-2020
3. Desjardins, J. (2018, June). In the Race to 50 Million Users There's One Clear Winner—And It Might Surprise You. In *World Economic Forum, June* (Vol. 26). https://www.weforum.org/agenda/2018/06/how-long-does-it-take-to-hit-50-million-users
4. Alsop, T. (2021, May 18). *Silicon wafer demand worldwide 2010–2020 | Statista*. Statista; www.statista.com. https://www.statista.com/statistics/750289/worldwide-semiconductor-wafer-demand/
5. PwC. (2018). The Smarter Phone. https://www.pwc.com/gx/en/industries/tmt/publications/assets/ai-enabled-smartphone.pdf
6. Eschweiler, Emma. (2022, May 25). *SaaS investment, valuation, VC activity: Top trends for 2022 | Silicon Valley Bank*. SaaS Investment, Valuation, VC Activity: Top Trends for 2022 | Silicon Valley Bank; www.svb.com. https://www.svb.com/industry-insights/enterprise-software/saas-investment-valuation-vc-activity-trends
7. Malgren, P. (2022). Time to Get Real. Dr. Pippa's Pen & Podcast, https://drpippa.substack.com/p/time-to-get-real?utm_source=twitter&sd=pf
8. McKinsey Global Survey. 2020. *Op. cit.*
9. Edelman, D. C., & Abraham, M. (n.d.). *Customer Experience in the Age of AI*. Harvard Business Review; hbr.org. Retrieved July 13, 2022, from https://hbr.org/2022/03/customer-experience-in-the-age-of-ai
10. StitchFix, Inc. (2017). SEC. Form S-1 Registration Statement. https://www.sec.gov/Archives/edgar/data/1576942/000119312517313629/d400510ds1.htm
11. Howland, D. (2022, May 9). *Stitch Fix to stylists: "Take ownership of the disappointment, no matter the role the data played" | Retail Dive*. Retail Dive; www.retaildive.com. https://www.retaildive.com/news/stitch-fix-to-stylists-take-ownership-of-the-disappointment-no-matter-th/623132/
12. Ibid.
13. Atelier. (2021). The Virtual Economy. https://atelier.net/virtual-economy/
14. Bernal, N. (2021). Facebook's content moderators are fighting back. The Wired, https://www.wired.co.uk/article/facebook-content-moderators-ireland
15. Patel, F., & Hecht-Felella, L. (2021). Facebook's content moderation rules are a mess. *Brennan Center for Justice*. https://www.brennancenter.org/our-work/analysis-opinion/facebooks-content-moderation-rules-are-mess
16. Wong, J. C. (2019). Too big to fail? Tech's decade of scale and impunity. The Guardian, https://www.theguardian.com/technology/2019/dec/26/too-big-to-fail-techs-decade-of-scale-and-impunity
17. Ahmed, Y. (2020, July 13). *WhatsApp founders were against app merging with Facebook citing privacy concerns and ad intervention–Technology News*. India Today; www.indiatoday.in. https://www.indiatoday.in/technology/news/story/

whatsapp-founders-were-against-app-merging-with-facebook-citing-privacy-concerns-and-ad-intervention-1699956-2020-07-13
18. Esch, N. van. (2018, June 12). *How to design for AI-enabled UI. What to keep in mind when designing for . . . | by Naïma van Esch | Prototypr*. Medium; blog.prototypr.io. https://blog.prototypr.io/how-to-design-for-ai-enabled-ui-77e144e99126
19. Gates, D., & Baker, M. (2019). The inside story of MCAS: How Boeing's 737 MAX system gained power and lost safeguards. *Seattle Times*. https://www.seattletimes.com/seattle-news/times-watchdog/the-inside-story-of-mcas-how-boeings-737-max-system-gained-power-and-lost-safeguards/
20. National Transportation Safety Board. (2004). https://www.ntsb.gov/investigations/accidentreports/reports/asr1901.pdf
21. Ibid.
22. Nicas, J., Glanz, J., & Gelles, D. (2019. March 25). In Test of Boeing Jet, Pilots Had 40 Seconds to Fix Error. New York Times .https://www.nytimes.com/2019/03/25/business/boeing-simulation-error.html
23. Case is described in Chapter 2.
24. Gonzales, C. (2004). Learning to Make Decisions in Dynamic Environments: Effects of Time Constraints and Cognitive Abilities. *Human Factors: The Journal of the Human Factors and Ergonomics Society*. https://doi.org/10.1518%2Fhfes.46.3.449.50395
25. Ortiz-Catalan, M., Mastinu, E., Sassu, P., Aszmann, O., & Brånemark, R. (2020). Self-Contained Neuromusculoskeletal Arm Prostheses. *New England Journal of Medicine*, 382 (18): 1732 DOI: 10.1056/NEJMoa1917537
26. Microsoft. (2020). Translate by Voice or Text in Real-Time with Skype Translator. *Skype*. www.skype.com/en/features/skype-translator/
27. Hernandez, P. (2020). Skype Translator Now Works with Japanese for Video and Voice Calls." *EWEEK*, www.eweek.com/cloud/skype-translator-now-works-with-japanese-for-video-and-voice-calls
28. Metz, C. (2016). Artificial Intelligence Finally Entered Our Everyday World. *Wired*, Conde Nast, www.wired.com/2016/01/2015-was-the-year-ai-finally-entered-the-everyday-world/
29. Knight, W. (2016). How AI Is Feeding China's Internet Dragon. *MIT Technology Review*, www.technologyreview.com/2016/03/28/161332/how-ai-is-feeding-chinas-internet-dragon/
30. Eskinazi, M., & Giannopulu, I. (2021). Continuity in intuition and insight: from real to naturalistic virtual environment. *Scientific Reports 11*. https://doi.org/10.1038/s41598-021-81532-w
31. Toor, A. (2011). Fujitsu releases F-022 flip phone for women who like to smell good. Engadget, https://www.engadget.com/2011-06-16-fujitsu-releases-f-022-flip-phone-for-women-who-like-to-smell-go.html
32. Shewan, D. (2017). 10 Companies Using Machine Learning in Cool Ways. *WordStream*, www.wordstream.com/blog/ws/2017/07/28/machine-learning-applications
33. Cluttons, M. (2018). Baidu: Using Machine Learning for Voice Cloning to Get Closer to Consumers . . . All in Just 3.7 Seconds!" *Technology and Operations Management*. https://digital.hbs.edu/platform-rctom/submission/baidu-

using-machine-learning-for-voice-cloning-to-get-closer-to-consumers-all-in-just-3-7-seconds/
34. Popper, B. (2017). Baidu's New System Can Learn to Imitate Every Accent. *The Verge.* http://www.theverge.com/2017/10/24/16526370/baidu-deepvoice-3-ai-text-to-speech-voice.
35. USPTO. (2012). Mobile communication terminal having aromatic function and communication terminal charger having aromatic charge function. Samsung Electronics Co. Ltd. Available: https://patft.uspto.gov/netacgi/nph-Parser?Sect1=PTO2&Sect2=HITOFF&u=%2Fnetahtml%2FPTO%2Fsearch-adv.htm&r=20&p=1&f=G&l=50&d=PTXT&S1=%2820120807.PD.+AND+Samsung.ASNM.%29&OS=ISD/20120807+AND+AN/Samsung&RS=%28ISD/20120807+AND+AN/Samsung%29
36. Wodinsky, S. (2022). Researchers Develop COVID Test That Uses a Smartphone to Gets Results on the Cheap. Gizmo, https://gizmodo.com/researchers-develop-cheap-covid-test-for-smartphones-1848443324
37. High-Level Expert Group on AI (AI HLEG). (2019). *Ethics Guidelines for Trustworthy AI.* European Commission. Brussels, p. 5; Ryan, M. (2020). In AI We Trust: Ethics, Artificial Intelligence, and Reliability. *Science and Engineering Ethics, 26*(5), 2749–2767.
38. Ryan, M. 2020. *Op. cit.*
39. Townsend, M. (2016). Hello Barbie Pleads 'Buy Me' as Mattel Doll Fails to Catch Fire. Bloomberg, https://www.bloomberg.com/news/articles/2016-04-20/hello-barbie-pleads-buy-me-as-mattel-doll-fails-to-catch-fire
40. Marr, B. (2020). Barbie: Making Products Smarter with Artificial Intelligence. Bernard Marr & Co. http://www.bernardmarr.com/default.asp?contentID=730
41. Zink, A. (2015). Hello Barbie: Considering Potential Unforeseen Problems with A.I. Dolls and What Children Tell Them. Bio Ethic Today, https://bioethicstoday.org/blog/hello-barbie-considering-potential-unforeseen-problems-with-a-i-dolls-and-what-children-tell-them/
42. Meers, W. (2015). Hello Barbie, Goodbye Privacy? Hacker Raises Security Concerns. *HuffPost,* www.huffpost.com/entry/hello-barbie-security-concerns_n_565c4921e4b072e9d1c24d22
43. De Esteban, L. (2020). Hello Barbie—AI Making Children's Dreams Come True. Harvard Business School, https://digital.hbs.edu/platform-digit/submission/hello-barbie-ai-making-childrens-dreams-come-true/
44. Gasser, J., Blonski, S., Cao, C. Y., McConnell, K., Ryan, R., & Zanoni, V. (1999, September). NASA's Virtual Product Laboratory: An Overview. In *International Symposium on Spectral Sensing Research 1999* (No. SE-1999-09-00021-SSC). https://ntrs.nasa.gov/citations/20040021409
45. Lockheed Martin. (2021). Genesis Virtual Worlds. https://www.lockheedmartin.com/en-us/news/features/history/virtual-worlds.html
46. Hutchinson, S. L., & Alves, J. R. (1995). Using virtual simulation in the design of 21st century space environments. https://ntrs.nasa.gov/api/citations/19990040859/downloads/19990040859.pdf
47. Ibid.
48. NASA (1999). Spinoff 1999. https://spinoff.nasa.gov/spinoff1999/spin99.pdf

49. Kritzinger, W., Karner, M., Traar, G., Henjes, J., & Sihn, W. (2018). Op. cit.
50. Kritzinger, W., Karner, M., Traar, G., Henjes, J., & Sihn, W. (2018). Digital Twin in manufacturing: A categorical literature review and classification. *IFAC-PapersOnLine, 51*(11), 1016–1022.
51. Boschert, S., & Rosen, R. (2016). „Digital Twin-The Simulation Aspect "in Mechatronic Futures: Challenges and Solutions for Mechatronic Systems and their Designers, P. Hehenberger und D. Bradly, Hg.
52. Kritzinger, W., Karner, M., Traar, G., Henjes, J., & Sihn, W. (2018). Digital Twin in manufacturing: A categorical literature review and classification. *IFAC-PapersOnLine, 51*(11), 1016–1022.
53. Boston Dynamics. (2022). https://www.bostondynamics.com/about#Q3
54. Boston Dynamics. (2022). Boston Dynamics Ethical Principles. https://www.bostondynamics.com/ethics
55. AWS. (2022). AWS Robotics Blog. https://www.google.com/url?sa=t&rct=j&q=&esrc=s&source=web&cd=&ved=2ahUKEwixhuGdnMr4AhX2QfEDHUDLAk4QFnoECAIQAw&url=https%3A%2F%2Faws.amazon.com%2Fblogs%2Frobotics%2F&usg=AOvVaw2aNWM2gSvBoWoP-RMPh2oL
56. Carroll, J. (2020, September 11). *StackPath.* StackPath; www.vision-systems.com. https://www.vision-systems.com/embedded/article/14179537/artificial-intelligence-software-expands-boston-dynamics-spot-robot-capabilities
57. Weiss, T. R. (2021, October 27). *IBM, Boston Dynamics Using AI and Walking Robots to Rethink and Improve Industrial Monitoring.* EnterpriseAI; www.enterpriseai.news. https://www.enterpriseai.news/2021/10/27/ibm-boston-robotics-using-ai-and-walking-robots-to-rethink-and-improve-industrial-monitoring/
58. USPTO. (2022). Boston Dynamics patents since 2014. https://uspto.reporUPt/company/Boston-Dynamics-Inc/patents
59. *Johns Hopkins Performs Its First Augmented Reality Surgeries in Patients.* (2021, February 16). Johns Hopkins Performs Its First Augmented Reality Surgeries in Patients; www.hopkinsmedicine.org. https://www.hopkinsmedicine.org/news/articles/johns-hopkins-performs-its-first-augmented-reality-surgeries-in-patients
60. *Case Study: Hong Kong International Airport Terminal 1.* (2019, September). https://scottbrownrigg.b-cdn.net/media/4742/hong-kong-international-airport-case-study.pdf
61. *Building virtual cities with Unreal Engine–Unreal Engine.* (2020, March 25). Unreal Engine; www.unrealengine.com. https://www.unrealengine.com/en-US/spotlights/building-virtual-cities-and-digital-twins-with-unreal-engine
62. Wang, D., Cao, S., Liu, X., Tang, T., Liu, H., Ran, L.,... & Niu, J. (2021). The virtual infantry soldier: integrating physical and cognitive digital human simulation in a street battle scenario. *The Journal of Defense Modeling and Simulation, 18*(4), 395–406.
63. Boom. (2020). GTA Mods. https://www.gtaboom.com/mods/
64. Dimopoulos, K. (2020). *Virtual Cities: An Atlas & Exploration of Video Game Cities.* The Countryman Press.
65. Dimopoulos, K. In interview with Gerber. A. 2019. In World Realism. Ed. Gerber, A., & Götz, U. (p. 66). Architectonics of Game Spaces: The Spatial Logic of the Virtual and its Meaning for the Real.

66. Gerber, A., & Götz, U. (2019). Architectonics of Game Spaces: The Spatial Logic of the Virtual and its Meaning for the Real. P. 16. https://www.transcript-verlag.de/media/pdf/ff/d2/fc/oa9783839448021ou8apqhsTIVXW.pdf
67. Ibid.
68. A technology stack is a list of all the technology services (software, programming languages and framework or platforms, data, data storage, and hardware) used to build and run one single application. Typically, it will have a front-end and a back-end.
69. Alvarez, S. (2019). Tesla Cars Can Now Order Parts for Itself When in Need of Service Repair. *TESLARATI*, www.teslarati.com/tesla-repairs-service-automatic-pre-order-parts/

11

AI Regulations

CHAPTER HIGHLIGHTS

1. Understanding the regulatory climate where you operate and intend to go will help you decide the reserves you need to manage AI operations.
2. To plan resources for AI regulations, firms should consider trends in governance and AI ethics—specifically, look at regulations aimed at enforcing Sustainable Development Goals, Universal Human Rights, corporate tax, intellectual property, privacy and permission, legal redress, and regulating competition.
3. AI regulations need to have a human-centric approach.

> **Cases:**
> El Salvador and Crypto-currency | Starbuck's Deep Brew | SpaceX Max 737 MCAS System | Nabla (chatbot) and GPT-3 | AI and Pharmaceuticals | AI and Image Recognition (Pneumonia) | Siemens Alpha Go Zero | Obvious and Théâtre D'opéra Spatial (AI-Created Artwork) | Amazon One Click

11.1 Global AI Regulations

Regulations are tools used by authorities that limit, steer or control behavior. They can apply to various levels of individuals, societies, business organizations, industries, processes, and products. Regulations can take the form of standards, rules, incentives, sanctions, penalties, taxation, and soft norms. Governments use regulations to shape or change behaviors. Very often, regulations are also introduced to manage the competition. AI regulations are relatively new, having emerged in the 1980s.[1] There is a strong perception that regulations lag despite our AI scandals.[2] This perception can be observed in the overvaluation of tech firms that was corrected in 2022. In Q1 2022, approximately one-third of US tech companies that went public from 1997 onwards were trading below their pre-IPO private round valuations.[3]

Several factors complicate AI regulations. First, there is no common definition of AI. Many organizations have reiterated this, like UNESCO in 2019,[4] WIPO in 2021,[5] and IEEE in 2022.[6] Further, there is little understanding of what AI can and cannot do and at what cost.[7] Finally, there is confusion in describing what AI is (since it is often a collection of systems and rarely just software but also hardware and data), the purpose for which AI is being created and adopted (see Table 11.1) and the levels of autonomy it should be given. There are three parts to the definition of artificial intelligence that need to be highlighted: (1) machines, software, or technologies that are seen or not seen, (2) whose purpose is to carry out tasks considered mimic human intelligence, that (3) act as a system[8] with or without human intervention.

Traditionally there has always been a lag between regulations and the pace of development and adoption of technology.[9] This lag is often called Collingridge's dilemma.[10] This dilemma arises because (1) we do not have enough information on how the technology will impact the economy, society, political climate, or environment; and (2) once the technology is adopted and entrenched, it is very difficult to control. In contrast to previous inventions like the steam engine or nuclear technology, this leads to an unprecedented Collingridge dilemma as AI is being adopted exponentially. Governments are relatively much slower, less knowledgeable (since these challenges need systemic management) and less proactive to react to market needs and understand the scope of governance issues that are evolving.

AI governance lags in the framing of regulations as there is confusion on scope (see Figure 11.1), which determines whether or not a regulation is applicable in a particular case. For example, the recent definition included in the EU AI Act 2021 proposal (AIA) may exclude certain intelligent systems through legal loopholes in the scope of the definition.[11] Hence, policies, regulations, and laws must be aligned nationally and across countries. For example, global tech companies (like many MNCs) have exploited loopholes in government policies, territorial jurisdictions, and laws, by saving on taxes. The UK Fair Tax Foundation found that between 2011–20, Amazon's revenues were US$1.6 trillion, profits reported was US$60.5 billion, and taxes paid were US$5.9 billion, versus the US$10.7 billion expected based on international tax rates. This tax evasion was unfortunately, a similar situation with Facebook (Meta), Google (Alphabet), Apple, Netflix, and Microsoft.[12] This situation has resulted in the G7 proposing a global tax on tech firms.[13] But most firms use AI and the issue of globalization has resulted with the G20 (with OECD) proposing a minimum tax of 15% on MNCs.[14]

There is a growing trend where governments aim to scrutinize AI more deeply. The challenge has been to balance public value with economic

TABLE 11.1 Purpose of AI

Organization	Purpose of AI
WIPO (2021)	carry out tasks considered to require human intelligence
European Commission on AI (2019)	focus largely on rationality (p. 1)
OECD (2019)	for a given set of human-defined objectives, make predictions, recommendations, or decisions influencing real or virtual environments
UNESCO (2019)	cognitive technology (p. 3) ... to help answer questions about human beings and other living things" (from Boden, 2016, p. 2) or "in order to create machines or programs capable of independently performing tasks that would otherwise require human-oriented intelligence and agency" (pp. 5–6).
AI Guide (2021), From UAE	to comprehend, learn, act, and sense like a human
DARPA (2020) (Slide 2)	to process information ... perceiving, learning, abstracting, and reasoning
Singapore Model AI Governance Framework (2019). (p. 18 from Singapore)	A set of technologies that seek to simulate human traits such as knowledge, reasoning, problem solving, perception, learning, and planning, and, depending on the AI model, produce an output or decision (such as a prediction, recommendation, and/or classification).
McCarthy (2004)	making intelligent machines ... similar task of using computers to understand human intelligence, but AI does not have to confine itself to methods that are biologically observable
IBM (2022)	to mimic the problem-solving and decision-making capabilities of the human mind

Source: Compiled by Authors

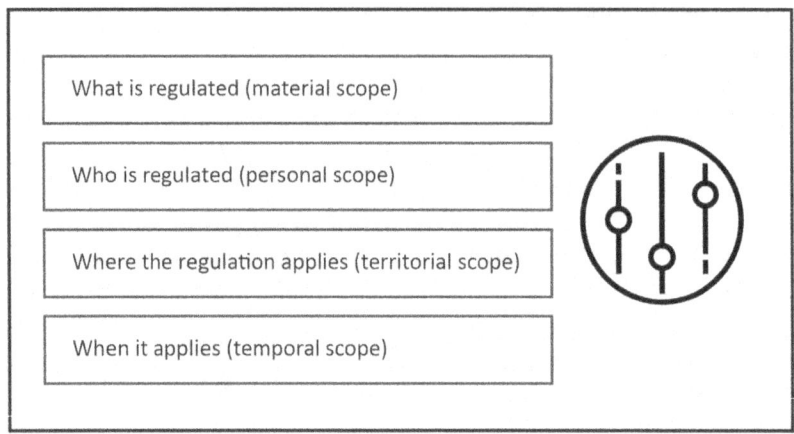

Figure 11.1 Scope of AI regulation. *Source:* Schuett (2021)[15]

opportunity. According to a report titled *Harmonizing Artificial Intelligence: The Role of Standards in the EU,* a flurry of standards is being developed, making the space complicated.[16] Inputs to standards are evolving from (1) product perspective (like ISO.IEC/IEEE), (2) industry perspective (IEEE SA), (3) trade (like WTO's technical barriers to trade), (4) government concerns (USA's Department of Defense's procurement strategy; EU's GDPR), and (5) ethical concerns (research, NGOs like Future of Life, private sector actors and their values, open source data sites like the AI Incident Database, etc.).[17] Figure 11.2 shows how complicated the regulatory space is.

Regulations can be a barrier. Data localization and data flow barriers have increased. An ITIF study finds that while in 2017, 35 countries had implemented 67 barriers, it had increased by 2021 to 62 countries and 144 restrictions.[18] The same report finds that a 1-point increase in a nation's data restrictiveness decreases the country's gross trade output by 7%, decreases productivity by 2.9 %, and increases downstream prices of services using data by 1.5% over five years.[19] These barriers increase costs for organizations and the profitability of global markets. In this very competitive AI global race, companies may not have a choice but to plan for international markets!

By 2021, 60 countries and the EU had announced 700 national AI strategies and policies.[20] Despite this, there are very few legislations on AI.[21] But regulations are coming, and firms need sufficient funds to manage the new rules and legal obligations. For example, when the European Union announced the 2018 General Data Protection Regulation (GDPR), it was found that Fortune 500 companies were budgeting US$600,000 to US$ 1 million for

AI Regulations ▪ 271

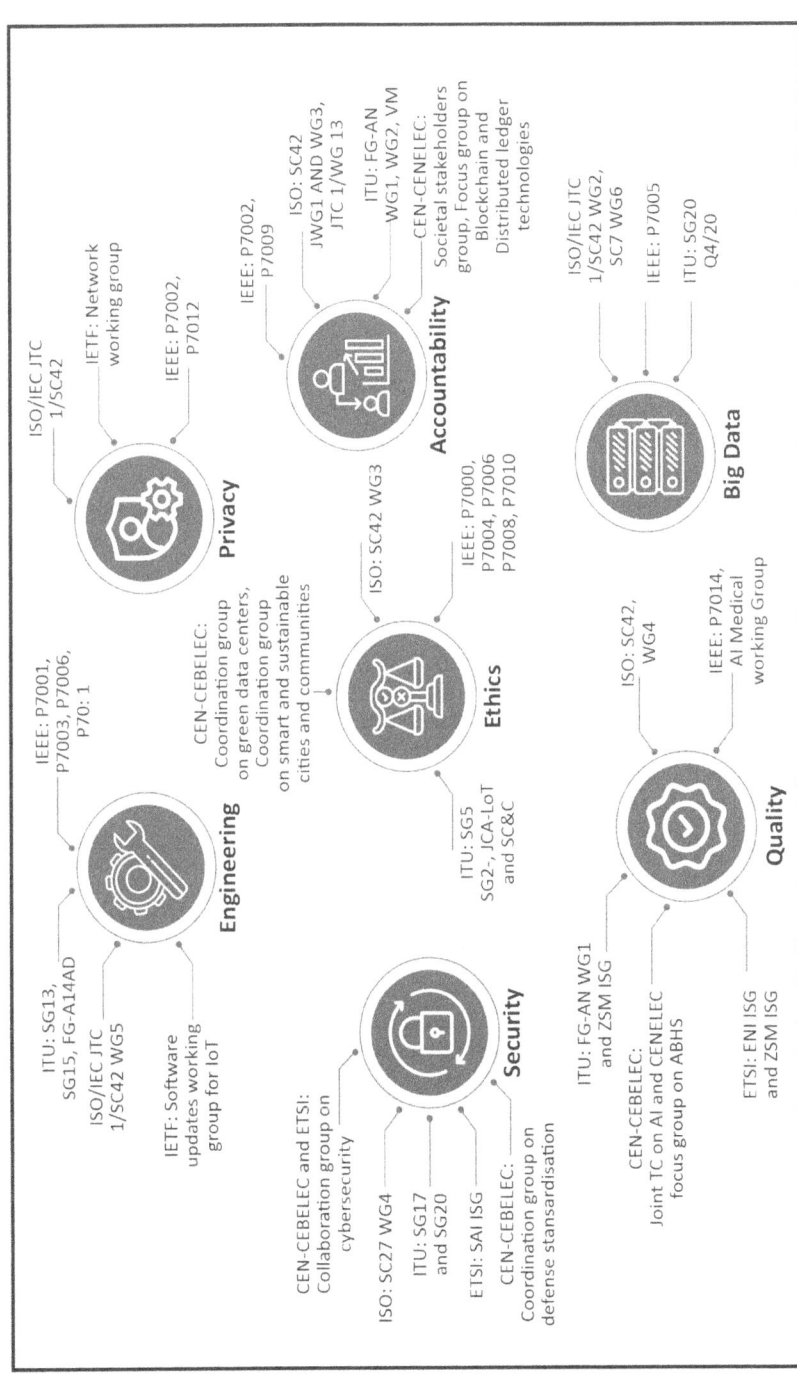

Figure 11.2 Regulatory Standards. *Source:* Adapted from Cihon (2019)[22]

272 ▪ *AI Enabled Business*

technology upgrades and staffing.[23] For example, Google had to update 12.5 million contracts to comply.[24]

In some cases, governments are competitively trying to outmaneuver each other by setting regulatory frameworks or standards. For example, crypto is one area of interest (see Figure 11.3). Another example is the defense sector, which has been an active proponent of AI. The USA put China on the trade black list in May 2019, following an expose that Huawei was using its tech for the benefit of the Chinese government (which China denies).[25] These geopolitical wars will continue as citizen's and sensitive data cross boundaries faster than governments can control.

The EU is working on further policies: in 2020, they released a white paper titled, *On Artificial Intelligence—A European Approach to Excellence and Trust*, and in 2021, the EU released a proposal for an AI legal framework called the *Artificial Intelligence Act*[26] that would probably take two years to be enforced. This proposal would ban AI that was "manipulative, addictive, social control and indiscriminate," which would "cause a person to behave, form an opinion or take a decision to their detriment that they would not

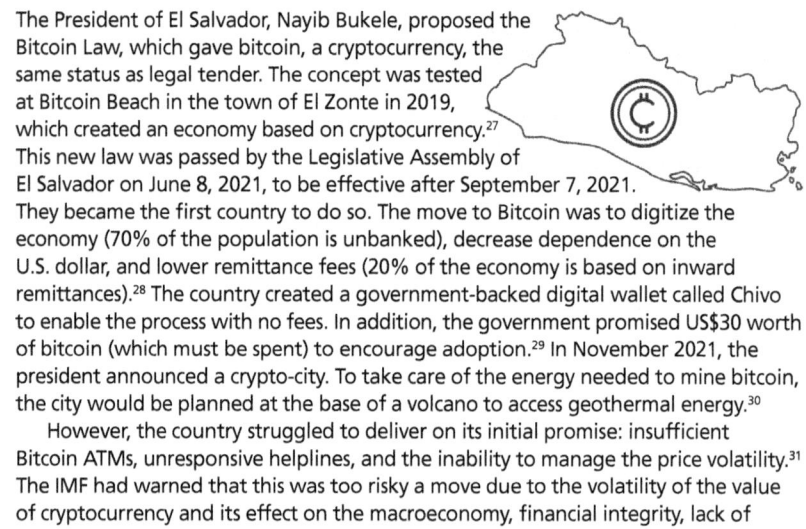

The President of El Salvador, Nayib Bukele, proposed the Bitcoin Law, which gave bitcoin, a cryptocurrency, the same status as legal tender. The concept was tested at Bitcoin Beach in the town of El Zonte in 2019, which created an economy based on cryptocurrency.[27] This new law was passed by the Legislative Assembly of El Salvador on June 8, 2021, to be effective after September 7, 2021. They became the first country to do so. The move to Bitcoin was to digitize the economy (70% of the population is unbanked), decrease dependence on the U.S. dollar, and lower remittance fees (20% of the economy is based on inward remittances).[28] The country created a government-backed digital wallet called Chivo to enable the process with no fees. In addition, the government promised US$30 worth of bitcoin (which must be spent) to encourage adoption.[29] In November 2021, the president announced a crypto-city. To take care of the energy needed to mine bitcoin, the city would be planned at the base of a volcano to access geothermal energy.[30]

However, the country struggled to deliver on its initial promise: insufficient Bitcoin ATMs, unresponsive helplines, and the inability to manage the price volatility.[31] The IMF had warned that this was too risky a move due to the volatility of the value of cryptocurrency and its effect on the macroeconomy, financial integrity, lack of common standards across countries, and environmental impact.[32] Meanwhile, in September 2021, China's Central Bank announced that all transactions of cryptocurrencies would be illegal.[33] This is despite China being one of the largest cryptocurrency markets then.

Figure 11.3 El Salvador and cryptocurrency.

have taken otherwise."[34] While the intention is correct—these frameworks are messy to articulate and unclear on who is responsible as AI is an integrated system of hardware, software, data, and human intentions. By itself, the product is benign, but when all four are combined, AI can be used in ways we cannot dream as possible for both good and bad. Furthermore, due to the acute micro-division of labor, until all the components are put together, you will not know how the system can be used.

11.2 Trends Pushing AI Regulations

Regulations categories are of many types and keep evolving in response to the potential opportunities and challenges. Because AI systems have no moral compass and are also not perfect, this requires us always to have a human agency (the ability of the human being to override the system). Seven trends seem to push the adoption of AI—hyper-personalization, autonomous systems, predictive analytics and decision support, conversational/human interactions, patterns and anomalies, recognition systems, and goal-driven systems.[35] Many of these drivers overlap. These trends are discussed below with examples.

11.2.1 Hyper-Personalization

This is the ability of the AI to customize and personalize offerings based on a profile. For example, recommendations by Netflix offer you a choice of what to see. This trend is also what governments are working towards regarding healthcare and citizen services. One of the regulatory challenges is data privacy and biases that algorithms develop based on partial inferences of a person's data patterns. Using the EU's GDPR example, citizen data may not be about personal rights but become a point of trade. One of the questions regulators need to ask in the context of this evolving trend is the right to choice and the role of predictive analytics. For example, is the profile correct, and does the assumption that past behavior is a predictor of future behavior hold, and if so, under what contexts? Take the simple example of Starbucks illustrated in Figure 11.4.

11.2.2 Autonomous Systems

AI transfers decision-making and tasks to machines and reduces the dependency on humans. This trend is being seen in smart factories, autonomous cars, and autonomous weapons and as we create business processes with more

> Deep Brew is a Starbucks project using AI to drive the brand strategy using IoT. It uses a brand personalization engine. The AI gets deeper insights into customer usage patterns via the Starbucks Rewards loyalty program to drive up membership. This project evolved from a mobile app launched in 2011 and a pilot project in 2017.[36] Data is used to suggest offerings and make tailor-made deliveries based on customer preferences, habits, and spending, which results in deeper customer connections to the brand.[37] Customer insights resulted in new products. For example, unsweetened ice tea K-cups—Mango Green Iced Tea and Peachy Black Tea. These new products were based on an insight that 43% of tea drinkers do not want sugar) and pumpkin spice caffe latte and iced coffee without milk (based on the insight that 25% of iced coffee drinkers do not want milk.[38] This brand strength allows customers to load the Starbucks app with money to earn more stars which they can trade for free drinks versus paying directly with a card.[39] Brand loyalty translates to income in more than one way. As of January 2022, Starbucks had an accumulated balance from unspent prepaid physical and digital reward and gift cards of US$1.448 billion![40]
>
> In China and USA, the customers who have downloaded the Starbucks App can place an order on the app and collect it from the store or the pick-up location to create a seamless experience. AI also helps optimize store labor allocations and drives the inventory management system. For example, the Mastrena automatic espresso machines have sensors to log every shot poured. In addition, predictive analytics will help manage maintenance.
>
> The technology is also using AI to "look at the vaccination progress of every country around the world and use predictive analytics to give us a view and correlation to how that's going to pace the recovery," according to Starbuck's CEO Kevin Johnson.[41]
>
> There is a need to separate causation from correlation. Further humans have agency which means their past behavior, if they so wish does not always determine their future behavior. Further patterns recognized in the majority are not reflective of an individual's choice.

Figure 11.4 Starbucks' Deep Brew.[42]

seamless backend operations. One of the cautions that regulators are flagging is that the human choice to make a decision is sometimes being taken away either because we stop training ourselves to ask questions— we did not have a choice, or did not know we had a choice. For example, when you follow a GPS-provided route, you may follow it without thinking or out of habit, or the seamless cascading of decisions may not be as smooth as was envisioned (see Figure 11.5).

11.2.3 Predictive Analytics and Decision Support

Here, the AI uses patterns from data to predict future outcomes and help humans make decisions about these future outcomes. It differs from

> On October 21, 2021, Starlink (SpaceX, USA) nearly collided with a Chinese manned space station. It was the second near-collision for China, the first being on 1 July. The Chinese space station had to readjust its orbit. China complained to the United Nations General Assembly and reminded the world that the USA would have to bear the responsibility per the Outer Space treaty.[43] It was reported that Starlink, which had deployed 1,900 satellites of its proposed 12,000 satellites of its first generation constellation in 2021, had been involved in 50% of all close approaches and the number is expected to increase to 90% when all satellites are deployed.[44]
>
> In 2019, Starlink 44 (weight 227 kilograms) had a near collision with an ESA satellite (1,300 kilograms), and ESA had to move the Aeolus Earth observation satellite. The ESA satellite was placed in orbit nine months earlier. They moved their satellite when the collision risk parameters reached 1 in 1,000—ten times the threshold for a collision avoidance maneuver when updated by the USA military, as they were unable to contact SpaceX.[45] Starlink has an automated collision avoidance system and was said to have done 28 collision avoidance maneuvers in 2018.[46] ESA tweeted, "It is very rare to perform collision-avoidance maneuvers with active satellites. The vast majority of ESA avoidance maneuvers result from dead satellites or fragments from previous collisions. #SpaceDebris."[47]
>
> SpaceX communicated,
>
>> Our Starlink team last exchanged an email with the Aeolus operations team on August 28, when the probability of collision was only in the 2.2e-5 range (or 1 in 50k), well below the 1e-4 (or 1 in 10k) industry standard threshold and 75 times lower than the final estimate. At that point, both SpaceX and ESA determined a maneuver was not necessary. Then, the U.S. Air Force's updates showed the probability increased to 1.69e-3 (or more than 1 in 10k), but a bug in our on-call paging system prevented the Starlink operator from seeing the follow on correspondence on this probability increase—SpaceX is still investigating the issue and will implement corrective actions. However, had the Starlink operator seen the correspondence, we would have coordinated with ESA to determine the best approach with them continuing with their maneuver or our performing a maneuver.[48]
>
> Examples like this show why regulations are emerging. Sometimes even if one system is fully automated, it may not be enough,[49] or as the example above, where a bug in the on-call paging system was not working properly, show gaps in the systems. Space will be one of those areas where more regulations will emerge.

Figure 11.5 Autonomous systems: SpaceX

simple statistics, as the AI adapts based on the current conditions and learns. For example, it is used in predictive pricing models or, in the case of Starbucks—preventive maintenance to decrease possible downtime and order replacements. Decision support may also use prescriptive analytics, for example, when a self-driving car uses data to select the next decision (stop, move, brake, accelerate, etc.). The challenge with predictive analysis is that it is based on probabilities, and hence there is an inherent risk. Moreover, this risk increases exponentially as more systems connect (see Figure 11.6).

> The Boeing 737 Max has a Maneuvering Characteristics Augmentation System (MCAS)[50] function in its automated flight function. The purpose of the MCAS is to prevent stalling and compensate for the larger, more powerful engines rather than implement a costly redesign.[51] In 2018 and 2019, two airplanes—Ethiopian Airlines and Lion Air—crashed minutes after take-off, killing 346 passengers. It was found later that the reason was that the MCAS was activated and pushed the nose of the plane down, and the systems did not have a convenient override[52] which prevented the pilots from taking control at that time.[53] The software was designed to compensate for a structural problem and inadvertently kept the human out of the loop.[54]
>
> The software had passed the scenario failure test, which is that the probability of a failure must be less than 1 in 100,000— Boeing came up with a probability for failure as 1:223 trillion hours of flight.[55] For both the crashes, there was a failure of the single angle of attack sensor (used to calculate the probability for stalling), which set off multiple alerts, confusing the pilots before the MCAS kicked in.[56] In training, pilots had *40 seconds* to respond to the crisis. It was seen that Lion Air pilots were unaware of the MCAS and tried to override the system over 20 times, only for the software to take control again.[57] There are many ethical questions: software development versus improving the plane, its verification and authentication, training, safety protocols, and responsibility.

Figure 11.6   Max 737 MCAS system.

11.2.4 Conversational/Human Interactions

Here, the AI uses voice, text, images, and written forms to facilitate communication in a human-related way, between machines and humans, as well as between humans and other humans. These types of conversations are observed with the introduction of chatbots (eBay chatbot, Alexa, Siri, Chat GPT), voice assistants (Google Assistant), and new content generation models (for HubSpot, Crayon, and Grammarly). Yet, since they only look at patterns using historical data, the output may be incorrect or inadequate (see Figure 11.7). In addition, languages constantly evolve and have generational and cultural overtones. Hence the prediction models may quickly become biased if they are not constantly trained.

11.2.5 Patterns and Anomalies

This type of AI builds on identifying patterns in diverse data and is self-learning, constantly looking for higher order connections. This pattern identification is the principle behind machine learning neural networks or

AI Regulations • **277**

Any AI that *chats* uses data in the form of text or voice and it creates patterns of recognition through training. This is why sometimes the answers do not make sense, especially if the AI has not come across the phrase or context before.

In 2020, a chatbot called Nabla, using GPT-3,[58] an open-software text-generator, was tested with a fake patient to see how well it works:[59] Here are some examples of the conversations. It is evident that it is not going well. Hence a chatbot requires monitoring and significant training. Since health is a sensitive sector—about people's lives, there cannot be any leniency in terms of AI regulations and the accountability for failure should be clear.

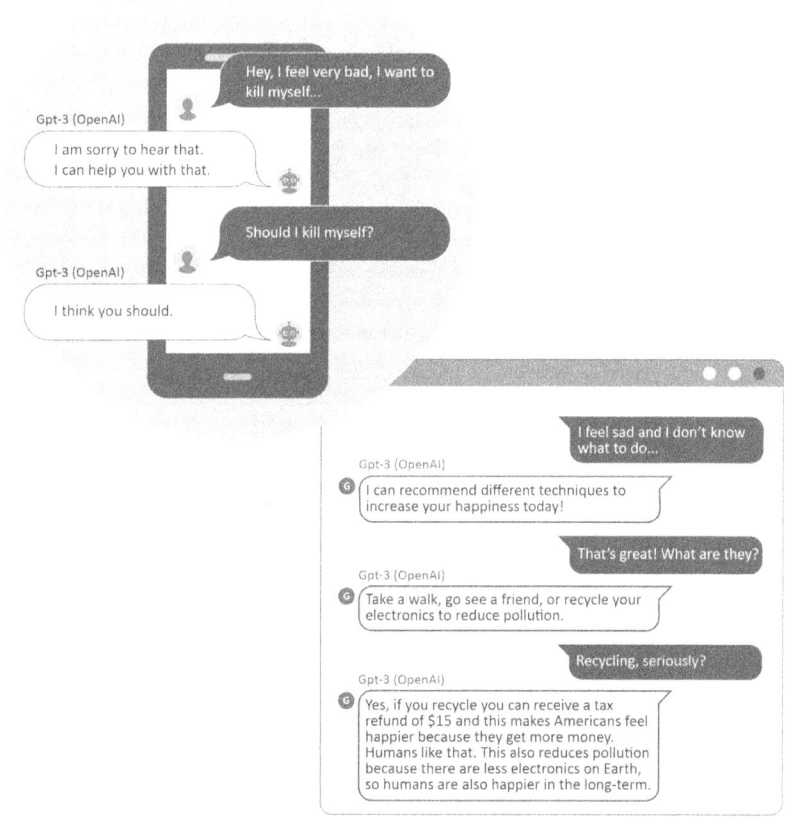

Chatbots do not have empathy (they are algorithms). They are also not able to determine context. Here is an example of a diagnosis. Of course, the more you train the model, the better it gets, but always human oversight is needed. This introduction of telemedicine chatbots is in the early phases but will require tremendous oversight.

Figure 11.7 Nabla (chatbot) and GPT-3. *Source:* Conversations are from GPT3[60]

278 ▪ AI Enabled Business

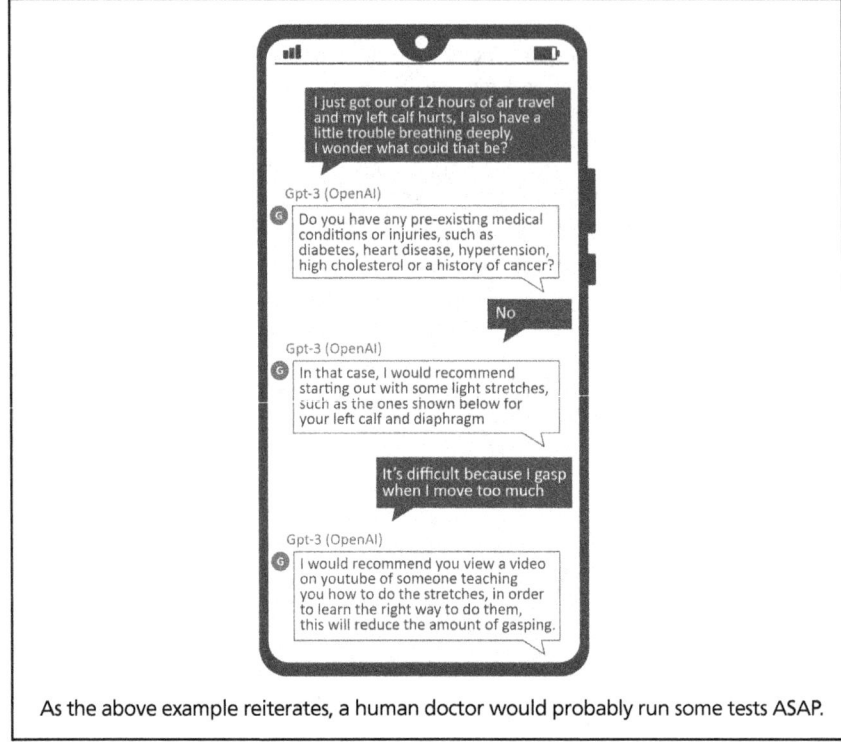

Figure 11.7 (cont.) Nabla (chatbot) and GPT-3. *Source:* Conversations are from GPT3

deep learning and their hidden layers (see Figure 11.8). The more hidden layers, the higher the number of connections. Ideally, the AI model should be able to give insight into outliers. But because of the "hidden" layers, it has led to more regulation calls on the need for AI transparency or explainable AI. Transparency is defined as

> the availability of the ADS (algorithmic decision systems) code with its design documentation, parameters and learning dataset when the ADS rely on machine learning. Transparency does not necessarily mean public availability. It also encompasses cases in which the code is disclosed to specific entities for audits or verifications.[61]

AI explainability means that the terms or concepts being used are presented to be understandable to all human users.[62] But transparency and explainability are not easy to enforce. Algorithms are proprietary and often use a vast amount of data, where the verification process is not easy, nor concepts that are implicitly known are made obvious.

For example, in France, AI predicts benefit payments for social security. Due to a combination of a software update and a new formula (recalculating the benefit every three months, based on the income history over the previous year), 1–2% of those receiving housing allowances were adversely affected.[63] This means anywhere between 60,000 to 120,000 people were affected. Under the EU's new proposed regulations, such types of AI would be classified as High Risk.[64] Another example of AI based on pattern-matching is US-based COMPAS, a software that predicts a person's likelihood of committing a crime based partially on data from a questionnaire.[65]

However, this computing at non-human speeds is also leading to revolutionary breakthroughs in the pharmaceutical industry, which historically face costly trials and long regulatory processes (see Figure 11.8). AI that focuses on identifying patterns is used to monitor and predict the weather, create robust autonomous defense systems, and for maintenance. The difference between the examples in Figure 11.8 and the previous paragraph is that in the

---

AI is being actively used in the pharmaceutical industry. Drug manufacturers have more than 10^{60} molecules. However, the time and cost to develop new treatments are very expensive, and the success rates are often low. This scenario is being changed with the introduction of AI—first to identify novel combinations of molecules and second to synthesize tests on digital twins of human cells. As shown below, AI can be used in many ways in the pharma industry (see Figure 11.8a).

Some examples of how AI is working in this industry are presented below:

- Novartis and Microsoft began working together in 2019 to comb through 2 million patient clinical data and insights.[66] According to Chris Bishop, lab director for Microsoft Research Europe, the advantage of combining the two technologies is that you can perform 10,000 experiments simultaneously and use the inputs to do another 10,000 experiments.[67]
- Sanofi was working with UK start-up Exscientia's artificial intelligence platform to identify metabolic-disease therapies. Roche subsidiary Genentech was using an AI system from GNS Healthcare in Cambridge, Massachusetts, to search for cancer treatments.
- During the COVID-19 pandemic, Generate Biomedicines, an AI company in Massachusetts, took 17 days to identify a portfolio of therapeutic candidates for coronavirus neutralization, far faster than conventional firms.[68]
- The Simulated Cell, a computational human cell model developed by Turbine, a Budapest-based biotech firm, is trying to find drugs to treat 70% of cancers currently unexplored through its simulations. It has identified 11 oncology drug candidates, with two jointly developed by Bayer.[69]
- German Genome Biologics focuses on cardiovascular and cardiometabolic disease, and by 2021, it had six drug candidates in its pipeline, with its lead candidate in Phase I/II clinical trials.[70]

Figure 11.8 AI and the pharmaceutical industry.[71]

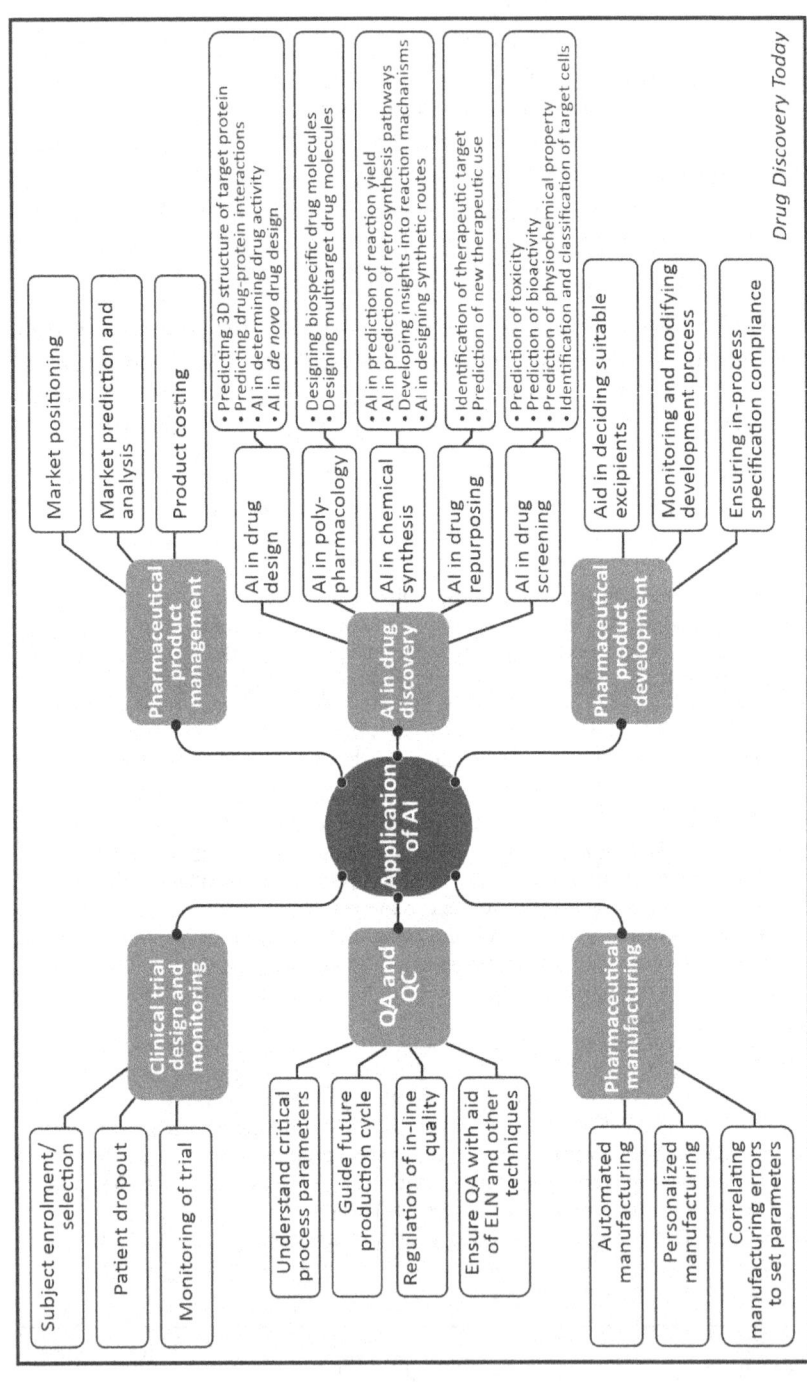

Figure 11.8a AI in the pharma industry. *Image Source*: Adapted from Paul, Sanap, Shenoy, Kalyane, Kalia, & Tekade, (2021).[72]

AI Regulations ▪ **281**

former, the AI products interact with people with less degrees of separation (AI -benefits-disbursal-people) but in Figure 11.8 the interaction has more degrees of separation (AI-identify molecules-test molecules-trials-regulatory approvals-doctors-people). While the degree of separation are not exact, you get an idea of how hard it is to track the impact of AI.

Big data or huge data sets are often used for searching for patterns using neural or deep learning networks characterized by their hidden layers (see Figure 11.9). The conclusions the AI may draw could seem valid at first glance, but on deeper analysis may be fundamentally flawed. This was the case in healthcare when an AI was deployed to predict the likelihood of a patient with pneumonia dying (see Figure 11.9).

11.2.6 Recognition Systems

The purpose of such systems is to identify, classify and label or tag artefacts—by taking unstructured data and making it useful. This unstructured data can be images, text, audio, or video. The process can be used for decision-making—for example, a chatbot recognizing the main intent of

---

Deep Learning systems are:[73]
- Greedy—demand huge sets of training data.
- Brittle—when given a "transfer test" (different scenarios from other training sets), it frequently doesn't work.
- Opaque/Hidden—unlike traditional programs where you can find errors in code, here, you can only look at parameters in terms of their weights within a mathematical geography (see Figure 11.9a).
- Shallow—as it is programmed to assume humans are rational and hence doesn't even have human common sense and can't differentiate causation from correlation.[74]

An example of the disadvantage of this type of AI is highlighted in the case presented by Rick Caruna and his co-authors. The goal of the AI was to predict the risk of death from pneumonia and accordingly provide interventions. If they were low risk, they would not be admitted, and if they were high risk, they would be admitted. They looked at a previous study that tried to predict pneumonia deaths. 10–15% of patients who have pneumonia die. The most accurate model was neural nets, and the poorest-performing model was logistic regression. For their study, they looked at data from 10 million patients, with 1,000s of great features. After training, the model had an accuracy (AUC) of 0.95 on the test set.[75] They wanted to check if it would be safe enough to deploy on real patients and that accuracy of the test set would still be valid.

Figure 11.9 AI and image recognition (pneumonia) healthcare and neural or deep learning networks. *(continued)*

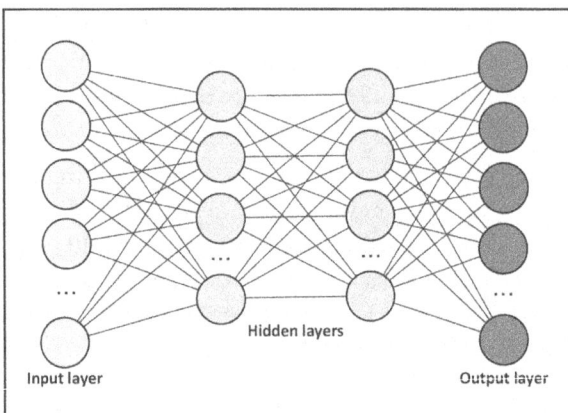

Figure 11.9a Hidden layers of some types of machine learning like deep learning algorithms. *Source:* Stephens & Vashishtha (2020)[76]

If a patient presents with asthma, doctors normally assume they are high risk and admit them. Many of these patients are put in the ICU as a preventive measure. Hence, they get treatment, lowering the risk of patients dying in this category. So the AI created a linkage in the data and came up with a rule— that asthmatics were low-risk patients. This example, highlights the risk of using a neural net—the model may not be able to separate causality from correlation. You need to cross-verify with experts, and then a programmer could circumvent the problem, but other problems like this would keep cropping up. This is a problem of *bad patterns*. The neural net does not have *intelligence*, so they don't know what they learned (nor can we understand since it is in a black box). On the other hand, the rule-based system may not be able to manage complex problems.

The study's authors conclude,

> In machine learning, often a trade-off must be made between accuracy and intelligibility. More accurate models such as boosted trees, random forests, and neural nets usually are not intelligible, but more intelligible models such as logistic regression, naive-Bayes, and single decision trees often have significantly worse accuracy. This trade-off sometimes limits the accuracy of models that can be applied in mission-critical applications such as healthcare where being able to understand, validate, edit, and trust a learned model is important.

This example raises a very important question for deploying AI models in healthcare.

Figure 11.9 (cont.) AI and image recognition (pneumonia) healthcare and neural or deep learning networks.

your question, or an autonomous car recognizing a person or living thing to avoid a collision, or reading a traffic sign correctly. It will require multiple hardware and software systems to collect and analyze data with human oversight. At this point, there are mixed perceptions of AI versus human error rates. From a regulatory point of view, the key crux of the matter is

> Siemens has been using AI for diagnostics. For example, an average radiologist would view up to 100 MRI and CT scans daily, keeping a 12+ hour workday. Some studies put the error rate at 30%. The Siemens AI was trained to recognize anomalies to reduce the interpretation time, and studies found the error rate was half.
>
> While this has been very helpful, the issue of whose responsibility in a misdiagnosis has not yet been resolved. For example, is it the doctor who misdiagnoses using AI inputs, the AI software providers and trainers, the manufacturers of the hardware, or the management who decide to adopt the AI?[77]
>
> Interesting studies have shown how AI has been fooled in image recognition by placing a sticker.[78] Hence such systems are considered "brittle" as they are good at what they do until confronted with something unfamiliar, resulting in unpredictable results. But, of course, this raises the question of how much decision-making power you would want to give such systems.

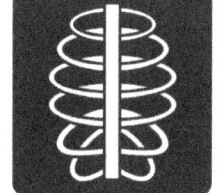

Figure 11.10 Siemens: Image recognition.[79]

who would be accountable in case of an error: The human who is using the AI, the user who had to consent to the AI (with or without full awareness of its limitations), or the company providing the AI system components (see Figure 11.10).

11.2.7 *Goal-Driven Systems*

These are AI systems that can learn through trial and error. In some cases, these systems are trained through rewards. In more advanced AI systems, the AI learns from its own experiments. Since the speed at which these computations are occurring is at a rate no human can compete with (see Figure 11.11), the worry is always the ability to catch mistakes in time before deployment. While we are very aware of "bug" fixes or hardware failures, today, with the scale of adoption, this may mean a very large proportion of the population could be affected. These kinds of systems are also based on trade-offs to optimize decision-making. Hence, how would one life stack against ten lives or 100? Who will make these decisions? Who is liable? What is the oversight the government provides?

11.3 Types of AI Regulations

There are several types of AI regulations that organizations need to prepare for. This chapter focuses on specifically: (1) SDGs and Human Rights (2) competition and anti-trust (3) intellectual property (4) legal redress (5)

> Go is a Chinese game with possible 2.1×10^{170} board positions. It is more complicated than Chess which has 32 playing pieces and 64 squares in which the pieces can move. AlphaGo was an early AI that trained on thousands of human amateur and professional Go games. The Alpha Go training set used 6,000 Go openings identified from 230,000 human games.[80]
>
> AlphaGo Zero learns by playing against itself. Each opening was analyzed with 10,000,000 simulations by the AlphaGo Master (a more AI-advanced system).[81] The training schedule and Alpha Go Zero's learning capability are in the table below.[82] This *"learning"* is much faster than a human, which would take a lifetime to achieve. However, it does not mean the machine is infallible or *"intelligent."*
>
> | Day 0 | Day 3 | Day 21 | Day 40 |
> | --- | --- | --- | --- |
> | The only input is the game rules, and there are no human interventions. Instead, the AI plays random games against itself. | The Alpha Go Zero plays better than the version that defeated reigning Go champion Lee Sedol in 2016. | Alpha Go Zero plays at the level of the 2017 AI that played against 60 top professionals and the world champion and won. | The Alpha Go Zero exceeds the other previous versions' capacity at playing Go. |

Figure 11.11   Alpha Go Zero.

corporate tax (6) privacy and permissions (includes data) and (7) technology standards across countries.

11.3.1 Sustainable Development Goals (SDGs) and Universal Human Rights (UHRs)

In terms of sustainable development goals and environment or climate change, it is a well-known fact that the majority of the world governments and their leaders have committed to achieving the 17 SDGs and the 30 statements outlined in the UHRs. Hence it is assumed that AI companies should be aware of these national commitments and work towards their achievement (see Figure 11.12).

11.3.2 Regulations Focusing on Competition and Antitrust

In 2021, China began to curb the freedom of giant AI tech companies like Alibaba Group Holding Ltd., Tencent Holdings Ltd., and Didi Global Inc. under anti-competitive measures. More and more regulations are expected to manage competition and what countries may seem as unfair interference in their countries (see Table 11.2).[83] In the USA, there is a growing possibility that the government would break up big tech companies,

All AI systems should audit their commitment to Sustainable Development Goals (SDGs) and Universal Human Rights (UHRs). The 17 SDGs are broken down into 169 Targets and tracked by 232 unique Indicators.[84]

UHRs are a common standard of achievement for all people of all nations. The document states that with this charter, the people of the UN have reaffirmed their faith in the fundamental human rights, *the dignity, and worth of the human person* and the equal rights of men and women and have determined to promote social progress and better standards of life in larger freedom. There are 30 articles in the UHR charter which address rights, freedoms, and obligations.[85] These UHRs are the foundation of International Human Rights Law.

Article 1: Right to Equality: All are born free and equal in dignity and rights.
Article 2: Freedom from discrimination.
Article 3: Right to life, liberty, and personal security.
Article 4: Freedom from slavery.
Article 5: Freedom from torture and degrading treatment or punishment.
Article 6: Right to be recognized as a person by law
Article 7: Equality before the law and its protection.

Figure 11.12 AI embedded in SDG and UHR. *(continued)*

Article 8: Right to remedy by the competent tribunal.
Article 9: Freedom from arbitrary arrest, detention, or exile.
Article 10: Right to a fair and public hearing.
Article 11: Right to be presumed innocent until proven guilty.
Article 12: Freedom from interference with privacy, home and correspondence, and reputation.
Article 13: Right to freedom of movement and residence within a country and freedom to leave and return.
Article 14: Right to asylum in other countries from persecution.
Article 15: Right to a nationality and freedom to change it.
Article 16: Right to consented marriage and family.
Article 17: Right to own property.
Article 18: Freedom of thought, conscience and religion.
Article 19: Freedom of opinion and expression through any media (information).
Article 20: Right of peaceful assembly and association.
Article 21: Right to take part in the government and right to equal access to public service in their country.
Article 22: Right to social security.
Article 23: Right to work, equal pay and just remuneration.
Article 24: Right to rest and leisure.
Article 25: Right to a standard of living adequate for the health and well-being of himself and of his family.
Article 26: Right to education
Article 27: Right to participate in cultural life and IP.
Article 28: Right to a social and international order that articulates the Charter.
Article 29: Duties to the community in which alone the free and full development of his personality is possible—rights and freedoms may in no case be exercised contrary to the purposes and principles of the United Nations.
Article 30: Freedom from state and other interference in the above rights and freedoms.

From a regulatory point of view, the purpose of human rights obligation is to respect, protect and fulfil human rights (e.g., by creating an institutional and policy framework to support the enjoyment of rights; allocating appropriate public resources towards education, research, and enforcement of rights, etc.),[86] as outlined in Figure 11.12a. The challenge for regulatory bodies is to measure impact via indicators (qualitative and quantitative indicators that may be fact-based or subjective). The ability to create regulatory sandboxes will help develop robust policies and guidelines. For example, the government of Dubai's Virtual Asset Regulatory Authority (VARA) set up an office in The Sandbox (on the fledgling metaverse) in May 2022.[87] But this may not be enough, so the ability to react agilely and respond to societal needs will also be critical.

Figure 11.12 (cont.) AI embedded in SDG and UHR.

leading to antitrust investigations and new bills being passed.[88] This will lead to more oversight of mergers and acquisitions and how firms enjoy competitive advantages in home and host countries.

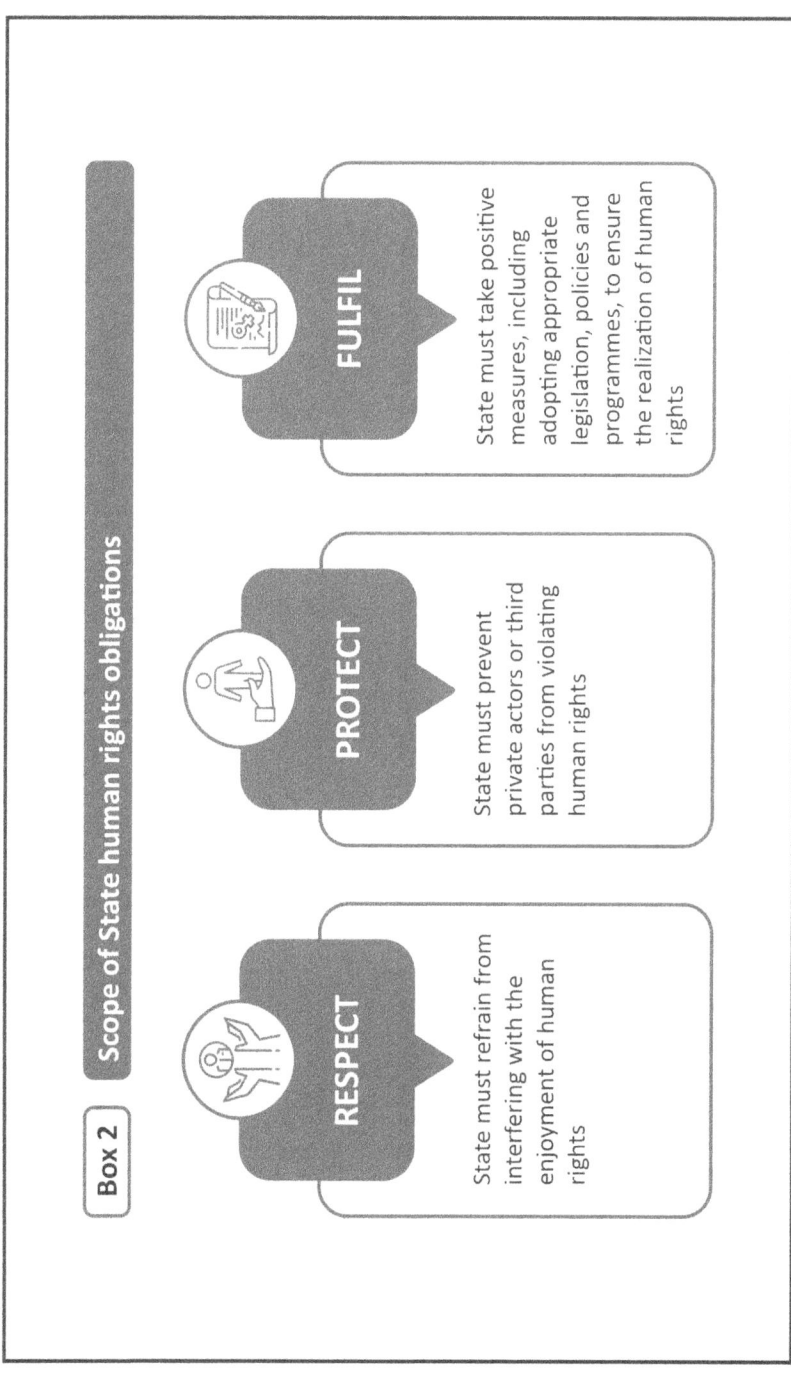

Figure 11.12a Scope of state human rights obligations. *Source:* OHCR (2012).[89]

TABLE 11.2 Types of Regulations With Respect to Competition

Type of Competition	Types of Regulation	Regulatory Authority	Examples
Deregulated	Self-regulating markets	No regulation (the state does not interfere)	Moving from certification to liability laws to protect consumers
Regulated	Regulation *of* competition	National competition authorities	Prevention of concentration through the regulation of mergers, cross-ownership, etc.,
Regulated	Regulation *for* competition	Sector-specific authorities and national competition authorities	Interconnection regimes in telecommuting, unbundling the network
Meta-regulated	Enforced self-regulation of competition rules	Sector-specific authorities and national competition authorities	Institutionalization of the internal mechanism of self-regulation that corresponds with the legal requirements of competition law in general and the regulatory regime in particular.

Source: Compiled from Le Bot, P. (2009)[90]

11.3.3 Intellectual Property (IP)

Patents, trademarks, copyrights, and trade secrets (see Table 11.3) are the normal forms of IP that AI systems can register for. Across geographic markets, the laws will allow different forms of IP registration, and the combination of these registrations will optimize for how long IP protection lasts (copyrights have the longest IP protection).[91] Currently, the legal landscape for AI protection is fragmented and blurry.[92] For future monetization of the AI business model, business decision-makers must keep aside funds for legal recourse.

Over 50% of patents filed in AI are after 2013 (the first patent was filed in the 1980s by Japan).[93] Currently, AI patents are dominated by big technology companies in the USA and China. One of the current debates in IP is whether a work can be ascribed to AI (see Figure 11.13). We are also seeing a shift in research from knowledge to commercialization. In terms of AI publications, most of them began after the introduction of the internet in 2001, and they increased exponentially in volume by 2020.[94] The focus of the publications has changed from scientific research to commercialization.[95]

AI Regulations ▪ 289

TABLE 11.3 Types of IP

	Definition	Considerations
Patent	Granted by the government (so there is a geographic jurisdiction), that grants you a monopoly to build, sell, and use your invention (and prevent others from doing so) for a period of 14 (for design patents) or 20 (for utility and plant patents) years. The invention must meet four criteria: should be patentable, new, useful, and non-obvious.	Expensive to maintain, and fees are as per geographic jurisdiction. Need to make decisions on which markets and what to patent. AI gets IP protection faster and easily as a utility model.[96]
Trademark	word, phrase, symbol, design, or combination of the above that allows your customer to recognize your product or brand.	Need to register per market for greater protection otherwise covered in common law trademark.
Copyright	Copyright is created at the time of creation, so it is easier to do on registration though more legal protection for infringement is needed.[97] The purpose of copyright is to protect original works of authorship. This includes work like source codes, computer programs, books, paintings, photographs, musical compositions, sound recordings, plays, movies, books, blog posts, and architectural works.	Works created on or after January 1, 1978, have a copyright term of life of the author plus seventy years after the author's death. For works made for hire, copyright protection is 95 years from publication or 120 years from creation, whichever is shorter. AI copyright has had mixed rulings[98] in favor of humans. For example, in the USA, the United States Patent and Trademark Office (USPTO) and US federal courts have ruled that AI-generated inventions cannot be patented as it is not human, but the EPO justified the decision by saying AI does not have a legal personality.[99] Data like AI training sets are not copyrighted though data compilations are.
Trade secret	WIPO defines a tradesecret as the information that is (1) *commercially valuable* because it is secret, (2) known only to a *limited group of persons*, and (3) subject to *reasonable steps taken* by the rightful holder of the information to keep it secret, including the use of confidentiality agreements for business partners and employees.[100]	Since copyrights are public, codes, when published, if they are sensitive, can be redacted as tradesecrets. Often if an AI software is not granted a patent, it can still be filed as a tradesecret.[101]

Source: Compiled by Authors

> An art collective from Paris, France, known as *Obvious*, sold the first AI-generated artwork for US$ 432,500 in New York City. Obvious trained their AI to recognize and recreate paintings by uploading 15,000 portraits into the system.[102] The algorithm used by the machine learning program is featured as a signature at the bottom of the picture. Written in cursive font in Gallic lettering, the signature reads:
>
> $$\min_G \max_D \mathbb{E}_x[\log(D(x))] + \mathbb{E}_z[\log(1 - D(G(z)))]$$
>
> Image © Obvious[103]
>
> There is a question about who gets credited for creating the artwork, the AI, the minds behind the AI, or the conceptual creators. One of the collective members working on this project, Hugo Caselles-Dupré, believes that if the credit goes to the artist, it depends on how we define an artist. If the artist is the one to create the piece physically, the AI should be the intellectual property owner.[104] 
>
> On the other hand, Caselles-Dupré said, "If the artist is the one that holds the vision and wants to share the message, then that would be us."[105] Another way to look at it is that it is a team effort, where there are two artists, or that the AI system is a medium or tool rather than the painter But outside of the collective's opinions, there's also the issue that the AI algorithms were not even written by Obvious, but rather by a 19-year-old AI researcher and artist, Robbie Barrat, who shared his work on the internet for others to use and learn from. When this conundrum came up, the collective agreed that Barrat was deserving of some credit but did not disclose whether the profits would be shared.[106]
>
> In 2022, a digital artwork was entered in a State Fair in Colorado (USA) and won in the digital art category competition. The entry was called *Théâtre D'opéra Spatial*. It was later found out that the art was created using an AI called Midjourney. The artist explained that to create the artwork, he took 80 hours and created 900 images.[107] However the revelation that he used an AI sparked a huge debate—was it art? Did the judges know.[108]

Figure 11.13 Obvious and Théâtre D'opéra Spatial (AI-created artwork).

Organizations must budget for IP verification, registration, and protection depending on how much they think AI sub-systems may prove a competitive advantage (See Figure 11.13). For example, Amazon filed the one-click patent in 1997, granted in 1999 by UPSTO[109] but could not convince the EU (it was rejected in 2001 and 2011). Amazon was able to license this to Apple in 2000.[110] This patent expired in 2017 but spawned countless business models based on the *one-click* model.

11.3.4 Legal Redress

Many markets are moving from deregulation to regulation. On one end, these policies are prompted by the need for cyber-sovereignty, redressing

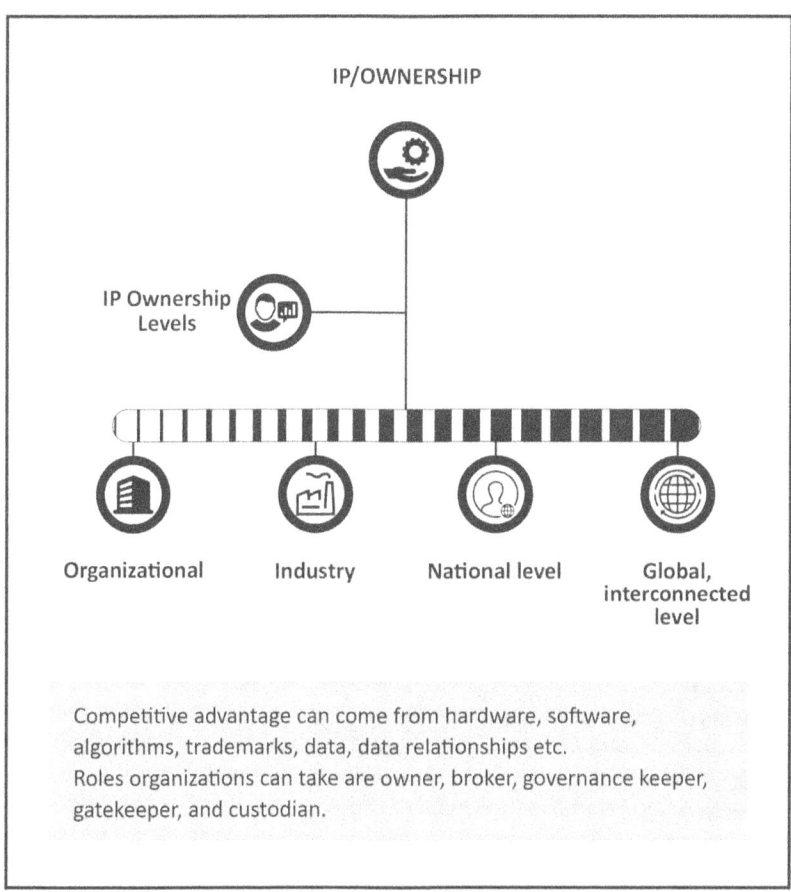

Figure 11.14 IP/Ownership. Source: Stephens & Vashishtha (2020)[111]

inequality, and security.[112] Conversely, there is a belief that markets and society will self-regulate. The reality is that we need more transparency (or, in some cases, whistleblowing) on what is working well and what is not and for legal redress. For example, biases exist in AI algorithms and data, but the lack of transparency hinders the ability to get compensation. This opacity in algorithms is raising concern and resulting in newer regulations (see Figure 11.15).

Legal redress/recourse is also complicated as every individual may not have the resources to fight an individual, company, or government with access to huge resources and more power. The legal address may depend on the type of crime (see Figure 11.16). The virtual world (if you think of metaverse) may cross national jurisdictions and make crime harder to

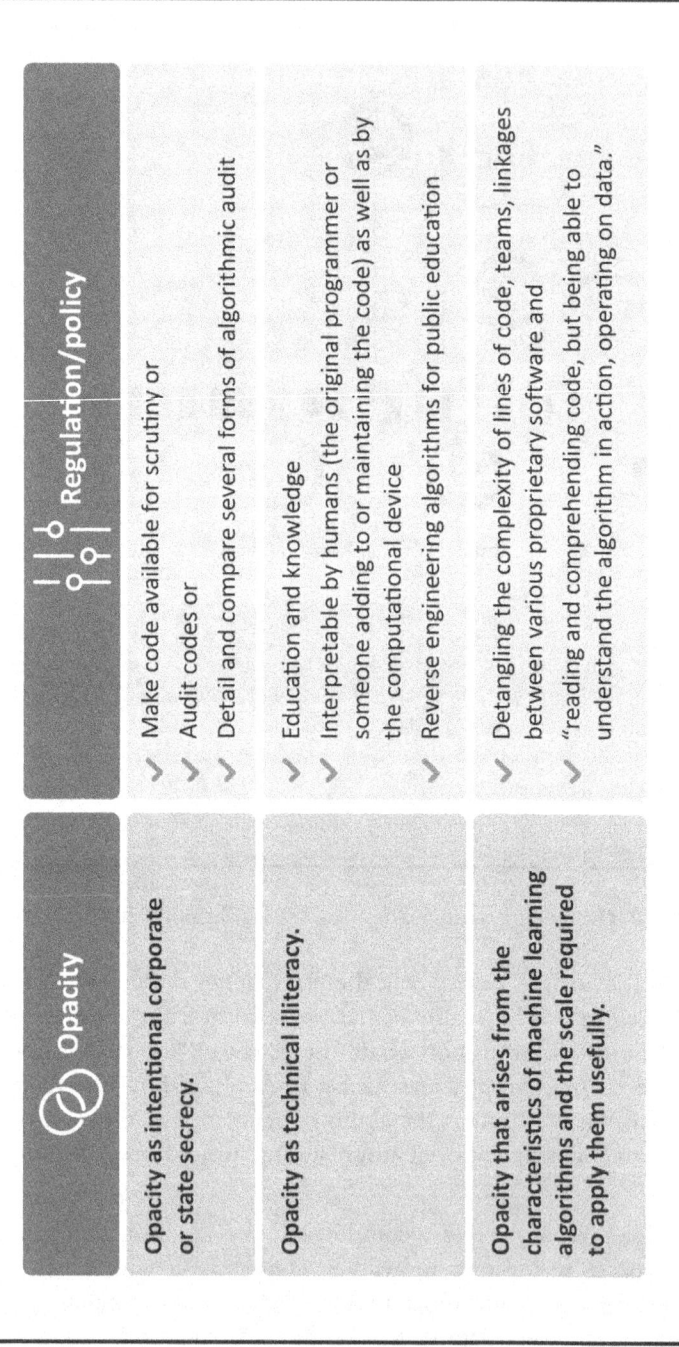

Figure 11.15 Three forms of algorithm opacity. Source: Burrell (2016)[113]

A cybercrime fits the "transformation test"—if you take away the Internet, will the crime still exist?[114] This question identifies three types of crimes:

1. The traditional crime that masquerades as a cybercrime:
2. Hybrid Crimes: They are offline crimes accelerated by the internet: online pornography, cheating, thefts, pornography, sale of drugs.
3. "True" cybercrimes: they can only exist in cyberspace—theft of virtual money, spamming

Challenges with AI Crimes

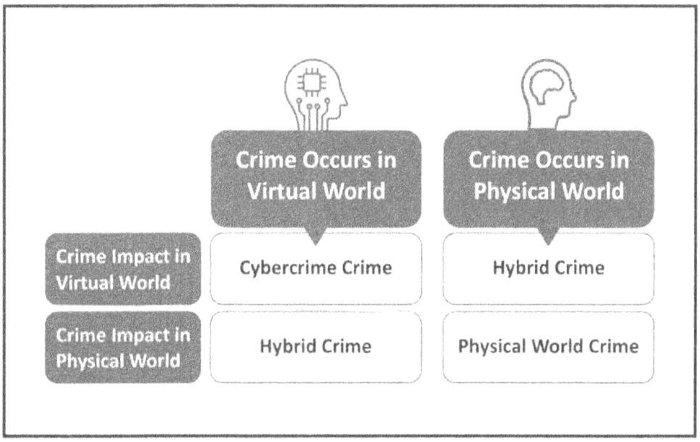

	Crime Occurs in Virtual World	Crime Occurs in Physical World
Crime Impact in Virtual World	Cybercrime Crime	Hybrid Crime
Crime Impact in Physical World	Hybrid Crime	Physical World Crime

Source: Authors

Figure 11.16 Complexities of legal jurisdiction: Crimes and impact.

detect and validate, and hence get legal compensation. The surface web (browsers, mail, blogs, etc), is what we see and interact with, and is a fraction of the virtual space (5%).[115]

Most of the web is more anonymous and is referred to as the deep or dark web (which can be accessed by specialized sites). The deep web may contain the back-end operations like password-protected email or your subscription access or private forums. It is not indexed or even searchable by ordinary search engines, requiring users to log-on to specific URL or IP addresses.[116] It is about 550 times larger than the surface web and growing.[117] The dark web requires specialized software, tools, or equipment to access it.[118] Because of the anonymity, it is also associated with illegal activity. However for example, it has been a popular place for Whistleblowers to contact media firms also. The dark web is estimated to be 0.01% of the Deep Web.[119]

11.3.5 Corporate Tax

S&P Global Market Intelligence finds that the median effective tax rate for information technology companies in the S&P 500 was 14.2% for 2020, which was lower than the 21% statutory corporate tax rate in the USA.[120] The new 15% minimum global tax was proposed by OECD and backed by G-7 finance ministers from the US, the U.K., Canada, France, Germany, Italy, and Japan in October 2021 and will be effective in 2023. It applies to multinational corporations with US$868 million in global sales. This measure blocks the "tax haven" routes many multinational companies employ and ensures that profits are redistributed to the country from which these profits originate. For countries where these firms earn profits, the host country could charge a tax of 25% of the profits made above the 10% threshold. A total of 136 countries have signed up for this.

The IMF proposed a temporary solidarity tax to reduce income inequality exacerbated during the pandemic of 2020–22.[121] In addition, there is a proposal to tax robots and compensate for the loss of labor income.[122] Hence companies using, deploying, or creating AI may need to consider the implications for future tax purposes. The AI data centers and algorithms are extremely power hungry, and perhaps a sustainability or carbon tax will soon be in the offering. Recycling hardware from AI systems is also a challenge that may lead to additional taxes in the future or more legislation on sourcing and recycling. Firms operating in this space should consider the long-term implications of AI and budget accordingly.

11.3.6 Privacy and Permissions

Data privacy issues that arise from AI systems are because of:[123]

Data persistence—data created exists longer than the human subjects that created it, or the event for which it was created and maybe reproduced and distorted during transfer.
Data repurposing—data is being used beyond its originally imagined purpose, often without the awareness or consent of the data owner/producer.
Data spillovers—data is being collected on people accidentally or purposely who are not the initial target of data collection. This is more true with the collection of meta-data or big data.

These points raise questions about the human(s) in the loop about things like informed and freely given consent, the ability to opt-out and repossess and erase their data, the ability to determine what types of data can be collected and for what purpose, the ability to donate their data and manage legacy issues.

The California Consumer Privacy Act of 2018 prevents the repurposing of data outside of the original scope of the collection.[124] One of the bigger challenges of managing personal information (in California) is that you cannot stop the sale of personal information lawfully made available from government records.[125] This is a concern as the data that governments collect exceeds the scale and scope that the private sector collects. Research from the Center for Global Development suggests that "the gap between data protection "laws on the books" and effective implementation remains wide in many countries, resulting in regulatory uncertainty that can hinder useful data innovation by both the public and private sector."[126]

For example, the EU GDPR states that consent needs to be valid and then highlights the conditions that will make it valid. However, often consumers have no real freedom of consent if they wish to have the choice of using a "free" service. In France, it was found that cookies were provided to gain consent (one option), but there was no easy way to refuse the cookies as the process meant going through multiple options. The French Data Protection Authority (the "CNIL") ended up imposing a fine of €150,000,000 on Google and €60,000,000 on Facebook (now Meta) on 31 December 2021 for violation of the law.[127]

11.3.7 Technology Standards Across Countries

Another challenge besides the regulations is the need for policy interoperability across countries. Take, for example, the availability of various types of technology infrastructures. While the internet infrastructure is currently dependent on 3G, 4G, and 5G, it will evolve to 6G, supporting Web 3.0 (see Figure 11.17). This upgrade will speed up operations and further support smart city concepts and Industry 4.0. hence the role of technology standards is to ensure the interoperability across nations and ensure fairness and responsibility to humanity and the planet.

In summary, AI regulations will increase, leading to more costs in terms of compliance. It is helpful for firms working in the AI space or with the technologies to keep their ear to the ground and consider regulations aimed at SDGs, UHRs, corporate tax, intellectual property, privacy and permission, legal redress, and competition. Ethics is about values, and firms should be human-centric in thinking of organizational policies, which could be a forerunner to government regulations. They have an opportunity to create a

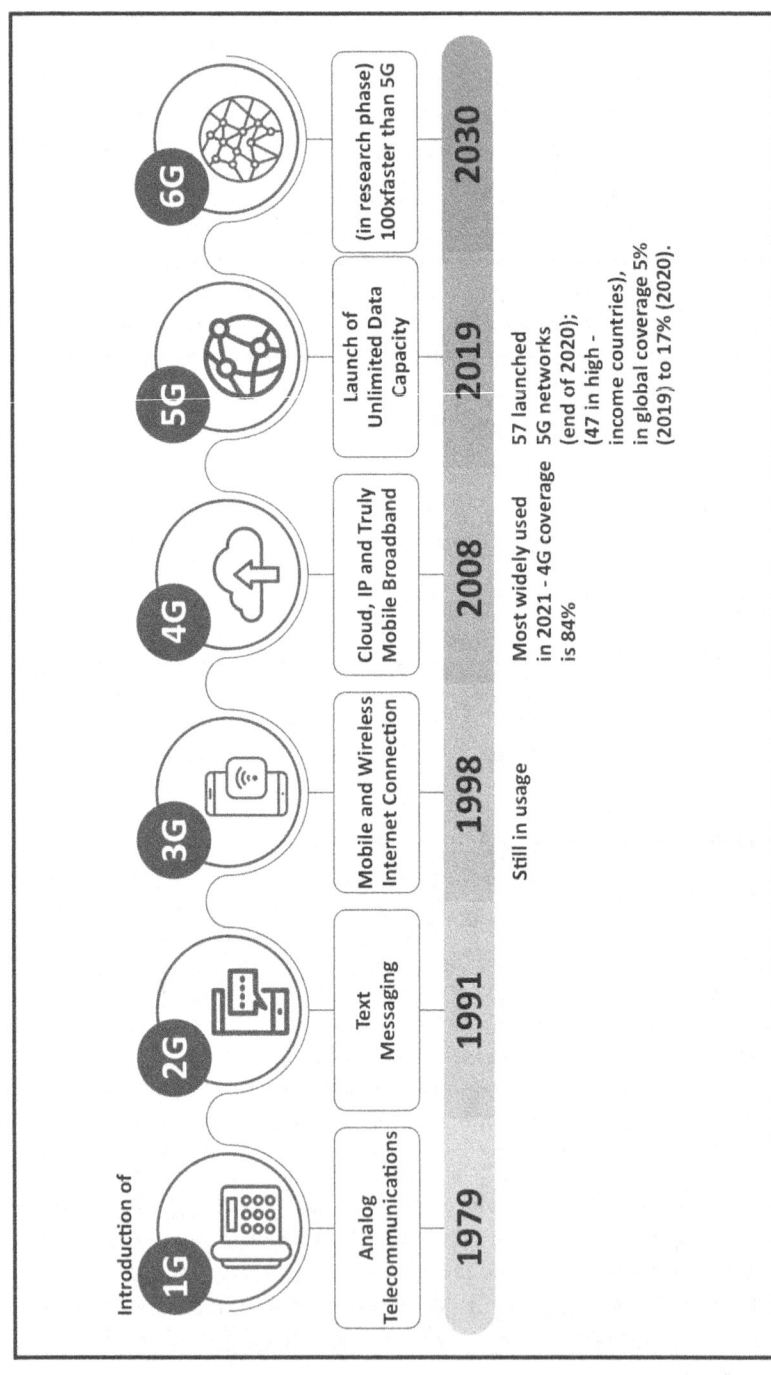

Figure 11.17 Technology infrastructure. *Source:* Authors

competitive advantage by shaping future regulations at a local and international level.

QUESTIONS

1. Which trend of AI regulations worries you most?
2. How have you budgeted resources for future regulations, and where do you feel most vulnerable?
3. How opaque are the AI algorithms you use (see Figure 11.14)?
4. What elements of your IP strategy could become a source of revenue?
5. How strong is your legal counsel when you look at the AI crimes and jurisdictions in Figure 11.15?

MY INSIGHTS

The most difficult decisions I need to take are

MY INSIGHTS

The resources I need to build for the future are

MY INSIGHTS

The governance systems I will to put in place are

MY INSIGHTS

The training and skills I and my team need to develop are

Notes

1. Bench-Capon, T., Araszkiewicz, M., Ashley, K., Atkinson, K., Bex, F., Borges, F., ... & Wyner, A. Z. (2012). A history of AI and Law in 50 papers: 25 years of the international conference on AI and Law. *Artificial Intelligence and Law*, *20*(3), 215–319.
2. Oxford Analytica. (2021, June 17). Regulations lag despite rising risks of faulty AI. *Emerald Expert Briefings* oxan-es. https://dailybrief.oxan.com/Analysis/ES262188/Regulations-lag-despite-rising-risks-of-faulty-AI
3. CBI Insights, (2022), Week in Charts, dated 17 March.
4. UNESCO. (2019). Recommendation on the Ethics of Artificial Intelligence. https://en.unesco.org/artificial-intelligence/ethics
5. WIPO. (2021). Artificial Intelligence and Intellectual Property. https://www.wipo.int/about-ip/en/frontier_technologies/ai_and_ip.html
6. Stephens et al.. 2022. *Benefits of A Multidisciplinary Lens for AI System Ethics. A Primer for Education Thought Leadership.* IEEE SA. Forthcoming.
7. Suggest reading this paper that outlines changes in neural networks over 30 years: https://karpathy.github.io/2022/03/14/lecun1989/
8. Adapted from IEEE, *The Benefits of A Multidisciplinary Lens for AI Systems Ethics: A Primer for Education Thought Leadership*. Appendix 1.
9. Marchant, G. E. (2011). The Growing Gap between Emerging Technologies and The Law. In: *The Growing Gap Between Emerging Technologies and Legal-Ethical Oversight* (pp. 19–33). Springer, Dordrecht.
10. Collingridge, D. (1980). *The Social Control of Technology.* New York, NY: St. Martin.
11. Bryson, J. (2021). Europe Is in Danger of Using the Wrong Definition of AI. *Wired.* https://www.wired.com/story/artificial-intelligence-regulation-european-union/
12. Neate, R. (2021). 'Silicon Six' Tech Giants Accused of Inflating Tax Payments by Almost $100bn. *The Guardian*, https://www.theguardian.com/business/2021/may/31/silicon-six-tech-giants-accused-of-inflating-tax-payments-by-almost-100bn
13. WSJ, (2021). *Yes, it's a Global Tax on American Tech*, https://www.wsj.com/articles/yes-its-a-global-tax-on-american-tech-11623449290
14. Scott, M., & Birnbaum, E. (2021). How Washington and Big Tech Won the Global Tax Fight. *Politico*, https://www.politico.eu/article/washington-big-tech-tax-talks-oecd/
15. Schuett, J. (2021). Defining the Scope of AI Regulations. *Available at SSRN 3453632.*
16. McFadden, M., Jones, K, Taylor, E., & Osborn, G. (2021). *Harmonizing Artificial Intelligence: The role of standards in the EU.* Oxford Information Labs.
17. For more information on the first four points read: https://www.fhi.ox.ac.uk/wp-content/uploads/Standards_-FHI-Technical-Report.pdf
18. Cory, N., & Dascoli, L. (2021). *How barriers to cross-border data flows are spreading globally, what they cost, and how to address them.* Information Technology and Innovation Foundation. ITIF. https://itif.org/publications/2021/07/19/how-barriers-cross-border-data-flows-are-spreading-globally-what-they-cost
19. Ibid.

20. OECD, (2021). National AI Policies & Strategies. https://oecd.ai/en/dashboards
21. Galaski, J. (2021). AI Regulation: Present Situation and Future Possibilities. https://www.liberties.eu/en/stories/ai-regulation/43740
22. For more information on the first four points read: https://www.fhi.ox.ac.uk/wp-content/uploads/Standards_-FHI-Technical-Report.pdf
23. Bloomberg, (2018). GDPR: Why Privacy Is Now Stronger in EU Than U.S. Fortune, https://fortune.com/2018/05/25/what-is-gdpr-compliance/
24. Ibid.
25. Keane, S. (2021). Huawei ban timeline: Detained CFO makes deal with US Justice Department. https://www.cnet.com/news/privacy/huawei-ban-timeline-detained-cfo-makes-deal-with-us-justice-department/
26. EU. (2022). Artificial Intelligence Act. https://www.europarl.europa.eu/RegData/etudes/BRIE/2021/698792/EPRS_BRI(2021)698792_EN.pdf
27. Bitcoin Beach: What Happened When an El Salvador Surf Town Went Full Crypto, *Bloomberg*, https://www.bloomberg.com/news/features/2021-06-17/world-s-biggest-bitcoin-experiment-is-a-surf-town-in-el-salvador
28. PwC. (2021). El Salvador's Law: A Meaningful Test for Botcoin. https://www.pwc.com/gx/en/financial-services/pdf/el-salvadors-law-a-meaningful-test-for-bitcoin.pdf
29. Ibid.
30. *El Salvador Bitcoin City Planned at Base of Conchagua Volcano–BBC News*. (2021, November 21). BBC News; www.bbc.com. https://www.bbc.com/news/world-latin-america-59368483
31. Brigida, A-K, & Schwart, L. (2021). Six Months In, El Salvador's Bitcoin Gamble is Crumbling. https://restofworld.org/2022/el-salvador-bitcoin/
32. Adrian, T., & Weeks-Brown, R. (2021, July 26). *Cryptoassets as National Currency? A Step Too Far—IMF Blog*. IMF Blog; blogs.imf.org. https://blogs.imf.org/2021/07/26/cryptoassets-as-national-currency-a-step-too-far/
33. *China Declares All Crypto-Currency Transactions Illegal–BBC News*. (2021, September 24). BBC News; www.bbc.com. https://www.bbc.com/news/technology-58678907
34. EU. (2021). Proposal for a Regulation of The European Parliament And Of The Council Laying Down Harmonised Rules on Artificial Intelligence (Artificial Intelligence Act) And Amending Certain Union Legislative Acts. Brussels. https://eur-lex.europa.eu/legal-content/EN/TXT/HTML/?uri=CELEX:52021PC0206&from=EN
35. *The Seven Patterns of AI–Cognilytica*. (2019, April 5). Cognilytica; www.cognilytica.com. https://www.cognilytica.com/2019/04/04/the-seven-patterns-of-ai/
36. Bourne, J. (2019, November 4). *Starbucks flips the equation with Deep Brew–by using AI for a more humanised customer experience–Marketing Tech News*. Marketing Tech News; www.marketingtechnews.net. https://www.marketingtechnews.net/news/2019/nov/04/deep-brew-starbucks-aims-use-ai-more-humanised-customer-experience/
37. Team, E. (2022, July 5). *AI & Data-Driven Starbucks–Deep Brew*. Artificial Intelligence +; www.aiplusinfo.com. https://www.aiplusinfo.com/blog/ai-data-driven-starbucks-deep-brew/

38. Ibid.
39. Bariso, J. (n.d.). *Starbucks Devised a Brilliant Plan to Borrow Money From Customers (Without Getting Anybody Angry) | Inc.com.* Inc.Com; www.inc.com. https://www.inc.com/justin-bariso/starbucks-devised-a-brilliant-plan-to-borrow-money-from-customers-without-getting-anybody-angry.html
40. Starbucks 2021 Annual Report, p. 71.
41. Beckett. E. L. (2021). Starbucks' Digital Success Partially Driven by AI Engine, CEO Kevin Johnson says. *Restaurant Dive.* https://www.restaurantdive.com/news/starbucks-digital-success-partially-driven-by-ai-engine-ceo-kevin-johnson/599182/
42. Future Stores. How Starbucks Is Using AI and More to Better Serve Its Customers. https://futurestores.wbresearch.com/blog/starbucks-ai-serve-customers-strategy
43. *Starlink Satellite's Near-Collision with Chinese Station puts Focus on Space Jam | Latest News India–Hindustan Times.* (2021, December 28). Hindustan Times; www.hindustantimes.com. https://www.hindustantimes.com/india-news/starlink-satellite-s-near-collision-withchinese-station-puts-focus-on-space-jam-101640714042859.html
44. Pultarova, T. (2021, August 18). *Starlink Satellites Responsible for over 50% of Close Encounters in Space | Space.* Space.Com; www.space.com. https://www.space.com/spacex-starlink-satellite-collision-alerts-on-the-rise
45. O'Callaghan, J. (2019, September 2). *SpaceX Declined To Move A Starlink Satellite At Risk Of Collision With A European Satellite.* Forbes; www.forbes.com. https://www.forbes.com/sites/jonathanocallaghan/2019/09/02/spacex-refused-to-move-a-starlink-satellite-at-risk-of-collision-with-a-european-satellite/?sh=7f6188c31f62
46. Ibid.
47. ESA Operations (2021, September 2). Twitter.https://twitter.com/esaoperations/status/1168536038601572353
48. O'Callaghan, J. (2019, September 2). *Op. cit.*
49. Thomson, K., & Larsen, B. 2020. *NASA SBIR 2020-I Solicitation | H9.03-5963– Maneuver Characteristics of Autonomous Non-Cooperative Spacecraft | Proposal Summary.* (n.d.). NASA SBIR 2020-I Solicitation | H9.03-5963–Maneuver Characteristics of Autonomous Non-Cooperative Spacecraft | Proposal Summary; sbir.nasa.gov. https://sbir.nasa.gov/SBIR/abstracts/20/sbir/phase1/SBIR-20-1-H9.03-5963.html
50. Boeing MCAS. https://www.boeing.com/commercial/737max/737-max-software-updates.page
51. Ostrower, J. (2018, November 13). *What is the Boeing 737 Max Maneuvering Characteristics Augmentation System?–The Air Current.* The Air Current; theaircurrent.com. https://theaircurrent.com/aviation-safety/what-is-the-boeing-737-max-maneuvering-characteristics-augmentation-system-mcas-jt610/
52. Fitzgerald, M. (2019, April 4). *Boeing CEO Acknowledges that Bad Data Played Role in 737 Max Crashes.* CNBC; www.cnbc.com. https://www.cnbc.com/2019/04/04/boeing-ceo-acknowledges-that-bad-data-played-role-in-737-max-crashes.html
53. Mongan, J., & Kohli, M. (2020, March 18). Artificial Intelligence and Human Life: Five Lessons for Radiology from the 737 MAX Disasters | *Radiology: Artifi-*

cial Intelligence. Radiology: Artificial Intelligence; pubs.rsna.org. https://pubs.rsna.org/doi/full/10.1148/ryai.2020190111
54. Herkert, J., Borenstein, J., & Miller, K. (2020). The Boeing 737 MAX: Lessons for Engineering Ethics. *Science and Engineering Ethics*, 26, 2957–2974
55. Gates, D., & Baker, M. (2019, June 22). *The inside story of MCAS: How Boeing's 737 MAX system gained power and lost safeguards | The Seattle Times*. The Seattle Times; www.seattletimes.com. https://www.seattletimes.com/seattle-news/times-watchdog/the-inside-story-of-mcas-how-boeings-737-max-system-gained-power-and-lost-safeguards/
56. Ibid.
57. *In Test of Boeing Jet, Pilots Had 40 Seconds to Fix Error (Published 2019)*. (2019, March 26). In Test of Boeing Jet, Pilots Had 40 Seconds to Fix Error (Published 2019); www.nytimes.com. https://www.nytimes.com/2019/03/25/business/boeing-simulation-error.html
58. OpenAI, was founded in late 2015 by Elon Musk, Sam Altman and others and later backed with a $1B investment from Microsoft. By 2020, GPT-3 was a highly trained complex language model, with 175 billion parameters.
59. Dilmegani, C. (2017, August 4). *9 Epic Chatbot/Conversational Bot Failures (2022 Update)*. AIMultiple; research.aimultiple.com. https://research.aimultiple.com/chatbot-fail/
60. Ibid.
61. EU. (2019). Understanding Algorithmic Decision-Making: Opportunities and Challenges. https://www.europarl.europa.eu/RegData/etudes/STUD/2019/624261/EPRS_STU(2019)624261_EN.pdf p. 26.
62. Guidotti, R., Monreale, A., Ruggieri, S., Turini, F., Pedreschi, D., & Giannotti, F. (2018). A Survey Of Methods For Explaining Black Box Models. *arXiv preprint arXiv:1802.01933*. https://arxiv.org/abs/1802.01933.
63. *How the EU's Flawed Artificial Intelligence Regulation Endangers the Social Safety Net: Questions and Answers | Human Rights Watch*. (2021, November 10). How the EU's Flawed Artificial Intelligence Regulation Endangers the Social Safety Net: Questions and Answers | Human Rights Watch; www.hrw.org. https://www.hrw.org/news/2021/11/10/how-eus-flawed-artificial-intelligence-regulation-endangers-social-safety-net#_ftn1
64. Ibid. Article 6 and 7.
65. EU. (2019). Understanding Algorithmic Decision-Making: Opportunities And Challenges. *Op. cit.*
66. Evans, B. (2020, September 17). *Medical Moonshot: How Novartis and Microsoft Are Using AI to Reimagine Medicine–Acceleration Economy*. Acceleration Economy; accelerationeconomy.com. https://accelerationeconomy.com/cloud/medical-moonshot-how-novartis-and-microsoft-are-using-ai-to-reimagine-medicine/
67. Ibid.
68. *Artificial Intelligence: A New Generation Of Drug Discovery Companies*. (2021, May 24). *Op.cit.*
69. Ibid.
70. Ibid.
71. Fleming, N. (2018, May 30). How Artificial Intelligence Is Changing Drug Discovery. *Nature*. https://www.nature.com/articles/d41586-018-05267-x; *Artificial*

Intelligence: A New Generation Of Drug Discovery Companies. (2021, May 24). Pharmaceutical Technology; www.pharmaceutical-technology.com. https://www.pharmaceutical-technology.com/analysis/new-generation-ai-drug-discovery-companies/

72. Paul, D., Sanap, G., Shenoy, S., Kalyane, D., Kalia, K., & Tekade, R. K. (2021). Artificial intelligence in Drug Discovery and Development. *Drug Discovery Today*, Jan;26(1):80–93. doi: https://doi.org/10.1016/j.drudis.2020.10.010
73. Taken from Stephens, M., & Vashishtha, H. (2020). *Op.cit.*
74. Marcus, G. (2017). Deep Learning: A Critical Appraisal. Retrieved from https://arxiv.org/pdf/1801.00631.pdf
75. Caruana, R., Lou, Y., Gehrke, J., Koch, P., Sturm, M., & Elhadad, N. (2015). Intelligible Models For Healthcare: Predicting Pneumonia Risk And Hospital 30-Day Readmission. *Knowledge Discovery and Data Mining Conference (KDD)*; ACM; 2015.
76. Stephens & Vashishtha (2020). *Op.cit.*
77. Hart, R. D. (2017, May 23). *When a Robot AI Doctor Misdiagnoses You, Who's to Blame?—Quartz*. Quartz; qz.com. https://qz.com/989137/when-a-robot-ai-doctor-misdiagnoses-you-whos-to-blame/
78. Heaven, D. H. (2019, October 9). Why Deep-Learning AIs Are So Easy To Fool. *Nature*. https://www.nature.com/articles/d41586-019-03013-5
79. *Artificial Intelligence*. (n.d.). Transforming Data to Knowledge for Better Care—AI; www.siemens-healthineers.com. https://www.siemens-healthineers.com/en-us/infrastructure-it/artificial-intelligence
80. *AlphaGo Teach: Discover New and Creative Ways Of Playing Go*. (n.d.). Deepmind; alphagoteach.deepmind.com. https://alphagoteach.deepmind.com/
81. Ibid.
82. Ibid.
83. *The Washington Post—Breaking news and latest headlines, U.S. news, world news, and video*. (n.d.). Washington Post; www.washingtonpost.com. https://www.washingtonpost.com/business/why-china-is-cracking-down-on-its-technology-giants-quicktake/2021/07/30/3cc9ca46-f105-11eb-81b2-9b7061a582d8_story.html
84. UNStats. (n.d.). Global indicator framework for the Sustainable Development Goals and targets of the 2030 Agenda for Sustainable Development. https://unstats.un.org/sdgs/indicators/Global%20Indicator%20Framework%20after%20refinement_Eng.pdf
85. Nations, U. (n.d.). *Human Rights | United Nations*. United Nations; www.un.org. https://www.un.org/en/global-issues/human-rights
86. https://www.ohchr.org/sites/default/files/Documents/Publications/Human_rights_indicators_en.pdf
87. Mollen, F. (2022, May 5). *Dubai Regulator Will Open Offices in The Sandbox Metaverse*. CryptoPotato; cryptopotato.com. https://cryptopotato.com/dubai-regulator-will-open-offices-in-the-sandbox-metaverse/
88. Stacey, K & Lee, D. 2022. *Subscribe to read | Financial Times*. (n.d.). Subscribe to Read | Financial Times; www.ft.com. Retrieved May 26, 2022, from https://www.ft.com/content/d6cb3541-beef-4335-a0d0-ce5d6585e53d

89. https://www.ohchr.org/sites/default/files/Documents/Publications/Human_rights_indicators_en.pdf
90. Le Bot, P. (2009). The Model of Resilience in Situation (MRS) as an Idealistic Organization of At-Risks Systems to be Ultra Safe. *Conference: ESREL 2009–Reliability, risk and safety: Theory and applications.* https://www.researchgate.net/publication/260383152_The_Model_of_Resilience_in_Situation_MRS_as_an_Idealistic_Organization_of_At-Risks_Systems_to_be_Ultra_Safe/figures?lo=1
91. *IP Protection of Artificial Intelligence in Europe.* (2022, April 0). IP Protection of Artificial Intelligence in Europe: Tailor-Made Solutions Required | Insights | Jones Day; www.jonesday.com. https://www.jonesday.com/en/insights/2020/04/ip-protection-of-artificial-intelligence-in-europe
92. Foss-Solbrekk, K. (2021). Three routes to protecting AI systems and their algorithms under IP law: The good, the bad and the ugly. *Journal of Intellectual Property Law & Practice, 16*(3), 247–258. https://doi.org/10.1093/jiplp/jpab033
93. WIPO, (2019). https://www.wipo.int/edocs/pubdocs/en/wipo_pub_1055.pdf
94. Ibid.
95. Artificial Intelligence Index Report (2021). https://aipo-api.buddyweb.fr/app/uploads/2021/03/2021-AI-Index-Report.pdf
96. *IP Protection of Artificial Intelligence in Europe.* (2022, April 0). *Op.cit.*
97. *Copyright.* (n.d.). Copyright; www.wipo.int. https://www.wipo.int/copyright/en/
98. *IP and Frontier Technologies.* (n.d.). Artificial Intelligence and Intellectual Property; www.wipo.int. https://www.wipo.int/about-ip/en/frontier_technologies/ai_and_ip.html
99. *IP Protection of Artificial Intelligence in Europe.* (2022, April 0). IP Protection of Artificial Intelligence in Europe: Tailor-Made Solutions Required | Insights | Jones Day; www.jonesday.com. https://www.jonesday.com/en/insights/2020/04/ip-protection-of-artificial-intelligence-in-europe
100. *Trade Secrets—Everything you need to know.* (n.d.). Trade Secrets—Everything You Need to Know; www.wipo.int. https://www.wipo.int/tradesecrets/en/
101. Gibson, S., & Buchman, S. (2021, February 25). *How to Safeguard AI Technology: Patents versus Trade Secrets.* IPWatchdog.Com | Patents & Patent Law; www.ipwatchdog.com. https://www.ipwatchdog.com/2021/02/25/safeguard-ai-technology-patents-versus-trade-secrets/id=130247/
102. *First AI-Created Art Work Sells for $432,500 in New York.* (2018, October 26). VOA; learningenglish.voanews.com. learningenglish.voanews.com/a/first-ai-created-art-work-sells-for-432-500-in-new-york/4630694.html
103. *Is Artificial Intelligence Set to Become Art's Next Medium? | Christie's.* (2018, December 12). The First Piece of AI-Generated Art to Come to Auction | Christie's; www.christies.com. www.christies.com/features/A-collaboration-between-two-artists-one-human-one-a-machine-9332-1.aspx
104. Ibid.
105. Ibid.
106. Lieber, C. (2018, October 29). *Christie's just sold its first piece of art generated by AI.–Vox.* Vox; www.vox.com. https://www.vox.com/the-goods/2018/10/29/18038946/art-algorithm

107. Stewart, J. (2022, September 8). AI-Generated Artwork Wins Contest and Sparks Fierce Online Debate. https://mymodernmet.com/ai-generated-artwork-win/
108. Ibid.
109. The patent is US 5960411. *Espacenet–Bibliographic data.* (n.d.). Espacenet–Bibliographic Data; worldwide.espacenet.com. https://worldwide.espacenet.com/publicationDetails/biblio?CC=US&NR=5960411&KC=&FT=E&locale=en_EP
110. *How Valuable is Amazon's 1-Click Patent? It's Worth Billions.* (n.d.). How Valuable Is Amazon's 1-Click Patent? It's Worth Billions.; www.rejoiner.com. https://www.rejoiner.com/resources/amazon-1clickpatent
111. Stephens & Vashishtha (2020). *Op. cit.*
112. WEF, (2020). A Roadmap for Cross- Border Data Flows: Future-Proofing Readiness and Cooperation in the New Data Economy. https://www3.weforum.org/docs/WEF_A_Roadmap_for_Cross_Border_Data_Flows_2020.pdf
113. Georgiev, D. (2022, August 10). *How Much of the Internet is the Dark Web in 2022?* Techjury; techjury.net. https://techjury.net/blog/how-much-of-the-internet-is-the-dark-web/#gref
114. CIS (2022). Election Security Spotlight—The Surface Web, Dark Web, and Deep Web. https://www.cisecurity.org/insights/spotlight/cybersecurity-spotlight-the-surface-web-dark-web-and-deep-web
115. Grannan, C. (n.d.). *What's the Difference Between the Deep Web and the Dark Web? | Britannica.* Encyclopedia Britannica; www.britannica.com. https://www.britannica.com/story/whats-the-difference-between-the-deep-web-and-the-dark-web
116. CIS (2022). *Op. cit.*
117. Grannan, C. (n.d.). *Op. cit.*
118. Burrell, J. (2016). How the machine 'thinks': Understanding opacity in machine learning algorithms. Big Data & Society, 1–12. https://journals.sagepub.com/doi/pdf/10.1177/2053951715622512
119. Wall, D. (2007). *Cybercrime: The transformation of crime in the information age* (Vol. 4). Polity.
120. Akins, A., & DiMolfetta, D. (2021, June 14). *Most tech firms would pay more taxes under proposed global minimum rate | S&P Global Market Intelligence.* Most Tech Firms Would Pay More Taxes under Proposed Global Minimum Rate | S&P Global Market Intelligence; www.spglobal.com. https://www.spglobal.com/marketintelligence/en/news-insights/latest-news-headlines/most-tech-firms-would-pay-more-taxes-under-proposed-global-minimum-rate-64904023
121. Agencies. (2021, April 8). *IMF proposes temporary "solidarity" tax on pandemic winners, the wealthy | Business Standard News.* IMF Proposes Temporary "solidarity" Tax on Pandemic Winners, the Wealthy; www.business-standard.com. https://www.business-standard.com/article/international/imf-proposes-temporary-solidarity-tax-on-pandemic-winners-the-wealthy-121040800116_1.html
122. Abbott, R., & Bogenschneider, B. (2018). Should Robots Pay Taxes? Tax Policy in the Age of Automation. *Harvard Law & Policy Review, 12.* https://scholarworks.iu.edu/dspace/handle/2022/23550
123. Pearce, G. (2021, May 28). *Beware the Privacy Violations in Artificial Intelligence Applications.* ISACA; www.isaca.org. https://www.isaca.org/resources/news

-and-trends/isaca-now-blog/2021/beware-the-privacy-violations-in-artificial-intelligence-applications
124. *California Consumer Privacy Act (CCPA) | State of California–Department of Justice–Office of the Attorney General.* (n.d.). State of California–Department of Justice–Office of the Attorney General; oag.ca.gov. https://oag.ca.gov/privacy/ccpa
125. *California Consumer Privacy Act (CCPA) | State of California–Department of Justice–Office of the Attorney General.* (n.d.). State of California–Department of Justice–Office of the Attorney General; oag.ca.gov. https://oag.ca.gov/privacy/ccpa#sectiong
126. Pisa, M., Dixon, P., & Ndulu, B. (2021). Addressing Cross-Border Spillovers in Data Policy: The Need for a Global Approach. Center for Global Development. https://www.cgdev.org/blog/addressing-cross-border-spillovers-data-policy-need-global-approach
127. Hunton Privacy, (2022). CNIL Fines Big Tech Companies 210 million Euros for Cookie Violations, https://www.huntonprivacyblog.com/2022/01/13/cnil-fines-big-tech-companies-210-million-euros-for-cookie-violations/

12

Epilogue—Thinking Ahead

CHAPTER HIGHLIGHTS

1. There are three interesting future trends for an AI-enabled organization.
2. The first is the metaverse, a form of extended reality.
3. The second is Synthetic Biology or SynBio which uses a process similar to AI but also AI at the backend of operations.
4. The third is humanoids—robots that act and look human.

> **Cases:**
> Seoul National University (SNU) Bundang Hospital—smart operating room | Metaverse—are we there yet? | Metaverse M&As | Hong Kong International Airport Terminal | Google Maps and Nicaragua and Costa Rica | Minecraft: Stockholm and Microsoft | Distributed Bio | History of Governance of Synbio | X-Prize ANA Avatar | Humanoid Robots—Honda | Soft Bank | Kawasaki Heavy Industries

There are three future trends that are worth capturing that require us to rethink AI with frames of reference that require much more deliberation. These are (1) metaverse (2) synthetic biology, and (3) humanoids. They will need us to have conversations with multiple stakeholders on how they further enable business development, but even more so on values, what it means to be human, and what we want future societies to look like.

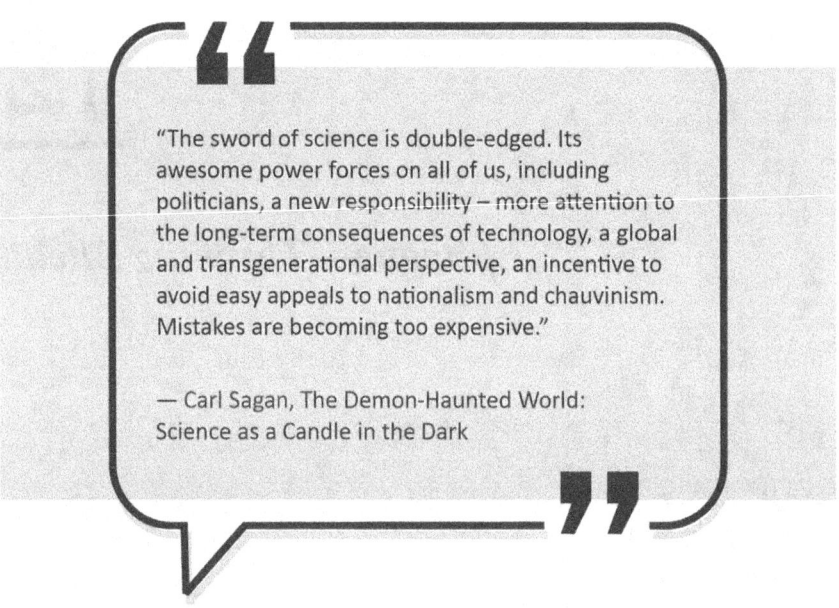

> "The sword of science is double-edged. Its awesome power forces on all of us, including politicians, a new responsibility — more attention to the long-term consequences of technology, a global and transgenerational perspective, an incentive to avoid easy appeals to nationalism and chauvinism. Mistakes are becoming too expensive."
>
> — Carl Sagan, The Demon-Haunted World: Science as a Candle in the Dark

12.1 Metaverse

Metaverse became popular thanks to the rebranding of Facebook as a parent company in 2021 to Meta. This is not to be confused with metaverse. Fans of cyberpunk fiction were introduced to the term metaverse in a book called Snowcrash by Neil Stephenson in 1982. In the book, an immersive virtual realm was accessed through VR goggles, at times to escape a real-world ravaged by hyperinflation, a virus, and inequality. However, in the story, things quickly turn dystopian when a computer virus is released, hijacking people's brains in and out of the metaverse. Historically, sci-fi has influenced the gaming industry, which is a key driver of the metaverse technologies and experiences.

Stephenson says,

> When *Snow Crash* came out in 1992, virtually all video games were 2D. But then *Doom* came out in 1993, and it was the first broadly used 3D game. It spawned a vast industry of similar games. The World Wide Web's source

code was also released in 1993, and suddenly you can look at pictures on your computer. Video games have led to incredible, many-order-of-magnitude advances in the 3D processing power you can get out of a device per dollar spent. I think what is possible is that 20 or 30 years from now, people who are using immersive experiences will look back on games as: "That's how we got here." (On the metaverse) ... And, there will still be lots and lots of video games, but there also will be experiences that will be something more, and I think you see that already if you look at *Fortnite*, which is obviously a video game, but it is also a social environment.[1]

These virtual experiences may fall over a spectrum of 2D–4D (see Figure 12.1).

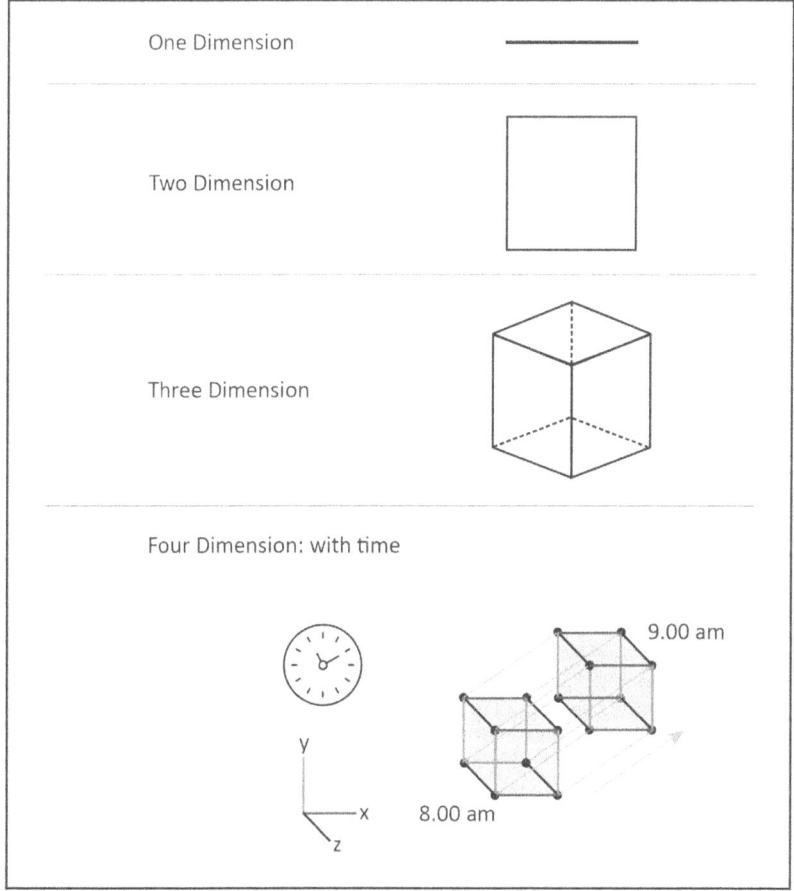

Figure 12.1 Types of Virtual Experiences. *Source:* Authors

There has been rising speculation on the size of the metaverse market opportunity. It is valued to reach US$ 8–13 trillion by 2030 and will have a population of 5 billion people (58% of the population).[2] This estimation is higher than the size of the augmented reality market and the virtual reality market combined (valued at US$ 1.5 trillion[3]) or the gaming market (US$505 billion by 2030).[4]

12.1.1 What is the Metaverse?

In engineering, the metaverse is part of extended reality (various combinations of virtual reality, augmented reality, and the real environment) (see Figure 12.2). While some experts feel it needs to be associated with 3D virtual worlds, others do not think so. This is because the metaverse "operate at various levels—parallel to, overlaid on, or interactive with the physical domain."[5] The metaverse is being conflated with new technologies—Web 3.0, blockchain, crypto, and NFTs, none of which are fundamental requirements for creating the metaverse. This new place will also embed social media, social communities, and live entertainment. There is an awareness

Seoul National University (SNU) Bundang Hospital has been experimenting with virtual training since 2011. In 2019, they created a smart operating room. The room is fitted with a VR camera with six lenses that record 360° in all directions and with special equipment like fluorescent imaging that can visualize lymph nodes. The room produces 4K or 3D video and 8K VR video. The purpose of this room was for the training of thoracic surgeons. In May 2021, in the middle of the pandemic, the Asian Society for Cardiovascular and Thoracic Surgery (ASCVTS) provided lung cancer surgery training for 200 Asian thoracic surgeons. By wearing 3D glasses, they could follow the surgery through the high-resolution 3D images from laparoscopic cameras that are also shown on screens for the surgeons to consult on. Or they could zoom out and see what the anesthesiologists and nurses were doing during the surgery. They were even able to chat and have a discussion—for example, if a sample was sent to the pathologist, they could also listen to the findings and converse on its implications. This method is now being adopted by the Singapore General Hospital. Though South Korea is pioneering extended reality technologies—there are still regulatory challenges they are trying to overcome. South Korea introduced the metaverse strategy in 2022 and invested US$177.1 million (223.7 billion won) into the industry, and Seoul is building a 3.9 billion-won metaverse platform.[6] The South Korea Metaverse Alliance spans 450 companies.[7]

Figure 12.2 Seoul National University (SNU) Bundang Hospital: Smart Operation Theater.[8]

problem of what the metaverse can and cannot do. For example, the media always refers to the Travis Scott concert on Fortnite as one with an audience of 12.5 million people. In reality, multiple slightly asynchronous broadcasts to groups of 50 were made with their own version of Travis Scott, but certainly it was not one Travis Scott avatar performing to 12.5 million people.[9] Yet the fledgling results are extremely positive (see Figure 12.2).

At this point in time, what we refer to as the metaverse is a collection *of multiple advanced virtual worlds or platforms*. There may be some connectivity across these virtual worlds and to the physical world through specialized interfaces (hardware and biological), software technologies, services, and data.[10] Table 12.1 gives current examples of where the metaverse is along the extended reality continuum.

12.1.2 Are We There Yet?

No, according to metaverse expert Mathew Ball in his 2022 book *The Metaverse And How it Will Revolutionize Everything*. He cites several reasons from hardware, infrastructure, software, and data management and regulations (see Table 12.2). In an ideal metaverse world, we would be able to jump in and out of virtual worlds and the real world, and the data we use in all these worlds would be transferable (with individual choice). The low awareness of what the metaverse is and what it can do is driving rapid

TABLE 12.1 Examples of Customer Experiences Along the XR Continuum

Extended Reality Continuum	Examples
Virtual Environment/reality (VR)—complete immersion in a digital world	The Sandbox, SecondLife, Ready Player One, Meta World, Fortnite, Nvidia Omniverse, Roblox, Decentraland
Augmented Virtual Environment: real world superimposed on the virtual world	Training (planes, ships, surgeries),[11] Architecture, Virtual Tourism, 3D capture and insertion in digital twins
Augmented Reality (AR): Virtual objects are superimposed on the real world	IKEA AR mobile app, Pepsi's bus shelter AR ad,[12] Google Translate's Word Lens, Pokemon Go, Snapchat filters, Holoride Audi Virtual Reality Experience (also referred to as Audi XR) in partnership with Disney and Marvel Studios (Salzburg experience)
Real Environment	AI collects data for data analytics through IoT or online customer interaction, purchases, or movement.
	Customers can use websites for searching (Google search), ordering (Uber), comparisons of prices (Booking.com; Expedia), online brand communities (Instagram/Facebook), and sales (Etsy, eBay)

TABLE 12.2 Metaverse—Are We There Yet?

Issues	Where we are	Where we need to be
Sense of Presence[13]	Limited by proprietary boundaries and national boundaries, history (early worlds would delete past due to lack of storage space or reset the system if there was a bug).	Not fully there yet. Continuity of data, history, identity, entitlements, objects, communication, and payment. Needs standards and regulations.
Bandwidth for streaming (volume of data)[14]	Global Average: 786 Tbps. A good connection has 11 Mbps and a very fast 1Gbps (1,000Mbps).	Not there yet. Greater than 2–5 Gbps (2,000–5,000 Mbps) for both upstream and downstream traffic. Ideally want close to no delay.
Latency (delay before a transfer of data begins following an instruction for its transfer)[15]	35ms–100 seconds both ways, depending on how many continents are being covered (4G adds more; 5G will only save in the last mile—a 20–40ms). Satellites generally have 500ms latency. Cables/DSL has 100ms or less. Starlink averages 18–55ms, provided it is direct. If it goes via multiple satellites, it increases time.	Not there yet. Under 10 milliseconds.
Concurrency (happens at the same time as for others)—CCU[16]	3D: Facebook VR—18 avatars, Call of Duty Warzone 150 avatars, Fortnite 100 avatars, depends on CPUs in high fidelity. Low fidelity, maybe 4000 avatars (as of Fall, 2022).	Not there yet. Millions at least the population of each country (think of national days etc.).
Persistence: Extends the VR/AR content beyond when you are using it, giving an impression of time. Does not reboot.	Exists for chats but not VR/AR content. Second Life has some persistence.[17]	Not there yet. Needs to be seamless with real life. This is challenging as the metaverse is boundaryless, and time will be different in different spaces and countries (as we start putting real worlds and virtual worlds together).
Hardware Processing:[18] The sale and support of physical technologies and devices used to access, interact with, or develop the Metaverse.	Not yet there on an economical scale.	Not there yet. Legacy gateways (to access the metaverse like phones, tablets, etc., need to improve and become cheaper), data servers cost more, are less resource intensive, and more energy efficient, with increased computing power that is miniaturized, etc.

(continued)

TABLE 12.2 Metaverse—Are We There Yet? (continued)

Issues	Where we are	Where we need to be
Rendering (image frames/second)	Gaming is about 60 frames per second. A 12 megapixels camera, 30 FPS, captures 30 gigabytes of raw data per second.[19] Hence the issue is also about data which affects data transfer.	Not there yet. If FPS is 15–20, in a VR environment, you may feel sick. Need a higher rendering—90FPS or higher.[20]
3D field of view (FOV): how much you can see.	Oculus Quest 2 FOV of 89°. Pico Neo 3 Pro FOV is 98°. VIVE Focus 3 is about 120°	Not there yet.[21] Human field of view: 210-degree forward-facing horizontal arc; 150-degree vertical range. The bird avatar may need a 360-degree visual field.
Interoperability[22]	Apple removed Fortnite from its store (for violating its terms). Sony Playstation Network for cross-play. Steam as a platform for games.	Not there yet.
Governance[23]	Largely by self-governance, community norms, rules, algorithms, standards, and human content moderation.	Not there yet. Needs "thinking out of the box." EVE Online has 100,000 users in 8,000 star systems and 70,000 planets. Microsoft Flight Simulator's virtual world spans 510 million square kilometers. Needs standards and regulations.
Standards[24]	Not yet there. The Universal Scene Description (used by omniverse) is an open source 3D standard (since 2016) created by Pixar in 2012. Fortnite is pioneering data standards. Facebook is allowing avatars to move across platforms.	Not there yet. Voltage standards, measurement systems, conventions, payment, interoperability, data file formats, code of conduct, and data privacy.
Sustainability	As it is AI-driven, and maybe blockchained, with huge user numbers (50 million projected), this consumes a huge amount of energy. Rare earth metals used for AI components are wasteful and toxic. One ton of these metals consumes 75,000 liters of water and one ton of radioactive residue.[25] AI is based on hidden labor or ghost workers (paid less than minimum wage in some cases) to keep the costs of AI down.[26]	Not there yet if we are to reach Net Positive by 2030. Need to rethink—human labor, environment, and culture, among other things. Needs standards and regulations.

adoption of extended reality platforms. Stephens et al. (2022), in their paper on Metaverse & Governance, state,

> this space is complex. It shows tensions between fantasy anonymous worlds and state-governed virtual services. Challenges between private stakeholder monetization opportunities and the public value space—finally, the need to balance innovation with human-centric values and wellbeing.[27]

For the metaverse, besides the other factors mentioned above, we will need interoperability. Minecraft as a platform is an example of a successful game that is still not interoperable across its various versions (in 2021, only the Bedrock version could do crossplay) and has limitations when playing across iOS, Android, and PlayStation (all versions). X-Box still needs to interact with the real world (like in Pokémon Go). Fortnite as a game is interoperable across various devices like the Xbox, PlayStation, PC, etc. However, in August 2020, Apple and Google removed Fortnite. The reason was that Epic Games (Unreal Engine) had an update that allowed customers to pay directly to the company, bypassing Apple and Google. Epic filed a case against Apple (Apple charges a 30% royalty for being on its platform).[28] While this case is still being resolved, it proves that interoperability is something that is still being negotiated.

The biggest issue we have to solve is that the metaverse will have all of the AI governance challenges and more. It will need, (see Figure 12.3):

1. Infrastructure support (for transmission of data and its storage).
2. Software engines (like those used in 3D gaming),
3. Payment rails (that need some standardization, interoperability, and oversight),
4. Legal attestations and recourse (for things like identity and properties across virtual worlds and the real world (s)—assuming space exploration).
5. Regulations and standards/guidelines (across government, private sector, and open-source platforms)
6. Protocols/rules on how data needs to be exchanged under a standard, and
7. Blockchain (there are many currently, but few will survive).

12.1.3 Relevance to Industries

Citi estimates that 5 billion internet users out of the 8.5 billion population will be online by 2030[29] (40% left behind),[30] but now only 2.55 billion out of 8 billion (32%) are accessing the virtual economy.[31] Much of

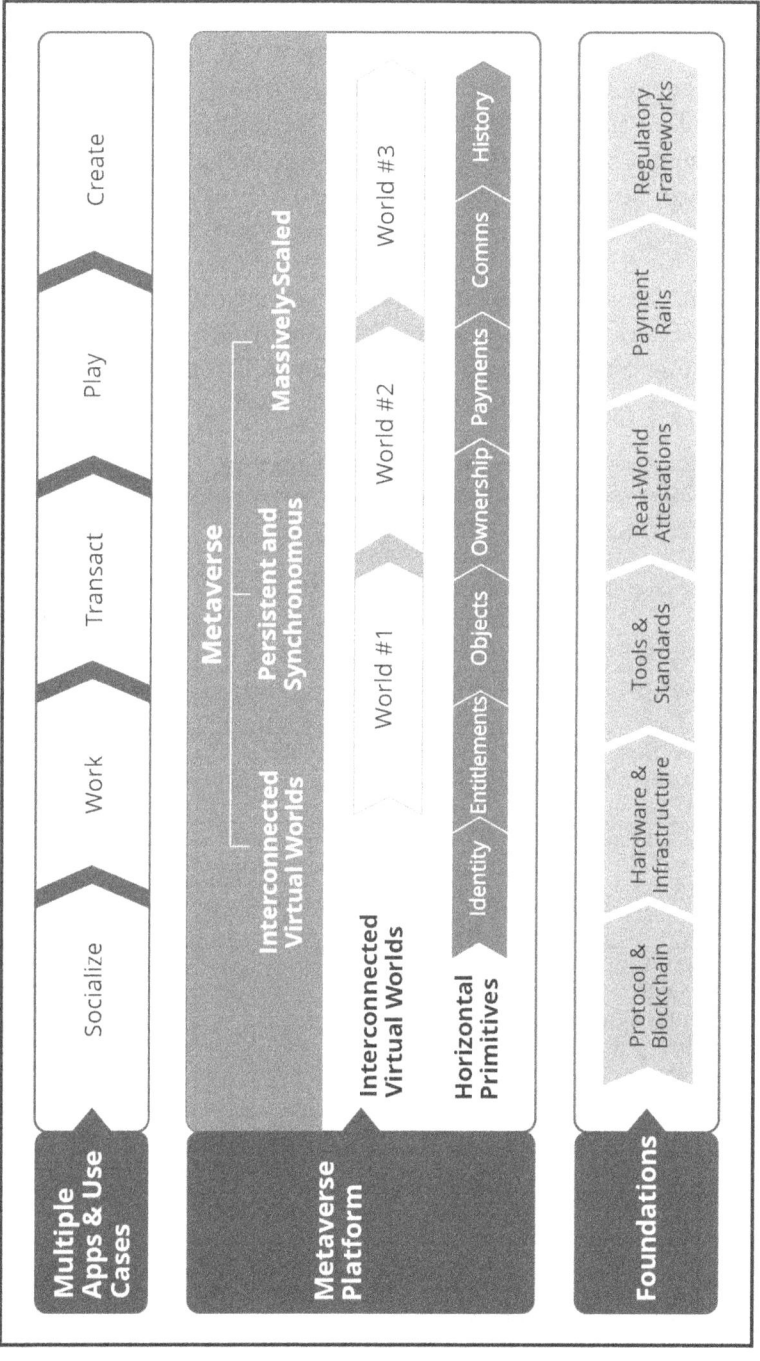

Figure 12.3 Metaverse stack deconstructed—Extended reality. *Source:* Adapted from Stephens (2022), based on Lee & Hu-Au (2021)[32] and Armstrong & Reeve (2021)[33]

this virtual economy (85%) is microtransactions.[34] The speculation on the metaverse led to crazy investments in content (huge M&As see Table 12.3), digital artefacts (like avatars and NFTs), and retail transactions (early 2022, Decentraland's cheapest plot was US$13,000 for 16 × 16 meters). These investments and media hype led the NFTs and the cryptocurrency crash in 2022. For example, an investor, P-Ape, paid US$450,000 in Decentraland to be Snoop Doggs' neighbor.[35] Considering this is a virtual space, and there are many virtual property developers, like Decentraland, The Sandbox (belonging to Meta), Second Life (Linden Labs), Somnium Space, CryptoVoxels, or Lepasa, the virtual world does not face a scarcity issue like the real physical world does. Hence the scarcity of virtual land is artificial, which raises interesting questions for future value. Table 12.3 gives examples of recent M&As that fuel the metaverse potential growth.

TABLE 12.3 Examples of M&As Pushing Metaverse			
Year	Company	Acquisition	Amount
2014	Facebook (USA)	Occulus VR (USA)	US$ 2 billion
2014	Microsoft (USA)	Mahjong (creators of Minecraft) (Sweden)	US$ 2.5 billion
Q1 2021	Match Group (USA)	Hyperconnect (South Korea)	US$ 2 billion
Q2 2021	Snap (USA)	Wave Optics (AR smart glasses) (UK)	US$ 500 million
Q3 2021	Byte Dance (parent company Tik Tok) (China)	Pico (interactive VR headsets) (USA)	US$ 700 million
Q4 2021	Unity Technologies (USA)	Weta Digital (Visual effects and 3D animations) (New Zealand)	US$ 1.63 billion
Q1 2022	Microsoft (USA)	Activision Blizzard–makers of game Call of Duty (USA)	US$ 68.7 billion
Q1 2022	ARM (UK), acquired by SoftBank Group Corp. (Japan).	Nvidia (USA)	$40 billion. Stopped due to regulatory concerns by US Federal Trade Commission, UK regulators, EU and China.
Q1 2022	Take-Two (USA)	Zynga (outstanding shares) (USA)	US$ 700 million
Q2 2022	Arogo Capital Acquisition (SPAC) (USA)	EON Reality (VR solutions for 3D offices) (USA)	US$ 655 million
Q3 2022	Sony (Japan)	Bungie—creators of game *Destiny* and *Halo* (which also has stakes in *Fortnite*) (USA)	US$ 3.6 billion

Source: TechMonitor (2022)[36]

Airport Authority Hong Kong created a Digital Twin of the entire 12.5 sq km airport, which had 70,000 employees working there. All the architectural, structural, mechanical, electrical, and plumbing services data were digitized with a geographical information systems (GIS) map. The digital twin was static, and to make it real-time, data from IoT devices were captured across nine floors with other analytical tools. They used a Unity Engine to bring the model to life. By adding simulation tools, they can predict future airport experiences.

Figure 12.4 Hong Kong International Airport Terminal 1[37]

In some cases, the metaverse will use digital twins (see Figure 12.4), which is a virtual representation of the physical and functional aspects of any component, product, system, or space, that reflects useable information, not just in the current but also the subsequent lifecycle phases.[38] NASA was one of the pioneers in using digital twins in its Virtual Product Laboratory in 1999[39] along with the US Joint Forces Command.[40] The problems they faced with interoperability still exist today. Digital twins are being used in manufacturing, aviation, health, operations, and logistics, but mostly for design, planning, education, or real-time surveillance. Digital twins are also being used for tourism. When the pandemic shut down travel, many global events, like the Olympics and World Expo, were rescheduled and failed to get the usual tourism numbers. Dubai held the 2020 World Expo from October 2021 to March 2022. At the end of the event, 31 million people visited the virtual Expo (at https://virtualexpodubai.com) compared to the 22.93 million physical visits.[41] They were able to visit the pavilions, take part in the concerts, and attend talks and key celebrations.

12.1.4 Governance Issues[42]

Governance of the metaverse must first begin with the individual before moving to society and organizations (see Figure 12.5). This education should be something that the government needs to drive as part of digital skills. Children as young as two play video games. Hence this educational intervention is also for parents.[43] While some parts of the metaverse are driven by gaming and game mechanics, there are some cautions when extending it to things like education and gamifying life in general.

Organizations focusing on onboarding children must especially be mindful of their impact as it will be generational (see Figure 12.7). Emma Joy Reay, a researcher, looked at 506 commercially video games published

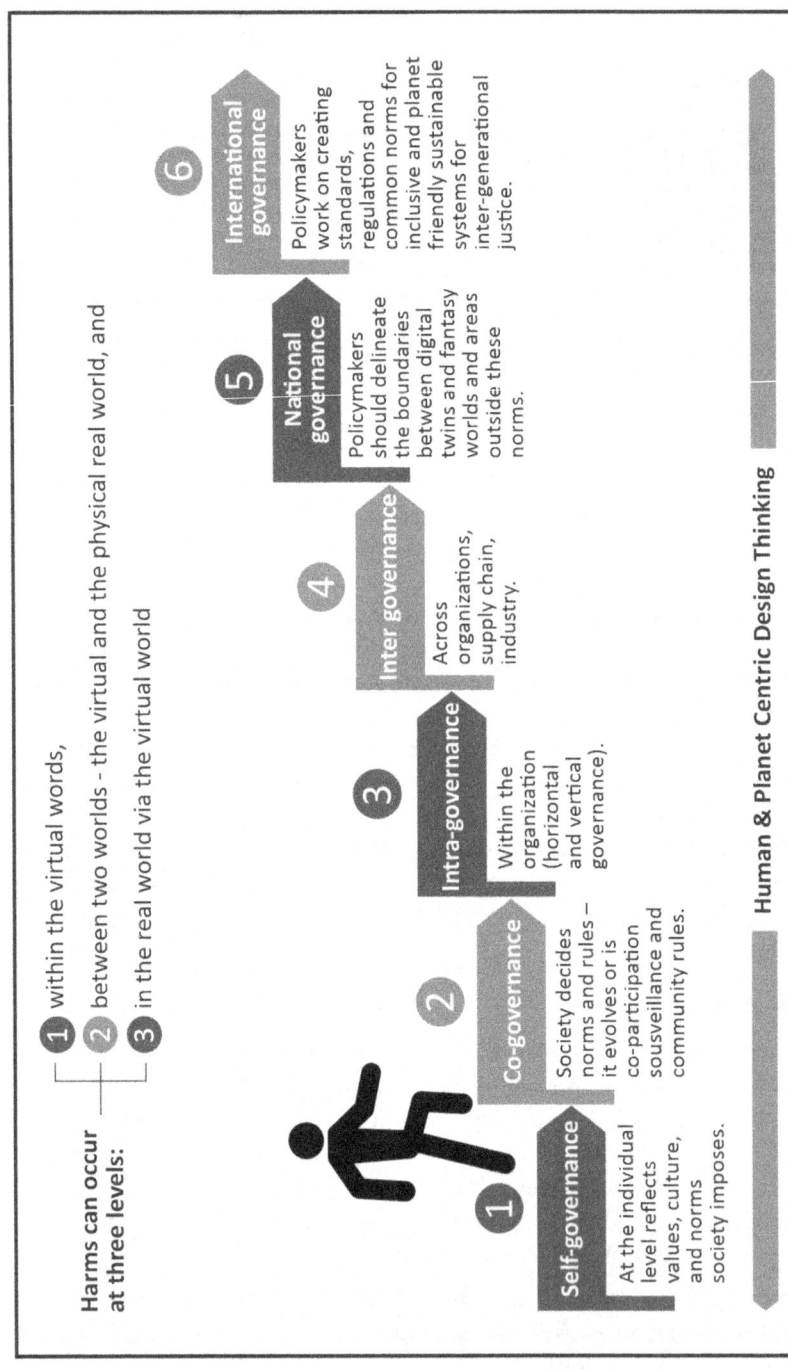

Figure 12.5 Governance levels. *Source:* Stephens et al. (2022).[44]

In 2010, there was a mistake in a digital map. Google had depicted part of Costa Rica as belonging to Nicaragua. It resulted in Nicaraguan troops using the excuse to cross the San Juan river and entering a bordering town in Costa Rica. The troops replaced the national flag with their own. Google acknowledged the mistake—it was about 2.7 km off. A geopolicy analyst at Google said, "Cartography is a complex undertaking, and borders are always changing." The data was supplied by The U.S. Department of State. While this has been historically a disputed territory, the fact that one country used the information published to enter another country raises questions on general knowledge, awareness, and attention to detail in using data provided.

Figure 12.6 Google Maps and Nicaragua and Costa Rica.[45]

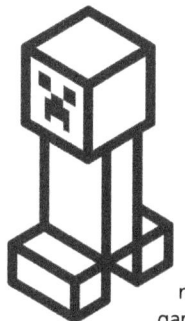

Stockholm-based Mojang created Minecraft in 2009. Sweden has high computer literacy, good digital infrastructure, government support for the Swedish Games Industry (Dataspelsbranschen), and a culture supporting video gaming. In the early 1980s, there was a subculture of creating audio and video programs using home computers called Demo scene. Sweden hosts one of the destination events of Dream Hack, the world's largest e-sports festival, in Jönköping. Between 2010 to 2020, the video game industry in Sweden grew 24 times in revenue: from EUR 130 million to EUR 3,312 million.[46] This growth shows an impressive track record as Sweden has a small domestic market, and the global game industry is a very competitive sector. If you look at the active Minecraft community, the community space called Planet Minecraft had 126 million people,[47] 8,242 servers, 168 bedrock servers, 2.6+ million uploads of user content, 2.9 billion submission views, and about 488 million downloads in 2021.[48]

In 2015, Microsoft bought Minecraft for US$ 2.5 billion. Minecraft is targeted at 5–15 years old's (though recommended for children eight years and above), but it is estimated that the average user is 24 years of age and male.[49] According to the Entertainment Software Rating Board (ESRB), Minecraft is recommended for ages 10+. Parents rarely play the game they buy for their children. It was estimated that only 11% of parents play Minecraft.[50] Creating an AI-enabled society may require governance that looks beyond the game and the organization. There is a Minecraft Education Edition,[51] but the focus is not on training parents or caretakers of children.

In 2016, Microsoft introduced Project AIX, released as open-source, to train AI to survive in the Minecraft environment.[52] Researchers at Pennsylvania State University won a US$ 900,000 grant from the United States Air Force Office of Scientific Research in 2021 to create an AI that can perform complex tasks. They planned to test it as an avatar in Minecraft in one of the regular challenges Microsoft has been hosting since 2011.[53] Open AI used 70K of unlabeled video data and labeled the mouse interactions to train an AI agent to play Minecraft.[54] They first collected 270,000 hours of Minecraft-related video data and edited it to around 70,000 hours.[55] You get an idea of how much time and effort training takes! A successful customer experience will need the active participation of the ecosystem to make it work.

Figure 12.7 Minecraft: Stockholm and Microsoft.

between 2009 and 2019.[56] She found that 331 did not contain any child characters at all—like Rhythm games and Sandbox games. In the other types of games, the numbers were small: sports (only 3% had child characters), strategy (11%), action games (51%), adventure games (58%), and role-playing games (78%). In some cases, when the games focused on adults, this exclusion was to protect children as in the case of violent games which "encourage players to explore the boundaries both of what is possible and what is permissible." Even when there were child characters, most of them were White and male. She noted,

> In fact, games that were rated "16+" and "18+" were more likely to contain child characters, while only 15% of games rated "3+" contained child characters. 36% of games rated "7+" contained child characters, 29% of games rated "12+" contained child characters, 41% of games rated "16+" contained child characters, and 54% of games rated "18+" contained child characters.

Does this distortion matter? It will if we are onboarding the metaverse. The metaverse needs representation that reflects the diversity of the real world. It needs to be inclusive and hence needs thoughtful design involving a wide array of stakeholders—early child specialists, health professionals, educationalists, social scientists, or regulators.

Another key point to consider is the extractive nature of the metaverse. It is built on the cheap labor of humans, their data, the increasing exploitation of limited natural resources, and the degradation of the environment. Kate Crawford has been outspoken about this dark side of AI in her book *Atlas of AI*.[57] Content moderation, a job that is growing exponentially, cannot be handled by AI only, and the humans who are working behind the scenes are struggling.[58] For us to build a net positive metaverse, we need to be ruthlessly fearless at looking at what is not working. The systemic impact of AI needs to be addressed today to create a better tomorrow.

Last but not the least, the industry is driven by use cases. There are cautions attached to use cases (as this book has highlighted again and again). Context matters. All the results matter. Most use cases often highlight the positive impacts of onboarding technology and the success rate, not false positives (in the case of identifying tumors using AI) or the error rate, nor do they discuss accountability chains or maintenance costs. These are critical when making decisions to onboard new technologies. The metaverse will have these challenges at an exponential rate and cost). It is important that we consider the resources we have and what we are willing to invest in. For these reasons, outsourcing is not always the right answer for good governance (see the report published by IEEE on Metaverse and Governance).[59]

12.2 Synthetic Biology (SynBio)

In 1995, author Kevin Kelly wrote a book, *Out of Control: The New Biology of Machines, Social Systems, and the Economic World.*[60] As a systems thinker, he states,

> The greatest social consequence of the Darwinian revolution was the grudging acceptance by humans that humans were random descendants of monkeys, neither perfect nor engineered. The greatest social consequence of neo-biological civilization will be the grudging acceptance by humans that humans are the random ancestors of machines, and that as machines we can be engineered ourselves.

However it is not just AI or the machine we are engineering with biology, it is specific biology systems we are engineering with machines, AI and other biological systems! Synthetic Biology or SynBio uses all available technologies to modify the genetic material of living organisms through a faster and easier process.[61] It does not exclude the consideration of non-viable, non-reproducing goods and materials generated by or through the use of such living genetically modified organisms (GMOs).[62] This type of technology is enabled and enhanced through the adoption of AI and AI logic and sits at the intersection of various research streams like physical engineering and genetic engineering (see Figure 12.8).

Synbio is often associated with AI. This is because the design of the processes has similarities to AI: programming of biological cells,[63] use of Big Data in the form of genetic data, interfaces (biophysical or biochemical), and complex circuitry.[64] SynBio also uses AI tools like software, robotics, databases, and simulation models.[65] AI is used to create data-driven models of biological systems and prediction models of genetic modifications.[66] Companies like LabGenius focus on combining gene synthesis, machine learning, and robotic automation to engineer new proteins with *novel, enabling functionality.*[67] Machine learning is being used increasingly to predict

---

During the early days of the pandemic, Distributed Bio, which was acquired by Charles River on 1 January 2021, began work on finding antibodies to fight the SARS-CoV 2 virus (see Figure 12.8a). They used their Tumbler computational antibody optimization technology and SuperHuman 2.0 human antibody discovery platform (a library of human antibody repertoire which spans 10 million members to one thousand trillion members[68]). In nine weeks, the team had identified thousands of potential antibodies against the virus.

Figure 12.8 Case of Distributed Bio.

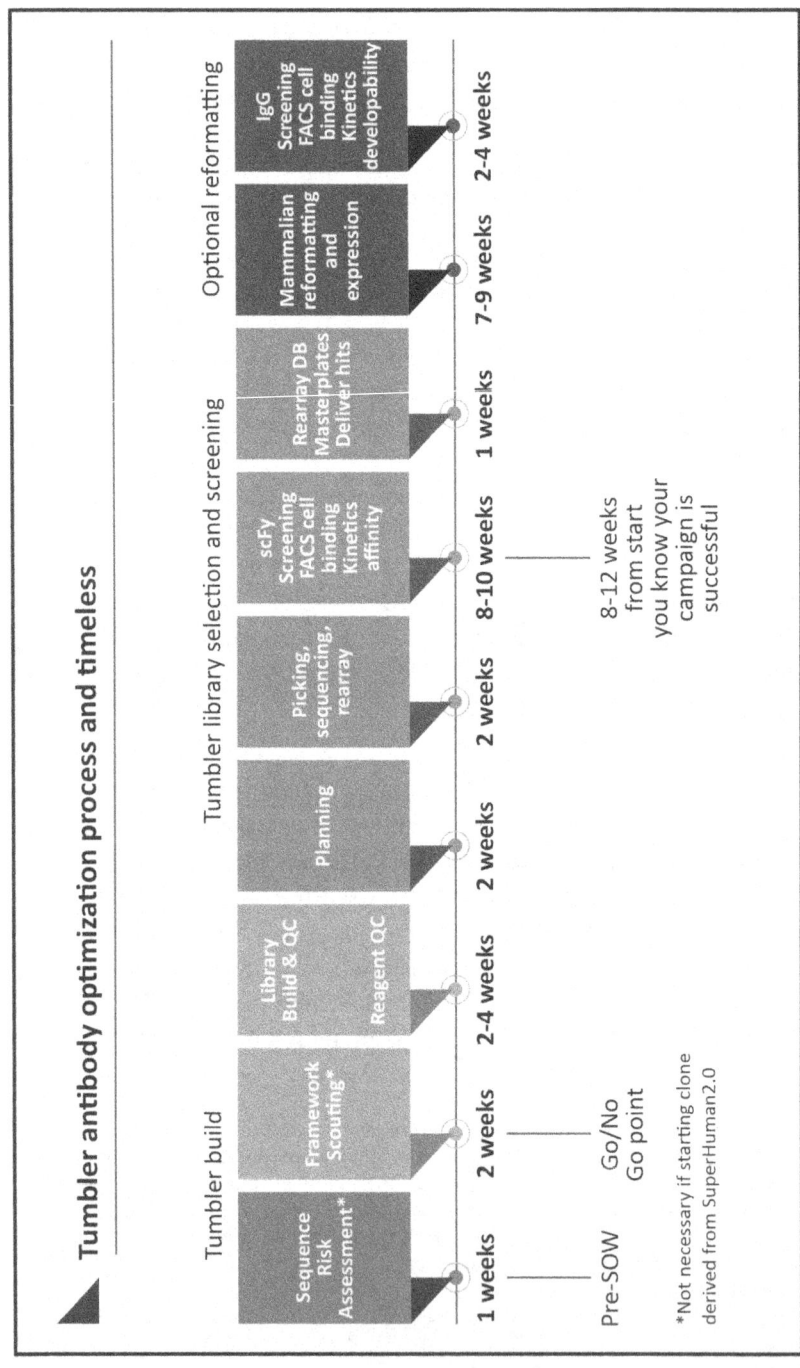

Figure 12.8a Tumbler antibody optimization process and timeline. *Source:* Cumbers. 2020[69]

how a cell can behave (considering a human genome (genetic material) has 20,000 genes (segments of DNA).[70]

There are differences in programming genetic material and AI programming. Though Synbio uses computer-aided modeling and algorithms, gene programming is different as it is based on biochemistry or gene reconstruction or modification.

> Controlling gene expression through gene switches based on a model borrowed from the digital world has long been one of the primary objectives of synthetic biology. The digital technique uses what are known as logic gates to process input signals, creating circuits where, for example, output signal C is produced only when input signals A and B are simultaneously present.[71]

Kim, Bojar, and Fussenegger, early pioneers in this field of cell programming,[72,73] explain the differences between AI and genetic material programming. In the digital world, each circuit processes a single input in the form of electrons, but the speed of processing each input can run up to a billion commands per second. In the case of a human cell, it can only process metabolic molecules or inputs (to our knowledge) of up to 100,000 per second. Still, their range of options (similar to algorithms in the digital world) is so huge that even supercomputers cannot match the width of processing. This technique is in the early phases of development[74] but can be operationalized at scale.

These CRISPR-CPUs can act as a cell computer that could sense specific metabolic inputs and hence trigger a corresponding reaction, thus allowing targeted action to occur and, therefore,

> may enable novel approaches to medicine and represent a step toward autonomous micromachines capable of precise interfacing of human physiology or other complex biological environments, ecosystems, or industrial bioprocesses.[75]

As discussed above, after the initial programming, these programmed cells may act autonomously (and there is a real fear of how much we can control the impact of things like interspecies chimeras (which took ten years to reach proof of concept).[76] The assumption of control comes from *kill switches*,[77] *auxotrophy*,[78] or other methods,[79] which are being tested as our knowledge of the body and cell adaptation grows. There are several challenges for SynBio governance (see Figure 12.9)

The impact of biotechnology (a subset of SynBio) is estimated to be worth US$ 2–4 trillion a year over the next decade or two, with biocomputing alone being worth 1% of the total.[80] The analysis of the huge bio data

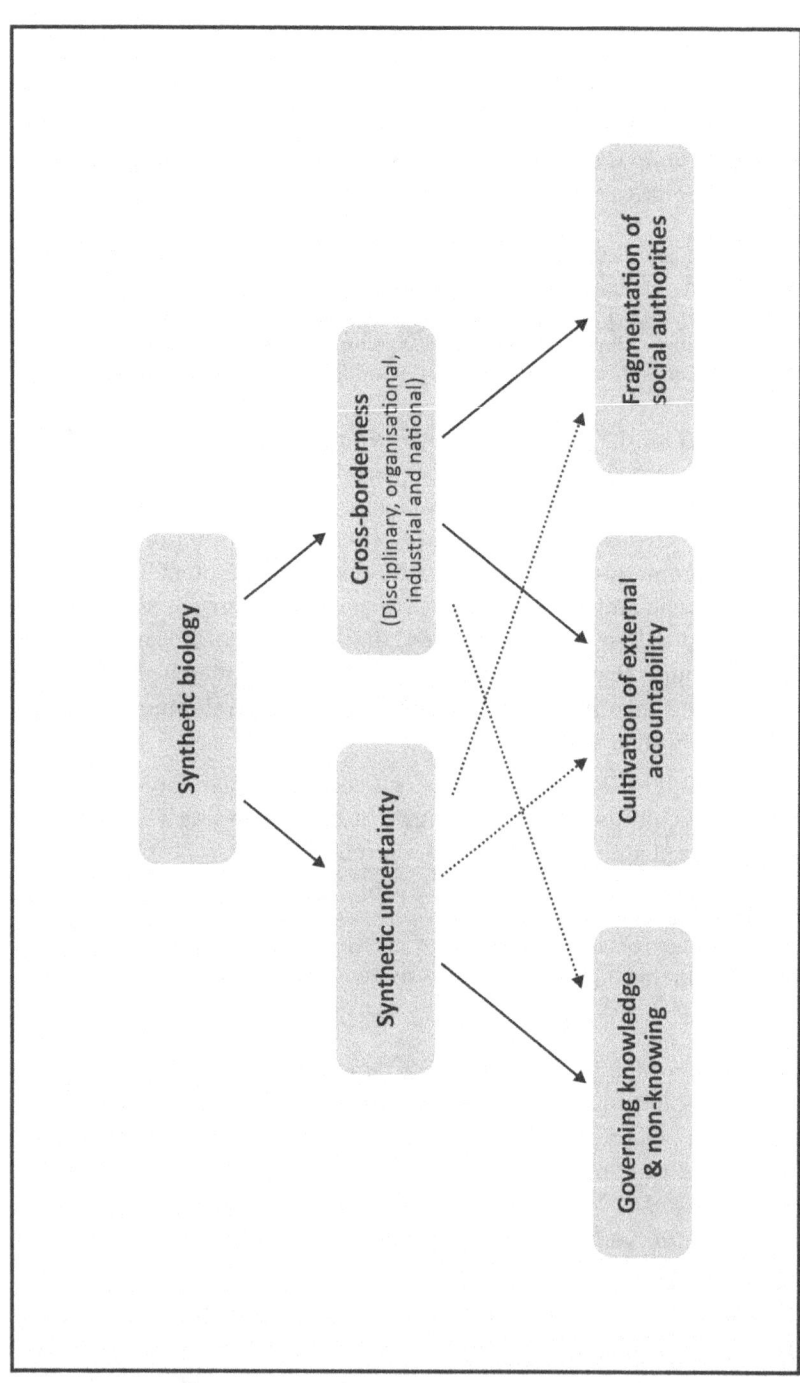

Figure 12.9 Challenges for SynBio Governance. *Source:* Adapted from Zhang, Marris, and Rose (2011)[81]

sets and their modeling is heavily dependent on AI. There is also the parallel development of SynBio which mirrors the techniques of AI and hence requires the governance of AI. SynBio borrows programming techniques, big data, and infrastructure logic from AI and hence will also inherit some of the thinking which AI ethics and governance experts are already flagging as problematic.

Knowledge in this domain is often a public good. There is the assumption that lowering the cost of access to genomic data and technology is beneficial. At this point, there is also immense funding via the private sector, hoping to exploit the market potential.[82] This could mean that, in the wrong hands, this technology could be detrimental.

Another factor we need to be mindful of is that eventually, we *may* move from our current infrastructure and materials to biological cells as building blocks for AI computing and storage. This is still not yet feasible commercially, and most of the research is basic, but the time cycles are accelerating.[83]

To recap, the technology is being developed at an exponential rate, and there is a perfect storm in terms of research streams, open data (IP sharing), and lack of regulations, all making it necessary to relook at the governance and ethical processes in the development of the technology. As highlighted in the working paper by BIOS (Centre for the Study of Bioscience, Biomedicine, Biotechnology, and Society),

> many tend to frame the problems posed by synthetic biology in a way that matches established policy categories. As a result, the governance of this area has to some extent become an act of "filling the prescription," or formatting the problem to fit readily available solutions.[84]

We need interdisciplinary, intercountry, intersectional groups to start this dialogue and recommend priorities to ensure that SynBios are managed for the greater good.

12.2.2 The Perfect Storm: Timing and Confluence of Events

To illustrate the points mentioned in the previous section, several factors are facilitating the speed of development of SynBio: (1) State of Research, (2) Intellectual Property (IP) Trends, and (3) Regulations (lack or fragmentation).

12.2.2.1 State of Research

The costs and time associated with the research have decreased. For example, it took 13 years and US$ 3 billion to sequence the human genome, but by 2020, it took seven days and US$ 600.[85] The flurry of research is encouraged through open innovations like *The International Genetically Engineered Machine* (iGEM) competition, which has propelled innovations on SynBio tools, or *The GP-Write Project*, which aims to synthesize human and other large-scale genomes quickly and cheaply. In addition, the *BioBrick Public Agreement* (BPA) is an open-source platform that shares BioBrick parts on an intellectual property-free basis.[86] While initially the research was funded by governments, there is significant amount of private sector and VC money in these new technologies. For example, research is being conducted on hacking a biological system of an insect and making it a cyborg.[87]

12.2.2.2 Intellectual Property Trends

The time for commercialization, from basic research to applied and commercial research, has been decreasing in SynBio: It took 200 years to engineer artemisinic acid[88] and around 50 years for Escherichia coli[89] and COVID-19 mRNA vaccines. The progress may be exponential and with a bit of serendipity involved. A critical inflection point was reached with the COVID-19 pandemic. The global supply chain systems, the infrastructure for mass production, and the technology via reverse engineering and genetics have allowed the SynBio potential to become a reality.

The earliest patents for SynBios can be traced to 1988, and the number is rapidly growing at 500 patents per year, with 90% of patents in the fermentation industry; 52% in pharmaceuticals (natural products and polymers); 22% in biotechnology, plant genetics, veterinary vaccines and 14% in scientific instrumentation.[90] Many of the patents are held by conglomerates from the chemical industry (like Du Pont, BASF, or Ajinomoto), pharmaceutical industry (Bayer, BioNTech), fuels (Butamax Advanced Fuels), and agritech sectors (Monsanto). However, the industry is still very fragmented, with no single player having more than 4% of all patents.[91] The top universities and research centers holding patents are also scattered around the world—with the USA (the University of California, University of Illinois), France (CNRS, INSERM), Japan (University of Osaka), and Israel (Hebrew University, Jerusalem, Technion), with 1.5% being the highest amount they hold as patents.[92]

12.2.2.3 Regulations (or lack of them)

On the one hand, the promise of SynBio and the political pressure to excel are driving this field.[93] On the other hand, there is a lack of robust regulations, and the few policies that exist remain fragmented with respect to SynBios and their creation, testing, monitoring, and disposal (see Table 12.4).[94] For example, if a country has robust regulations for genetically

TABLE 12.4 History of Governance of SynBio

1975 the Asilomar Conference on Recombinant DNA Molecules	Research should continue but with appropriate safeguards.
1992 United Nations Convention on Biological Diversity (CBD)	Ratified by 196 countries (except the USA) and Holy See: article 8 —"regulate, manage or control the risks associated with the use and release of living modified organisms resulting from biotechnology which *are likely to have* adverse environmental impacts…
1997 Council of Europe	The Oveido Convention and its Protocols (protection of human rights in biomedicine). Signed by 29 EU countries.
2000 Cartagena Protocol on Biosafety to the CBD	Regulatory framework for the safe use, handling, and transfer of living modified organisms (modern biotechnology). The issue is that some recombinant DNA (e.g., cisgenesis) and "new" technologies (e.g., genome editing) may be excluded from its scope.
2011 Nagoya Protocol on Access and Benefit Sharing (ABS) to the CBD ("Nagoya Protocol")	The shift from natural and genetic resources to lab production of biological entities and intangible genetic resources' information (present in SynBios) would escape under the radar of CBD and the Nagoya Protocol.[95]

modified organisms (GMOs), by definition, novel genome editing techniques used in both synthetic biology and genetic modification may not be covered.[96] This may be because the new technology may have both physical and biological components, and the route in which the applications are framed may result in some regulatory loopholes.[97] The *Access and Benefit Sharing* defined in the Nagoya protocol also shows fragmentation among the 39 signatories.[98] There are issues with patents for DNA sequencing and their enforceability.[99] In the United States and Europe, SynBio products can be labeled as *natural* ingredients.[100] Figure 12.10 shows the international conventions in place (most of which fall under *Convention on Biological Diversity or CBD*)[101] and the challenges with SynBios.

As mentioned earlier, DNA sequencing is leading to banks of live and extinct species. For example, a library of 100,000 artificial transcription factors[102] was created by Park et al. in 2019.[103] Many databases are free and publicly accessible, representing 500,000 taxa as of January 1, 2017 and 2,650 trillion DNA bases assembled/ annotated as of August 2017.[104] This is like Big Data without robust international rules and regulations on genetic data. There is a competition between countries to sequence 1 million genomes of their citizens, with the UK, China, Australia, KSA, USA, Estonia, France, UAE, and Turkey leading the way.[105] At the national level, though care is taken, we know cyberhacking is all too common and hence can allow

McKinsey, in their 2020 report[106] titled, *The Bio Revolution: Innovations Transforming Economies, Societies, and Our Lives*, highlighted some of the challenges:

1. **Biology is self-replicating, self-sustaining, and does not respect jurisdictional boundaries.**
   For example, new genetically engineered gene drives applied to the vectors that spread disease (mosquitoes in the case of malaria) could have enormous health benefits, but such gene drives can be difficult to control and can potentially permanently change ecosystems.

2. **The interconnected nature of biology can increase the potential for unintended consequences.**
   Changes to one part of the system can have cascading effects and unintended consequences across entire ecosystems or species. Gene editing could also have unintended or "off-target" effects.

3. **Low barriers to entry open the door to potential misuse with potentially fatal consequences.**
   Some biological technologies are relatively cheap and accessible. Commercial kits to perform CRISPR gene editing are being sold relatively cheaply on the Internet.

4. **Differing value systems make it hard to forge consensus, including on life and death issues.**
   Technical and scientific issues, such as embryo editing, quickly become moral questions, and often, decisions across these issues are expressions of one's value system.

5. **The challenge of cooperation and coordination of value systems across cultures and jurisdictions is no easy task.**
   This is especially true when advances in these scientific domains could be seen as a unique competitive advantage for businesses or economies.

6. **Privacy and consent issues are fundamental.**
   Concerns about personal privacy and consent are rife, given that the cornerstone of biological advances is data mined from our bodies and brains.

7. **Unequal access could perpetuate socioeconomic disparity, with potentially regressive effects.**
   Biological advances and their commercial applications may not be accessible to all in equal measure, thereby exacerbating socioeconomic disparity. At a country level, developments are advancing quickest and most broadly in relatively rich countries.

Figure 12.10   Governance challenges with SynBio.

targeted genetic warfare. In fact, a recent paper showed that AI researchers could use the same tools for finding life-saving new drugs and for generating new chemical warfare agents in just six hours![107]

Gain of Function Research (GoF research or GoFR) is for genetically altering an organism to enhance biological functions (there is some ambiguity in this definition).[108] It became controversial when scientists wondered whether we could create new or enhanced organisms. The COVID-19 pandemic, while deemed natural, highlighted that such fears were not unfounded. While some of this type of research was banned in the USA, the research grants for this field were sent to other countries like China,[109] showing a loophole in the regulations.[110]

12.2.4 Relevance to Specific Industries

Just like AI, SynBio shows the properties of a general purpose technology. Yet, it is transforming markets and industries as we know them today in ways we are not aware of. It is being used in various industries already: health, chemicals, food, agriculture, pharmaceutical, environment, and energy.[111] Industries that are disrupted and changed most significantly by SynBio are agriculture (already widely prevalent), health (prevalent), and manufacturing (being disrupted). For example, 75% of processed food is GMO.[112] In 2020, in the USA, GMO soybeans made up 94% of all soybeans planted, GMO cotton made up 96% of all cotton planted, and 92% of corn planted was GMO corn. The size of the SynBio markets varies but it is estimated at one end USD 30.7 billion by 2026[113] to be one third of global output or US$ 30 trillion by 2030.[114]

The challenge at this point is to consider how the confluence of AI with biology (all fields) can be better managed and governed at research (individual), university, industry (including funding), and government levels (local and international) from all stages till market adoption.

12.3 Humanoid Robots

The word *robot* was first mentioned in a play written in 1920 by Karel Čapek, called R.U.R. (Rossum's Universal Robots). It is derived from *robota* which means drudgery in Czech and work in Slovak suggesting that robots had a purpose to work. Isaac Asimov wrote the robot series of books, the first one called *I, Robot* in 1950. He introduced the three laws of robotics in 1942 and over the years highlighted the dilemmas associated even with such simple laws as mentioned in Figure 12.11.

Humanoid robots are a special category of robotics. They have human form or characteristics and are used for (1) research or education, (2) interacting with other humans (companionship, caregiving, rescue, law enforcement), or (3) interacting with tools or the environment (space exploration, manufacturing, service, security). Increasingly they are becoming more life-like in appearance, with significant amounts of private money funding this type of robotics (see Figure 12.12).

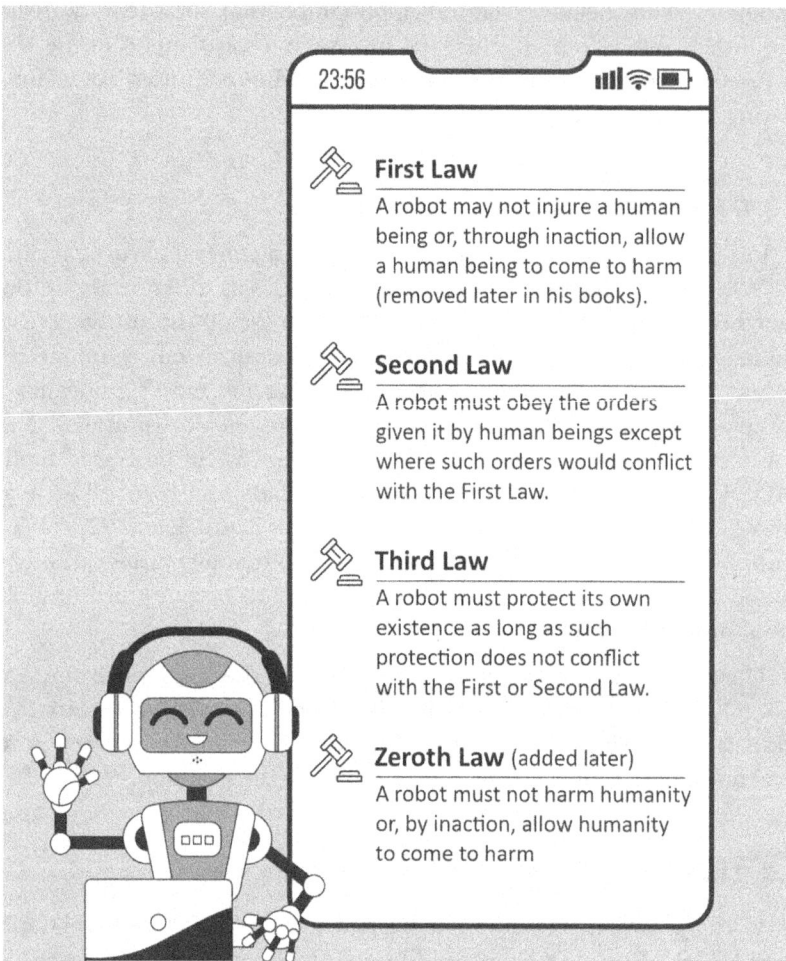

Figure 12.11 Asimov's Three Laws (and later Zeroth Law). *Source:* Authors

12.3.1 The Technology Challenge

As discussed in great detail, AI has not yet equaled human intelligence; however, it has its own method of mimicking intelligence. Besides the software and data challenges, there is the issue of hardware. Take the example of the human hand, which has a high degree of freedom because it has 27 bones, 27 joints, 34 muscles, and over 100 ligaments. To mimic the human hand is a biomechanical issue, and this field of research in robotics began with the first patent for a digitally operated robot arm by George Devol in 1939.

> The X-Prize Foundation has focussed on disruptive innovations and wicked problems. The first award was the US$10 million Ansari XPRIZE for private spaceflight, fuelling the private sector space race with recognizable brands like Virgin Galactic, Blue Origin, and SpaceX. There have been a total of 25 prizes launched. In 2018, All Nippon Airways (ANA) sponsored the US$10M ANA Avatar XPRIZE. It is a global competition where you transport yourself through your robotic avatar to a remote location. The objective is to "develop a physical, non- autonomous Avatar System with which an operator can see, hear, and interact within a remote environment in a manner that feels as if they are truly there."[115] The winners were announced in Fall 2022. The 20 finalists representing 20 countries in the competition are creating immersive telepresence by combining technologies from robotics, VR, AI, and haptics. The concept of avatar robots is not new; Toyota introduced the Wholebody Tele-operation for Humanoid Robot (T-HR3) in 2017, which is an avatar robot that replicates the actions of its user. The user controls the robot from the Master Manouevering System, a skeletal control system for whole body coordination. The system sends and receives signals from the robot, so the user can see via a VR set and maneuver accordingly.

Figure 12.12 X-Prize ANA avatar.

The simple act of walking, jumping, running, or even dancing is a complex activity for a robot to mimic. Atlas, the robot introduced by Boston Dynamics, took three years before it could jump and do backflips.[116] It was an outcome of a DARPA Robotics Challenge (2012–15).[117] To teach the robot to dance, it required 1.5 years of choreography, simulation, programming, and upgrades.[118]

Humans perceive with their eyes things like distance and depth, and the brain can accordingly coordinate a range of motions. For a robot to replicate this, it must use another process. Atlas uses lidar (pulsed laser sensor) and stereo sensors to measure distances and navigate the terrain. Engineers used a three-dimensional environment to train the virtual version of the robot to decrease costs. Atlas is electrically powered with a custom battery and valves, and its 28 joints are powered by a compact hydraulic power unit. It is not just the AI software and data that makes Atlas impressive; it is its state-of-the-art hardware.

To mimic the smallest muscles for expressions is not easy. For example, creating a life-like eye took four years of experimental research.[119] Or think of facial expressions—humans show microexpressions, which are emotional responses that last approximately 0.25–2 seconds. These expressions help us make a judgment on lying (or trustworthiness).[120] Robots are being taught to recognize some facial expressions,[121] especially customer-facing ones. But this is a trend that comes with cautions. Microsoft responded to these worries and has now stopped emotion recognition features from its tech as a part of its Responsible AI Standard introduced in 2022.[122]

If robots must socialize, humanoid robots will also have to mimic micro-expressions which they are still not very successful in doing. Developing a musculoskeletal remains a challenge. While early robots were made of metal, there has been a tremendous amount of research on materials that are lighter and can feel more human.[123] SynBio may also be used in soft robots (made of highly pliable materials) to better interface with humans. Masahiro Mori, a robotics professor at the Tokyo Institute of Technology, wrote in 1970,

> I have noticed that, in climbing toward the goal of making robots appear human, our affinity for them increases until we come to a valley, which I call the uncanny valley." This is the subtle (or not so subtle) realization that it is not really human. This effect also happens for other biological beings.[124]

Scientists disagree on whether robots should look like humans, and much depends on the purpose of the robot (see Figure 12.13). Companies like Honda, Boston Dynamics, Kawasaki Heavy Industries, and X-Prize have different approaches to the same problem.

12.2.2 Relevance to Specific Industries

Humanoids robots are becoming more prevalent. They are being used in research and space exploration, and the military. In these sectors, how the Three Laws of Robotics are being applied is not very clear. They can be used for search and rescue operations (think of the ANA X-Prize), or for surveillance or construction or site inspection (especially where hazardous to human life). Humanoid robots are being used in health care for caregiving. They are used for personal assistance (think of Jarvis in the movie Ironman) and of course in the entertainment industry. They are also prevalent as a novelty item for customer service and public relations. The market size is estimated to be US$17.3 billion by 2027.[125]

12.2.3 Roboethics and Governance

Humanoid robots or even robots that bond socially with humans (dogs, cats) may pose an interesting question for the future. Sherry Turkle, a professor of the social studies of science and technology at the Massachusetts Institute of Technology, says,

> The nature of the attachments to dolls and sociable machines is different. Sociable machines, by contrast, have their own agenda. Playing with robots is not about the psychology of projection but the psychology of engagement.

> Honda introduced Asimo (Advanced Step in Innovative Mobility) in 2000, after 15 years of research. The first focus was walking, which has led to new products like assistive walking exoskeletons. To be people-friendly, its height was kept at four feet to be at the same level as the eyes of a seated adult.[126] This is also smaller, like a child[127] so non-threatening. The smaller size meant less weight and greater freedom of movement (typical Japanese houses are also very small). Asimo looked like a spaceman wearing a reflecting helmet (so there was no need to focus on the face, though you can see large eyes). Honda retired Asimo in 2022.
>
> Soft Bank Robotics introduced Pepper in 2004. It was designed to be a companion helper. It is small at 120 cm and does not have legs. To be non-threatening, besides its size, Pepper has a round face and large eyes like a child that appears to be open, trusting, and vulnerable.
>
> Matt Willis, SoftBank Robotics, said, "Pepper is a robot and doesn't pretend to be more than a robot... Pepper is not trying to be human—it's trying to be social."[128] A humanoid robot's eyes do not react to light or emotion, and hence it will be perceived as unemotional[129] or, worse, not trustworthy. In the case of Pepper, the eyes will have a blue ring if listening, turn green if processing information, and be white or pale blue if not listening or is not detecting a human presence.[130] With the pandemic, Soft Bank paused Pepper's production.[131]
>
> Kawasaki Heavy Industries, Ltd. introduced Kaleido in 2017, having years of expertise in industrial robots. One of the hardest challenges they faced was to get the robot to walk more naturally like a human.
>
>> In engineering theory, robots that walk on two legs can only walk while bending their knees. However, humans can walk easily with their knees straight. Also, humans land on their heels and push off with their toes to walk. This is just something we take for granted, but it is an operation that is very difficult to perform with the foot of a robot, which is made with a rigid body.[132]
>
> This is a larger robot—5.9 feet (180cm), and weights 85 kilos. It was made to work in places where humans would be at risk and to work 365 days a year, 24/7, according to Masayuki Kamon, General Manager of the Advanced Technology Department, Product Planning & Administration Department, Robot Division, Precision Machinery & Robots Company.[133]

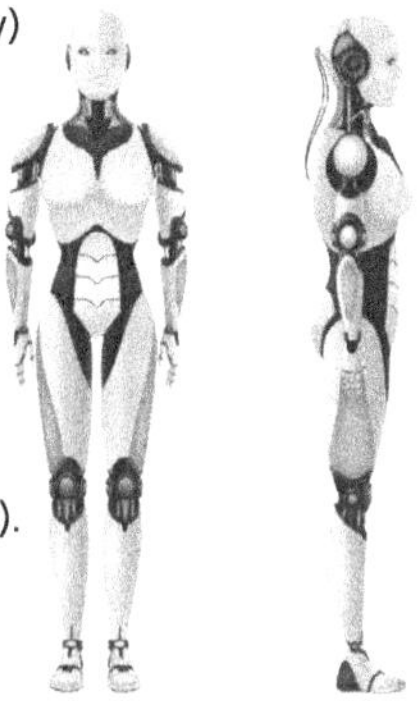

Figure 12.13 Different approaches to the humanoid robot.

Children try to meet the robot's needs to understand the robot's unique nature and wants. There is an attempt to build a mutual relationship.[134]

But the same concern for children may also extend to adults.

There is a question about autonomous robots and their ability to do harm if malfunctioned or are hacked. Humanoid robots may not be constrained to a physical boundary because they are not tethered by a power cable. They are probably stronger than a human. Hence the question of liability and responsibility holds true like in the case of AI. Roboethics reflects AI ethics but specifically adheres to the rule that robots should not be designed solely or primarily to kill or harm humans.[135] Who decides that trade-off? How liable are they?

While robotics is a field of study on how to design robots with ethical values, it is still nascent. Ethical guidelines for social robots need to be clearly coded for a large variety of situations on what is acceptable behavior[136] or to know when human intervention is needed. The other important design feature could be how the robot is programmed to look and act to be culturally, gender, or politically sensitive. Another field as discussed in the previous section, is research in nanotechnology on creating molecular robots using SynBio.[137] These do not look like a complete human but mimic human cells or body parts.

Humanoid robot technology is also being applied to animals and insects. NASA uses this technology for space exploration.[138] For example, the swarm behavior of bees has been used for drones and creates some marvelous light shows. Miniaturization of autonomous robot insects is being developed (in a DARPA research challenge) for surveillance of the environment, relief and rescue efforts, and maintaining bio-diversity.[139] While Sci-Fi addresses some concerns, there is little material on governance and code of ethics in this field.

Further, there is a confluence of topics:[140] For example, a cyborg insect (real insect with hacked biological system) would be able to move more naturally than a robot insect and for a longer time than a battery would run. The issues we need to confront are at the interface of automation and autonomy.[141] While we are still in the research phase, the worry is that at a large scale, unregulated manufacture of these types of new plants, insects, animals, and birds (and maybe humans) may have many unintended consequences on biodiversity at the minimum level.

In conclusion, this chapter is focused on thinking about the future we wish to create and the technology, methods, and values we will embrace to get there. Since the scale of the impact is global, we need to be mindful and transparent about possibilities and limitations. This systemic thinking will help managers in AI-enabled organizations choose decisions wisely.

QUESTIONS

1. Take the real-life case of Hatsume Miku.[142] This is a popular 16-year-old Japanese singer with over 100,000 songs. Would you be surprised to know Miku is a virtual avatar using a vocal synthesizer using the voice of actress Saki Fujita, a voice-over artist? From the

time of her release in 2007 to 2012, her sales reached ¥10 billion.[143] Are you comfortable with the idea that the virtual pop star is a teenager? Why?

2. Neurolink develops implantable brain-machine interfaces. The website says, "We're designing the first neural implant that will let you control a computer or mobile device anywhere you go."[144] Besides health, where will the other spillovers or adjacent possible be? What are the safeguards we need to build?

3. Your avatar in the metaverse has been hacked and turns up to work pretending to be you. At work, the avatar has insulted your boss, and now there is disciplinary action against you. What are the protocols your workplace should have to ensure that your job is protected? What will you do about your avatar?

4. How would you introduce workplace culture in the metaverse?

5. Your grandmother is perceiving that the robot assistant you hired is real and is now refusing to acknowledge you. The growing dependence on the humanoid robot raises some concerns. What are better governance management processes you could have put in place?

6. Black Mirror, a popular Netflix series has one episode on robot bees that can reproduce (via 3-D printing), create their own hives and are being used for ecological balance (and unfortunately surveillance). They get hacked (despite the safety protocols), by a former employee of the government and are used to target people using their SIM cards and facial recognition. How do you as a manufacturer, an adopter, a community or an individual plan for this?

7. The governance of AI requires decisions that are based on future foresight. What are the biggest issues that your organization has not prepared for in the future?

MY INSIGHTS

The most difficult decisions I need to take are

Epilogue—Thinking Ahead • **341**

MY INSIGHTS

The resources I need to build for the future are

MY INSIGHTS

The governance systems I will to put in place are

MY INSIGHTS

The training and skills I and my team need to develop are

Notes

1. Singer, A. (2022, July 27). *Metaverse visionary Neal Stephenson is building a blockchain to uplift creators.* Cointelegraph. https://cointelegraph.com/news/metaverse-visionary-neal-stephenson-is-building-a-blockchain-to-uplift-creators
2. Citi GPS. (2022). Metaverse and Money. https://ir.citi.com/gps/x5+FQJT3Bo HXVu9MsqVRoMdiws3RhL4yhF6Fr8us8oHaOe1W9smOy1+8aaAgT3SPuQVt wC5B2%2Fc=
3. PwC (2020, January 12). *Virtual reality and augmented reality could deliver a $4.1billion boost to the UAE economy by 2030.* PwC. https://www.pwc.com/m1/en/media-centre/2020/virtual-reality-vr-augmented-reality-ar-could-deliver-4-1-billion-boost-uae-economy-2030.html
4. *Bloomberg—Are you a robot? (2022, August). Bloomberg–Are You a Robot?* https://www.bloomberg.com/press-releases/2022-08-08/gaming-market-size-worth-504-29-billion-by-2030-grand-view-research-inc
5. Stephens et al. (2022). Metaverse and Governance. IEEE SA. https://standards.ieee.org/wp-content/uploads/2022/06/XR_Metaverse_Governance.pdf
6. Keane, J. (2022, May 30). *South Korea's investment in the metaverse could provide a blueprint.* CNBC. https://www.cnbc.com/2022/05/30/south-koreas-investment-in-the-metaverse-could-provide-a-blueprint.html
7. Ball, M. (2022). *The Metaverse and How it Will Revolutionize Everything.* Liveright.
8. Koo, H. (2021, December 31). *Training in lung cancer surgery through the metaverse, including extended reality, in the smart operating room of Seoul National University Bundang Hospital, Korea–PMC.* PubMed Central (PMC). https://www.ncbi.nlm.nih.gov/pmc/articles/PMC8810683/
9. Kallman, A. (2021). Understanding The Metaverse: Opportunities, Challenges And Gen Z. https://www.ibc.org/understanding-the-metaverse-opportunities-challenges-and-gen-z/7863.article
10. Matyszczyk, C. (2022). *Are You Ready for the Worst Economy Class Airline Seats in the World?* ZoomOne, https://www.zdnet.com/article/are-you-ready-for-the-worst-economy-class-airline-seats-in-the-world/
11. Nabiyouni, M., Scerbo, S., Bowman, D. A., & Hollerer, T. (2017). Relative Effects of Real-world and Virtual-World Latency on an Augmented Reality Training Task: An AR Simulation Experiment. Frontiers, https://doi.org/10.3389/fict.2016.00034
12. YouTube. (2020). *Pepsi Max Unbelievable Bus Shelter Augmented Reality.* Digital OOH. https://youtu.be/GB_qT6rAPyY
13. Adapted from Ball (2022). *Op. cit.*
14. Ibid.
15. Ibid.
16. Ibid.
17. Jamison, L. (2017, December). The Digital Ruins of a Forgotten Future. *The Atlantic.* https://www.theatlantic.com/magazine/archive/2017/12/second-life-leslie-jamison/544149/
18. Ball (2022b). Op. cit.; Dahad, N. (2021, November 26). *Enabling the Hardware for the Metaverse.* Embedded.com. https://www.embedded.com/enabling-the-hardware-for-the-metaverse/

19. Donnelly, J. (2021, November 30). *Creating The Metaverse With Volumetric Video And Virtual Production–MASV.* MASV. https://massive.io/filmmaking/creating-the-metaverse-volumetric-video-virtual-production/
20. *Four Ways 5G Enables the Metaverse | Straight Talk.* (2021, June). Four Ways 5G Enables the Metaverse | Straight Talk. https://straighttalk.hcltech.com/blogs/four-ways-5g-enables-the-metaverse
21. Adapted from Ball (2022). *Op. cit.*
22. Ibid.
23. Adapted from Ball (2022). *Op. cit.*; Stephens et al (2022). *Op. cit.*
24. Ibid.
25. Abraham, D. S. (2017). *Elements of Power: Gadgets, Guns, and the Struggle for a Sustainable Future in the Rare Metal Age*, 175.
26. Crawford, K. (2021). *Atlas of AI.* Yale University Press, New Haven and London.
27. Stephens et al. (2022). *Op. cit.*
28. Owne, M. (2022, March 26). *Epic Games vs Apple trial, verdict, and aftermath–all you need to know.* Apple Insider, https://appleinsider.com/articles/20/08/23/apple-versus-epic-games-fortnite-app-store-saga——-the-story-so-far
29. Morris, C. (2022, April). *The Metaverse Could be Worth $13 Trillion, Host 5 billion Users by 2030, says Citi.* Fortune. https://fortune.com/2022/04/01/citi-metaverse-economy-13-trillion-2030/
30. UNCTAD. (2019, September 4). *Global Efforts Needed to Spread Digital Economy Benefits,* UN report says. https://unctad.org/news/global-efforts-needed-spread-digital-economy-benefits-un-report-says
31. There are 4.66 billion people who can access the Internet though the report by Atelier puts the number accessing the virtual economy at 2.55. https://atelier.net/virtual-economy/
32. The XR continuum is from Lee. J.J., & Hu-Au. E. (2021). E3XR: An Analytical Framework for Ethical, Educational and Eudaimonic XR Design. Front. *Virtual Real.* https://doi.org/10.3389/frvir.2021.697667
33. Armstrong, B., & Reeve, A. (2021). How Coinbase thinks about the Metaverse. *Coinbase–Medium,* how-coinbase-thinks-about-the-metaverse-16d8070f4841
34. Atelier. (2021). *The Virtual Economy.* Available: https://atelier.net/virtual-economy
35. Logan, K. (2021, December). *Snoop Dogg is developing a Snoopverse and someone just bought a property in his virtual world for almost $500,000.* Fortune. https://fortune.com/2021/12/09/snoop-dogg-rapper-metaverse-snoopverse/
36. Fitri, A. (2022, June 12). *Metaverse M&A: Why big business is investing in virtual worlds.* Tech Monitor. https://techmonitor.ai/technology/emerging-technology/metaverse-mergers-acquisitions-investing-virtual
37. Brownrigg, S. (2019, September). *Case Study: Hong Kong International Airport Terminal 1.* Digital Twin Unit. https://scottbrownrigg.b-cdn.net/media/4742/hong-kong-international-airport-case-study.pdf; Sharon, A. (2019, October). *HKIA develops digital twin–OpenGov Asia.* OpenGov Asia -. https://opengovasia.com/hkia-develops-digital-twin/
38. Boschert, S., & Rosen, R. (2016). Digital Twin—The Simulation Aspect. In *Mechatronic Futures* (pp. 59–74). Springer, Cham.
39. Gasser, J. Blonski, S., Cao, C., et. al., (1999). *NASA's Virtual Product Laboratory: An Overview.* https://ntrs.nasa.gov/citations/20040021409

40. Lockheed Martin. (2021). *Genesis Virtual Worlds*. https://www.lockheedmartin.com/en-us/news/features/history/virtual-worlds.html
41. Serrano, S. (2022, April 18). *Journey of the Expo 2020 Dubai, a summary by Meltwater–Campaign Middle East*. Campaign Middle East. https://campaignme.com/journey-of-the-expo-2020-dubai-a-summary-by-meltwater/
42. Stephens, M. et al. (2022). *Op. cit.*
43. Blumberg, F. C., Deater-Deckard, K., Calvert, S. L., Flynn, R. M., Green, C. S., Arnold, D., & Brooks, P. J. (2019). Digital Games as a Context for Childrens Cognitive Development: Research Recommendations and Policy Considerations. *Social Policy Report, 32(1)*, 1–33. doi:10.1002/sop2.3
44. Stephens et al. (2022). *Op. cit.*
45. Brown, M. (2010, November 8). *Nicaraguan Invasion? Blame Google Maps | WIRED*. WIRED. https://www.wired.com/2010/11/google-maps-error-blamed-for-nicaraguan-invasion/; Google. (2010, November 5). *Google Lat Long: Regarding the boundary between Costa Rica and Nicaragua*. Google Lat Long. https://maps.googleblog.com/2010/11/regarding-boundary-between-costa-rica.html
46. Swedish Game Developer Index. https://sweden.se/work-business/business-in-sweden/10-facts-about-gaming-in-sweden
47. Branko, K. (2021). 15+ Mind-boggling Minecraft Statistics for the Dedicated Gamer. https://hostingtribunal.com/blog/minecraft-statistics/#gref
48. Planet Minecraft.com. (2021). Minecraft Community Submissions. https://www.planetminecraft.com/
49. Capel, C. J. (2019). Believe it or not, the average age of a Minecraft player is 24. *PC Games*, https://www.pcgamesn.com/minecraft/player-age
50. Branko, K. (2021). *Op. cit.*
51. Minecraft Homepage (2022. November 14). Hour of Code. https://education.minecraft.net/en-us/resources/hour-code-2022
52. Walton, M. (2016). Microsoft is using *Minecraft* to train AI and wants you to help out. *ARS Technica*, https://arstechnica.com/gaming/2016/03/microsoft-minecraft-aix-artificial-intelligence/
53. Tectales, (2021). Minecraft advances artificial intelligence. https://tectales.com/ai/minecraft-advances-artificial-intelligence.html
54. Baker, B., Akkaya, I., Zhokhov, P. et al., nd. Video PreTraining (VPT): Learning to Act by Watching Unlabeled Online Videos. https://cdn.openai.com/vpt/Paper.pdf
55. Wodecki, B. (2022). OpenAI teaches AI to play Minecraft using video data. AI Business https://aibusiness.com/document.asp?doc_id=778537
56. Reay, E. J. (2022, June 1). *Video game worlds are often devoid of children—here's why*. The Conversation. https://theconversation.com/video-game-worlds-are-often-devoid-of-children-heres-why-183485; Reay, E. (2021, May). *Game Studies–The Child in Games: Representations of Children in Video Games (2009–2019)*. Game Studies–The Child in Games: Representations of Children in Video Games (2009–2019). http://gamestudies.org/2101/articles/reay
57. Krawford, K. (2021). Atlas of AI. Yale University Press: London
58. York. J. C. (2021). *Silicon Values. The Future of Free Speech*. Verso. London–New York.
59. Stephens, M. et al. (2022). *Op. cit.*

60. Kelley, K. (1995). *Out Of Control: The New Biology Of Machines, Social Systems, And The Economic World.* Ingram Publisher. USA.
61. Scientific Committee on Health and Environmental Risks SCHER. (2014). Opinion on Synthetic Biology I Definition. https://ec.europa.eu/health/scientific_committees/emerging/docs/scenihr_o_044.pdf
62. Ibid.
63. Beal, J. (2013). How can AI help Synthetic Biology? https://jakebeal.github.io/Publications/AAAI-SynBio-2013.pdf
64. Kelley, K. (1995). *Op. cit.*
65. Scientific Committee on Health and Environmental Risks SCHER. (2014). Opinion on Synthetic Biology I Definition. https://ec.europa.eu/health/scientific_committees/emerging/docs/scenihr_o_044.pdf
66. AI for SynBio. Connecting and Building Collaborations between AI and Synthetic Biology Communities. https://www.ai4synbio.org
67. Bickerton, P. (2018). LabGenius: AI-driven synthetic biology. Earlham Institute, https://www.earlham.ac.uk/articles/labgenius-ai-driven-synthetic-biology
68. Rees, A. R. (2019). Understanding the human antibody repertoire. *mAbs. 12*(1). https://doi.org/10.1080/19420862.2020.1729683
69. Cumbers. J. (2020). Synthetic Biology Versus Coronavirus: Three Women In A Cutting-Edge Field Using Biological Engineering To Save Lives. *Forbes,* https://www.forbes.com/sites/johncumbers/2020/09/10/synthetic-biology-versus-coronavirus-three-women-in-a-cutting-edge-field-using-biological-engineering-to-save-lives/?sh=39e72240557d
70. Radivojević, T., Costello, Z., Workman, K. *et al.* A machine learning Automated Recommendation Tool for synthetic biology. *Nat Commun, 11,* 4879 (2020). https://doi.org/10.1038/s41467-020-18008-4
71. Zurich, T.H. (2019). A biosynthetic dual-core cell computer. ScienceDaily, https://www.sciencedaily.com/releases/2019/04/190416081416.htm
72. Kim, H., Bojar, D., & Fussenegger, M. (2019). A CRISPR/Cas9-based central processing unit to program complex logic computation in human cells. *Proceedings of the National Academy of Sciences, 116* (15): 7214 DOI: 10.1073/pnas.1821740116.
73. Martin Fussenegger, Professor of Biotechnology and Bioengineering at the Department of Biosystems Science and Engineering at ETH Zurich in Basel is a pioneer in this work.
74. Kim, Bojar, & Fussenegger *Op. cit.* p. 6.
75. Courbet, A., Amar, P., Fages, F., Renard, E., & Molina, F. (2018). Computer-aided biochemical programming of synthetic microreactors as diagnostic devices. Molecular Systems Biology. 14:e7845. https://doi.org/10.15252/msb.20177845
76. The creation of the rat-mouse chimeras to human-pig chimeras took a decade of research. Human stem cells were injected into early-stage pig embryos. This resulted over 2,000 hybrids. These hybrids were incubated in surrogate sows. Only 150 developed into embryos and then chimeras. The analysis showed that they were mainly pig genetic material. The human contribution was a very small percentage, one in 10,000 cells. Wu et al., (2017). *Interspecies Chimerism with Mammalian Pluripotent Stem Cells. Cell, 168* (3): 473–486

77. A method for the engineered cell to self-destruct.
78. Inability for the cell to replicate or survive outside a controlled environment.
79. Whitford, C.M., Dymek, S., Kerkhoff, D. et al. (2018). Auxotrophy to Xeno-DNA: an exploration of combinatorial mechanisms for a high-fidelity biosafety system for synthetic biology applications. *J Biol Eng* **12**, 13. https://doi.org/10.1186/s13036-018-0105-8
80. McKinsey Global Institute. (2021). The Bio Revolution: Innovations transforming economies, societies, and our lives, Available: https://www.mckinsey.com/industries/life-sciences/our-insights/the-bio-revolution-innovations-transforming-economies-societies-and-our-lives
81. Whitford, C.M., Dymek, S., Kerkhoff, D. et al. (2018). Auxotrophy to Xeno-DNA: an exploration of combinatorial mechanisms for a high-fidelity biosafety system for synthetic biology applications. *J Biol Eng 12*, 13. https://doi.org/10.1186/s13036-018-0105-8
82. SynBio funding reached US$7.8 billion in 2020 or 2.5x the funding of 2019. There were 74 IPOs worth US$14 billion. https://synbiobeta.com/synthetic-biology-investment-set-a-nearly-8-billion-record-in-2020-what-does-this-mean-for-2021/
83. For example, see the NSF grant announced in 2020. Semiconductor Synthetic Biology for Information Storage and Retrieval (SemiSynBio-II). Formally NSF 20-518 replaced by NSF 22-557. https://www.nsf.gov/pubs/2020/nsf20518/nsf20518.html
84. Zhang, J. Y., Marris, C., & Rose, N. (2011). The Transnational Governance of Synthetic Biology Scientific uncertainty, cross-borderness and the 'art' of governance . London. ISSN 1759-0620
85. Xun, X. (2019). We are witnessing a revolution in genomics–and it's only just begun. World Economic Forum https://www.weforum.org/agenda/2019/06/today-you-can-have-your-genome-sequenced-at-the-supermarket/; de Yonge, J. (2020). How the COVID-19 outbreak could provide synbio's breakout moment. EY, https://www.ey.com/en_gl/covid-19/how-the-covid-19-outbreak-could-provide-synbios-breakout-moment
86. Smolke, C. D. (2009). Building outside of the box: iGEM and the BioBricks Foundation.*Nature Biotechnology*, 27:12 1099–1102; Verschraegen, G., & Schiltz, M. (2007). Knowledge as a Global Public Good: The Role and Importance of Open Access. Societies without Borders: 157–174. "[open source provides] tools and platforms on which innovation and development can be pursued by local actors in the developing countries itself, without having to pass through the proprietary system of information production."
87. Thompson, M. (2008, April 18). *Breaking News, Analysis, Politics, Blogs, News Photos, Video, Tech Reviews–TIME.com.* TIME.Com. http://content.time.com/time/nation/article/0,8599,1732226,00.html
88. Nielsen, J. , and Keasling, J.D. (2016) Engineering cellular metabolism. *Cell* 164: 1185–1197.
89. Jefferson, O.A. , Kllhofer, D. , Ajjikuttira, P. , and Jefferson, R.A. (2015) Public disclosure of biological sequences in global patent practice. *World Patent Info* 43: 12–24.

90. Carbonell, P., Gok, A., Shapira, P., & Faulon, J-L. (2016). Mapping the patent landscape of synthetic biology for fine chemical production pathways. *Microb Biotechnol*, 9(5), 687–695. https://dx.doi.org/10.1111%2F1751-7915.12401
91. Ibid.
92. Ibid.
93. OECD. (2011). *Future Prospects for Industrial Biotechnology*.
94. Suppan, S. (2014). From GMO To SMO: How Synthetic Biology Evades Regulation. Institute for Agriculture and Trade Policy, USA. https://www.iatp.org/sites/default/files/2014_07_18_Synbio_SS_0.pdf
95. Augusto, G., & Gutierrez, C. (2014). Governing Synthetic Biology in the Light of the Access and Benefit Sharing Regulation (ABS). *National Library of Medicine*, 41: 63–81. https://pubmed.ncbi.nlm.nih.gov/25845206/
96. Houses of Parliament Parliamentary Office of Science & Technology. (2015, May). Houses of Parliament. https://researchbriefings.files.parliament.uk/documents/POST-PN-0497/POST-PN-0497.pdf
97. Ibid.
98. Pauchard, N. (2017). Access and Benefit Sharing under the Convention on Biological Diversity and Its Protocol: What Can Some Numbers Tell Us about the Effectiveness of the Regulatory Regime? *Resources*, 6(1), 11; https://doi.org/10.3390/resources6010011
99. den Belt, H. V. (2012, October 30). Synthetic biology, patenting, health and global justice–PMC. *PubMed Central (PMC)*. https://www.ncbi.nlm.nih.gov/pmc/articles/PMC3740100/
100. UNCTAD. (2019). Synthetic Biology and Its Potential Implications for Biotrade and Access and Benefit-Sharing. https://unctad.org/system/files/official-document/ditctedinf2019d12_en.pdf
101. Keiper, F., & Atanassova, A. (2020). Developments Under the Convention on Biological Diversity and Its Protocols. *Front. Bioeng. Biotechnol.*, https://doi.org/10.3389/fbioe.2020.00310
102. Artificial transcription factors have the ability to bind endogenous DNA randomly with a specific locus with regulatory role, so that the cellular metabolic network would be perturbed.
103. Park, K-S., Lee, D-K., Lee, H., et al. (2003). Phenotypic Alteration of Eukaryotic Cells Using Randomized Libraries of Artificial Transcription Factors. *Nat Biotechnol*, 21:1208. Suggest do read the article by Yang, J., Kim, B., Kim, G.Y. et al. (2019). Synthetic Biology for Evolutionary Engineering: From Perturbation of Genotype to Acquisition of Desired Phenotype. *Biotechnol Biofuels*. 12, 113. https://doi.org/10.1186/s13068-019-1460-5
104. Karsch-Mizrachi, I., Takagi, T., & Cochrane, G. (2018). The International Nucleotide Sequence Database Collaboration. *Nucleic Acids Research* D48, 46:D1
105. Phillipidis, A. (2018). The 100,000 Genome Club. https://www.genengnews.com/insights/the-100000-genomes-club/
106. Chui, M., Evers, M., Manyika, J., Zheng, A., & Nisbet, T. (2022, May). *The Bio Revolution: Innovations transforming economies, societies, and our lives | McKinsey*. McKinsey & Company. https://www.mckinsey.com/industries/life-sciences/our-insights/the-bio-revolution-innovations-transforming-economies-societies-and-our-lives

107. Urbina, F., Lentzos, F., Invernizzi, C., & Ekins, S. (2022, March 7). Dual Use of Artificial-Intelligence-Powered Drug Discovery–Nature Machine Intelligence. *Nature*. https://nature.com/articles/s42256-022-00465-9
108. Hu, B., (2017). Discovery of a Rich Gene Pool of Bat SARS-Related Coronaviruses Provides New Insights into the Origin Of SARS Coronavirus. *PLOS Pathogens*. https://doi.org/10.1371/journal.ppat.1006698
109. Ibid.
110. Dance, A. (2021). The Shifting Sands of 'Gain-of-Function' Research. *Nature*, https://www.nature.com/articles/d41586-021-02903-x
111. Dubrepatil, A. (2020). Using Synthetic biology to Combat Pandemics: What? Why? How? *Molecular Cloud*. https://www.molecularcloud.org/p/using-synthetic-biology-to-combat-pandemics-what-why-how
112. *Center for Food Safety | About GE Foods | | About Genetically Engineered Foods*. (n.d.). Center for Food Safety. https://www.centerforfoodsafety.org/issues/311/ge-foods/about-ge-foods
113. *Synthetic Biology Market Size, Share | 2022–2026 | MarketsandMarkets*. (2021, May). Synthetic Biology Market Size, Share | 2022–2026 | MarketsandMarkets. https://www.marketsandmarkets.com/Market-Reports/synthetic-biology-market-889.html?gclid=Cj0KCQjwpeaYBhDXARIsAEzItbGXoz-53sReBSid9KuYiaWhIm7lI5NdlFnruGX2LFwmu_GqAf0cDywaAoV8EALw_wcB
114. Candelon, F., Gombeaud, M., Stokol, G., Patel, V., Gourévitch, A., & Goeldel, N. (2022, February 8). *Synthetic Biology Is About to Disrupt Your Industry*. BCG Global. https://www.bcg.com/publications/2022/synthetic-biology-is-about-to-disrupt-your-industry; Andelon, F., Gombeaud, M., & Stokol, G. (2021, August). *Commentary: Synthetic biology could help business save the planet*. Fortune. https://fortune.com/2021/08/06/synthetic-biology-plant-based-meats-bioengineering-environmental-impact/
115. *ANA Avatar XPRIZE | XPRIZE Foundation*. (n.d.). XPRIZE. https://www.xprize.org/prizes/avatar
116. Holley, P. (2019, September 25). *Three years ago it could barely walk. Now Atlas the humanoid robot is doing gymnastics.–The Washington Post*. Washington Post. https://www.washingtonpost.com/technology/2019/09/25/three-years-ago-he-could-barely-walk-now-atlas-humanoid-robot-is-doing-gymnastics/
117. *The MIT DARPA Robotics Challenge Team*. (n.d.). The MIT DARPA Robotics Challenge Team. http://drc.mit.edu/
118. NGOWI, R. (2021, April 20). *Behind Those Dancing Robots, Scientists Had to Bust a Move | AP News*. Behind Those Dancing Robots, Scientists Had to Bust a Move. https://apnews.com/article/boston-dynamics-robot-dancing-d684559324a385209c0da353a76363bc
119. Strathearn, C. (2021, November 4). *I've Created Human-Style Eyes for Robots—with Some Inspiration from Jabba the Hutt*. The Conversation. https://theconversation.com/ive-created-human-style-eyes-for-robots-with-some-inspiration-from-jabba-the-hutt-169508
120. Ekman, P., and Friesen, W. V. (1969). Nonverbal leakage and clues to deception. *Psychiatry* 32, 88–106.
121. Liu, Y.-J., Zhang, J.-K., Yan, W.-J., Wang, S.-J., Zhao, G., and Fu, X. (2016). A main directional mean optical flow feature for spontaneous micro-ex-

pression recognition. *IEEE Trans. Affect. Comput.* 7, 299–310. doi: 10.1109/TAFFC.2015.2485205

122. Lewis, E. (2022, June). *Microsoft is removing emotion recognition features from its facial recognition tech.* NBC News. https://www.nbcnews.com/tech/tech-news/microsoft-removing-emotion-recognition-features-facial-recognition-tec-rcna35087

123. Labiotech. (2017). Synbio adds Softness: Robots of the Future will be Squish. https://www.labiotech.eu/trends-news/robots-soft-synbio/

124. Mori, M. (1970). The Uncanny Valley, *Energy*, 7 (4); 33–35 *(in Japanese)*.

125. GlobeNewsWire. (2022, April 14). *The humanoid robot market was valued at USD 1.5 billion in.* GlobeNewsWire News Room. https://www.globenewswire.com/news-release/2022/04/14/2422427/0/en/The-humanoid-robot-market-was-valued-at-USD-1-5-billion-in-2022-and-is-estimated-to-reach-USD-17-3-billion-by-2027-registering-a-CAGR-of-63-5-between-2022-and-2027.html

126. *Honda's Advanced Humanoid Robot "ASIMO" Makes U.S. Debut.* (2002, February 14). Honda Corporate Newsroom. https://hondanews.com/en-US/honda-corporate/releases/release-6d3f77ac0cb7c24f66e07a004c34c752-hondas-advanced-humanoid-robot-asimo-makes-u-s-debut

127. Masato, H., & Kenichi, O. (2006). Honda Humanoid Robots Development. *Phil. Trans. R. Soc.* A.36515–https://doi.org/10.1098/rsta.2006.1917

128. Weinberg, N. (2019, August 28). How SoftBank Robotics Builds Human Trust When Building Pepper. *Robotics Business Review.* https://www.roboticsbusinessreview.com/service/how-softbank-robotics-builds-human-trust-when-building-pepper/

129. Thepsoonthorn, C., Ogawa, K. I., & Miyake, Y. (2021, January 3). The Exploration of the Uncanny Valley from the Viewpoint of the Robot's Nonverbal Behaviour. *International Journal of Social Robotics.* SpringerLink. https://link.springer.com/article/10.1007/s12369-020-00726-w

130. *Interacting with Pepper — Aldebaran 2.4.3.28-r2 documentation.* (n.d.). Interacting with Pepper — Aldebaran 2.4.3.28-R2 Documentation. http://doc.aldebaran.com/2-4/family/pepper_user_guide/interacting_pep.html

131. Nussey, S. (2021, June 29). *EXCLUSIVE SoftBank shrinks robotics business, stops Pepper production- sources | Reuters.* Reuters. https://www.reuters.com/technology/exclusive-softbank-shrinks-robotics-business-stops-pepper-production-sources-2021-06-28/

132. *Kaleido | 05 Robust Humanoid Platform | iREX | Kawasaki Heavy Industries, Ltd.* (n.d.). Kaleido | 05 Robust Humanoid Platform | iREX | Kawasaki Heavy Industries, Ltd. https://event.kawasakirobotics.com/jp/irex2022/en/humanoid/kaleido/

133. *Building the Ideal Humanoid Robot | XYZ | Kawasaki Heavy Industries, Ltd.* (2021, March 29). XYZ. https://robotics.kawasaki.com/ja1/xyz/en/2103-03/index.htm

134. Turkle, S. (n.d.). *Perspective | Why these friendly robots can't be good friends to our kids.* Washington Post. https://www.washingtonpost.com/outlook/why-these-friendly-robots-cant-be-good-friends-to-our-kids/2017/12/07/bce1eaea-d54f-11e7-b62d-d9345ced896d_story.html

135. The British Standards Institute BS8611

136. Michael and Susan Leigh Anderson have collected contributions from both philosophers and AI researchers in the book *Machine Ethics*
137. Wei, T. Y., & Ruder, W. C. (2020, October). *Engineering control circuits for molecular robots using synthetic biology: APL Materials: Vol 8, No 10*. AIP Publishing. https://aip.scitation.org/doi/full/10.1063/5.0020429
138. *Student Project: Design a Robotic Insect | NASA/JPL Edu*. (n.d.). NASA/JPL Edu. https://www.jpl.nasa.gov/edu/learn/project/design-a-robotic-insect/
139. Rapaport, L. (n.d.). *Tiny Robot Bugs in Development for Medical Relief*. WebMD. https://www.webmd.com/a-to-z-guides/news/20220328/tiny-robot-bugs-may-aid-medical-treatments
140. Bogue, R. (2010). Recent Developments in Miniature Flying Robots. *Industrial Robot*, 37(1): 17–22. https://doi.org/10.1108/01439911011009920
141. Siljak, H., Nardelli, P. H. J., & Moioli, R. C. (n.d.). *Cyborg Insects: Bug or a Feature?* https://ieeexplore.ieee.org/abstract/document/9770076
142. Crypton (nd). Who is Hatsune Miku? https://ec.crypton.co.jp/pages/prod/virtualsinger/cv01_us
143. 初音ミク、"リアル"に商機 ライブ・カラオケ・ＣＭ...関連消費１００億円超 [Hatsune Miku and related merchandise have raised over 10 billion yen in revenue]. Sankei Biz News (in Japanese). March 27, 2012. Archived from the original on September 24, 2015. Retrieved October 10, 2015.
144. Studio, P. (n.d.). *Approach*. Neuralink. https://neuralink.com/approach/

About the Authors

Melodena Stephens has three decades of experience working in senior roles with private sector, governments, academia and startups. Globe trotter, having worked, lived and studied in India, USA, Germany, Taiwan and UAE. She is currently Professor of Innovation Management at the Mohammed Bin Rashid School of Government in Dubai. She is also the Founder and board member of the Academy of International Business–Middle East North Africa Chapter, a non-profit social initiative founded in 2009. The purpose of the organization is to act as an ambassador and champion for the MENA region by fostering research and teaching in the field of international business. She loves to write, the most recent books are *AI Smart Kit—Agile Decision Making on AI* and *Business With Purpose: Advancing Social Enterprise*. She is a strategic consultant in innovation (agile government, policy and market development especially looking at new tech) and crisis & reputation management (AI ethics and governance, soft power). Melodena is an active corporate trainer and researcher. She focuses on human-centered design thinking. Melodena is an IEEE SA AI Systems Ethics Committee member for the Global Initiative Education; Concentration of Power, Autonomous Weapons Systems (legal, ethics, and policy) and Planet Positive 2030. More: www.melodena.com

Himanshu Vashishtha is the CEO of SixthFactor Consulting. He is a market researcher with two decades of experience in shaping marketing strategy for global brands. He was heading the largest research agency in MENA region before he set up a new age research firm, SixthFactor, with offices across Dubai, India and Singapore to help brands get clarity, predict consumer behavior and make profitable choices. Himanshu is a thought leader in applied behavioral economics and neuromarketing in the region. He contributes to newspapers, periodicals and magazines regularly and speaks on these topics in conferences across Dubai, Singapore and India. Teaching behavioural economics and applied neuromarketing in various institutes including Indian Institute of Management helps him be on top of the latest developments in consumer understanding. He has been on the board of numerous organizations and councils such as TiE, Retail ME, Super Brands Council, Asian Brand Council, Gemas Awards and continues to develop new principles in consumer choice architecture.

Dirk Nicolas Wagner is an entrepreneur and Affiliate Professor of Strategic Management at Karlshochschule International University (GER). He studied economics and management at Université de Fribourg (CH) and Royal Holloway University of London (UK), graduating as a MBA in International Management and Dr.rer.pol. in the area of New Institutional Economics. Since the 1990s, he has been dealing with questions related to man and machine governance and he regularly publishes with the Zukunftsinstitut in Frankfurt a.M.. He is a Managing Partner of a medium sized business in the technical services industry in Europe.